11 Years

CBSE

Class 10

SCIENCE

Previous Year-wise

Solved Papers (2013 - 2023) for with Value Added Notes

DISHA Publication Inc.
45, 2nd Floor, Maharishi Dayanand Marg,
Corner Market, Malviya Nagar, new Delhi -110017
Tel: 49842349/ 49842350

By:
Sanjeev Kumar Jha
Kalpana Bhargav
Rashi Chauhan

Typeset By
DISHA DTP Team

Write To Us At
feedback_disha@aiets.co.in

CONTENTS

IMPORTANT POINTS & FORMULAE i-xii

1. CBSE Board Solved Paper (All India 2023) 2023-1-12
2. CBSE Board Solved Paper (Delhi 2023) 2023-1-12
3. CBSE Board Solved Paper (All India 2022) Term-II 2022-1-6
4. CBSE Board Solved Paper (All India 2022) Term-I 2022-7-16
5. CBSE Board Solved Paper (All India 2020) 1-12
6. CBSE Board Solved Paper (Delhi 2020) 13-24
7. CBSE Board Solved Paper (All India 2019) 25-36
8. CBSE Board Solved Paper (Delhi 2019) 37-48
9. CBSE Board Solved Paper (All India 2018) 49-60
10. CBSE Board Solved Paper (All India 2017) 61-70
11. CBSE Board Solved Paper (Delhi 2017) 71-82
12. CBSE Board Solved Paper (All India 2016) 83-94
13. CBSE Board Solved Paper (Delhi 2016) 95-104
14. CBSE Board Solved Paper (All India 2015) 105-114
15. CBSE Board Solved Paper (Delhi 2015) 115-124
16. CBSE Board Solved Paper (All India 2014) 125-136
17. CBSE Board Solved Paper (Delhi 2014) 137-148
18. CBSE Board Solved Paper (Delhi 2013) 149-160

Chapterwise Division of Questions

The table below presents the chapter-wise division of the questions of the 18 papers. So this book can be put to dual usage-yearwise as well as chapter-wise. To find questions of a chapter just follow the question numbers in its row against the 18 papers. This table also depicts the Trend Analysis of 2023-2013 papers.

Ch. No.	Chapter Name	Year of Examination																		
		2023		2022		2021	2020		2019		2018	2017		2016		2015		2014		2013
		All India	Delhi	All India Term-I	All India Term-II		All India	Delhi	All India	Delhi	All India	(All India) Term-II	(2016-2017) Term-I	(2015-2016) Term-I	(Delhi) Term-II	(All India) Term-II	(2014-2015) Term-I	(2013-2014) Term-I	(Delhi) Term-II	All India
1.	Chemical Reactions and Equations	3, 12, 21, 30	1, 2, 3, 17, 21(A), 27(ii)	1, 4, 6, 7, 10, 25, 29, 32		Not held in 2021 due to Covid-19 Pandemic	15, 25 (or)	5 (or), 6, 15	6	13(or)	12, 25		1, 26	10, 12, 29, 34			1, 10, 13, 27, 36	1, 10, 25, 27		
2.	Acids, Bases and Salt	2, 4, 17, 28	4, 5, 6, 21(B), 28	5, 8, 9, 26, 30, 31			11, 16 (or)	7, 8, 16 (or)	7 (or) 22 (or), 23	21	10 (or)	25	10, 14, 22, 25, 28, 29, 34	2, 14, 22, 25, 26, 27, 28	34	25, 34	22, 25, 26, 28, 29	14, 22, 26, 28, 29, 30	25, 26	25, 26, 27
3.	Metals and Non-Metals	48, 20, 37	7, 21(i), 37	2, 3, 27, 28	6		2 (or), 14	25	4 (or), 8	15, 27 (or)	18, 24		12, 13, 23, 27	13, 23			7, 14, 23	6, 7, 12, 13, 23		
4.	Carbon and its Compounds	34	34		7, 12		1, 13, 26	1, 13, 17	3, 9	20 (or), 26	11	1, 7, 8, 19, 26, 27, 34			1, 7, 8, 19, 25, 26, 27	1, 7 8, 19, 26, 27			8, 20, 27, 28, 29	20, 28, 29
	Periodic Classification of Elements *				13		12 (or), 17	26 (or)	5, 16 (or)	5 (or), 14	5, 20	9, 10			9, 10	9, 10			1, 10, 11	1, 10, 11
5.	Life Processes	5, 19, 23, 27	8, 9, 19, 23, 24, 29	11, 12, 13, 14, 15, 16, 35, 36, 37, 38, 41, 42, 53, 54, 55, 56			19, 27	27 (or)	10, 11 (or), 25	4, 11, 22, 23 (or)	19 (or), 27		18, 24, 32, 33, 36	17, 24, 32, 33, 36		2	16, 18, 24, 32, 33, 34	18,24, 36,37,38, 39, 40, 41, 42		
6.	Control and Coordination	6, 29	11				4, 7	18(or)	17 (or)	9, 10	3, 9		3, 7, 17, 19	3, 18, 19			3, 12, 17, 19	3, 17, 19		
7.	How do Organisms Reproduce?	14, 35	35, 38		3 (or), 4, 5		28(or)	3, 19, 28	12, 24 (or)	19 (or)	7, 17, 22 (or)	2, 11, 12, 13, 20, 28, 35			2, 11, 12, 13, 20, 28, 35	11, 12, 13, 20, 28, 35			4, 13, 21, 22, 38, 39	8, 12, 13, 21, 22, 38, 39, 42
8.	Heredity	9, 38	10, 12, 18, 22		11, 15 (or)		20, 21	20, 29	18	12 (or)	2	14, 15, 21, 29			14, 15, 21, 29	14, 15, 21, 29			2, 9, 14, 15, 40, 41, 42	2, 4, 9, 14, 15, 40, 41
9.	Light-Reflection and Refraction	7, 28, 39	30, 31, 39	17, 18, 19, 20, 22, 23, 57, 58, 59, 60			9, 22, 24, 30 (or)	9 (or), 21 (or), 29 (or)	13 (or), 26	18, 24	4, 6 (or), 23	4, 16, 22, 23, 30, 31, 32, 36			4, 16, 22, 23, 30, 31, 32, 36	4, 16, 22, 23, 30, 31, 32, 36			5, 16, 17, 23, 30, 31, 32, 33, 36, 37	5, 16, 17, 23, 30, 31, 32, 33, 36, 37
10.	Human Eye and Colourful World	13, 16, 31	25	21, 24, 34			5	22	19, 26 (or)	3, 8	21 (or)	17, 24, 33			17, 24, 33	17, 24, 33		11	18, 24, 34, 35	18, 24, 34, 35
11.	Electricity	24, 36	13, 15, 36		9 & (or), 10		6, 29,	10 (or), 23, 24	2, 20, 27	2, 16 (or), 25 (or)	8, 15, 16, 26		2, 6, 9, 11, 15, 16, 20, 30, 31, 35	1, 20, 30, 35			2, 16, 20, 30, 31, 35	2, 15, 16, 20, 31, 32, 33, 34, 35, 36	12	
12.	Magnetic Effect of Electric Current	15, 26, 32	14, 16, 20, 32		2 & (or), 14 & (or)		23	2, 13, 30	21	17			21	7, 11, 21			9, 11, 21	9, 21		
	Sources of Energy *						3	12, 14	14	1,	1,		4, 5, 8	9, 31			4, 5, 6, 8	4, 5, 8		
13.	Our Environment	10, 33	26		1 (or), 8		9, 18 (or)	4,	15	6 (or)	14	3		4, 5, 6, 8, 15, 16	3, 18	3, 5, 6, 18	15		6, 7, 19	3, 6, 19
	Management of Natural Resources *						8 (or)	11	1	7	13	5, 6, 16, 18			5, 16				3	7
		39	39	60	15		30	30	27	27	27	36	36	36	36	36	36	42	42	42

Note: * The highlighted chapters are removed from the NCERT

All India 2023

CBSE Board Solved Paper

Time Allowed : 3 hrs. | *Maximum Marks : 80*

General Instructions:

Read the following instructions very carefully and strictly follow them :

(i) This question paper consists of **39** questions. **All** questions are compulsory.
(ii) Question paper is divided into **FIVE** sections – **Section A, B, C, D** and **E.**
(iii) In **section A** – question number 1 to 20 are multiple choice questions (MCQs) carrying **1** mark each.
(iv) In **section B** – question number 21 to 26 are very short answer (VSA) type questions carrying **2** marks each. Answer to these questions should be in the range of 30 to 50 words.
(v) In **section C** – question number 27 to 33 are short answer (SA) type questions carrying **3** marks each. Answer to these questions should in the range of 50 to 80 words.
(vi) In **section D** – question number 34 to 36 are long answer (LA) type questions carrying **5** marks each. Answer to these questions should be in the range of 80 to 120 words.
(vii) In **section E** – question number 37 to 39 are of 3 **source based/case based units of assessment** carrying **4** marks each with sub-parts.
(viii) There is no overall choice. However, an internal choice has been provided in some sections.

SECTION - A

Select and write one most appropriate option out of the four options given for each of the questions 1 - 20:

1. Metal oxides generally react with acids, but few oxides of metal also react with bases. Such metallic oxides are: **1**

I. MgO II. ZnO
III. Al_2O_3 IV. CaO
(a) I and II (b) II and III
(c) III and IV (d) I and IV

2. Few drops of aqueous solution of ammonium chloride are put on a universal indicator paper. The paper turns pink. **1**

Study the following table and choose the correct option.

	Nature	Ammonium chloride is a salt of	Range of pH
(a)	acidic	weak acid and strong base	less than 7
(b)	basic	weak acid and strong base	more than 7
(c)	acidic	strong acid and weak base	less than 7
(d)	basic	strong acid and strong base	7

3. Select the appropriate state symbols of the products given as X and Y in the following chemical equation by choosing the correct option from table given below:

$$Zn_{(s)} + H_2SO_{4(l)} \longrightarrow ZnSO_{4(X)} + H_{2(Y)}$$ **1**

	(X)	(Y)
(a)	(s)	(l)
(b)	(aq)	(g)
(c)	(aq)	(s)
(d)	(g)	(aq)

4. Two salts 'X' and 'Y' are dissolved in water separately. When phenolphthalein is added to these two solutions, the solution 'X' turns pink and the solution 'Y' does not show any change in colour, therefore 'X' and 'Y' are **1**

	(X)	(Y)
(a)	Na_2CO_3	NH_4Cl
(b)	Na_2SO_4	$NaHCO_3$
(c)	NH_4Cl	Na_2SO_4
(d)	$NaNO_3$	Na_2SO_4

5. In the given diagram of a closed stomata: (1), (2), (3) and (4) respectively are: 1

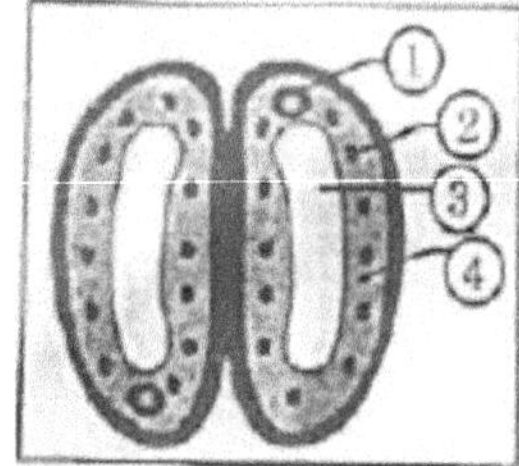

(a) nucleus, chloroplast, guard cell, vacuole

(b) nucleus, chloroplast, vacuole, guard cell

(c) chloroplast, nucleus, vacuole, guard cell

(d) vacuole, guard cell, nucleus, chloroplast

6. Walking in a straight line and riding a bicycle are the activities which are possible due to a part of the brain. Choose the correct location and name of this part from the given table: 1

	Part of the Brain	Name
(a)	Fore brain	Cerebrum
(b)	Mid brain	Hypothalamus
(c)	Hind brain	Cerebellum
(d)	Hind brain	Medulla

7. A student wants to obtain an erect image of an object using a concave mirror of 10 cm focal length. What will be the distance of the object from mirror? 1

(a) Less than 10 cm

(b) 10 cm

(c) between 10 cm and 20 cm

(d) more than 20 cm

8. Bronze is an alloy of 1

(a) Copper and Zinc

(b) Aluminium and Tin

(c) Copper, Tin and Zinc

(d) Copper and Tin

9. In an experiment with pea plants, a pure tall plant (TT) is crossed with a pure short plant (tt). The ratio of pure tall plant to pure short plants in F_2 generation will be 1

(a) 1 : 3 (b) 3 : 1

(c) 1 : 1 (d) 2 : 1

10. Study the given figure of a Food web and identify the primary consumer in the food web: 1

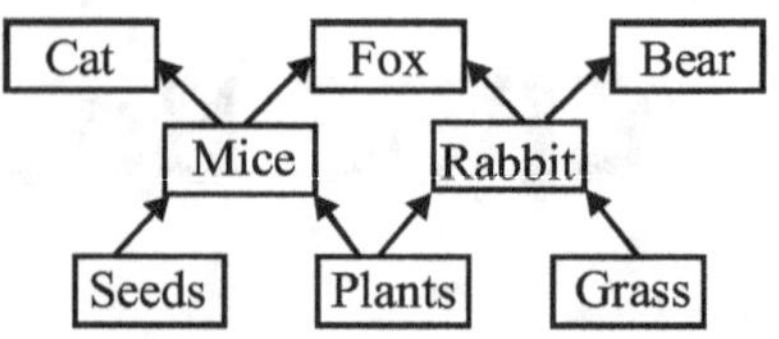

(a) Mice and Bear (b) Rabbit and Cat

(c) Rabbit and Fox (d) Mice and Rabbit

11. Chooe the correct order of the stages of binary fission in Leishmania. 1

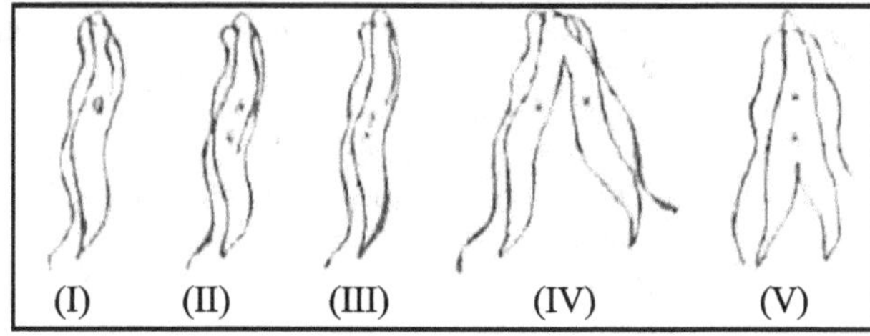

(a) I, II, III, IV, V (b) I, III, II, V, IV

(c) I, III, V, II, IV (d) I, II, III, V, IV

12. Consider the following chemical equation I and II

I. $Mg + 2HCl \rightarrow MgCl_2 + H_2$

II. $NaOH + HCl \rightarrow NaCl + H_2O$

The correct statement about these equations is – 1

(a) 'I' is a displacement reaction and 'II' is a decomposition reaction.

(b) 'I' is a displacement reaction and 'II' is double displacement reaction.

(c) Both 'I' and 'II' are displacement reactions.

(d) Both 'I' and 'II' are double-displacement reactions.

13. In the following diagram showing dispersion of white light by a glass prism, the colours 'P' and 'Q' respectively are- 1

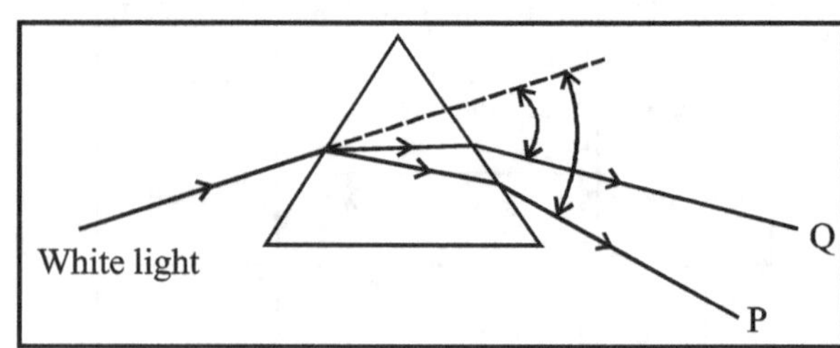

(a) Red and Violet (b) Violet and Red

(c) Red and Blue (d) Orange and Green

14. Consider the following three flowers namely X, Y and Z. Which flower(s) would develop into a fruit? **1**

Flower X	Flower Y	Flower Z

(a) 'X' only (b) 'Z' only

(c) 'X' and 'Y' only (d) 'Y' and 'Z'

15. The magnetic field inside a long straight current carrying solenoid: **1**

(a) is zero

(b) decreases as we move towards its end.

(c) increases as we move towards its end.

(d) is same at all points.

16. In human eye the part which allows light to enter into the eye is –

(a) Retina (b) Pupil

(c) Eye lens (d) Cornea

For Questions 17-20 are Assertion – Reasoning based questions.

These consists of two statements - Assertion (A) and Reason (R). Answer these questions selecting the appropriate option given below:

(a) Both Assertion (A) and Reason (R) are true and Reason (R) is the correct explanation of Assertion (A).

(b) Both Assertion(A) and Reason (R) are true, but Reason (R) is not the correct explanation of Assertion (A).

(c) Assertion (A) is true, but Reason (R) is false.

(d) Assertion (A) is false, but Reason (R) is true.

17. Assertion (A) : It is advised that while diluting an acid one should add water to acid and not acid to water keeping the solution continuously stirred.

Reason (R) : The process of dissolving an acid into water is highly exothermic.

18. Assertion (A) : The energy which passes to the herbivores does not come back autotrophs.

Reason (R) : The flow of energy in a food chain is unidirectional.

19. Assertion (A) : Amoeba takes in food using finger like extensions of the cell surface.

Reason (R) : In all unicellular organisms, the food is taken in by the entire cell surface.

20. Assertion (A) : Melting point and boiling point of ethanol are lower than that of sodium chloride.

Reason (R) : The forces of attraction between the molecules of ionic compounds are very strong.

SECTION - B

Q. No. 21 to 26 are Very Short Answer Questions.

21. State whether the given chemical reaction is a redox reaction or not. Justify your answer. **2**

$MnO_2 + 4HCl \rightarrow MnCl_2 + 2H_2O + Cl_2$

22. (a) List two difference between the movement of leaves of a sensitive plant and the movement of a shoot towards light. **2**

OR

(b) What happens at synapse between two neurons? State briefly. **2**

23. Give the name of the enzyme present in the fluid in our mouth cavity. State the gland which produces it. What would happen to the digestion process if this gland stops secreting this enzyme? **2**

24. Let the resistance of an electrical device remain constant, while the potential difference across its two ends decreases to one fourth of its initial value. What change will occur in the current through it? State the law which helps us in solving the above stated question. **2**

25. A light ray enters from medium A to medium B as shown in the figure. **2**

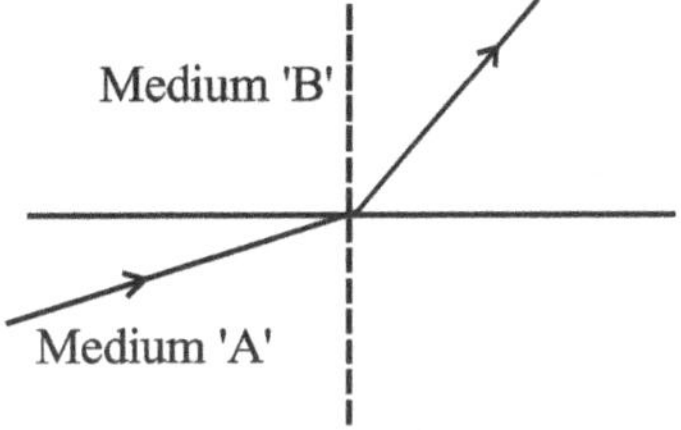

(a) Which one of the two media is denser w.r.t. other medium? Justify your answer. 1

(b) If the speed of light in medium A is v_a and in medium B is v_b, what is the refractive index of B with respect to A. 1

OR

(a) A ray of light starting from diamond is incident on the interface separating diamond and water. Draw a labelled ray diagram to show the refraction of light in this case. 1

(b) Absolute refractive indices of diamond and water are 2.42 and 1.33 respectively. Find the value of refractive index of water w.r.t. diamond. 1

26. State the rule to determine the direction of a (a) magnetic field produced around a straight conductor carrying current and (b) force experienced by a current carrying straight conductor placed in a magnetic field which is perpendicular to it. 2

SECTION - C

Q. No. 27 to 33 are Short Answer Questions.

27. Explain the process of transport of oxygenated and deoxygenated blood in a human body. 3

28. (a) A substance 'X' is used as a building material and is insoluble in water. When it reacts with dil. HCl, it produces a gas which turns lime water milky. 3

(i) Write the chemical name and formula of 'X'.

(ii) Write chemical equations for the chemical reactions involved in the above statements.

OR

(b) A metal 'M' on reacting with dilute acid liberates a gas 'G'. The same metal also liberates gas 'G' when reacts with a base.

(i) Write the name of gas 'G'.

(ii) How will you test the presence of this gas?

(iii) Write chemical equations for the reactions of the metal with (1) an acid and (2) a base. 3

29. (a) Name the gland and the hormone secreted by it in scary situations in human beings. List any two responses shown by our body when this hormone is secreted into the blood. 3

OR

(b) In the given diagram 3

(i) Name the parts labelled A, B, and C.

(ii) Write the functions of A and C.

(iii) Reflex arcs have evolved in animals? Why?

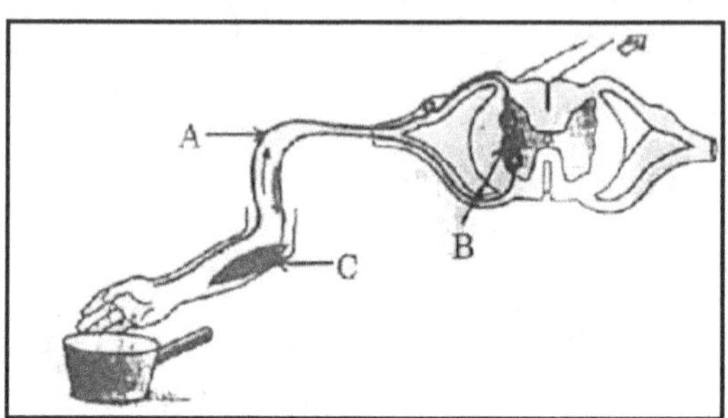

30. With the help of an appropriate example. Justify that some of the chemical reactions are determined by

(a) Change in temperature.

(b) Evolution of a gas, and

(c) Change in colour

Give chemical equation for the reaction involved in each case. 3

31. State reasons for Myopia. With the help of ray diagrams, show the 3

(a) image formation by a myopic eye, and

(b) correction of myopia using an appropriate lens.

32. What is a solenoid? When does a solenoid behave as a magnet? Draw the pattern of the magnetic field produced inside it showing the directions of the magnetic field lines. 3

33. (a) Write the percentage of (i) solar energy captured by the autotrophs and (ii) energy transferred from autotrophs to the next level in a food chain.

(b) What are trophic levels? Why do different food chains in an ecosystem not have more than four to five trophic levels? Give reason. 3

SECTION - D

Q. No. 31 to 36 are Long Answer Questions.

34. (a) (i) A compound 'A' with a molecular formula of $C_2H_4O_2$ reacts with a base to give salt and water. Identify 'A', state its nature and the name of the functional group it possesses. Write chemical equation for the reaction involved.

(ii) When the above stated compound 'A' reacts with another compound 'B' having molecular formula C_2H_6O in the presence of an acid, a sweet smelling compound 'C' is formed.

(1) Identify 'B' and 'C'.

(2) State the role of acid in this reaction. **5**

(3) Write chemical equation for the reaction involved.

OR

(b) (i) Name the compound formed when ethanol is heated at 443 K in the presence of conc. H_2SO_4 and draw its electron dot structure. State the role of conc. H_2SO_4 in this reaction.

(ii) What is hydrogenation? Explain it with the help of a chemical equation. State the role of this reaction in industry. **5**

35. Give reason for the following:

(a) During reproduction inheritance of different proteins will lead to altered body designs.

(b) Fertilization cannot take place in flowers if pollination does not occur.

(c) All multicellular organisms cannot give rise to new individuals through fragmentation or regeneration.

(d) Vegetative propagntion is practised for growing only some type of plants.

(e) The parents and off-springs of organisms reproducing sexually have the same number of chromosomes.

36. (a) (i) What is meant by resistance of a conductor? Defne its SI unit.

(ii) List two factors on which the resistance of a rectangular conductor depends.

(iii) How will the resistance of a wire be affeted if its

(1) length is doubled, and

(2) radius is also doubled?

Give justification for your answer.

OR

(b) In an electric circuit three bulbs of 100 W each are connected in series to a source. In another circuit set of three bulbs of the same wattage are connected in parallel to the same source.

(i) Will the bulb in the two circuits glow with the same brightness? Justify your answer.

(ii) Now, let one bulb in both the circuits get fused. Will the rest of the bulbs continue to glow in each circuit? Give reason for your answer. **5**

SECTION-E

Q. No. 37 to 39 are case based/data based questions with 2 to 3 short sub-parts. Internal choice is provided in one of these sub-parts.

37. On the basis of reactivity metals are grouped into three categories-

(i) Metals of low reactivity

(ii) Metals of medium reactivity

(iii) Metals of high reactivity

Therefore metals ae extracted in pure form from their ores on the basis of their chemical properties.

Metals of high reactivity are extracted from their ores by electrolysis of the molten ore.

Metals of low reactivity are extracted from their sulphide ores, which are converted into their oxides. The oxides of these metals are reduced to metals by simple heating.

(a) Name the process of reduction used for a metal that gives vigorous reaction with air and water both.

(b) Carbon cannot be used as a reducing agent to obtain aluminium from its oxide? Why?

(c) Describe briefly the method to obtain mercury from cinnabar. Write the chemical equation for the reactions involved in the process.

OR

(c) Differentiate between roasting and calcination giving chemical equation for each.

38. All human chromosomes are not paired. Most human chromosomes have a maternal and a paternal copy, and we have 22 such pairs. But one pair called the sex chromosomes, is odd in not always being a perfect pair. Women have a perfect pair of sex chromosomes. But men have a mismatched pair in which one is normal sized while the other is a short one. **4**

(a) In humans, how many chromosomes are present in a Zygote and in each gamete?

(b) A few reptiles rely entirely on environmental cues for sex determination. Comment.

(c) "The sex of a child is a matter of chance and none of the parents are considered to be responsible for it." Justify it through flow chart only.

OR

(c) Why do all the gametes formed in human females have an X chromosome?

39. A student took three concave mirrors of different focal lengths and performed the experiment to see the image formation by placing an object at different distances with these mirrors as shown in the following table. **4**

Case No.	Object-distance	Focal length
I	45 cm	20 cm
II	30 cm	15 cm
III	20 cm	30 cm

Now answer the following questions:

(a) List two properties of the image formed in Case I.

(b) In which one of the cases given in the table, the mirror will form real image of same size and why?

(c) Name the type of mirror used by dentists. Give reason why do they use type of mirrors.

OR

(c) Look at the table and identify the situation (object distance and focal length) which resembles the situation in which concave mirrors are used as shaving mirrors? Draw a ray diagram to show the image formation in this case.

Solutions

1. **(b)** Amphoteric oxides react with both, acids and bases. ZnO and Al_2O_3 are amphoteric in nature. **(1 mark)**

Amphoteric nature of ZnO and Al_2O_3:

$ZnO + 2HCl \longrightarrow ZnCl_2 + H_2O$

$ZnO + 2NaOH \longrightarrow Na_2ZnO_2 + H_2O$

$Al_2O_3 + 6HCl \longrightarrow 2AlCl_3 + 3H_2O$

$Al_2O_3 + 2NaOH \longrightarrow 2NaAlO_2 + H_2O$

2. **(c)** Ammonium chloride (NH_4Cl) is a salt of a strong acid HCl and a weak base NH_4OH.
Thus, there will be an excess of H^+ ions and the PH of the solution will be less than 7. **(1 mark)**

3. **(b)** The reaction between Zn and H_2SO_4 gives an ionic compound $ZnSO_4$ that remains in aqueous state along with the release of H_2 gas.
Thus, X = (aq.), Y = (q) **(1 mark)**

4. **(a)** Phenalphthalein is an indicator that turns pink in alkaline medium.
Therefore, solution 'X' must be an alkaline solution or a solution of a salt of a weak acid and strong base. Thus, 'X' must be Na_2CO_3 and 'Y' must be NH_4Cl. **(1 mark)**

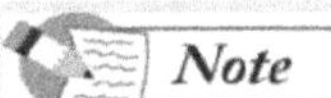

Phenolphthalein is a pH indicator that is colourless at pH between 0 to 8.3, has pink colour at pH between 8.3 and 10.0, and is again colourless at pH above 10.0

5. **(d)** 1- nucleus, 2- chloroplast, 3- vacuole, 4- guard cell **(1 mark)**

Guard cells are pairs of epidermal cells that control gas diffusion by regulating the opening and closure of stomatal pores.

6. **(c)** Walking in a straight line and riding a bicycle are voluntary actions and are controlled by cerebellum. Cerebellum control voluntary actions such as body posture and balance of the body. Involuntary actions such as vomiting, blood pressure are under the control of medulla of hind brain. **(1 mark)**

7. **(a)** In concave mirror, image is erect only when object is between focus (F) and pole (P). So, distance of object from the mirror should be less than focal length i.e. less than 10 cm. **(1 mark)**

8. **(d)** Bronze is an alloy of Cu and Sn.
Brass is an alloy of Cu and Zn. **(1 mark)**

9. **(c)** In pea plants, a pure tall plant (TT) is crossed with a short plant (tt). The ratio of pure tall plant to short plants inF_2 is 1:1
Following combinations of genotype emerge is F_2 generation : TT (1), tt (1) and Tt (2).
This shows that ratio of pure tall (TT) to pure short (tt) is 1:1. **(1 mark)**

10. **(d)** Mice and rabbit are the primary consumers they are dependent on producers like seeds, plants and grass for food. **(1 mark)**

Primary consumers are also known as herbivorous.

11. **(a)** Leishmania undergoes binary fission like Amoeba. Leishmania divides into two daughter cells longitudinally and such a type of binary fission is called longitudinal binary fission. In Leishmania, binary fission occurs in a definite orientation. Nuclear division is followed by the appearance of a constriction in the cell membrane. The membrane grows transversely inwards from the middle of the dividing cell. Cytoplasm separates into two equal parts having one nucleus each. **(1 mark)**

12. **(b)** 'I' is a displacement reaction as it involves displacement of H^+ ions from HCl and formation of $MgCl_2$.
'II' is a double displacement reaction as it involves exchange of ions between NaOH and HCl. **(1 mark)**

13. **(b)** Red colour bend and deviate the least, whereas violet colour bend and deviate the most. So 'P' is violet and 'Q' is red. **(1 mark)**

Dispersion takes place because different colours of light travels with different speed in the prism.

14. **(c)** 'X' and 'Y' only
In the given diagram, flower "X" and "Y" contains female reproductive parts of the flower. Flower 'X' contains both male and female reproductive parts necessary for fertilisation to occur and will facilitate the development of fruit. The female elements are collectively called the pistil. The top of the pistil is called the stigma, which is a sticky surface receptive to pollen and flower 'Z' contains male reproductive parts of the flowers. The male parts of the flower are called the stamens and are made up of the anther at the top and the stalk or filament that supports the anther. The ovary is the part of the female reproductive structure of the flower, the pistil. Ovary bears ovules inside it. Fruit is a ripened ovary of the plant that develops after fertilization. Ovules in the ovary develop into seed. For flower 'Y' the female reproductive part is present if cross fertilisation occurs then fruit will develop. **(1 mark)**

15. **(d)** For an ideal long solenoid, magnetic field inside the solenoid is along the axis and is uniform, and outside the solenoid it is zero. **(1 mark)**

16. **(d)** The front part of eye is cornea and it allows light to enter into the eye. **(1 mark)**

17. **(d)** While diluting an acid, we should add the acid to water to initially make a dilute solution as the process of dissolution is highly exothermic. Thus, Assertion (A) is false but Reason (R) is true. **(1 mark)**

18. **(a)** The flow of energy in a food chain is unidirectional as food chain is a linear sequence of transfer of energy. The energy that is captured by the autotrophs cannot be returned to the sun and the energy which passes to the herbivores cannot be returne back to autotrophs. As it moves successively through the various trophic levels, it is no longer available to the last trophic level. **(1 mark)**

19. **(c)** Amoeba possesses finger- like projections called as pseudopodia which are involved in fetching and consumption of prey but the entire cell surface is not involved in this process. **(1 mark)**

Amoeba are found in water bodies such as ponds, lakes and slow-moving rivers.

20. **(a)** Ethanol is a covalent compound that has weak attractive forces while NaCl is an ionic compound that has stronger electrostatic or coulombic forces of attraction. Therefore, the melting and boiling point of ethanol are lower than that of NaCl.
Thus, both, Assertion (A) and Reason (R) are correct and Reason (R) is a correct explanation of Assertion (A). **(1 mark)**

21. The given reaction involves conversion of MnO_2 into $MnCl_2$ in which the oxidation state of Mn changes from +4 to +2. Thus, it is reduced. **(1 mark)**
The oxidation state of Cl changes from –1 in HCl to 0 in Cl_2. Thus, it is oxidized. **(1 mark)**
Therefore, the given reaction is a Redox reaction.

22. (a) The movement of leaves may occur in response to touch. So the information that is touch is communicated by electrical chemical means transfer from cell to cell. The movement of shoot occurs due to phototropism that is the movement of shoot in direction of sunlight. **(2 marks)**

OR

(b) Transmission of nerve impulses occurs between two neurons via junction called the synapse. At the end of the axon, the electrical impulse sets releases some chemicals (neurotransmitters). These chemicals cross the gap or synapse and start a similar electrical impulse in the dendrite of the next neuron. **(2 marks)**

23. Enzyme present in the liquid of mouth cavity is salivary amylase. Gland which produces this enzyme is salivary gland this enzyme helps in digestion of starch in our mouth if this gland stop secreting this enzyme the digestion of starch will stop. **(2 marks)**

24. As R is constant, so by Ohm's law current through the conductor is directly proportional to potential difference across it. Therefore if potential difference is decreased to one-fourth of initial value, current will also decrease to one-fourth of initial value. **(2 marks)**

25. (a) As light is bending towards normal so ray is moving from rarer medium to denser medium. So medium 'B' is denser w.r.t. medium 'A'. **(1 mark)**

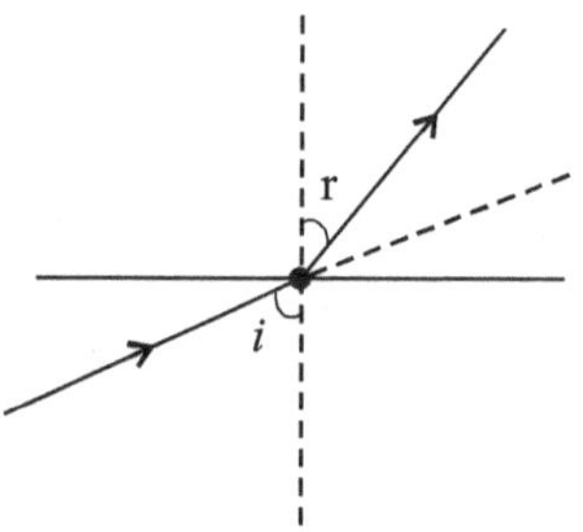

(b) Refractive index of 'B' w.r.t 'A' is given as

$$^{A}\mu_B = \frac{\mu_B}{\mu_A} = \frac{\frac{c}{v_B}}{\frac{c}{v_A}} = \frac{v_A}{v_B} = \frac{v_a}{v_b}$$

$[\because v_A = v_a \text{ and } v_B = v_b]$ **(1 mark)**

OR

(a) As ray is moving from diamond (denser) to water (rarer), so ray will bend away from normal. **(1 mark)**

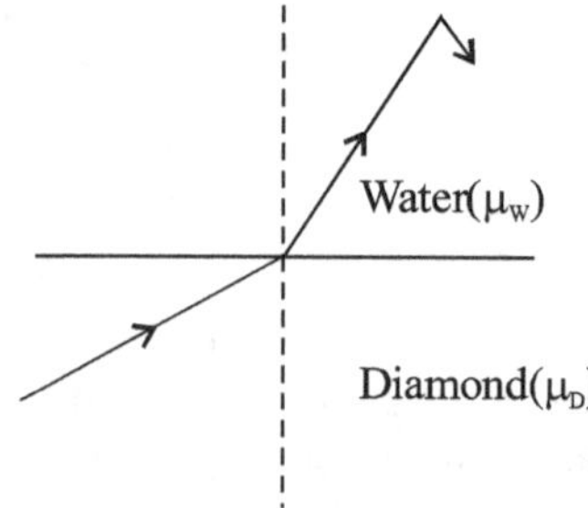

(b) Refractive index of water w.r.t diamond is given as

$$\frac{\mu_W}{\mu_D}$$

So, $\frac{\mu_W}{\mu_D} = \frac{1.33}{2.42} = \frac{133}{242}$ **(1 mark)**

26. (a) "Maxwell's Right- Hand Thumb Rule "can be used to determine the direction of magnetic field lines around a current-carrying straight conductor. **(1 mark)**

(b) "Fleming's Left Hand Rule" is used to find the direction of force acting on a current carrying conductor, placed in a magnetic field. **(1 mark)**

27. The heart is a muscular organ which is as big as our fist. Because both oxygen and carbon dioxide have to be transported by the blood, the heart has different chambers to prevent the oxygen-rich blood from mixing with the blood containing carbon dioxide. The carbon dioxide-rich blood has to reach the lungs for the carbon dioxide to be removed, and the oxygenated blood from the lungs has to be brought back to the heart. This oxygen-rich blood is then pumped to the rest of the body. We can follow this process step by step. Oxygen-rich blood from the lungs comes to the thin-walled upper chamber of the heart on the left, the left atrium. The left atrium relaxes when it is collecting this blood. It then contracts, while the next chamber, the left ventricle, relaxes, so that the blood is transferred to it. When the muscular left ventricle contracts in its turn, the blood is pumped out to the body. De-oxygenated blood comes from the body to the upper chamber on the right, the right atrium, as it relaxes. As the right atrium contracts, the corresponding lower chamber, the right ventricle, dilates. This transfers blood to the right ventricle, which in turn pumps it to the lungs for oxygenation. Since ventricles have to pump blood into various organs, they have thicker muscular walls than the atria do. Valves ensure that blood does not flow backwards when the atria or ventricles contract. **(3 marks)**

28. (a) (i) 'X' = Calcium carbonate, $CaCO_3$. **(1 mark)**

(ii) Equations:–

$$\underset{(S)}{CaCO_3} + 2HCl \longrightarrow CaCl_2 + H_2O + CO_2 \uparrow$$

$$\underset{\text{(lime water)}}{Ca(OH)_2 + CO_2} \longrightarrow \underset{\text{(milky solution)}}{CaCO_3 + H_2O}$$ **(2 marks)**

OR

(b) (i) The gas evolved in both the cases in Hydrogen. 'G' = H_2. **(1 mark)**

(ii) The presence of H_2 gas can be checked by bringing a burning candle near the gas. **(1 mark)**
A popping sound indicates the presence of H_2 gas.

(iii) Reactions:-

(1) $Zn + 2HCl \longrightarrow ZnCl_2 + H_2 \uparrow$

(2) $Zn + 2NaOH \longrightarrow \underset{\text{(sodium zincate)}}{Na_2ZnO_2} + H_2 \uparrow$

(1 mark)

29. (a) Adrenaline (epinephrine) is a hormone adrenal glands make to help human being to prepare for stressful or dangerous situations. Adrenaline is secreted directly into the blood and carried to different parts of the body. The target organs or the specific tissues on which it acts include the heart. As a result, the heart beats faster, resulting in supply of more oxygen to our muscles. The blood to the digestive system and skin is reduced due to contraction of muscles around small arteries in these organs. **(3 marks)**

OR

(i) A- Sensory neuron, B- Relay neuron, C- Effector muscle in arm

(ii) A sensory neuron carries impulses from the receptor to the CNS (brain or spinal cord). C- Effectors are muscles or glands which respond when they receive impulses from motor neurones. Examples of effectors are the biceps and triceps muscles in the arm. When stimulated, muscles contract get shorter).

(iii) A basic reflex arc consist of sensory neurons, motor neuron and the muscle or gland cells.

Reflex arc, have evolved in animals, in order to perform quick responses against the external stimuli, as the thinking process of brain is not fast enough. **(3 marks)**

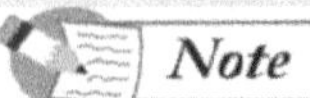
Note

The main difference between sensory and motor neuron is their function and structure.

30. (a) Chemical reaction detected by a change in temperature:-

$$\underset{\text{(Quick lime)}}{CaO} + H_2O \longrightarrow Ca(OH)_2 + \text{Heat}$$

This reaction involves release of heat (exothermic reaction) along with the formation of $Ca(OH)_2$.
Thus, the temperature of the system rises indicating a chemical change. **(1 mark)**

(b) Chemical Reaction detected by evolution of a gas:-

$$Zn + H_2SO_4 \longrightarrow ZnSO_4 + H_2 \uparrow$$

The H_2 gas produced here gives a popping sound upon burning, indicating a chemical change has taken place. **(1 mark)**

(c) Chemical reaction detected by a change in colour:-

$$\underset{\text{(Green)}}{FeSO_4} \xrightarrow{\text{Heat}} \underset{\text{(Brown–red)}}{Fe_2O_3} + SO_2 + SO_3$$

Here, the thermal decomposition of $FeSO_4$ causes it to give brown-reddish Fe_2O_3. **(1 mark)**

31. If the eyeball is too long or the eyelens is too spherical then final image is formed infront of retina and this condition is called myopia **(1 mark)**

(a) Image formation by myopic eye

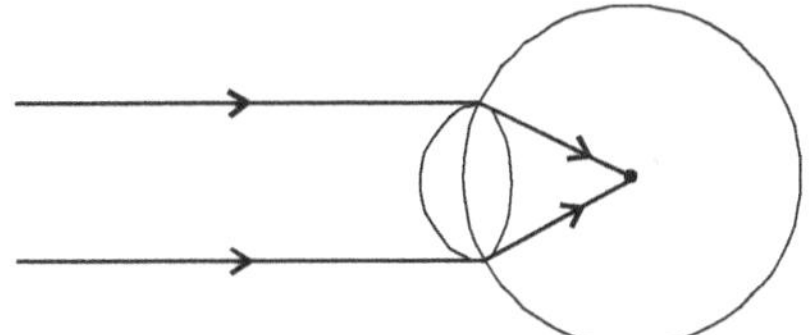

(1 marks)

(b) Correction of myopia by concave lens

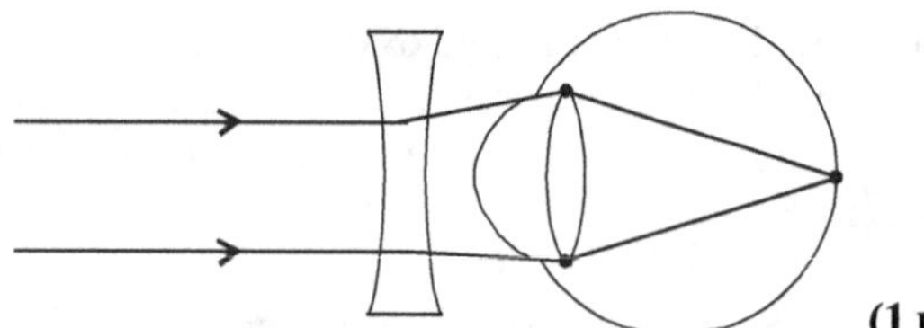

(1 mark)

32. A long coil of wire consisting of closely packed loop is called solenoid. **(1 mark)**

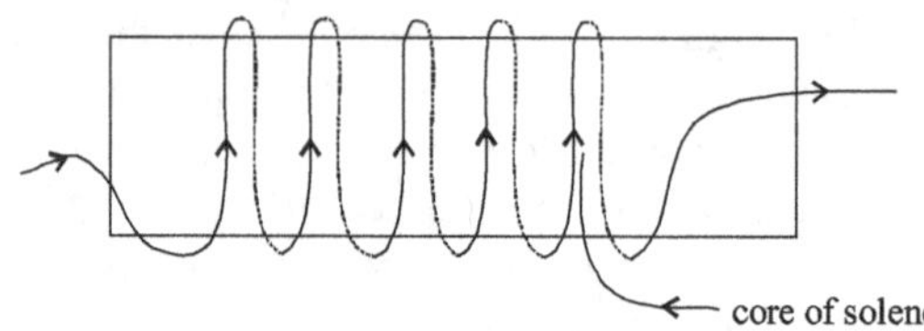

A solenoid acts as a magnet when current flows through it. **(1 mark)**

Pattern of magnetic field lines inside solenoid:-

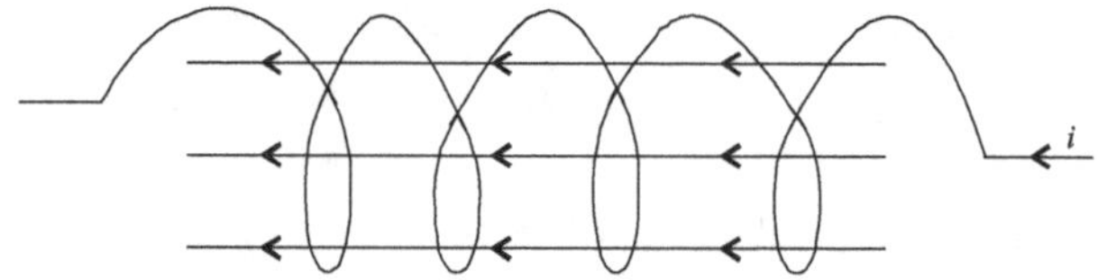

33. (a) (i) The green plants in a terrestrial ecosystem capture about 1% of the energy of sunlight that falls on their leaves and convert it into food energy.

(ii) When green plants are eaten by primary consumers, a great deal of energy is lost as heat to the environment, some amount goes into digestion and in doing work and the rest goes towards growth and reproduction. An average of 10% of the food eaten is turned into its own body and made available for the next level of consumers. Therefore, 10% can be taken as the average value for the amount of organic matter that is present at each step and reaches the next level of consumers. **(1½ marks)**

(b) Each step or level of the food chain forms a trophic level. There is only 10% flow of energy from one trophic level to the next. The loss of energy at each step is consistent that very little usable energy is available after four or five trophic levels. Hence only 4 to 5 trophic levels are present in each food chain. **(1½ marks)**

34. **(a)** (i) since the compound gives a salt and water upon reaction with a base, it is an acidic compound. The molecular formula $C_2H_4O_2$ represents a molecule of ethanoic acid CH_3COOH.

'A' = CH_3COOH

Ethanoic acid is a low-melting and boiling compound with vinegar smell.

Functional Group present = – COOH (Carboxylic group) **(1 mark)**

Chemical equation for the reaction -

$$CH_3COOH + NaOH \longrightarrow \underset{\text{(Sodium ethanoate)}}{CH_3COONa} + H_2O$$

(1 mark)

(ii) Ethanoic acid (A) reacts with ethanol (CH_3CH_2OHB) to give a sweet smelling ester (c).

(1) 'B' = CH_3CH_2OH (ethanol)

'C'= $CH_3COOC_2H_5$(ester) **(1 mark)**

(2) The presence of an acid (H^+) in this reaction catalyses the esterification reaction. **(1 mark)**

(3) $$CH_3COOH + CH_3 - CH_2OH \xrightleftharpoons{H^+} CH_3 - COOC_2H_5 + H_2O$$

(1 mark)

OR

(b) (i) $$\underset{\text{ethanol}}{CH_3 - CH_2 - OH} \xrightarrow[H_2SO_4, 443K]{\text{Hot conc.}} \underset{\text{ethene}}{CH_2 = CH_2} + H_2O$$ **(1 mark)**

Electron-dot structure of ethene:-

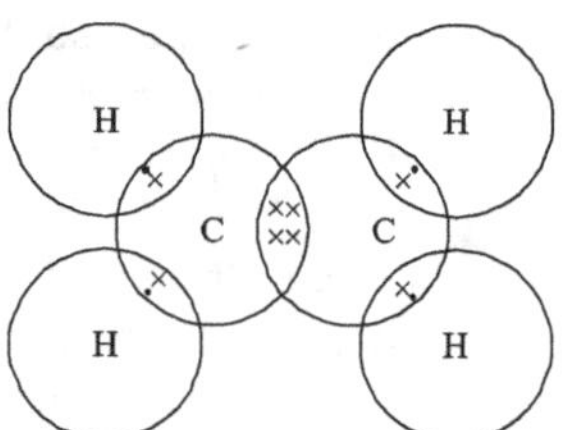

(1 mark)

Role of H_2SO_4 = It is used as a dehydrating agent. **(1 mark)**

(ii) Hydrogenation is an addition reaction in which a hydrogen molecule is added usually to an unsaturated organic compound. **(1 mark)**

$$\begin{matrix} R & & R \\ & C=C & \\ R & & R \end{matrix} \xrightarrow[H_2]{\text{Nickel Catalyst}} \begin{matrix} & H & H & \\ & | & | & \\ R- & C & -C & -R \\ & | & | & \\ & R & R & \end{matrix}$$ **(1 mark)**

Industrially, this reaction is used for the conversion of vegetable oils to saturated fats or ghee.

35. (a) Cellular DNA is the information source for making proteins in the cell. The DNA in the cell nucleus is the information source for making proteins. If the information is changed, different proteins will be made. Different proteins will eventually lead to altered body designs. Therefore, a basic event in reproduction is the creation of a DNA copy. **(1 mark)**

(b) Flower fertilization requires both male and female gametes. If pollination does not occur it means that the male gamete is not available, hence fertilization cannot take place. **(1 mark)**

(c) Complex multicellular organisms cannot give rise to new organism by using methods of reproduction like regeneration or fragmentation because the tissue and specialised cell make up the organs in the body. This is because of high degree of specialisation, multicellular organisms cannot reproduce by regeneration of a part of some tissue. **(1 mark)**

(d) The property of vegetative propagation is used in methods such as layering or grafting to grow many plants like sugarcane, roses, or grapes for agricultural purposes. Plants raised by vegetative propagation can bear flowers and fruits earlier than those produced from seeds. Such methods also make possible the propagation of plants such as banana, orange, rose and jasmine that have lost the capacity to produce seeds. **(1 mark)**

(e) Gametes of sexually-reproducing animals have half the number of chromosomes as that of the parents. Thus, during fertilization, when two gametes i.e. male and female gametes, fuse, the offspring produced will have the same amount of DNA or the same number of chromosomes as that of the parent. **(1 mark)**

36. (a)

(i) Resistance of a conductor is the opposition offered by it to flow of charge carriers (electron) inside it. Its SI unit is Ohm. **(1½ marks)**

(ii) Resistance depends on factors such as

(1) Nature of conductor

(2) Length of conductor

(3) Cross-sectional area of conductor **(1½ marks)**

(iii)

(1) As $R \propto l$

So if length is doubled, then resistance also get doubled. **(1 mark)**

(2) As $R \propto \frac{1}{A}$ i.e $R \propto \frac{1}{r^2}$ $\left[\because A = \pi r^2\right]$

So if radius is doubled, then resistance becomes one-fourth. **(1 mark)**

OR

(b) (i) Let us assume that resistance of each bulb is R Case (1)

Current in each bulb $= \frac{V}{3R}$ **(1 mark)**

Case (2)

Net current $= \frac{V}{R/3} = \frac{3V}{R}$ **(1 mark)**

Current will get equally divided in three bulbs $= \frac{I}{3} = \frac{V}{R}$

Bulbs in case (2) will glow with great brightness because current $\propto$ Brightness. **(1 mark)**

(b) Now if one bulb gets fused, in case (1), rest of bulbs will not glow because in series voltage eruption in one appliance will affect other appliances. **(1 mark)**

But in case (b) all other bulbs will glow as voltage eruption in one bulb does not affect the voltage of other bulbs. **(1 mark)**

37. (a) Highly reactive metals like Na are obtained by 'Electrolytic reduction'. **(1 mark)**

The metal is deposited at cathode of the electrolytic cell.

(b) Carbon cannot be used as a reducing agent to obtain aluminium from its oxide because Al lies up in the reactivity series of metals and for such metals, electrolytic reduction is a suitable method. **(1 mark)**

(c) Cinnabar (HgS) is a sulphide ore of Hg.

Hg lies low in the reactivity series. First, HgS is heated to give HgO which upon further heating, gives Hg. **(1 mark)**

$$2HgS(s) + 3O_2(g) \xrightarrow{\text{Heat}} 2HgO(s) + 2SO_2(g)$$

$$2HgO(s) \xrightarrow{\text{Heat}} 2Hg(l) + O_2(g)$$ **(1 mark)**

OR

(c) **Roasting:** It is the process of heating the sulphide ores in the excess of air to give corresponding metal oxides. **(½ mark)**

e.g: $2ZnS(s) + 3O_2(g) \xrightarrow{\text{Heat}} 2ZnO(s) + 2SO_2(g)$ **(½ mark)**

Calcination : It is the process of heating the ore in the absence of air to directly give the oxide of the metal. **(½ mark)**

e.g. $2ZnCO_3(s) \xrightarrow{\text{Heat}} ZnO(s) + CO_2(g)$ **(½ mark)**

38. (a) Zygote is formed due to the fusion of male and female gametes. Gametes are haploid cells. Thus fusion of two haploid cells results in the formation of a diploid cell. Therefore zygote is a diploid cell with 46 chromosomes. **(1 mark)**

(b) In few reptiles like crocodiles, alligators and turtles, the temperature of egg incubation has a significant influence on the sex determination of the developing embryos. **(1 mark)**

(c) Most human chromosomes have a maternal and a paternal copy, and we have 22 such pairs. But one pair, called the sex chromosomes, is odd in not always being a perfect pair. Women have a perfect pair of sex chromosomes, both called X. But men have a mismatched pair in which one is a normal-sized X while the other is a short one called Y. So women are XX, while men are XY. All children will inherit an X chromosome from their mother regardless of whether they are boys or girls. Thus, the sex of the children will be determined by what they inherit from their father. A child who inherits an X chromosome from her father will be a girl, and one who inherits a Y chromosome from him will be a boy. Thus, the sex of a child is a matter of chance and none of the parents are considered to be responsible for it. **(2 mark)**

OR

All children will inherit an X chromosome from their mother regardless of whether they are boys or girls. Thus, the sex of the children will be determined by what they inherit from their father. A child who inherits an X chromosome from her father will be a girl, and one who inherits a Y chromosome from him will be a boy. Thus, all the gametes formed in human females have an X chromosome. **(4 mark)**

39. (a) Here, $|u| = 45$ cm and $|f| = 20$cm

as $|u| > |2f|$ So image formed will be (i) real and inverted

(ii) Between f and 2f **(½ × 2 = 1 mark)**

(iii) Smaller than size of object

(b) In case (II), image will be formed at centre of curvature and will be real and size same as that of object. **(1 mark)**

(c) Dentist use concave mirror because when teeth is in between focus (F) and pole (P) of concave mirror, we get enlarged and erect image behind the mirror. **(2 mark)**

OR

(c) Case (III) is used as shaving mirror, because when face is between focus (F) and pole (P) of concave mirror, we get enlarged and erect image behind the mirror as shown in fig. below. **(1 mark)**

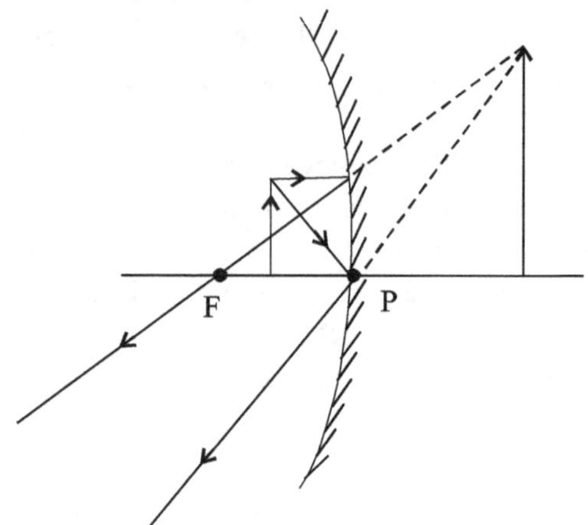

(1 mark)

Delhi 2023

CBSE Board Solved Paper

Time Allowed : 3 hrs. | *Maximum Marks : 80*

General Instructions:

Read the following instructions very carefully and strictly follow them :

(i) This question paper consists of **39** questions. **All** questions are compulsory.
(ii) Question paper is divided into **FIVE** sections – **Section A, B, C, D** and **E.**
(iii) In **section A** – question number 1 to 20 are multiple choice questions (MCQs) carrying **1** mark each.
(iv) In **section B** – question number 21 to 26 are very short answer (VSA) type questions carrying **2** marks each. Answer to these questions should be in the range of 30 to 50 words.
(v) In **section C** – question number 27 to 33 are short answer (SA) type questions carrying **3** marks each. Answer to these questions should in the range of 50 to 80 words.
(vi) In **section D** – question number 34 to 36 are long answer (LA) type questions carrying **5** marks each. Answer to these questions should be in the range of 80 to 120 words.
(vii) In **section E** – question number 37 to 39 are of 3 **source based/case based units of assessment** carrying **4** marks each with sub-parts.
(viii) There is no overall choice. However, an internal choice has been provided in some sections.

SECTION - A

(Multiple Choice Questions)

1. When Sodium bicarbonate reacts with dilute hydrochloric acid, the gas evolved is: **1**

(a) Hydrogen; it gives pop sound with burning match stick.

(b) Hydrogen; it turns lime water milky.

(c) Carbon dioxide; it turns lime water milky.

(d) Carbon dioxide; it blows off a burning match stick with a pop sound.

2. When aqueous solutions of potassium iodide and lead nitrate are mixed, an insoluble substance separates out. The chemical equation for the reaction involved is: **1**

(a) $KI + PbNO_3 \rightarrow PbI + KNO_3$

(b) $2KI + Pb(NO_3)_2 \rightarrow PbI_2 + 2KNO_3$

(c) $KI + Pb(NO_3)_2 \rightarrow PbI + KNO_3$

(d) $KI + PbNO_3 \rightarrow PbI_2 + KNO_3$

3. A metal ribbon 'X' burns in oxygen with a dazzling white flame forming a white ash 'Y'. The correct description of X, Y and the type of reaction is: **1**

(a) X = Ca; Y = CaO;
Type of reaction = Decomposition

(b) X = Mg; Y = MgO;
Type of reaction = Combination

(c) X = Al; Y = Al_2O_3;
Type of reaction = Thermal decomposition

(d) X = Zn; Y = ZnO;
Type of reaction = Endothermic

4. Acid present in tomato is: **1**

(a) Methanoic acid (b) Acetic acid
(c) Lactic acid (d) Oxalic acid

5. Sodium hydroxide is termed an alkali while Ferric hydroxide is not because: **1**

(a) Sodium hydroxide is a strong base, while Ferric hydroxide is a weak base.

(b) Sodium hydroxide is a base which is soluble in water while Ferric hydroxide is also a base but it is not soluble in water.

(c) Sodium hydroxide is a strong base while Ferric hydroxide is a strong acid.

(d) Sodium hydroxide and Ferric hydroxide both are strong base but the solubility of Sodium hydroxide in water is comparatively higher than that of Ferric hydroxide.

6. The name of the salt used to remove permanent hardness of water is: **1**

(a) Sodium hydrogen carbonate ($NaHCO_3$)

(b) Sodium chloride (NaCl)

(c) Sodium carbonate decahydrate ($Na_2CO_3 . 10H_2O$)

(d) Calcium sulphate hemihydrate ($CaSO_4 . \frac{1}{2}H_2O$)

7. The electron dot structure of chlorine molecule is: **1**

(a) 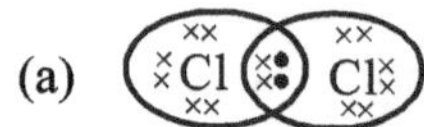

(b) 

(c) 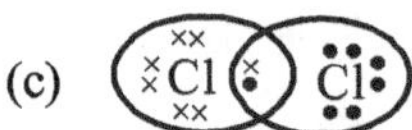

(d) 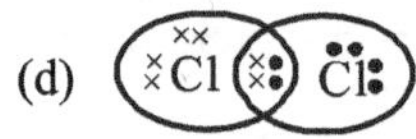

8. Observe the following diagram and identify the process and its significance from the following options: **1**

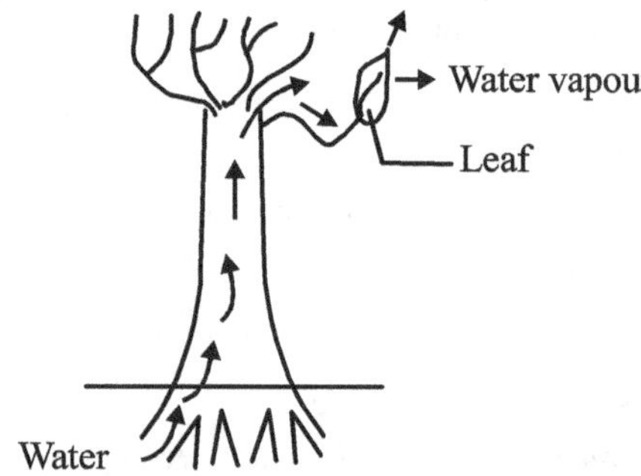

(a) Evaporation : maintains water contents in leaf cells.

(b) Transpiration : creates a suction force which pulls water inside the plant.

(c) Excretion : helps in excreting out waste water from the plant.

(d) Translocation : helps in transporting materials from one cell to another.

9. Opening and closing of stomata is due to: **1**

(a) High pressure of gases inside the cells.

(b) Movement of water in and out of the guard cells.

(c) Stimulus of light in the guard cells.

(d) Diffusion of CO_2 in and out of the guard cells.

10. A cross between pea plant with white flowers (vv) and pea plant with violet flowers (VV) resulted in F_2 progeny in which ratio of violet (VV) and white (vv) flowers will be: **1**

(a) 1 : 1 (b) 2 : 1

(c) 3 : 1 (d) 1 : 3

11. In plants the role of cytokinin is: **1**

(a) Promote cell division.

(b) Wilting of leaves.

(c) Promote the opening of stomatal pore.

(d) Help in the growth of stem.

12. The number of chromosomes in parents and offsprings of a particular species undergoing sexual reproduction remain constant due to: **1**

(a) 'doubling of chromosomes after zygote formation.

(b) halving of chromosomes after zygote formation.

(c) doubling of chromosomes before gamete formation.

(d) halving of chromosomes at the time of gamete formation.

13. Two LED bulbs of 12W and 6W are connected in series. If the current through 12W bulb is 0.06A the current through 6W bulb will be: **1**

(a) 0.04A (b) 0.06A

(c) 0.08A (d) 0.12A

14. The correct pattern of magnetic field lines of the field produced by a current carrying circular loop is: **1**

(a) 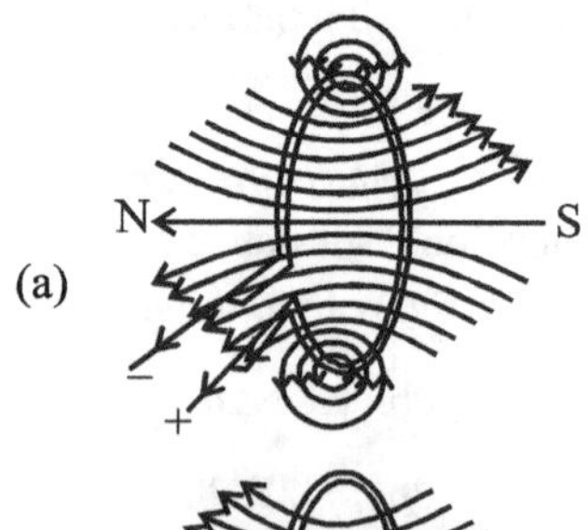

(b) 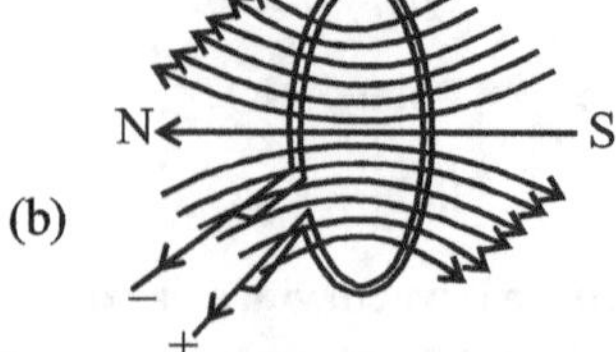

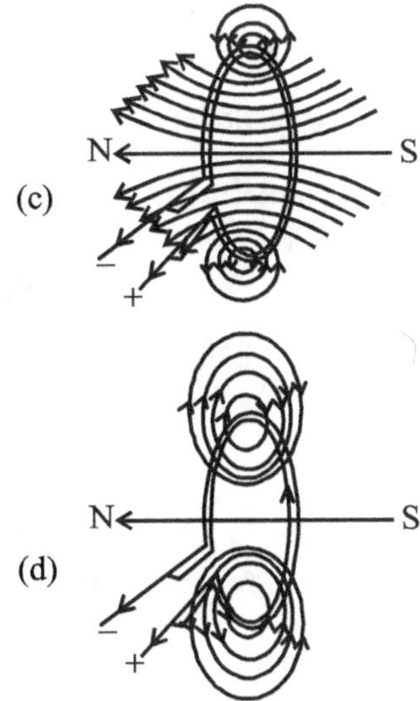

15. The resistance of a resistor is reduced to half of its initial value. If other parameters of the electrical circuit remain unaltered, the amount of heat produced in the resistor will become: **1**

(a) four times (b) two times

(c) half (d) one fourth

16. An alpha particle enters a uniform magnetic field as shown. The direction of force experienced by the alpha particle is: **1**

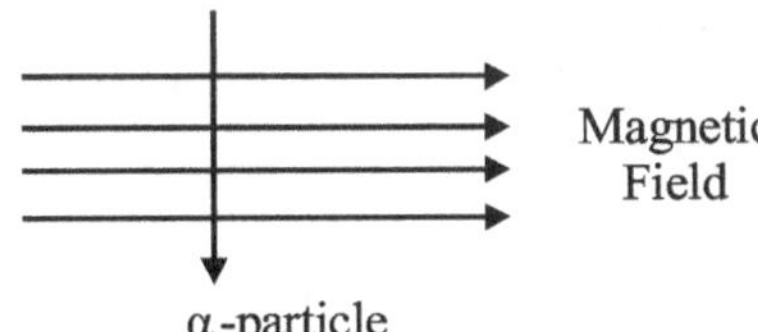

(a) towards right (b) towards left

(c) into the page (d) out of the page

For Questions 17-20, are Assertion – Reasoning based questions.

These consist of two statements - Assertion (A) and Reason (R). Answer these questions selecting the appropriate option given below:

(a) Both (A) and (R) are true and (R) is the correct explanation of (A).

(b) Both (A) and (R) are true, but (R) is not the correct explanation of (A).

(c) (A) is true, but (R) is false.

(d) (A) is false, but (R) is true.

17. **Assertion (A) :** Reaction of Quicklime with water is an exothermic reaction.

Reason (R) : Quicklime reacts vigorously with water releasing a large amount of heat. **1**

18. **Assertion (A) :** In humans, if gene (B) is responsible for black eyes and gene (b) is responsible for brown eyes, then the colour of eyes of the progeny having gene combination Bb, bb, or BB will be black only.

Reason (R) : The black colour of the eyes is a dominant trait. **1**

19. **Assertion (A) :** The inner walls of the small intestine have finger like projections called villi which are rich in blood.

Reason (R) : These villi have a large surface area to help the small intestine in completing the digestion of food. **1**

20. **Assertion (A) :** A current carrying straight conductor experiences a force when placed perpendicular to the direction of magnetic field.

Reason (R) : The net charge on a current carrying conductor is always zero. **1**

SECTION - B

Q. No. 21 to 26 are Very Short Answer Questions.

21. (A) A student took a small amount of copper oxide in a conical flask and added dilute hydrochloric acid to it with constant stirring. He observed a change in colour of the solution. **2**

(i) Write the name of the compound formed and its colour.

(ii) Write a balanced chemical equation for the reaction involved.

OR

(B) The industrial process used for the manufacture of caustic soda involves electrolysis of an aqueous solution of compound 'X'. In this process, two gases 'Y' and 'Z' are liberated. 'Y' is liberated at cathode and 'Z', which is liberated at anode, on treatment with dry slaked like forms a compound 'B'. Name X, Y, Z and B. **2**

22. (A) Name the part of brain which is responsible for the following actions: 2

(i) Maintaining posture and balance

(ii) Beating of heart

(iii) Thinking

(iv) Blood pressure

OR

(B) Where are auxins synthesized in a plant? Which organ of the plant shows: 2

(i) Positive phototropism

(ii) Negative geotropism

(iii) Positive hydrotropism

23. Write one specific function each of the following organs in relation with excretion in human beings: 2

(i) Renal Artery

(ii) Urethra

(iii) Glomerulus

(iv) Tubular part of nephron

24. Two green plants are kept separately in oxygen free containers, one in the dark and other in sunlight. It was observed that plant kept in dark could not survive longer. Give reason for this observation. 2

25. (A) Observe the following diagram and answer the questions following it: 2

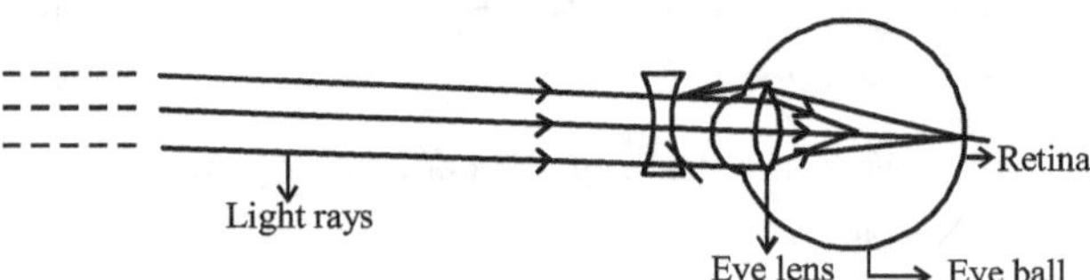

(i) Identify the defect of vision shown.

(ii) List its two causes.

(iii) Name the type of lens used for the correction of this defect.

OR

(B) The colour of clear sky from the earth appears blue but from the space it appears black. Why? 2

26. Use of several pesticides which results in excessive accumulation of pesticides in rivers or ponds, is a matter of deep concern. Justify this statement. 2

SECTION - C

(Short Answer Questions)

27. (i) While electrolysing water before passing the current some drops of an acid are added. Why? Name the gases liberated at cathode and anode. Write the relationship between the volume of gas collected at anode and the volume of gas collected at cathode. 3

(ii) What is observed when silver chloride is exposed to sunlight? Give the type of reaction involved.

28. (i) Suggest a safe procedure of diluting a strong concentrated acid. 3

(ii) Name the salt formed when sulphuric acid is added to sodium hydroxide and write its pH.

(iii) Dry HCl gas does not change the colour of dry blue litmus paper. Why?

29. (A) (i) How does Paramecium obtain its food? 3

(ii) List the role of each of the following in our digestive system:

(a) Hydrochloric acid

(b) Trypsin

(c) Muscular walls of stomach

(d) Salivary amylase

OR

(B) (i) What is double circulation? 3

(ii) Why is the separation of the right side and the left side of the heart useful? How does it help birds and mammals?

30. (A) Define the following terms in the context of a diverging mirror: 3

(i) Principal focus

(ii) Focal length

Draw a labelled ray diagram to illustrate your answer.

OR

(B) An object of height 10 cm is placed 25 cm away from the optical centre of a converging lens of focal length 15 cm. Calculate the image-distance and height of the image formed. **3**

31. The power of a lens is +4D. Find the focal length of this lens. An object is placed at a distance of 50 cm from the optical centre of this lens. State the nature and magnification of the image formed by the lens and also draw a ray diagram to justify your answer. **3**

32. (A) (i) Why is an alternating current (A.C.) considered to be advantageous over direct current (D.C.) for the long distance transmission of electric power?

(ii) How is the type of current used in household supply different from the one given by a battery of dry cells?

(iii) How does an electric fuse prevent the electric circuit and the appliances from a possible damage due to short circuiting or overloading.

OR

(B) For the current carrying solenoid as shown, draw magnetic field lines and give reason to explain that out of the three points A, B and C, at which point the field strength is maximum and at which point it is minimum?

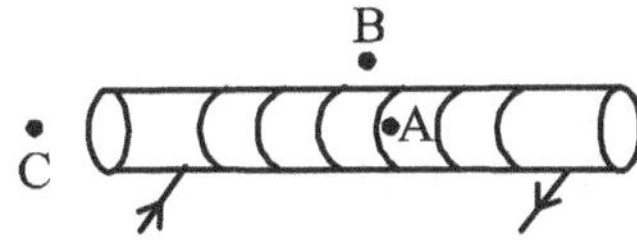

33. Write one difference between biodegradable and non-biodegradable wastes. List two impacts of each type of the accumulated waste on environment if not disposed off properly. **3**

SECTION - D

(Long Answer Questions)

34. (A) (i) Draw the structure of the following compounds:

(a) Butanoic acid (b) Chloropentane **5**

(ii) How are structure (a) and structure (b) given below related to one another? Give reason to justify your answer.

$$\underset{CH_3}{\overset{CH_3}{>}}CH-CH\underset{CH_3}{\overset{CH_3}{<}}$$

Structure (i)

$$CH_3-\overset{CH_3}{\underset{CH_3}{C}}-CH_2CH_3$$

Structure (ii)

Draw one more possible structure for above case.

(iii) Differentiate between saturated and unsaturated carbon compounds on the basis of their general formula.

OR

(B) (i) What happens when a small piece of sodium is dropped in ethanol? Write the equation for this reaction. **5**

(ii) Why is glacial acetic acid called so?

(iii) What happens when ethanol is heated at 443 K in the presence of conc. H_2SO_4? Write the role of conc. H_2SO_4 in this case.

(iv) Write an equation showing saponification.

35. (i) Name and explain the two modes of asexual reproduction observed in hydra. **5**

(ii) What is vegetative propagation? List two advantages of using this technique.

36. (i) How is electric current related to the potential difference across the terminals of a conductor? **5**

Draw a labelled circuit diagram to verify this relationship.

(ii) Why should an ammeter have low resistance?

(iii) Two V - I graphs A and B for series and parallel combinations of two resistors are as shown. Giving reason state which graph shows (a) series, (b) parallel combination of the resistors.

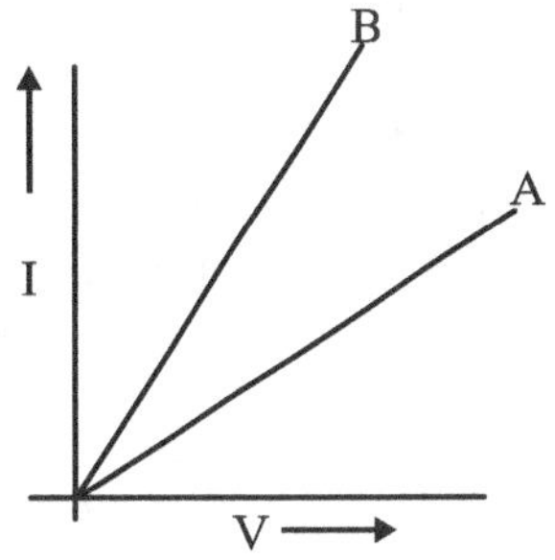

SECTION-E

(Source Based/Case Based Questions)

37. The melting points and boiling points of some ionic compounds are given below: **4**

Compound	Melting Point (K)	Boiling Point (K)
NaCl	1074	1686
LiCl	887	1600
$CaCl_2$	1045	1900
CaO	2850	3120
$MgCl_2$	981	1685

These compounds are termed ionic because they are formed by the transfer of electrons from a metal to a non-metal. The electron transfer in such compounds is controlled by the electric configuration of the elements involved. Every element tends to attain a completely filled valence shell of its nearest noble gas or a stable octet.

(i) Show the electron transfer in the formation of magnesium chloride. **1**

(ii) List two properties of ionic compounds other than their high melting and boiling points. **1**

(iii) (A) While forming an ionic compound say sodium chloride how does sodium atom attain its stable configuration? **2**

OR

(iii) (B) Give reasons: **2**

(i) Why do ionic compounds in the solid state not conduct electricity?

(ii) What happens at the cathode when electricity is passed through an aqueous solution of sodium chloride?

38. The most obvious outcome of the reproductive process is the generation of individuals of similar design, but in sexual reproduction they may not be exactly alike. The resemblances as well as differences are marked. The rules of heredity determine the process by which traits and characteristics are reliably inherited. Many experiments have been done to study the rules of inheritance. **4**

(i) Why an offspring of human being is not a true copy of his parents in sexual reproduction? **1**

(ii) While performing experiments on inheritance in plants, what is the difference between F_1 and F_2 generation? **1**

(iii) (A) Why do we say that variations are useful for the survival of a species over time? **2**

OR

(iii) (B) Study Mendel's cross between two plants with a pair of contrasting characters.

RRYY × rryy

Round Yellow × Wrinkled Green

He observed 4 types of combinations in F_2 generation. Which of these were new combinations? Why do new features which are not present in the parents, appear in F_2 generation?

39. The ability of a medium to refract light is expressed in terms of its optical density. Optical density has a definite connotation. It is not the same as mass density. On comparing two media, the one with the large refractive index is optically denser medium than the other. The other medium with a lower refractive index is optically rarer. Also the speed of light through a given medium is inversely proportional to its optical density. **4**

(i) Determine the speed of light in diamond if the refractive index of diamond with respect of vacuum is 2.42. Speed of light in vacuum is 3×10^8 m/s. **1**

(ii) Refractive indices of glass, water and carbon disulphide are 1.5, 1.33 and 1.62 respectively. If a ray of light is incident in these media at the same angle (say θ), then write the increasing order of the angle of refraction in these media. **1**

(iii) (A) The speed of light in glass 2×10^8 m/s and in water is 2.25×10^8 m/s. **2**

(a) Which one of the two is optically denser and why?

(b) A ray of light is incident normally at the water-glass interface when it enters a thick glass container filled with water. What will happen to the path of the ray after entering the glass? Give reason.

OR

(iii) (B) The absolute refractive indices of water and glass are 4/3 and 3/2 respectively. If the speed of light in glass is 2×10^8 m/s, find the speed of light in (i) vacuum and (ii) water. **2**

Solutions

1. **(c)** $NaHCO_3 + HCl \longrightarrow NaCl + H_2O + CO_2 \uparrow$
CO_2 gas turns lime water milky due to formation of $CaCO_3$. **(1 mark)**

The chemical reaction that takes place between Lime water and CO_2 is :-

$$Ca(OH)_2 + CO_2 \longrightarrow \underset{\text{(milky solution)}}{CaCO_3} + H_2O$$

The solution turns colourless when excess of CO_2 is passed through the solution due to the formation of bicarbonate.

$$CaCO_3 + CO_2 + H_2O \longrightarrow \underset{\text{(Colourless)}}{Ca(HCO_3)_2}$$

2. **(b)** Potassium iodide and lead nitrate react and undergo a double-displacement reaction to give a precipitate of lead Iodide (PbI_2)
$2KI + Pb(NO_3)_2 \longrightarrow PbI_2 \downarrow + 2KNO_3$ **(1 mark)**
3. **(b)** Mg bums in air with a dazzling flame to give white ashes of MgO.
Thus, 'X' = Mg, 'Y' = MgO
The given reaction is a combination reaction as only a single product is obtained. **(1 mark)**
4. **(d)** Oxalic acid is present in tomatoes. **(1 mark)**
5. **(b)** NaOH is a strong base and soluble in water.
That is why it is an alkali.
$Fe(OH)_3$ is a weak base and does not dissolve in water so it is not an alkali. **(1 mark)**
6. **(c)** Washing Soda ($Na_2CO_3.10H_2O$) is used for the removal of permanent hardness of water. **(1 mark)**

Permanent hardness of water causes formation of deposits that clogplumbing in electrical appliances.
The hardness is not removed by simple boiling. Boiling with washing soda gives insoluble salts and allow us to remove the permanent hardness.

$$MSO_4 + Na_2CO_3 \longrightarrow MCO_3 \downarrow + Na_2SO_4$$

7. **(c)** Each chlorine atom in Cl_2 shares one of its valence electrons to form a single covalent bond. **(1 mark)**
8. **(b)** The given diagram is showing the process of transpiration that involve water loss from the aerial parts of the plants (mainly leaves) in the form of water vapour is called transpiration. During evaporation of water through the stomata of leaves, a pull is formed inside the xylem tissue that helps in the upward movement of water into the xylem vessels. This pressure is called a transpiration pull/suction force that pulls water inside the plant via roots. **(1 mark)**
9. **(b)** Water in guard cells controls the opening and closing of the stomatal pore turgor pressure inside the guard cells is created due to osmotic flow of water inside the guard cells which causes opening of the stomatal apperture. **(1 mark)**
10. **(c)** According to the question the cross is made between the violet flower (VV) and white flower (vv)

F_1 generation

♀ \ ♂	v	v
V	Vv (violet)	Vv (violet)
V	Vv (violet)	Vv (violet)

(½ mark)

The offspring produced in the F_1 generation is Vv or the violet flower (considering violet as dominant).
Then the cross is again done between F_1 hybrids Vv × Vv.

F_2 generation

♀ \ ♂	V	v
V	Vv (violet)	Vv (violet)
v	Vv (violet)	vv (white)

(½ mark)

The F_2 generation obtained as result of the cross-three violets and one white.
The phenotypic ratio as a result of the cross is 3 : 1.

A monohybrid cross is the hybrid of two individual with homozygous genotype which result in opposite phenotype for a certain genetic trait.

11. **(a)** Cytokinin is a plant hormone that promotes cytokinesis, which is cell division. **(1 mark)**
12. **(d)** New offsprings are formed by the fusion of male and female gametes. Gametes are formed by meiotic division. Meiosis is a reduction division in which the number of chromosomes gets halved. Thus, the gametes have the number of chromosome as that of parent. Hence, gametes are haploid in number. **(1 mark)**
13. **(b)** In series same current flows through each circuit element irrespective of power.
So, current through 6 watt bulb
= current through 12 watt bulb
= 0.06 A **(1 mark)**
14. **(c)** If we look from left of a coil, we will find current to be flowing in anti-clockwise direction. So, left face of coil is north pole and therefore right face will be south pole. So, direction of magnetic field will be from south to north i.e., from right to left. **(1 mark)**

15. **(b)** As $H = \frac{V^2}{R}t \Rightarrow H \propto \frac{1}{R}$

$\Rightarrow \frac{H_2}{H_1} = \frac{R_1}{R_2} = \frac{R}{R/2} = 2$

So, $H_2 = 2H_1$ **(1 mark)**

16. **(d)** Direction of force is determined by right hand thumb rule i.e. put your right hand on $\vec{V}$ and curl it in direction of $\vec{B}$, then direction of thumb is in upward direction. So, direction of $\vec{B}$ is out of page. **(1 mark)**

17. **(a)** Quicklime (CaO) reacts with water to give limewater $Ca(OH)_2$) along with the release of heat.

$CaO + H_2O \longrightarrow Ca(OH)_2 + Heat$ **(1 mark)**

Thus, the reaction is a fast reaction and an exothermic reaction.

18. **(d)** (bb) is a homozygous recessive condition for brown eye color. Therefore, assertion is false. **(1 mark)**

19. **(a)** Both assertion and reason are correct and it is the correct explanation of assertion. **(1 mark)**

Villi are small intestine vascular projections that project into intestinal cavity, increasing the surface area of food absorption.

20. **(b)** Whenever a current carrying conductor is placed in direction perpendicular to magnetic field, it will always experience a force. So, (a) is correct.

When current flows, charge just moves from one part of conductor to other part. So overall charge within the conductor remain same. If initially it is zero, then during flow of current also it is zero.

So, (b) is correct. **(1 mark)**

We can clearly see (a) is not correct explanation of (b).

21. **(A)** (i) The compound formed in the reaction is copper (II) chloride ($CuCl_2$) which is blue-green in colour. **(1 mark)**

(ii) $CuO + 2HCl \longrightarrow CuCl_2 + H_2O$ **(1 mark)**

OR

(B) Caustic soda (NaOH) is prepared from brine solution (NaCl) using electrolysis. (Chlor-alkali process) compound electrolysed 'X' = NaCl. (Sodium Chloride) **(½ mark)**

Gas 'Y' at cathode = H_2 **(½ mark)**

Gas 'Z' at anode = Cl_2 **(½ mark)**

Compound 'B' formed by reaction of Cl_2 gas and dry slaked lime ($Ca(OH)_2$) = $CaOCl_2$ (Bleaching powder) **(½ mark)**

Electrolysis of a salt involves a Redox reaction in which one of the species is oxidized (at anode) and the other is reduced (at cathode).

The electrolytic solution carries the charges and more stable species are formed at the electrodes.

'Bleaching Powder' is represented in a simple form as $CaOCl_2$, although the actual composition is quite complex.

22. (A) (i) Hindbrain **(½ mark)**

(ii) Medulla **(½ mark)**

(iii) Cerebrum **(½ mark)**

(iv) Medulla **(½ mark)**

OR

(B) Auxins are plant growth promoters, generally produced by the growing apex of stem and root of the plants, from where they migrate to the regions of their action. **(½ mark)**

(i) shoot/stem **(½ mark)**

(ii) shoot/stem **(½ mark)**

(iii) Roots **(½ mark)**

23. (i) Renal artery carries blood from the heart to the kidneys. **(½ mark)**

(ii) The main function of urethra is to expel urine out of the body. **(½ mark)**

(iii) The function of glomerulus is to filter the blood passing through it and initiate urine formation. **(½ mark)**

(iv) Tubular part of nephron is involved in reabsorption of water, glucose, amino acids etc. **(½ mark)**

24. Plant kept in sunlight will survive longer, because it will be able to produce oxygen required for respiration by the process of photosynthesis. **(1 mark)**

Moreover, plant kept in the dark will not be able to photosynthesize and hence it will finally die due to non-availability of oxygen. **(1 mark)**

25. (A) (i) Myopia **(½ mark)**

(ii) It's two causes are :- **(½ × 2 = 1 mark)**

(1) Enlongation of eyeball

(2) Eyelens become too convexed

(iii) We use concave lens to treat myopia

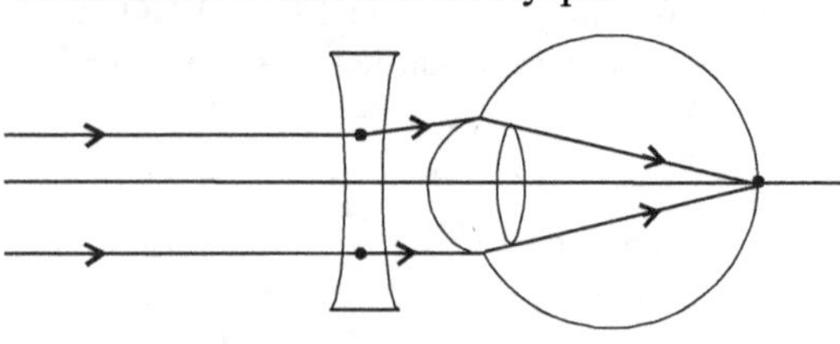

OR

(B) The color of the clear sky appears blue from the Earth due to a phenomenon called Rayleigh scattering. The Earth's atmosphere contains various gases and particles, including nitrogen and oxygen molecules. When sunlight passes through the atmosphere, these molecules scatter the sunlight in all directions, causing the blue light to be scattered more than other colors, giving the sky its blue color. **(1 mark)**

However, from space, the atmosphere is not visible, so the sky appears black because there is no medium for the scattering of sunlight. The light from the sun is not scattered, and there is no atmospheric interference, which makes the sky appear black. **(1 mark)**

26. Use of several pesticides which results in excessive accumulation of pesticides in rivers or ponds, is a matter of deep concern because these pesticides are chemicals which are either washed down into the soil or into the water bodies from the soil, these are absorbed by the plants along with water and minerals, and from the water bodies these are taken up by aquatic plants and animals. As these chemicals are not degradable, these get accumulated progressively at each trophic level. As human beings occupy the top level in any food chain, the maximum concentration of these chemicals get accumulated in our bodies this phenomenon is known as biological magnification. **(2 marks)**

27. (i) Addition of some drops of acid like dilute H_2SO_4 increases the conductivity of the solution to be electrolysed as water is a bad conductor of electricity. **(½ mark)**

$$2H_2O(\ell) \xrightarrow[H^+]{\text{electrolysis}} \underset{\text{at cathode}}{2H_2(g)} + \underset{\text{at anode}}{O_2(g)}$$ **(½ mark)**

Gas liberated at cathode = H_2

Gas liberated at anode = O_2 **(½ mark)**

According to the balanced chemical equation, the volume of hydrogen gas collected at the cathode is double the volume of the oxygen gas collected at the anode.

$$V(H_2) = 2V(O_2)$$ **(½ mark)**

(ii) AgCl turns grey in the presence of sunlight.

$$2AgCl(s) \xrightarrow{\text{Sunlight}} 2Ag(s) + Cl_2(g)$$ **(½ mark)**

This is a decomposition reaction.

28. (i) A strong concentrated acid is safely diluted by adding the acid in a beaker full of water gradually.

This gives a dilute solution and avoids splashing of the acid. **(1 mark)**

(ii) $$\underset{\text{Acid}}{H_2SO_4} + \underset{\text{Base}}{2NaOH} \longrightarrow Na_2SO_4 + 2H_2O$$

Salt formed = Sodium Sulphate (Na_2SO_4) **(½ mark)**

pH of the solution = 7 (Neutral) **(½ mark)**

(iii) Dry HCl gas does not change the colour of the dry blue litmus paper because HCl does not dissociate into H^+ ions. The colour will change in the aqueous solution only. **(1 mark)**

29. (A) (i) Paramecium is a unicellular organism. The cell exhibit a definite shape and food is taken in at a specific spot. Food is moved to this spot by the movement of cilia which cover the entire surface of the cell. **(1 mark)**

(ii) (a) The hydrochloric acid creates an acidic medium which facilitates the action of the enzyme pepsin. **(½ mark)**

(b) Trypsin is an enzyme involved in digestion of proteins. **(½ mark)**

(c) The muscular walls of the stomach help in mixing the food thoroughly with more digestive juices. **(½ mark)**

(d) Salivary amylase helps in breaking down of starch present in food into simple sugars. **(½ mark)**

OR

(B) (i) The circulation of blood in human is known as double circulation because the blood circulates in humans by two different pathways-

- **Pulmonary circulation :** Circulation of blood between the heart and the lungs. During this cycle, the deoxygenated blood from the heart enters the lungs for oxygenation. After oxygenation, the blood re-enters the heart.
- **Systemic circulation :** Circulation of blood between the heart and all body parts. During this cycle, the oxygenated blood is forced out of the heart into the body parts, and the used blood from the body parts is carried back to the heart. **(1½ marks)**

(ii) **Oxygen enters the blood in the lungs.**

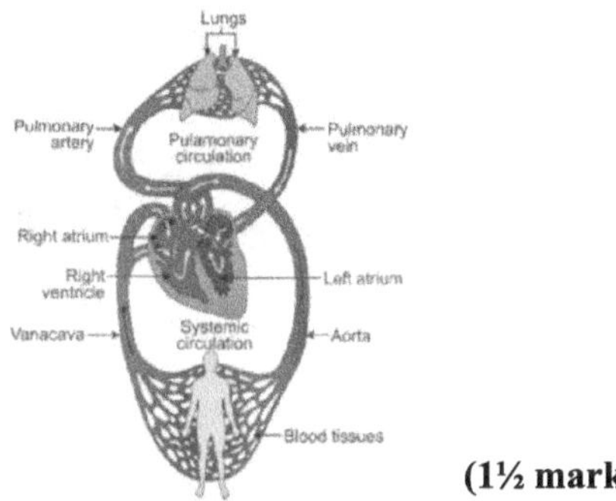

(1½ mark)

Fig. : Diagrametic representation of transport and exchange of oxygen and carbon dioxide

The separation of the right side and the left side of the heart is useful to keep oxygenated and de-oxygenated blood from mixing. Such separation allows a highly efficient supply of oxygen to the body. This is useful in animals that have high energy needs, such as birds and mammals, which constantly use energy to maintain their body temperature.

The pulmonary artery function is to transport deoxygenated blood from right side of heart to the lungs for oxygenation.

30. (A) For a diverging mirror :-

(i) **Principal focus** :- It is a point where ray parallel to principal axis appears to meet after reflection from the mirror. **(½ mark)**

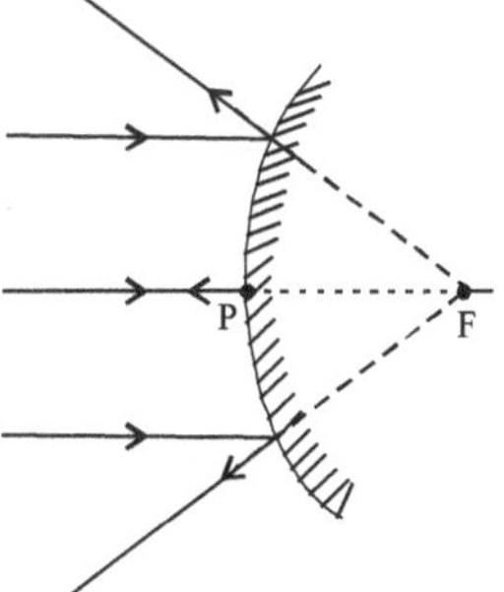

(½ mark)

(ii) **Focal length** :- It is distance between pole and principal focus. **(½ mark)**

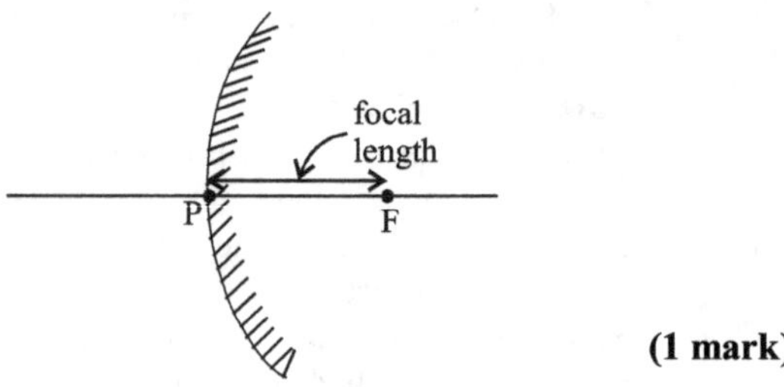

(1 mark)

(B) We have

$h_0 = 10$ cm, $u = -25$ cm and $f = 15$ cm

By lens formulae

$$\frac{1}{v}-\frac{1}{u}=\frac{1}{f} \quad \Rightarrow \frac{1}{v}-\frac{1}{-25}=\frac{1}{15}$$ **(1 mark)**

$$\Rightarrow \frac{1}{v}=\frac{1}{15}-\frac{1}{25} \quad \Rightarrow \frac{1}{v}=\frac{25-15}{25\times15}$$

$$\Rightarrow \frac{1}{v}=\frac{10}{25\times15} \quad \Rightarrow v=\frac{75}{2}\text{cm}$$ **(1 mark)**

as, $$m=\frac{v}{u}=\frac{h_i}{h_0} \quad \Rightarrow \frac{75}{-25\times2}=\frac{h_i}{10}$$

$$\Rightarrow h_i=\frac{75\times10}{-25\times2} \quad \Rightarrow h_i=-15\text{ cm}$$ **(1 mark)**

31. We have $f=\frac{1}{P}=\frac{1}{4}m=25\text{cm}$ **(½ mark)**

and, $u = -50$

By lens formulae

$$\frac{1}{v}-\frac{1}{u}=\frac{1}{f} \quad \Rightarrow \frac{1}{v}-\frac{1}{-50}=\frac{1}{25}$$ **(½ mark)**

$$\Rightarrow \frac{1}{v}=\frac{1}{25}-\frac{1}{50} \quad \Rightarrow \frac{1}{v}=\frac{2-1}{50}$$

$$\Rightarrow \frac{1}{v}=\frac{1}{50} \quad \Rightarrow v=50\text{ cm}$$ **(½ mark)**

So, $m=\frac{v}{u}=\frac{50}{-50}=-1$ **(½ mark)**

So, image will formed on the other side of lens and will be real inverted and same size as object as shown in figure **(½ mark)**

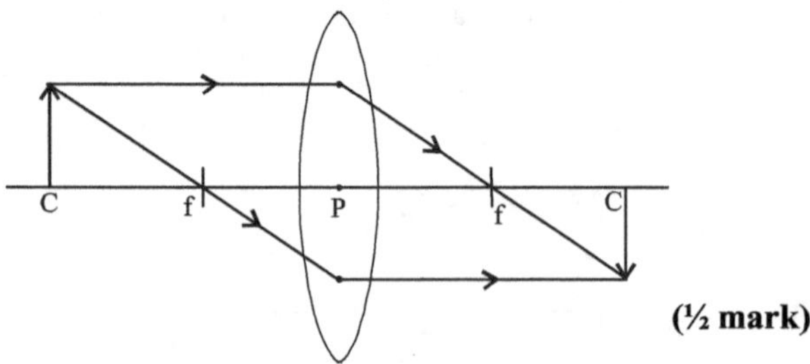

(½ mark)

32. (A) (i) Power wasted only depends on resistance and current in the circuit and does not depend on whether its AC or DC.

If P is the power transmitted, and R is the resistance of the line:

$P = IV$

$$\text{Power loss} = I^2R = \frac{V^2}{R}$$

It is better to have lower current and higher voltage to reduce losses. AC is much easier (therefore cheaper) to step up and down in voltage (using a transformer) than DC, and can be done more efficiently than the much more expensive and complex DC step-up/step-down systems. That is why AC is used for power transmission. **(1 mark)**

(ii) Current used, in household supply is AC and that given by battery of dry cells is DC. Difference between AC and DC is that DC remain constant with time and AC changes its direction after a fixed interval of time. **(1 mark)**

(iii) When an electric circuit gets overloaded or short-circuited, the fuse in live wire get heated up and melts due to low melting point. Due to which now circuit becomes open circuited and current cannot flow through it. Hence further damage will be prevented and the appliances will be saved. **(1 mark)**

OR

(B) Magnetic field lines through ideal solenoid is as shown below

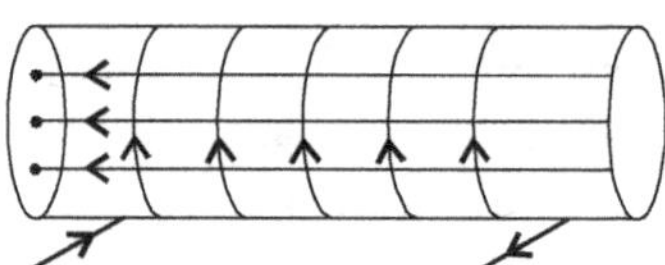

For an ideal solenoid, magnetic field outside the solenoid is zero and inside it is constant.

So, magnetic field will be maximum at 'B' and is zero and minimum at 'B' and 'C'. **(1 mark)**

One end of the solenoid behaves as a magnetic north pole, while the other behave as the south pole. The field lines inside the solenoid are in the form of parallel straight lines. This indicates that the magnetic field is same at all points inside the solenoid.

33. Biodegradable wastes are those substances which get degraded to their simpler and harmless substances over a peroid of time whereas the non-biodegradable wastes are those substances which do not get degraded to their simpler and harmless substances over a period of time. **(1½ marks)**

Biodegradable wastes cause less pollution in the environment and do not disturb the ecological balance in nature whereas non-biodegradable wastes cause more pollution and cause disturbance in the ecological balance if not disposed off properly. **(1½ marks)**

34. **(A)** (i) (a) Butanoic acid:-

$$\begin{array}{ccccccccc} & & H & & H & & H & & O \\ & & | & & | & & | & & \| \\ H & - & C & - & C & - & C & - & C-OH \\ & & | & & | & & | & & \\ & & H & & H & & H & & \end{array}$$

(1 mark)

(b) Chloropentane:

$$\begin{array}{ccccccccccc} & & H & & H & & H & & H & & H \\ & & | & & | & & | & & | & & | \\ H & - & C & - & C & - & C & - & C & - & C-Cl \\ & & | & & | & & | & & | & & | \\ & & H & & H & & H & & H & & H \end{array}$$

(1 mark)

(ii) Structure (i) and (ii) have the same molecular formula but different structures.

Therefore they are structural isomers. **(1 mark)**

Another structure for the compound

$$\begin{array}{ccccccccccccc} & & H & & H & & H & & H & & H & & H \\ & & | & & | & & | & & | & & | & & | \\ H & - & C & - & C & - & C & - & C & - & C & - & C-H \\ & & | & & | & & | & & | & & | & & | \\ & & H & & H & & H & & H & & H & & H \end{array}$$

(1 mark)

(iii) Saturated carbon compounds (Hydrocarbons) have the general formula of $C_n H_{2n+2}$ **(½ mark)**

Note

Homologous Series :-

Compounds in which the same functional group substitutes for hydrogen in a carbon chain are called Homologous compounds.

They are represented by a general formula in which each member differs by a $-CH_2-$ unit.

Unsaturated carbon compounds have the general formula of $C_n H_{2n}$ (alkenes) or $C_n H_{2n-2}$ (alkynes) **(½ mark)**

OR

(B) (i) When a small piece of sodium metal is dropped in ethanol, Hydrogen gas is evolved that gives a pop sound when a burning candle is brought near. **(1 mark)**

$$2CH_3CH_2-OH+2Na \longrightarrow 2CH_3CH_2-O^-Na^+ + H_2\uparrow$$

(1 mark)

(ii) The melting point of pure ethanoic acid is 290 K due to which it freezes during winter in cold climates. Therefore it is called 'Glacial acetic acid'. **(1 mark)**

(iii) Heating ethanol at 443 K in the presence of concentrates H_2SO_4 causes it to undergo dehydration to give ethene and water.

H_2SO_4 acts as a dehydrating agent here. **(1 mark)**

(iv) Saponification:

$$CH_3COOC_2H_5 \xrightarrow{NaOH} C_2H_5OH + CH_3COONa$$ **(1 mark)**

Note

Saponification is the process of preparation of soaps that are defined as the sodium or potassium salts of long chain carboxylic acids.

Esters are also used in the manufacture of perfumes and flavouring agents.

35. (i) Budding and regeneration are the two modes of asexual reproduction observed in *Hydra*.

1. **Budding in *Hydra* :** - Organisms such as *Hydra* use regenerative cells for reproduction in the process of budding. In *Hydra*, a bud develops as an outgrowth due to repeated cell division at one specific site. These buds develop into tiny individuals and when fully mature, detach from the parent body and become new independent individuals.

2. **Regeneration in *Hydra* :** - Parent *Hydra* body get cut or broken down into many pieces many of these pieces grow into separate individuals. However, regeneration is carried out by specialised cells. These cells proliferate and make large number of cells. From this mass of cells, different cells undergo changes to become various cell types and tissues. **(2½ marks)**

(ii) Vegetative propagation is an asexual mode of reproduction in plants in which the vegetative parts like root, stem and leaves are useful in development of new plants. This property of vegetative propagation is used in methods such as layering or grafting to grow many plants like sugarcane, roses, or grapes for agriculture purposes. Two advantages of using vegetative propagation are as follows:

(1) Plants raised by vegetative propagation can bear flowers and fruits earlier than those produced from seeds.

(2) Such methods also make possible the propagation of plants such as banana, orange, rose and jasmine that have lost the capacity to produce seeds. **(2½ marks)**

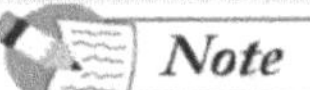

Note

Vegetative reproduction is any form of asexual reproduction occuring in plants in which a new plant grows from a fragment or cutting of parent plant.

36. (i) According to Ohm's law, current flowing through the conductor is directly proportional to potential difference across its end i.e. $i \propto V_A - V_B$ **(1 mark)**

$\Rightarrow$ $iR = V_A - V_B$, R = resistance of conductor

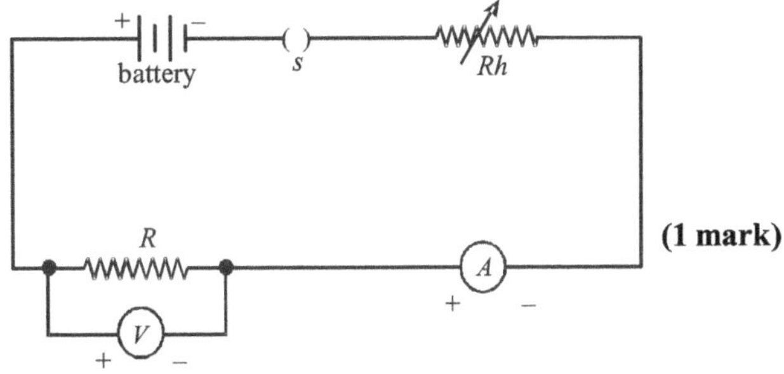

(1 mark)

(ii) The resistance of an ammeter should be low. An ammeter is used to measure the current in a circuit and it should always be connected in series. Resistance means the obstruction caused to the movements of electrons. If resistance is more, current will be less. So, if an ammeter has a high resistance then the current measured will be quite less as compared to the actual current which is undesirable. If an ammeter has zero resistance, then we will get the exact current in the circuit. But this is not possible as every material in this world has some internal resistance. **(2 mark)**

(iii) As $R_{series} > R_{parallel}$

$\Rightarrow$ $(Slope)_{series} > (Slope)_{parallel}$

[$\because$ R = slope of i – v curve]

As 'A' has less slope than 'B', so 'A' is parallel combination and 'B' is series combination. **(1 mark)**

37. (i) $\underset{2,8,2}{Mg} \longrightarrow \underset{2,8}{Mg^{2+}} + 2e^-$

$\underset{2,8,7}{Cl} + e^- \longrightarrow \underset{2,8,8}{Cl^-}$

$Mg: + 2\,{}^{\times\times}_{\times\times}\overset{\times}{Cl}{}^{\times}_{\times} \longrightarrow (Mg^{2+})[{}^{\times}_{\bullet}Cl{}^{\times}_{\times}]_2^-$ **(1 mark)**

(ii) **Properties of ionic compounds:**

(a) Ionic compounds are generally soluble in water.

(b) Their aqueous solutions conduct electricity. **(1 mark)**

(iii) (A) Sodium atom has one electron in its valence shell. Na loses that one valence electron to form the Na^+ cation and attains a stable configuration of 2,8

$\underset{2,8,1}{Na} \longrightarrow \underset{2,8}{Na^+} \longrightarrow e^-$ **(2 mark)**

Note

Electronic configuration of elements:

The distribution of all the electrons of an element in the shells is called its electronic configuration. The shells available are K, L, M, N and so on that can accommodate a maximum of 2, 8, 18 and 32 respectively.

OR

(B) (i) Ionic compounds do not conduct electricity in the solid state because the movement of ions is not possible due to the rigidity of the structures of the solid. **(1 mark)**

(ii) Sodium Chloride (NaCl) is electrolysed in its aqueous solution.

At cathode, reduction of H^+ and Na^+ ions takes place.

$$\underset{(eq)}{2H^+} \xrightarrow{2e^-} H_2(g)$$

$$\underset{(eq)}{Na^+} \xrightarrow{e^-} Na(s)$$

Hydrogen gas and sodium metal are obtained at cathode. **(1 mark)**

38. (i) Sexual reproduction is a process of creation of new organism by combining the genetic material of two organisms. As both parents contribute half of their chromosomes required for the gamete formation of offspring, the offspring will have traits of both parents, but will not be exactly like either parent. **(1 mark)**

(ii) The F_1 generation results from a cross between two purebred parents, while the F_2 generation results from a cross between two F_1 individuals. The F_1 generation is always heterozygous, which the F_2 generation may contain both homozygous and heterozygous individuals. **(1 mark)**

(iii) (A) Variation leads to genetic diversity. Organisms are better suited to face the struggle for existence due to the presence of variations as because of variation they can adapt themselves well for example. If there were a population of bacteria living in temperate waters and if the water temperature were to be increased by global warming most of these bacteria would die, but the few variants resistant to heat would survive and grow further. Variation is thus useful for the survival of species over time. **(2 mark)**

OR

(iii) (B) In crossing of RRYY (Round yellow) × rryy (wrinkled green) pair of contrasting traits in which more than traits are involved, the genes are likely to assort independently, irrespective of the combination of traits present in the parents. So, new combinations of genes appear in the offsprings leading to new traits. **(2 mark)**

39. (i) We have

$$V = \frac{c}{\mu} = \frac{3\times10^8}{2.42} = 1.24\times10^8\, m/s$$ **(1 mark)**

(ii) We know that,

$$\frac{\sin i}{\sin r} = \mu \Rightarrow \sin r = \frac{\sin i}{\mu}$$

So, if μ increases then sin r decreases i.e. r decreases.

Therefore, when μ = 1.62, r is minimum

when μ = 1.33, r is maximum

when μ = 1.5, r is greater than (μ = 1.62)

but less than (μ = 1.33) **(1 mark)**

(iii) (A)

(i) Glass is optically denser as speed of light in glass is less than that in water.

(ii) Path of light will remain straight throughout because for normal incidence, i = 0 and therefore r = 0.

OR

(iii) We have

(i) $c = \mu_g v_g \Rightarrow c = \frac{3}{2} \times 2 \times 10^8 = 3 \times 10^8$ m/s **(1 mark)**

(ii) $v_w = \frac{c}{\mu_w} = \frac{3\times10^8}{4/3} = 2.25 \times 10^8$ m/s **(1 mark)**

All India 2022

CBSE Board Solved Paper Term-II

Time Allowed : 2 Hours **_Maximum Marks : 40_**

General Instructions:

Read the following instructions carefully and strictly follow them.

(i) This question paper contains **15** questions. All questions are compulsory.

(ii) This question paper is divided into **three** sections viz. Section **A**, **B** and **C**.

(iii) Section A - Question numbers **1** to **7** are short answer type questions. Each question carries **two** marks.

(iv) Section B - Question numbers **8** to **13** are also short answer type questions. Each question carries **three** marks.

(v) Section C - Question numbers **14** and **15** are case based questions. Each question carries **four** marks.

(vi) Internal choices have been provided in some questions. Only one of the alternatives has to be attempted.

SECTION - A

1. In the following food chain, only 2J of energy was available to the peacocks. How much energy would have been present in Grass? Justify your answer.

GRASS → GRASSHOPPER → FROG → SNAKE → PEACOCK **2**

OR

(a) What is meant by garbage? List two classes into which garbage is classified.

(b) What do we actually mean when we say that the "enzymes are specific in their action"?

2. (a) Name the poles P, Q, R and S of the magnets in the following figures 'a' and 'b' : **1/2+1/2+1 = 2**

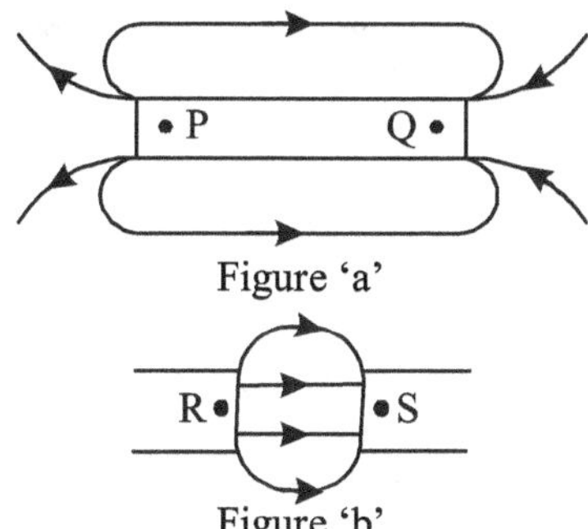

Figure 'a'

Figure 'b'

(b) State the inference drawn about the direction of the magnetic field lines on the basis of these diagrams.

OR

When is the force experienced by a current - carrying straight conductor placed in a uniform magnetic field. **1+1 = 2**

(i) Maximum;

(ii) Minimum ? **3**

3. Name the reproductive parts of an angiosperm. Where are these parts located? Explain the structure of its male reproductive part. **2**

OR

What is puberty? Mention any two changes that are common to both boys and girls in early teenage years.

4. (a) Name the reproductive and non-reproductive parts of bread mould (*Rhizopus*).

(b) List any two advantages of vegetative propagation. **2**

5. In the following figure showing a germinating gram seed, name the parts labelled as A, B and C : **1/2×4 = 2**

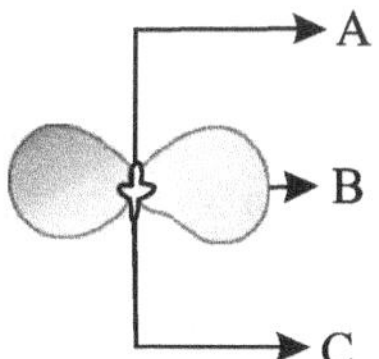

Why is part 'B' considered to be important during germination ?

6. A part of modern periodic table is given below. On its basis, answer the following questions: **1/2×4 = 2**

Group No.→ / Period ↓	1	2	13	14	15	16	17	18
2		A				B		
3	E			D			F	C

(a) Write the molecular formula of the compound formed by the combination :

(i) A and F (ii) E and B

(b) Which of the element is a

(i) noble gas? (ii) metalloid?

7. Write the chemical formula of two consecutive homologous of organic compounds having functional group – OH. What happens to the (i) boiling point and (ii) solubility of organic compounds of a homologous series as the molecular mass increases. **1/2×4 = 2**

SECTION - B

8. (a) We do not clean ponds or lakes, but an aquarium needs to be cleaned regularly. Why ? 1 + 2
   (b) Why is ozone layer getting depleted at the higher levels of the atmosphere ? Mention one harmful effect caused by its depletion.

9. (a) List the factors on which the resistance of a uniform cylindrical conductor of a given material depends. 2+1
   (b) The resistance of a wire of 0.01 cm radius is 10 Ω. If the resistivity of the wire is 50×10^{-8} Ω m, find the length of this wire.

OR

   (a) What is the meaning of electric power of an electrical device ? Write its SI unit. 1½
   (b) An electric kettle of 2kW is used for 2h. Calculate the energy consumed in
      (i) kilowatt hour and 1½
      (ii) joules.

10. In the given circuit determine the value of :
   (i) total resistance of the circuit 1½
   (ii) current flowing through the ammeter. 1½

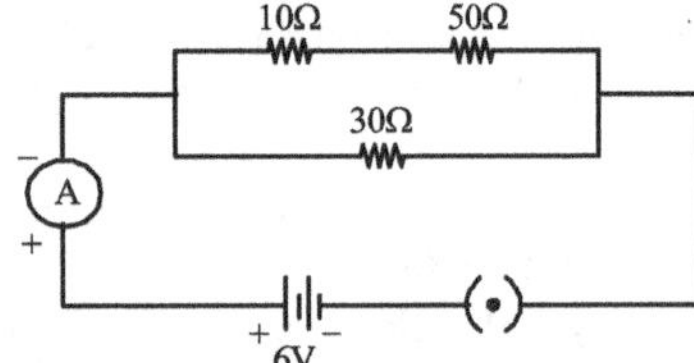

11. A green stemmed tomato plant denoted by (GG) is crossed with a tomato plant with purple stem denoted by (gg). 3
   (i) What colour of the stem would you expect in their F_1 progeny ?
   (ii) In what ratio would you find the green and purple coloured stem in plants of F_2 progeny ?
   (iii) What conclusion can be drawn for the above observations ?

12. Consider the following organic compounds : 3

```
     H  H  H                  H  H
     |  |  |                  |  |
(i) H—C—C—C=O       (ii) H—C—C=O
     |  |                     |
     H  H                     H
```

   (a) Name the functional group present in their compounds.
   (b) Write the general formula for the compounds of this functional group.
   (c) State the relationship between these compounds and draw the structure of any other compound having similar functional group.

OR

   (a) Draw the electron dot structure for ethyne. 1+2 = 3
   (b) List two differences between the properties exhibited by covalent compounds and ionic compounds.

13. (a) State Newland Law of Octaves. 1 + 1 + ½ + ½ = 3
   (b) With an example, explain Dobereiner's Triads.
   (c) List one limitation each of both the attempts mentioned in '*a*' and '*b*'.

SECTION - C

This section has 02 case based questions (14 and 15). Each case is followed by **03** sub-questions (a, b and c). Part (a) and (b) are compulsrory. However an internal choice has been provided in Part (c).

14. A student was asked to perform an experiment to study the force on a current carrying conductor in a magnetic field. He took a small aluminum rod AB, a strong horse shoe magnet, some connecting wires, a battery and a switch and connected them as shown. He observed that on passing current, the rod gets displaced. On reversing the direction of current, the direction of displacement also gets reversed. On the basis of your understanding of this phenomenon, answer the following questions : 4

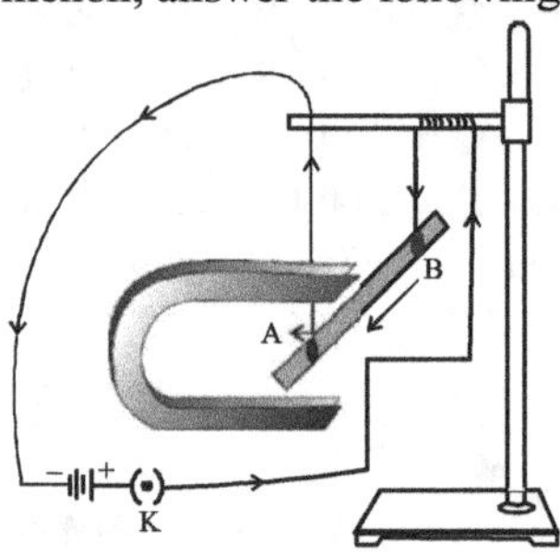

   (a) Why does the rod get displaced on passing current through it ?
   (b) State the rule that determines the direction of the force on the conductor AB.
   (c) (i) In the above experimented set up, when current is passed through the rod, it gets displaced towards the left. What will happen to the displacement if the polarity of the magnet and the direction of current both are reversed ?
      (ii) Name any two devices that use current carrying conductors and magnetic field.

OR

Draw the pattern of magnetic field lines produced around a current carrying straight conductor held vertically on a horizontal cardboard. Indicate the direction of the field lines as well as the direction of current flowing through the conductor.

15. Mendel blended his knowledge of Science and mathematics to keep the count of the individuals exhibiting a particular trait in each generation. He observed a number of contrasting visible characters controlled in pea plants in a field. He conducted many experiments to arrive at the laws of inheritance.
   (a) If only one pair of contrasting characters like tall and short plants is taken, plants obtained in F_1 generation are not of medium height. Why ?
   (b) Name the recessive traits in above case.
   (c) Mention the type of the new combinations of plants obtained in F_2 progeny along with their ratio, if F_1 progeny was allowed to self pollinate. 1+1+2 = 4

OR

If 1600 plants were obtained in F_2 progeny, write the number of plants having traits :
(i) Tall with round seeds
(ii) Short with wrinkled seeds
Write the conclusion of the above experiment.

Solutions

1. Energy present in Grass = 20000 J

Justification : According to the ten percent law of energy in a food chain, only ten % of energy is transferred to the next trophic level. Thus, the energy keeps on decreasing by 10% of each level.

Explanation

Energy available to grass = 20000 J **[1 Mark]**

Energy available to grasshopper

= 10% of 20000 = 2000 J

Energy available to frog = 10% of 2000 = 200 J

Energy available to snake = 10% of 200 = 20 J

Energy available to peacock = 10% of 20 = 2 J **[1 Mark]**

hence, justified.

OR

(a) The household waste or rubbish produced in our day-to-day life is called garbage. For example, spoilt food, vegetable peels, leaves, wood, glass, paper, plastic, etc. **[1 Mark]**

Garbage is classified into the following two types:

(i) Biodegradable garbage-
E.g.,-spoilt food, vegetable peels etc. **[½ Mark]**

(ii) Non-Biodegradable garbage-
E.g.,-plastic, metal cans, etc. **[½ Mark]**

(b) Enzymes are specific because different enzymes have differently shaped active sites. The shape of active site is complementary to shape of specific substrate. Salivary amylase, for instance, is an enzyme needed for the conversion of starin into simple sugars.

2. (a) In figure (a) P – North Pole : Q – South Pole
(b) R – North Pole : S – South Pole
[½ + ½ Mark]

(b) Magnetic field lines always starts from North Pole and end at South Pole. **[1 Mark]**

Note

All magnetic field lines are closed curves. They come out of the magnet from the side of north pole and go into it on the side of the south pole. They continue inside the magnet.

OR

The force experienced by a current-carrying straight conductor placed in a uniform field is

(i) maximum when the conductor is placed perpendicular to the magnetic field. **[1 Mark]**

(ii) minimum when the conductor is placed parallel to the magnetic field. **[1 Mark]**

3. In an angiospermic plant, the male reproductive part is stamen and female reproductive part is carpel. It is located in the flower. Male reproductive part consist of two parts- **[1 Mark]**

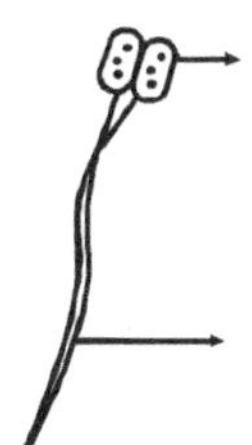

Anther (It develop male gametes called pollen grain)

Filament (It help to attach male reproductive part from the base of flower.) **[1 Mark]**

OR

– Puberty is the phase in humans, when a boy or girl reach to their sexual maturity. **[1 Mark]**

– Two changes that are common to both boys and girls in early teenage years are–

(i) Releasing of hormones (growth and sex). **[1 Mark]**

(ii) Growth of public hair, facial hair and increase in height.

4. (a) Reproductive part of bread mould is sporangium. While non-reproductive part of bread mould is hyphae. **[1 Mark]**

(b) Advantages of vegetative propagation are:

(i) Plants produce by vegetative propagation can bear flowers and fruits earlier than those produced from seeds. **[1 Mark]**

(ii) Useful for plants that have lost the capacity to produce seeds.

5. 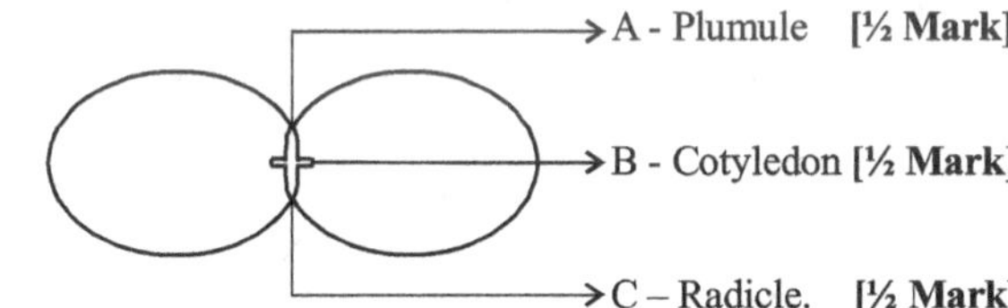

Cotyledons store food reserves in the seed, hence it supply nutrition to the developing embryo. **[½ Mark]**

6. (a)

(i) Element 'A' belongs to group 2nd therefore it must be divalent and element 'F' belongs to group 17 therefore it must be monovalent. Hence molecular formula should be

Valency : +2 ╳ 1
Elements : A ╳ F

$\therefore A_1 F_2$ or we can write it as AF_2 **[½ Mark]**

(ii) Element 'E' belongs to the group 1 therefore it should be monovalent and element 'B' belongs to group 16th therefore it must be divalent. Hence molecular formula should be

Valency : +1 ╳ 2
Elements : E ╳ B

$\therefore E_2B_1$ or E_2B **[½ Mark]**

(b)

(i) Element 'C' is a noble gas. **[½ Mark]**

(ii) Element 'D' is a metalloid. **[½ Mark]**

7. In a homologous series the consecutive members differ by $-CH_2$ unit. For alcohol functional group the consecutive homologous are

(a) CH_3OH **[½ Mark]**

(b) CH_3CH_2OH **[½ Mark]**

(i) Boiling point increases with increase in the molecular mass in the homologous series. **[½ Mark]**

(ii) Solubility in water decreases with increase in the molecular mass in the homologous series. **[½ Mark]**

In alcohol homologous series, as the size of alkyl group increases, solubility in water decreases due to increase in non-ionic interactions (van der Waal interaction) of long hydrocarbon chain.

8. (a) Ponds and Lakes are natural ecosystems as they contain decomposers which act as a cleaning agents, whereas an aquarium is an artificial ecosystem, which do not contain decomposers that clean it. Hence it need to be clean periodically. **[1 Mark]**

(b) Ozone layer is getting depleted at the higher levels of the atmosphere due to the effect of chlorofluorocarbons (CFCs).

Its harmful effect is skin cancer. **[2 Marks]**

CFCs are used as refrigerants and in fire extinguisher.

9. (a) The factors on which the resistance of a conductor depends are

(i) Length of the conductor (l): Resistance (R) of a conductor is directly proportional to length i.e., $R \propto l$

(ii) Area of cross-section (A): Resistance (R) of a conductor is inversely proportional to area of cross-section i.e., $R \propto \frac{1}{A}$

(iii) Material of the conductor: Resistance of a conductor depends on material of the conductor.

i.e., $R \propto \frac{l}{A}$ or, $R = \rho\frac{l}{A}$

Here, ρ = resistivity or specific resistance of the conductor which depends on the material of the conductor.

[2 Marks]

Resistance of a conductor depends on temperature also.

$R_t = R_0(1 + \alpha t)$

α = temperature coefficient of resistance

R_0 = resistance at 0°C

R_t = resistance at t°C

(b) According to question, resistance R = 10Ω, radius of the wire r = 0.01 cm = 0.01×10^{-2}m = 1×10^{-4}m, resistivity $\rho = 50 \times 10^{-8}\Omega$ m, length of the wire l = ?

using formula, $R = \rho\frac{l}{A} = \rho\frac{l}{\pi r^2}$

$$10 = \frac{50 \times 10^{-8} \times l}{3.14 \times (1 \times 10^{-4})^2} \Rightarrow l = \frac{3.14 \times 10 \times 10^{-8}}{50 \times 10^{-8}}$$

$= \frac{3.14}{5} = 0.628$ m **[1 Mark]**

$\therefore l = 62.8$ cm

OR

(a) Consider a current I flowing through a resistor or device of resistance R. Let the potential difference across it be V. Let t be the time during which a charge Q flows across. Therefore, the appliance supply energy = VQ in time t.

Hence electric power of an electric device = energy per unit time,

$$P = V\frac{Q}{t} = VI = I^2R \;[\because V = IR]$$

or, $P = V^2/R$ **[1 Mark]**

The SI unit of electric power is watt (w)

1 watt = 1 volt × 1 ampere = 1VA **[½ Mark]**

(b) (i) The commercial unit of electric energy is kilowatt hour (kwh) commonly known as unit.

1 kwh = 1000 watt × 3600 second = 3.6×10^6 watt second

= 3.6×10^6 J

As per question, electric kettle of 2 kw = 2000 watt and used for 2h = 2 × 3600 second

∴ Energy consumed in kilowatt hour

= 2000 × 2 × 3600

= $4 \times 3.6 \times 10^6$ J

= 4 kilowatt hour. **[1 Mark]**

(ii) Energy consumed in joules = $4 \times 3.6 \times 10^6$ J

= 144×10^5 Joules **[½ Mark]**

10. (i) In the given circuit diagram, resistances of 10 Ω and 50 Ω are in series and resistance of 30 Ω connected in parallel with them.

Therefore total resistance of the circuit (R)

$$\frac{1}{R} = \frac{1}{10+50} + \frac{1}{30} = \frac{1+2}{60} = \frac{3}{60}$$

$\therefore R = \frac{60}{3}\Omega = 20\,\Omega$ **[1½ Marks]**

(ii) Current flowing through the ammeter,

$I = \frac{V}{R} = \frac{6}{20} = 0.3$A **[1½ Marks]**

11. (i) Green stem Purple Stem **[1 Mark]**

Parent – GG gg

↓ ↓

gamete – G g

↓

F_1 Gen – Gg (green stem)

(i) F_1 progeny must be like their dominant parent with green stemmed tomato plant.

(ii) F_2 Gen **[1 Mark]**

	G	g
G	GG	Gg
g	Gg	gg

Phenotype ratio → GG : Gg : Gg : gg (GG : Gg : Gg — green stem; gg — purple stem)

Hence, the ratio for green stem and purple stem is 3:1 respectivily.

(iii) The above observation show law of dominance. **[1 Mark]**

Note

Law of dominance state that when parents with pure, contrasting traits are crossed together, only one form of trait appear in next generation.

12. (a) Aldehyde functional group (–CHO) is present in both the compounds (i) and (ii). **[1 Mark]**

(b) General Formula : $C_n H_{2n+1} CHO$ **[1 Mark]**

(c) These two compounds are homologous compound of (–CHO) functional group series. They differ by – CH_2 unit from each other. Another compound of the same functional group can be written as follows.

$CH_3 CH_2 CH_2 CHO$

Structural formula:

```
   H  H  H  H
   |  |  |  |
H—C—C—C—C=O
   |  |  |
   H  H  H
```

[1 Mark]

OR

(a) Ethyne HC ≡ CH

Electron dot structure:

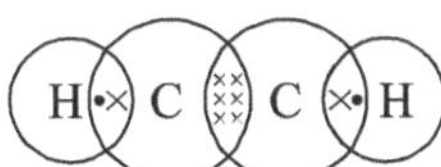

[1 Mark]

(b)

Covalent Compounds	Ionic Compounds
(i) Covalent compounds generally have low melting and boiling point. (ii) Covalent compounds are generally soluble in organic solvent and insoluble in water.	(i) Ionic compounds have high melting and boiling point because of the presence of strong electrostatic attraction between the ions. (ii) Ionic compounds are soluble in water and generally insoluble in organic solvent.

[2 Marks]

13. **(a)** Newland arranged the then known elements in the order of increasing atomic masses. He found that every eighth element had properties similar to that of the first element. He called it the 'law of octaves'. **[1 Mark]**

(b) Dӧbereiner arranged the elements with similar properties into groups having three elements in each group known as triad. Dӧbereiner showed that when the three elements in a triad are arranged in the order of increasing atomic masses, the atomic mass of the middle element was roughly the average of the atomic masses of the other two elements.

Li	6.9
Na	23.0
K	39.0

$$\text{Atomic mass of Na} = \frac{6.9 + 39.0}{2} = 22.95 \approx 23.0$$

which is approximately equal to the atomic mass of Na. **[1 Mark]**

(c) **Limitation of Law of octaves:** Law of octaves applicaple only up to calcium, after calcium every eighth element did not possess properties similar to that of the first. **[½ Mark]**

Limitation of Dӧbereiner Triad: Dӧbereiner could identify only three triads from the elements known at that time. Hence this system was not very usefull. **[½ Mark]**

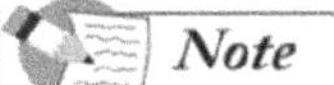

Note

Drawback of Newland's law of octaves is that he placed some unlike elements under the same note. For example, he placed Co and Ni, with F, Cl, Br which have very different properties than these elements. Therefore, this law worked well with lighter elements only.

14. (a) The rod get displaced on passing current through it because a force is exerted on the rod when it is placed in a magnetic field. **[1 Mark]**

(b) Fleming's left hand rule determines the direction of the force on the conductor AB.

According to this rule, stretch the thumb, forefinger and middle finger of your left hand such that they are mutually perpendicular. If the first finger points in the direction of magnetic field and the second finger in the direction of current, then the thumb will point in the direction of motion or the force acting on the conductor. **[1 Mark]**

(c) (i) If the polarity of the magnet and the direction of current both are reversed, the rod gets displaced towards the right. **[1 Mark]**

(ii) Two devices that use current carrying conductors and magnetic field are electric motor and electric generator. **[1 Mark]**

OR

Pattern of magnetic field lines produced around a current carrying straight conductor held vertically.

Also indicated the direction of field lines as well as the direction of current flowing through the conductor.

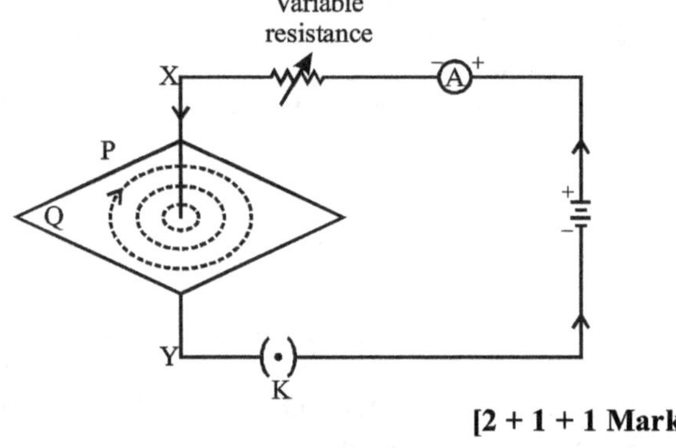

[2 + 1 + 1 Marks]

15. **(a)** If only one pair of contrasting characters is taken. F_1 generation either shows tall or short characterstic, as it follows law of dominance where only dominant character expresess itself. **[1 Mark]**

(b) Short plants have recessive trait. **[1 Mark]**

(c)

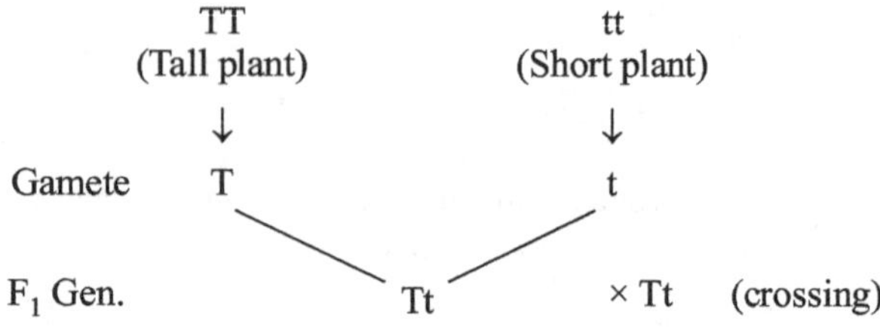

F_2 Gen. TT, Tt, Tt, tt **[2 Marks]**

Phenotype Ratio → 3 : 1

OR

F_2 progeny for dihybrid cross are

(i) Tall with round seeds – 9 = $\frac{9}{16}$ of 1600 = 900

[1 Mark]

(ii) Short with wrinkled seed – $1 = \frac{1}{16}$ of $1600 = 100$

[1 Mark]

- As it follow dihybrid cross, hence, F_2 generation is having phenotype ratio 9 : 3 : 3 : 1.
- It shows law of independent assortments. **[2 Marks]**

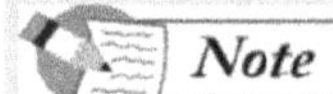

A monohybrid cross results in a phenotypic ratio of 3:1.
A dihybrid cross result in a phenotypic ratio of 9:3:3:1.

All India 2022

CBSE Board Solved Paper Term-I

Time Allowed : 90 Min. ***Maximum Marks : 40***

General Instructions:

Read the following instructions very carefully and strictly follow them :

(i) This question paper contains **60** questions out of which **50** questions are to be attempted. All questions carry equal marks.
(ii) The question paper consists three Sections – Section A, B and C.
(iii) Section – **A** consists of **24** questions. Attempt any **20** questions from Q. No. **1** to **24**.
(iv) Section – **B** also consists of **24** questions. Attempt any **20** questions from Q. No. **25** to **48**.
(v) Section – **C** consists of three Case Studies containing **12** questions and **4** questions in each case. Attempt any **10** from Q. No. **49** to **60**.
(vi) There is only one correct option for every Multiple Choice Question (*MCQ*). Marks will not be awarded for answering more than one option.
(vii) There is no negative marking.

SECTION - A

Section-A consists of **24** questions (Q. No. **1** to **24**). Attempt any **20** questions from this section. The first attempted 20 questions would be evaluated.

1. A student took Sodium Sulphate solution in a test tube and added Barium Chloride solution to it. He observed that an insoluble substance has formed. The colour and molecular formula of the insoluble substance is:
(a) Grey, Ba_2SO_4 (b) Yellow, $Ba(SO_4)_2$
(c) White, $BaSO_4$ (d) Pink, $BaSO_4$

2. Which of the following oxide(s) is/are soluble in water to form alkalies?
(i) Na_2O (ii) SO_2 (iii) K_2O (iv) NO_2
(a) (i) and (iii) (b) (i) only
(c) (ii) and (iv) (d) (iii) only

3. Study the diagram given below and identify the gas formed in the reaction.

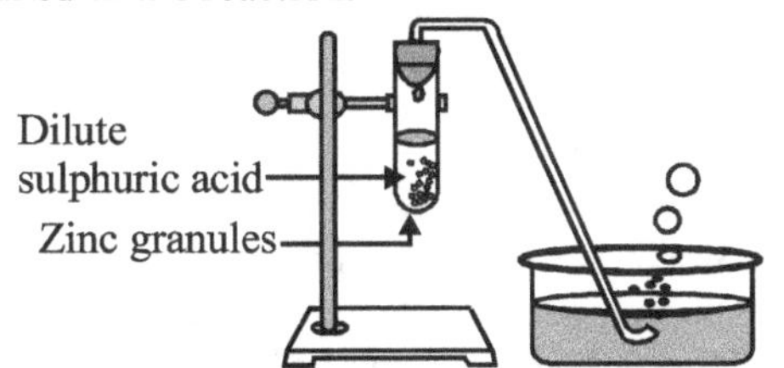

(a) Carbon di-oxide which extinguishes the burning candle.
(b) Oxygen due to which the candle burns more brightly.
(c) Sulphur dioxide which produces a suffocating smell.
(d) Hydrogen which while burning produces a popping sound.

4. Sodium reacts with water to form sodium hydroxide and hydrogen gas. The balanced equation which represents the above reaction is:
(a) $Na(s) + 2H_2O(l) \rightarrow 2NaOH(aq) + 2H_2(g)$
(b) $2Na(s) + 2H_2O(l) \rightarrow 2NaOH(aq) + H_2(g)$
(c) $2Na(s) + 2H_2O(l) \rightarrow NaOH(aq) + 2H_2(g)$
(d) $2Na(s) + H_2O(l) \rightarrow 2NaOH(aq) + 2H_2(g)$

5. Which of the options in the given table are correct?

Option	**Natural Source**	**Acid Present**
(i)	Orange	Oxalic acid
(ii)	Sour milk	Lactic acid
(iii)	Ant sting	Methanoic acid
(iv)	Tamarind	Acetic acid

(a) (i) and (ii) (b) (i) and (iv)
(c) (ii) and (iii) (d) (iii) and (iv)

6. $C_6H_{12}O_6(aq) + 6O_2(aq) \rightarrow 6CO_2(aq) + 6H_2O(l)$
The above reaction is a/an
(a) displacement reaction (b) endothermic reaction
(c) exothermic reaction (d) neutralisation reaction

7. Which of the following statements about the reaction given below are correct?
$MnO_2 + 4HCl \rightarrow MnCl_2 + 2H_2O + Cl_2$
(i) HCl is oxidized to Cl_2
(ii) MnO_2 is reduced to $MnCl_2$
(iii) $MnCl_2$ acts as an oxidizing agent
(iv) HCl acts as on oxidizing agent
(a) (ii), (iii) and (iv)
(b) (i), (ii) and (iii)
(c) (i) and (ii) only
(d) (iii) and (iv) only

8. Select from the following the statement which is true for bases.
(a) Bases are bitter and turn blue litmus red.
(b) Bases have a pH less than 7.
(c) Bases are sour and change red litmus to blue.
(d) Bases turn pink when a drop of phenolphthalein is added to them.

9. Study the following table and choose the correct option:

	Salt	Parent Acid	Parent Base	Nature of Salt
(a)	Sodium Chloride	HCl	NaOH	Basic
(b)	Sodium Carbonate	H_2CO_3	NaOH	Neutral
(c)	Sodium Sulphate	H_2SO_4	NaOH	Acidic
(d)	Sodium Acetate	CH_3COOH	NaOH	Basic

10. It is important to balance the chemical equations to satisty the law of conservation of mass. Which of the following statements of the law is incorrect?
(a) The total mass of the elements present in the reactants is equal to the total mass of the elements presents in the products.
(b) The number of atoms of each element remains the same, before and after a chemical reaction.
(c) The chemical composition of the reactants is the same before and after the reaction.
(d) Mass can neither be created nor can it be destroyed in a chemical reaction.

11. Consider the following statements in connection with the functions of the blood vessels marked A and B in the diagram of a human heart as shown.

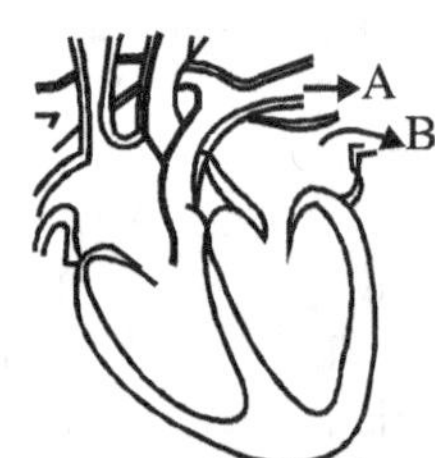

(i) Blood vessel A – It carries carbon dioxide rich blood to the lungs.
(ii) Blood vessel B – It carries oxygen rich blood from the lungs.
(iii) Blood vessel B – Left atrium relaxes as it receives blood from this blood vessel.
(iv) Blood vessel A – Right atrium has thick muscular wall as it has to pump blood to this blood vessel.

This correct statements are
(a) (i) and (ii) only (b) (ii) and (iii) only
(c) (ii), (iii) and (iv) (d) (i), (ii) and (iii)

12. In living organisms during respiration which of the following products are not formed if oxygen is not available?
(a) Carbon dioxide + Water
(b) Carbon dioxide + Alcohol
(c) Lactic acid + Alcohol
(d) Carbon dioxide + Lactic Acid

13. The correct statements with reference to single celled organisms are
(i) Complex substances are not broken down into simpler substances.
(ii) Simple diffusion is sufficient to meet the requirement of exchange of gases.
(iii) Specialised tissues perform different functions in the organism.
(iv) Entire surface of the organism is in contact with the environment for taking in food.
(a) (i) and (iii) (b) (ii) and (iii)
(c) (ii) and (iv) (d) (i) and (iv)

14. Which one among the following is not removed as a waste product from the body of a plant?
(a) Resins and Gums (b) Urea
(c) Dry Leaves (d) Excess Water

15. Which of the following statements are correct in reference to the role of A (shown in the given diagram) during a breathing cycle in human beings?

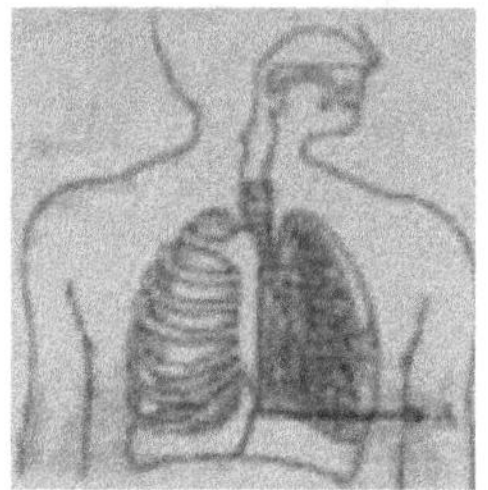

(i) It helps to decrease the residual volume of air in lungs.
(ii) It flattens as we inhale.
(iii) It gets raised as we inhale.
(iv) It helps the chest cavity to become larger.
(a) (ii) and (iv) (b) (iii) and (iv)
(c) (i) and (ii) (d) (i), (ii) and (iv)

16. Which one of the following conditions is true for the state of stomata of a green leaf shown in the given diagram?

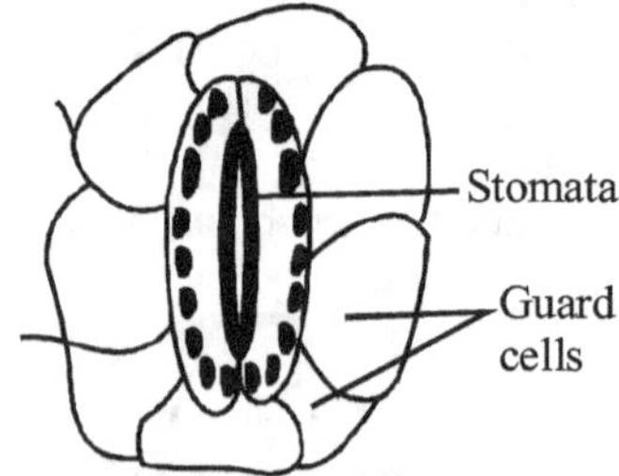

(a) Large amount of water flows into the guard cells.
(b) Gaseous exchange is occurring in large amount.
(c) Large amount of water flows out from the guard cells.
(d) Large amount of sugar collects in the guard cells.

17. In which of the following is a concave mirror used?
(a) A solar cooker
(b) A rear view mirror in vehicles
(c) A safety mirror in shopping malls
(d) In viewing full size image of distant tall buildings.

18. A student wants to obtain magnified image of an object AB as on a screen. Which one of the following arrangements shows the correct position of AB for him/her to be successful?

(a) 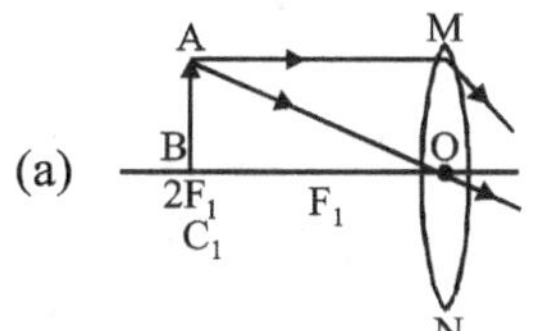

(b) 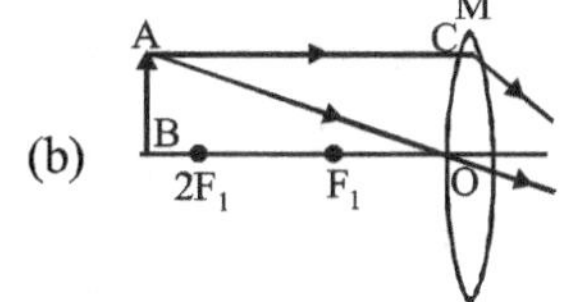

(c) 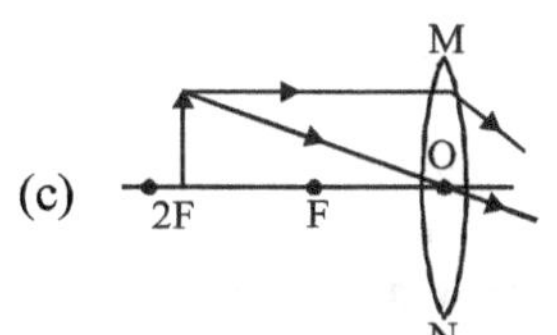

(d) 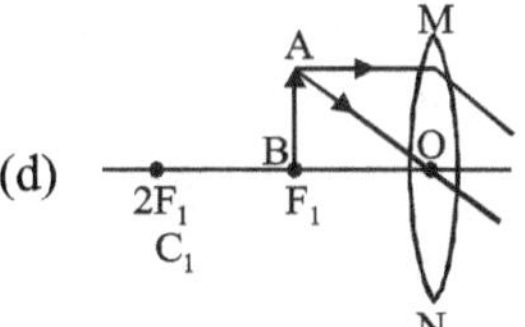

19. The following diagram shows the use of an optical device to perform an experiment of light. As per the arrangement shown, the optical device is likely to be a:

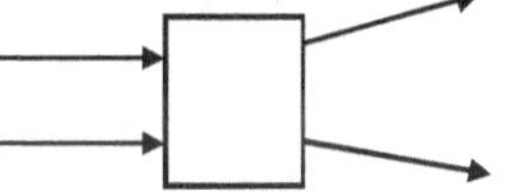

(a) Concave mirror
(b) Concave lens
(c) Convex mirror
(d) Convex lens

20. A ray of light starting from air passes through medium A of refractive index 1.50, enters medium B of refractive index 1.33 and finally enters medium C of refractive index 2.42. If this ray emerges out in air from C, then for which of the following pairs of media the bending of light is least?

(a) air-A (b) A-B (c) B-C (d) C-air

21. Which of the following statements is **not true** for scattering of light?

(a) Colour of the scattered light depends on the size of particles of the atmosphere.
(b) Red light is least scattered in the atmosphere.
(c) Scattering of light takes place as various colours of white light travel with different speed in air.
(d) The fine particles in the atmospheric air scatter the blue light more strongly than red. So the scattered blue light enters our eyes.

22.

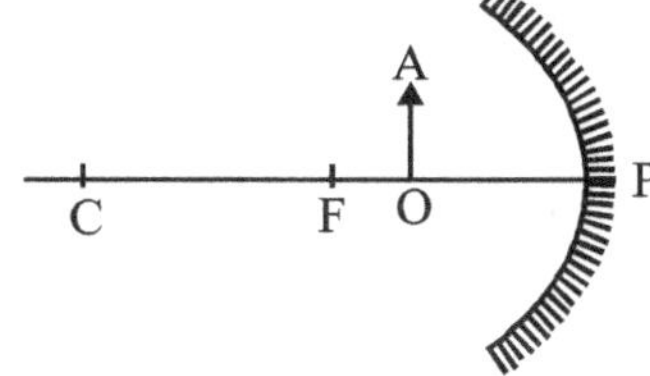

For the diagram shown, according to the new Cartesian sign convention the magnification of the image formed will have the following specifications:

(a) Sign - Positive, Value - Less than 1
(b) Sign - Positive, Value - More than 1
(c) Sign - Negative, Value - Less than 1
(d) Sign - Negative, Value - More than 1

23.

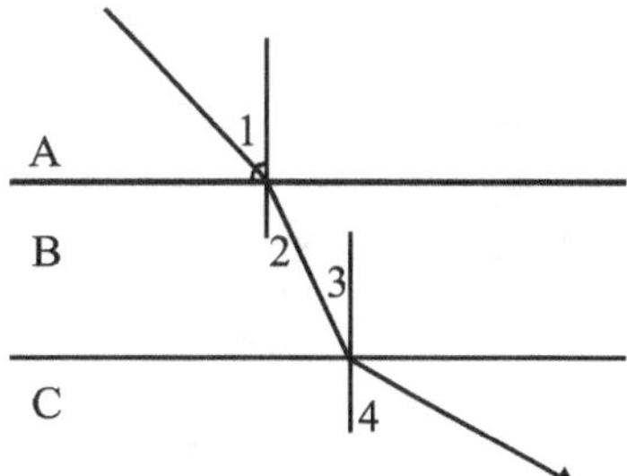

A ray of light is incident as shown. It A, B and C are three different transparent media, then which among the following options is true for the given diagram?

(a) $\angle 1 > \angle 4$
(b) $\angle 1 < \angle 2$
(c) $\angle 3 = \angle 2$
(d) $\angle 3 > \angle 4$

24. In the diagram given below, X and Y are the end colours of the spectrum of white light. The colour of 'Y' represents the

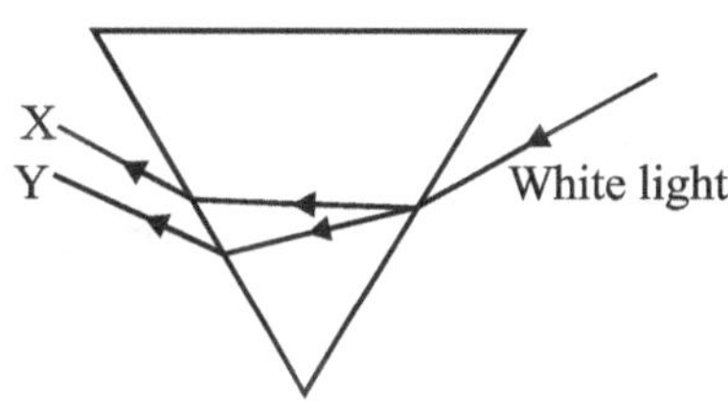

(a) Colour of sky as seen from earth during the day.
(b) Colour of the sky as seen from the moon.
(c) Colour used to paint the danger signals.
(d) Colour of sun at the time of noon.

SECTION - B

Section-B consists of **24** questions (Q. No. 25 to 48). Attempt any **20** questions from the section. The first attempted **20** questions would be evaluated.

25. Which one of the following reactions is categorised as thermal decomposition reaction?

(a) $2H_2O(l) \rightarrow 2H_2(g) + O_2(g)$
(b) $2AgBr(s) \rightarrow 2Ag(s) + Br_2(g)$
(c) $2AgCl(s) \rightarrow 2Ag(s) + Cl_2(g)$
(d) $CaCO_3(s) \rightarrow CaO(s) + CO_2(g)$

26. Consider the pH value of the following acidic samples:

S. No.	Sample	pH Value
1.	Lemon Juice	2.2
2.	Gastric Juice	1.2
3.	Vinegar	3.76
4.	Dil. Acetic acid	3.0

The decreasing order of their H^+ ion concentration is

(a) $3 > 4 > 1 > 2$ (b) $2 > 1 > 3 > 4$
(c) $2 > 1 > 4 > 3$ (d) $3 > 4 > 2 > 1$

27. Study the experimental set up shown in given figure and choose the correct option from the following:

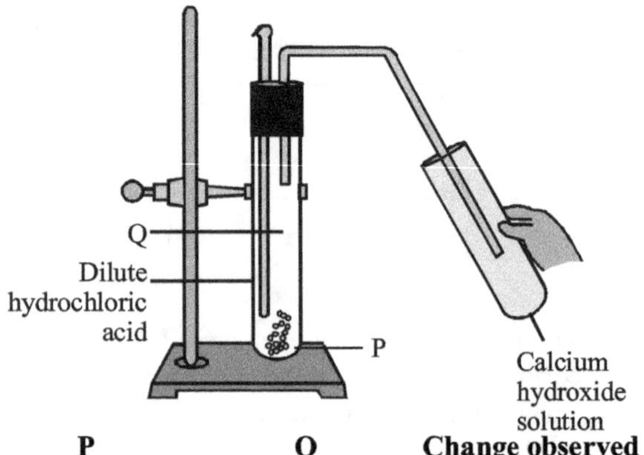

	P	Q	Change observed in calcium hydroxide solution
(a)	K_2CO_3	Cl_2 gas	No change
(b)	$KHCO_3$	CO_2 gas	No change
(c)	$KHCO_3$	H_2 gas	Turns milky
(d)	K_2CO_3	CO_2 gas	Turns milky

28. Which one of the following structures correctly depicts the compound $CaCl_2$?

(a) $Ca^{2+}[:\ddot{Cl}:]^{2-}$ (b) $[:\ddot{Ca}:]^{2+}[:\ddot{Cl}:]_2$

(c) $Ca^{2+}[:\ddot{Cl}:]_2$ (d) $[:\ddot{Ca}:]^{+}[:\ddot{Cl}:]^{-}_2$

29. The pair(s) which will show displacement reaction is/are

(i) $NaCl$ solution and copper metal
(ii) $AgNO_3$ solution and copper metal
(iii) $Al_2(SO_4)_3$ solution and magnesium metal
(iv) $ZnSO_4$ solution and iron metal

(a) (ii) only (b) (ii) and (iii)
(c) (iii) and (iv) (d) (i) and (ii)

30. Which of the following salts do not have the water of crystalisation?

(i) Bleaching Powder (ii) Plaster of Paris
(iii) Washing soda (iv) Baking soda

(a) (ii) and (iv) (b) (i) and (iii)
(c) (ii) and (iii) (d) (i) and (iv)

Question No. 31-35 consists of two statements - **Assertion (A)** and **Reason (R)**. Answer these questions selecting the appropriate option given below:

(a) Both (A) and (R) are true and (R) is the correct explanation of (A).
(b) Both (A) and (R) are true but (R) is not the correct explanation of (A).
(c) (A) is true, but (R) is false.
(d) (A) is false, but (R) is true.

31. **Assertion (A) :** Sodium hydrogen carbonate is used as an ingredient in antacids.

Reason (R) : $NaHCO_3$ is a mild non-corresive basic salt.

32. **Assertion (A) :** Burning of Natural gas is an endothermic process.

Reason (R) : Methane gas combines with oxygen to produce carbon dioxide and water.

33. **Assertion (A) :** Nitrogen is an essential element for plant growth and is taken up by plants in the form of inorganic nitrates or nitrites.

Reason (R) : The soil is the nearest and richest source of raw materials like Nitrogen, Phosphorus and other minerals for the plants.

34. **Assertion (A) :** Sun appears reddish at the time of Sunrise and Sunset.

Reason (R) : Distance travelled by sunlight in the atmosphere is lesser during sunrise and sunset as compared to noon.

35. **Assertion (A) :** Hydrochloric acid helps in the digestion of food in the stomach.

Reason (R) : Hydrochloric acid creates an acidic medium to activate protein digesting enzymes.

36. A student was asked to write a stepwise procedure to demonstrate that carbon dioxide is necessary for photosynthesis. He wrote the following steps. The wrongly worded step is –

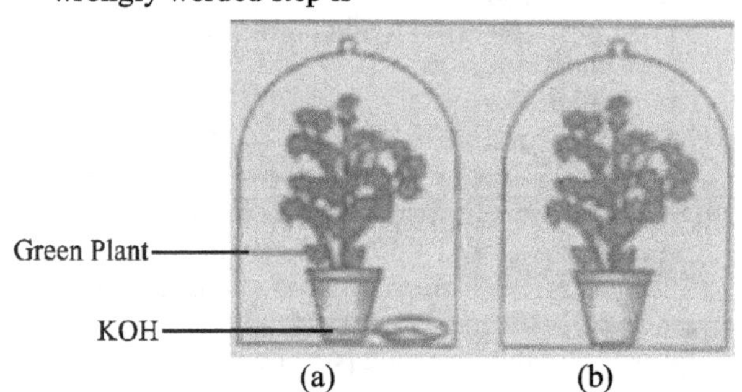

(a) Both potted plants are kept in dark room for at least three days.
(b) Bottom of the bell jars is sealed to make them air tight.
(c) Both potted plants are kept in sunlight after the starch test.
(d) A leaf from both the plants is taken to test the presence of starch.

37. Respiratory structures of two different animals a fish and a human being are as shown.

Observe (a) and (b) and select one characteristic that holds true for both of them.

(a) Both are placed internally in the body of animal.
(b) Both have thin and moist surface for gaseous exchange.
(c) Both are poorly supplied with blood vessels to conserve energy.
(d) In both the blood returns to the heart after being oxygenated.

38. Observe the diagram of an activity given below. What does it help to conclude, when the person exhales into the test-tube?

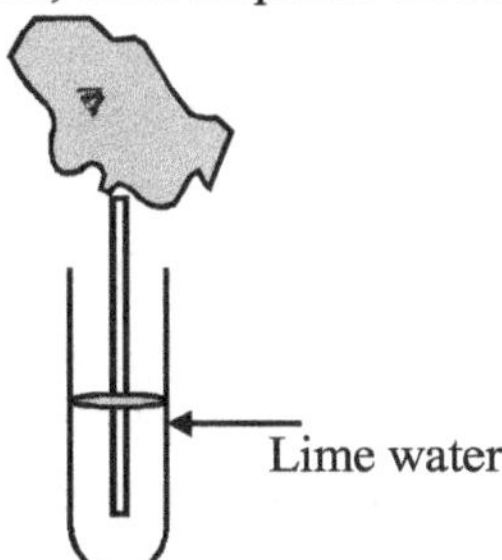

(a) Percentage of carbon dioxide is more in inhaled air.
(b) Fermentation occurs in the presence of oxygen.
(c) Percentage of carbon dioxide is more in the exhaled air.
(d) Fermentation occurs in the presence of carbon dioxide.

39. If a lens can converge the sun rays at a point 20 cm, away from its optical centre, the power of this lens is –
(a) + 2D (b) – 2D (c) + 5D (d) – 5D

40. The radius of curvature of a converging mirror is 30 cm. At what distance from the mirror should an object be placed so as to obtain a virtual image?
(a) Infinity
(b) 30 cm
(c) Between 15 cm and 30 cm
(d) Between 0 cm and 15 cm

41. The length of small intestine in a deer is more as compared to the length of small intestine of a tiger. The reason for this is –
(a) Mode of intake of food.
(b) Type of food consumed.
(c) Presence or absence of villi in intestines.
(d) Presence or absence of digestive enzymes.

42. Identify the two components of Phloem tissue that help in transportation of food in plants
(a) phloem parenchyma & sieve tubes
(b) sieve tubes & companion cells
(c) phloem parenchyma & companion cells
(d) phloem fibres and sieve tubes

43. A converging lens forms a three times magnified image of an object, which can be take on a screen. If the focal length of the lens is 30 cm, then the distance of the object from the lens is
(a) – 55 cm (b) – 50 cm
(c) – 45 cm (d) – 40 cm

44.

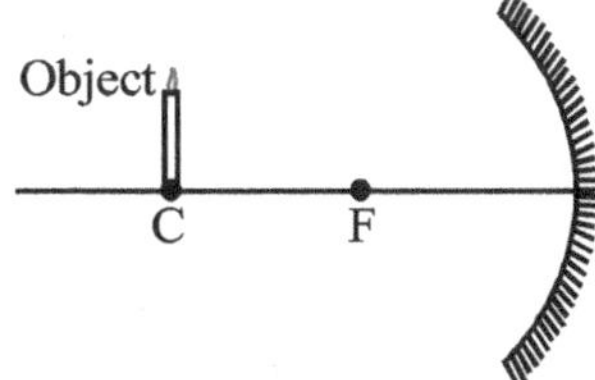

Which of the following statements is not true in reference to the diagram shown above?
(a) Image formed is real.
(b) Image formed is enlarged.
(c) Image is formed at a distance equal to double the focal length.
(d) Image formed is inverted.

45.

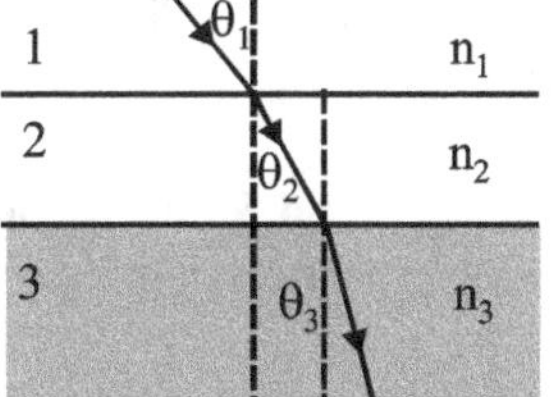

In the diagram shown above n_1, n_2 and n_3 are refractive indices of the media 1, 2 and 3 respectively. Which one of the following is true in this case?
(a) $n_1 = n_2$ (b) $n_1 > n_2$
(c) $n_2 > n_3$ (d) $n_3 > n_1$

46. The refractive index of medium A is 1.5 and that of medium B is 1.33. If the speed of light in air is 3×10^8 m/s, what is the speed of light in medium A and B respectively?
(a) 2×10^8 m/s and 1.33×10^8 m/s
(b) 1.33×10^8 m/s and 2×10^8 m/s
(c) 2.25×10^8 m/s and 2×10^8 m/s
(d) 2×10^8 m/s and 2.25×10^8 m/s

47. An object of height 4 cm is kept at a distance of 30 cm from the pole of a diverging mirror. If the focal length of the mirror is 10 cm, the height of the image formed is
(a) + 3.0 cm (b) + 2.5 cm
(c) + 1.0 cm (d) + 0.75 cm

48. 50.0 mL of tap water was taken in a beaker. Hydrochloric acid was added drop by drop to water. The temperature and pH of the solution was noted. The following graph was obtained. Choose the correct statements related to this activity.

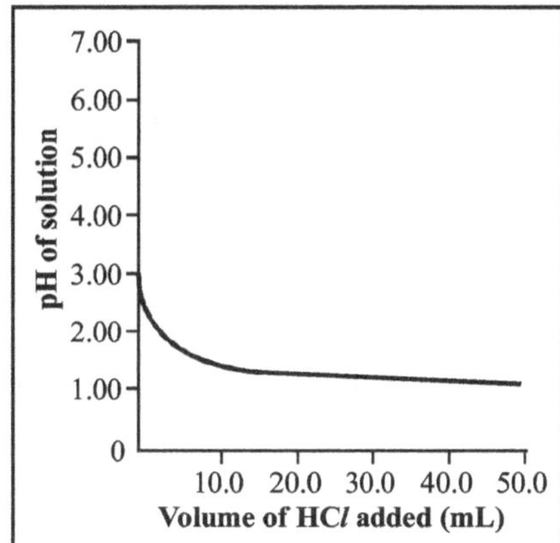

(i) The process of dissolving an acid in water is highly endothermic
(ii) The pH of the solution increases rapidly on addition of acid.
(iii) The pH of the solution decreases rapidly on addition of acid.
(iv) The pH of tap water was around 7.0.
(a) (i) and (ii) (b) (i) and (iii)
(c) (iii) and (iv) (d) (ii) and (iv)

SECTION - C

Section-**C** consists of **three** cases followed by questions. There are a total of **12** questions (Q. No. **49** to **60**) in this Section. Attempt any **10** questions from this section. The first attempted **10** questions would be evaluated.

Case-I :

A student, took four metals P, Q, R and S and carried out different experiments to study the properties of metals. Some of the observations were:

- All metals could not be cut with knife except metal R.
- Metal P combined with oxygen to form an oxide M_2O_3 which reacted with both acids and bases.
- Reaction with water.

  P – Did not react either with cold or hot water but reacted with steam

  Q – Reacted with hot water and the metal started floating

  R – Reacted violently with cold water

  S – Did not react with water at all

  Based on the above observations answer the following:

49. Out of the given metals, the one which needs to be stored used Kerosene is

(a) P (b) R
(c) S (d) Q

50. Out of the given metals, the metal Q is

(a) Iron (b) Zinc
(c) Potassium (d) Magnesium

51. Metal which forms amphoteric oxides is

(a) P (b) Q
(c) R (d) S

52. The increasing order of the reactivity of the four metals is:

(a) $P < Q < R < S$ (b) $S < R < Q < P$
(c) $S < P < Q < R$ (d) $P < R < Q < S$

Case-II:

The figure shown below represents a common type of dialysis called as Haemodialysis. It removes waste products from the blood. Such as excess salts, and urea which are insufficiently removed by the kidney in patients with kidney failure. During the procedure, the patient's blood is cleaned by filtration through a series of semi-permeable membranes before being returned to the blood of the patient. On the basis of this, answer the following questions.

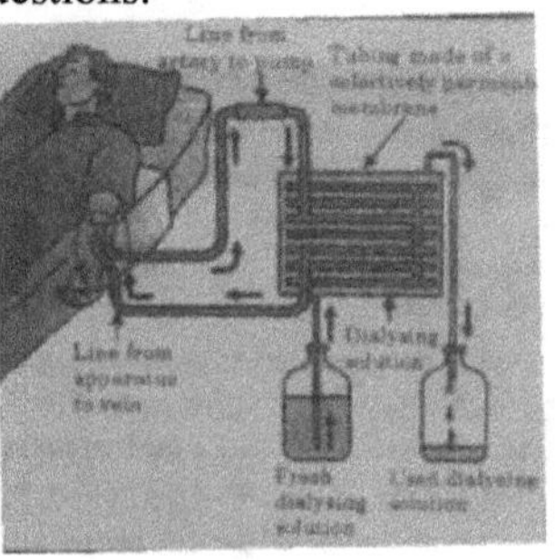

53. The hemodialyzer has semi-permeable lining of tubes which help to :

(a) To maintain osmotic pressure of blood.
(b) To filter nitrogenous wastes from the dialyzing solution.
(c) In passing the waste products in the dialyzing solution.
(d) To pump purified blood back into the body of the patient.

54. Which one of the following is not a function of Artificial Kidney?

(a) To remove nitrogenous wastes from the blood.
(b) To remove excess fluids from the blood.
(c) To reabsorb essential nutrients from the blood.
(d) To filter and purify the blood.

55. The 'used dialysing' solution is rich in:

(a) Urea and excess salts
(b) Blood cells
(c) Lymph
(d) Proteins

56. Which part of the nephron in human kidney, serves the function of reabsorption of certain substances?

(a) Glomerulus (b) Bowmans Capsule
(c) Tubules (d) Collecting duct

Case-III:

A compound microscope is an instrument which consists of two lenses L_1 called objective, forms a real, inverted and magnified image of the given object. This serves as the object for the second lens L_2; the eye place. The produces the final image, which is inverted with respect to the original object, enlarged and virtual.

57. What types of lenses must be L_1 and L_2?

(a) Both concave
(b) Both convex
(c) L_1 - concave and L_2 - convex
(d) L_1 - convex and L_2 - concave

58. What is the value and sign of magnification (according to the new Cartesian sign convention) of the image formed by L_1?

(a) Value = Less than 1 and Sign = Positive
(b) Value = More than 1 and Sign = Positive
(c) Value = Less than 1 and Sign = Negative
(d) Value = More than 1 and Sign = Negative

59. What is the value and sign of (according to new Cartesian sign convention) magnification of the image formed by L_2?

(a) Value = Less than 1 and Sign = Positive
(b) Value = More than 1 and Sign = Positive
(c) Value = Less than 1 and Sign = Negative
(d) Value = More than 1 and Sign = Negative

60. If power of the eyepiece (L_2) is 5 diopters and it forms an image at a distance of 80 cm from its optical centre, at what distance should the object be?

(a) 12 cm (b) 16 cm (c) 18 cm (d) 20 cm

Solutions

1. **(c)** When sodium sulphate reacts with barium chloride solution, then insoluble white precipitate of barium sulphate is formed.

$$BaCl_2(aq) + Na_2SO_4(aq) \longrightarrow \underset{\text{White PPt.}}{BaSO_4}\downarrow + 2NaCl(aq)$$

2. **(a)** When highly electropositive metal like Na and K reacts with oxygen, they will form basic oxides i.e. Na_2O and K_2O as basic oxides are soluble in water and form hydroxide while SO_2 and NO_2 are oxides of non-metal which are acidic in nature.

Bases which are soluble in water are called alkalis. NaOH and KOH, are bases as they generate OH^- ions in water.

3. **(d)** When zinc granules is added in dilute sulphuric acid, then zinc displaces the hydrogen and form zinc sulphate and hydrogen gas as zinc is more reactive than hydrogen. So, an evolved hydrogen gas on burning produces a popping sound.

$$Zn + H_2SO_4 \longrightarrow ZnSO_4 + H_2\uparrow$$

Generally, metal + dil. acid $\longrightarrow$ salt + $H_2(g)\uparrow$ the reactivity order is Mg > Al > Zn > Fe. copper does not show reaction with dil.acid as it is less active than hydrogen.

4. **(b)** When sodium reacts with water, it forms sodium hydroxide and hydrogen gas.
$Na(s) + H_2O(l) \longrightarrow NaOH(aq) + H_2(g)$
In reactant side; Na and H_2O is multiply by 2 and in product side; NaOH is multiply by 2 to balance the reaction.
Therefore; the balanced equation is:
$2Na(s) + 2H_2O(l) \longrightarrow 2NaOH(aq) + H_2(g)$

5. **(c)** (i) In orange, citric acid is present.
(ii) In sour milk, lactic acid is present.
(iii) In Ant sting, methanoic acid is present.
(iv) In Tamarind, tartaric acid is present.

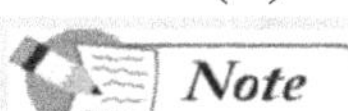

Methanoic acid (HCOOH) is also known as gormic acid.

6. **(c)** $C_6H_{12}O_6(aq) + 6O_2(aq) \longrightarrow 6CO_2(aq) + 6H_2O(l)$ + 686 Kcal
The given reaction is a type of exothermic reaction as energy is released during the reaction.

7. **(c)** HCl forms Cl_2 by losing 1'H' atom per molecule. Thus it gets oxidized itself and acts as reducing agent. Simultaneously, MnO_2 loses 2 'O' atoms per molecule and forms $MnCl_2$ thus, it gets reduced and acts as an oxidizing agent.

$$\overset{+4}{Mn}O_2 + 4H\overset{-1}{Cl} \longrightarrow \overset{+4}{Mn}Cl_2 + 2H_2O + \overset{0}{Cl_2}$$

HCl is oxidised to Cl_2, thus there is increase in oxidation state while MnO_2 is reduced to $MnCl_2$, thus there is decrease in oxidation state. Hence MnO_2 act as an oxidizing agent and HCl act as a reducing agent.

Note

Modern definiton of oxidatin Reduction process:

Loss of electron → Charge over element increases → Oxidation

Gain of electron → Charge over elements decreases → Reduction

$H\overset{-1}{Cl} \longrightarrow \overset{0}{Cl_2}$ *(charge increases by one unit) → Oxidation*

$\overset{+4}{Mn}O_2 \longrightarrow \overset{+2}{Mn}Cl_2$ *(charge decrease by two unit) → Reduction*

8. **(d)** Bases are bitter and turns red litmus to blue. The pH value for the bases are more than 7 and on addition of few drops of phenolpthalein turns bases into pink in color.

9. **(d)**
(a) Sodium chloride is a neutral salt of strong acid (HCl) and strong base (NaOH).
(b) Sodium carbonate is a basic salt of strong base (NaOH) and weak acid (H_2CO_3).
(c) Sodium Sulphate is a neutral salt of strong base (NaOH) and strong acid (H_2SO_4).
(d) Sodium Acetate is a basic salt of strong base (NaOH) and weak acid (CH_3COOH).

10. **(c)** The chemical composition of the reactants changes but total mass of the reactants remains same before and after the chemical reaction.

11. **(d)** Oxygen-rich blood from the lungs comes to the thin-walled upper chamber of the heart on the left, the left atrium. The left atrium relaxes when it is collecting this blood. It then contracts, while the next chamber, the left ventricle, relaxes, so that the blood is transferred to it. When the muscular left ventricle contracts in its turn, the blood is pumped out to the body. De-oxygenated blood comes from the body to the upper chamber on the right, the right atrium, as it relaxes. As the right atrium contracts, the corresponding lower chamber.

12. **(a)** Ethanol (in yeast) and lactic acids (in our muscle cells) are produce in the absence of oxygen during respiration process. While in the presence of oxygen (in mitochondria) glucose will break down ATP (energy, carbon dioxide and water molecules.

13. **(c)** In the case of a single-celled organism, no specific organs for taking in food, exchange of gases or removal of wastes may be needed because the entire surface of the organism is in contact with the environment. Simple diffusion will meet the requirements of all the cells.

14. **(b)** Urea is an excretory product which is generally produced by the breakdown of proteins. In humans, urea is mainly produced in the liver.

15. **(a)** When we breathe in, we lift our ribs and flatten our diaphragm, and the chest cavity becomes larger as a result. Because of this, air is sucked into the lungs and fills the expanded alveoli.
Inspiration can occur if the pressure within the lungs is less than atmospheric pressure inspiration is initiated by contraction of diaphgram which increases the volume of thoracic chamber.

16. **(b)** Tiny pores (called stomata) present on the surface of the leaves. Massive amounts of gaseous exchange takes place in the leaves through these pores for the purpose of photosynthesis.

17. **(a)** In solar cooker, concave mirror is used as it absorbs all the incident light and reflect it to a single focal point.

18. **(c)** To get magnified image of an object on a screen by a convex lens, object must be either at focus (F) or between F and 2F. When object at F image is at infinity. Hence (c) is the correct option.

Note

Concave mirrors form real images that can be projected outo a screen if the object is farther away than the focal points. If the object is closer than the focal point, the image is fomred up right and large but virtual i.e. cannot be projected onto a screen.

19. **(b)** Concave lens or, diverging lens diverges the incident ray of light.

20. **(b)** Since $\mu_{21} = \frac{\sin i}{\sin r}$
So the bending of light is least for pair of media (A) $\mu = 1.50$ to (B) $\mu = 1.33$

21. **(a)** According to Raleigh's law sccattering $\propto \frac{1}{\lambda^4}$ $\lambda_{Red} > \lambda_{Blue}$ so red light is least scattered in the atmosphere.

22. **(b)** As object is placed between pole (P) and focus (F) of a concave mirror so image formed is virtual, erect and magnified. Hence sign positive and value more than 1.

23. **(c)** Angle $\angle 3$ & $\angle 2$ are in same medium so $\angle 3 = \angle 2$ alternate angle.

24. **(c)** The colour of Y is red the colour used to paint the danger signal. When white ray of light passes through a prism it disperses into seven colours VIBGYOR. Red colour deviates or bends the least.

25. **(d)** $CaCO_3(s) \xrightarrow{\Delta} CaO(s) + CO_2(g)$; is a type of thermal decomposition reaction. When calcium carbonate is heated, it decomposes into calcium oxide and carbondioxide.

Note

Reaction (b) and (c) are the examples of photodecomposition reactions where decomposition takes place in the presence of light. Reaction in option (a) is the electrolytic process in which decomposition process takes place with electricity.

26. **(c)** The lower the pH value, the higher will be the concentration of hydrogen ions in the solution. The pH value of Gastric juice is the least and pH value of vinegar is the highest. Therefore the decreasing order of their H^+ ion concentration is $2 > 1 > 4 > 3$.

27. **(d)** The reaction is shown below:

$$K_2CO_3 + 2HCl \longrightarrow 2\,KCl + H_2O + CO_2 \uparrow$$

$$CO_2 + \underset{\text{Lime water}}{Ca(OH)_2} \longrightarrow \underset{\text{milky ppt.}}{CaCO_3 \downarrow}$$

28. **(c)** The structure of $CaCl_2$ is $[Ca^{2+}]\left[\times\ddot{\underset{..}{Cl}}:\right]_2$

29. **(b)** The reaction in which one element is replaced by another in a compound is known as displacement reaction.

$$Cu(s) + 2\,AgNO_3(aq) \longrightarrow Cu\,(NO_3)_2\,(aq) + 2Ag\,(s)$$

$$Al_2\,(SO_4)_3 + 3mg \longrightarrow 3MgSO_4 + 2Al$$

Note

Metals which are more reactive displaces less reactive metal from their salt solution. The order of reactivity is
Na > Mg > Al > Zn > Fe > Cu > Ag

30. **(d)** The formula of bleaching powder is $CaOCl_2$ and the formula of baking soda is $NaHCO_3$. Therefore, they do not have the water of crystalisation.

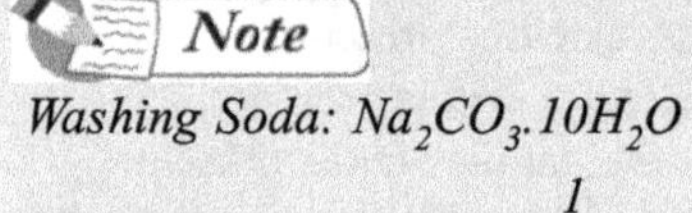
Note

Washing Soda: $Na_2CO_3.10H_2O$

Plaster of Paris: $CaSO_4.\frac{1}{2}H_2O$

31. **(a)** Due to non-corrosive nature of sodium hydrogen carbonate, it is used as an ingredient is antacids.

32. **(d)** Burning of natural gas is an exothermic process. When methane gas combines with oxygen, it will produce carbon dioxide and water.

$$CH_4 + 2O_2 \longrightarrow CO_2 + 2H_2O$$

33. **(b)** Nitrogen is the most frequently limiting nutrient for crop growth of all the essential nutrients. Nitrogen is the nutrient that typically produces the highest yield response in crop plants, promoting rapid vegetative growth and providing the plant with a healthy green colour.

Nitrogen is taken up by roots in the inorganic forms of nitrate $\mathbf{NO_3^-}$ and ammonium $\mathbf{NH_4^+}$ ions. Once inside the plant, NO_3 is converted to NH_2 and assimilated to form organic compounds.
Nitrogen addition is not recommended for legume crops such as soybean because they produce their own nitrogen supply. Nitrogen-fixing soil organisms (*Rhizobium*) associated with legume roots capture atmospheric nitrogen and provide it to the plant.

34. **(c)** Light from the sun overhead travelled relatively shorter distance.

35. **(a)** The digestion in stomach is taken care of by the gastric glands present in the wall of the stomach. These release hydrochloric acid, a protein digesting enzyme called pepsin, and mucus. The hydrochloric acid creates an acidic medium which facilitates the action of the enzyme pepsin.

36. **(c)** The following step for this experiment are-
(i) Take two healthy potted plants which are nearly the same size.
(ii) Keep them in a dark room for three days.
(iii) Now place each plant on separate glass plates. Place a watch-glass containing potassium hydroxide by the side of one of the plants. The potassium hydroxide is used to absorb carbon dioxide.
(iv) Cover both plants with separate bell-jars.
(v) Use Vaseline to seal the bottom of the jars to the glass plates so that the set-up is air-tight.
(vi) Keep the plants in sunlight for about two hours.
(vii) Pluck a leaf from each plant and check for the presence of starch as in the above activity.
During photosynthesis, plants take in carbon dioxide and convert carbon dioxide, water into oxygen and glucose.

37. **(b)** Both gill and lungs in fish and human respectively, having moist and thin surface for gaseous exchange.

38. **(c)** When person exhale into the test tube , the lime water present into test tube turns milky which indicate the presence of CO_2 .

$$\underset{\text{lime water}}{Ca(OH)_2} + CO_2 \longrightarrow \underset{\text{calcium carbonate}}{CaCO_3}$$

39. **(c)** As the lens converges the sun rays so lens is convex, so (f) focal length is +(ve). And power of lens

$$P = \frac{1}{f_{(\text{in metre})}} = \frac{1}{\frac{20}{100}} = +5D$$

40. **(d)** Virtual image is formed by a converging or concave mirror only when object is placed between pole and focal point i.e., between 0 cm and 15cm $\left(\because f = \frac{r}{2} \text{ and } r = 30 \text{ cm given}\right)$

41. **(b)** The small intestine of a deer (herbivore) is longer than that of a tiger (carnivore). This is due to the fact that cellulose (a component part of the plant cell wall) takes longer for deer to digest than flesh, which takes less time.

42. **(b)** Phloem is a permanent complex tissue of the plant that helps in the transportation of food. Sieve tubes and companion cells are the two components of phloem tissue that transport food bidirectional.
Sieve tubes are the cells that conduct food in angiosperms. Companion cells are also present in angiosperms.

43. **(d)** Given : magnification, $m = -3 \therefore$ if $u = x$ then $v = 3x$ cm and $f = 30$ cm.

Using lens formula, $\frac{1}{f} = \frac{1}{v} - \frac{1}{u} \Rightarrow \frac{1}{30} = \frac{1}{-3x} - \frac{1}{x}$

$= \frac{-1-3}{3x}$ or, $\frac{1}{30} = \frac{-4}{3x} \therefore x = \frac{-120}{3} = -40$ cm

Hence the distance of the object from the lens, $u = x = -40$ cm.

44. **(b)** As object is at the centre of curvature of the concave mirror so image formed is at the centre of curvature, real, inverted and of the same size as that of object.

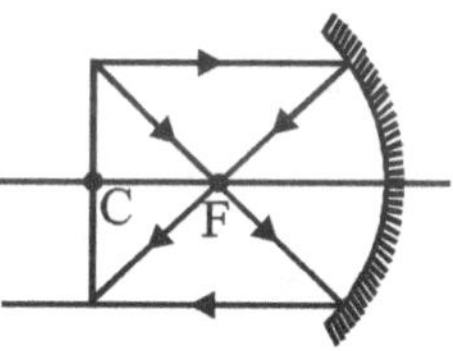

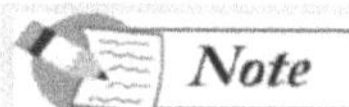

When object is placed beyond centre of curvature image formed is enlarged and diminished when object is placed between pole and centre of curvature.

45. **(d)** From the diagram,
$\angle\theta_1 > \angle\theta_2 > \angle\theta_3$
$\therefore \quad n_1 < n_2 < n_3$ or, $n_3 > n_1$ or n_2

46. **(d)** Speed of light in medium

$$V_{med} = \frac{\text{Speed of light in air}}{\text{Speed of light in medium}}$$

$$\therefore \quad V_A = \frac{3\times10^8}{1.5} = 2\times10^8 \text{ m/s}$$

$$\text{and } V_B = \frac{3\times10^8}{1.33} = 2.25\times10^8 \text{ m/s}$$

47. **(c)** Here object is placed at a distance of 30 cm i.e., between centre of curvature and infinity so image formed is virtual, erect, diminished between the pole P and focus F behind the mirror.

$u = -30$ cm, $h_O = 4$ cm, $f = +10$ cm given

using mirror formula, $\frac{1}{f} = \frac{1}{v} + \frac{1}{u}$ or $\frac{1}{+10} = \frac{1}{v} + \frac{1}{-30}$

$\Rightarrow \frac{1}{v} = \frac{1}{30} + \frac{1}{10} = \frac{1+3}{30} = +\frac{4}{30}$ $\quad \therefore v = 7.5$ cm

Now from formula, magnification $M = \frac{v}{u} = \frac{h_I}{h_O}$

$\therefore \frac{7.5}{30} = \frac{h_I}{4}$ $\quad \therefore h_I = 1$ cm

48. **(c)** The pH of solution decreases, on addition of acid and the pH value for tap water was around 7.0.

Case I (Qs. 49-52)

49. **(b)** The metal which reacted violently with cold water needs to be stored in kerosene.

50. **(d)** Magnesium reacts with hot water and the metal started floating.
$Mg + 2H_2O \rightarrow Mg(OH)_2 + H_2\uparrow$
Mg does not react with cold water.

51. **(a)** Metal P combined with oxygen to form an oxide M_2O_3 which reacted with both acids and bases. Hence, acts as an amphoteric oxide.

52. **(c)** The increasing order of reactivity of metal is:
$S < P < Q < R$.

Case II (Qs. 53-56)

53. **(c)** The haemodialyzer has a semi-permeable lining of tubes which help in passing the waste product into the dialyzing solution.
Dialysis is the process of solute transfer across a semi-permeable memberane.

54. **(c)** An artificial kidney does not reabsorb essential nutrient from the blood.

55. **(a)** The used dialysing solution is rich in waste products from the blood like urea and excess salts.

56. **(c)** Tubules of the nephron in the human kidney serves the function of reabsorption of certain substances.

Case III (Qs. 57 - 60) : Ray diagram for the formation of image by a compound microscope is shown below :

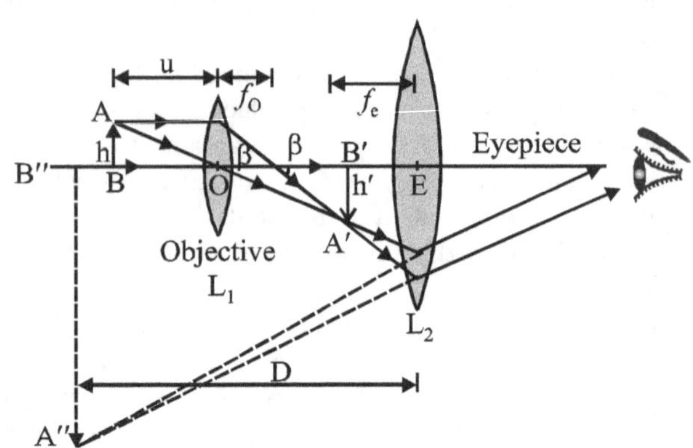

57. **(b)** From the diagram, both the lenses L_1 (objective) and L_2 (eyepiece) are convex.

58. **(d)** From the diagram, the image formed by the objective lens L_1 is magnified and inverted (A' B') so magnification

$M = \frac{\text{height of the image}}{\text{height of the object}}$.

Hence M value = more than 1 and sign = negative.

In compound microscope, magnification does not change appreciably if objective and eye-piece are interchanged.

59. **(b)** The image formed by the eyepiece L_2 is magnified and inverted (A″ B″) of the object A′ B′, so magnification M value = more than 1 and sign = positive.

60. **(b)** Power of a lens, $P = \frac{1}{f(\text{in metre})}$ or $5 = \frac{1}{f}$

$\therefore f = \frac{1}{5} \times 100$

or, $f = 20$ cm and $v = -80$ cm, $u = ?$

using lens formula, $\frac{1}{f} = \frac{1}{v} - \frac{1}{u}$ or, $\frac{1}{20} = \frac{1}{-80} - \frac{1}{u}$

$\therefore \frac{1}{u} = -\frac{1}{20} - \frac{1}{80} = \frac{-4-1}{80} = -\frac{5}{80}$

$\therefore u = 16$ cm from the optical centre of the lens L_2.

All India **2020**

CBSE Board Solved Paper

Time Allowed : 3 Hours | ***Maximum Marks : 80***

General Instructions:

Read the following instructions very carefully and strictly follow them :

(i) The question paper comprises three Sections, **A, B** and **C**. There are **30** questions in the question paper.

(ii) All questions are compulsory.

(iii) Section **A** - all questions / or parts (question no. **1** to **14**) there of in this section are **one** mark questions comprising MCQ, VSA type and Assertion-Reason type questions. They are to be answered in **one** word or in one sentence.

(iv) Section **B** - question no. **15** to **24** are short answer type questions, carrying **three** marks each. Answer to these questions should not exceed **50** to **60** words.

(v) Section **C** - question no. **25** to **30** are long answer type questions, carrying **five** marks each. Answer to these questions should not exceed **80** to **90** words.

(vi) Answer should be brief and to the point. Also the above mentioned word limit be adhered to as far as possible.

(vii) There is no overall choice in the question paper. However, an internal choice has been provided in some questions in each section. Only one of the choices in such questions have to be attempted.

(viii) In addition to this, separate instructions are given with each section and question, wherever necessary.

SECTION - A

1. How are covalent bonds formed?

2. Define electropositivity.

OR

The atomic radii of first group elements are given below :

Group-I element	Atomic Radii (pm)
Na	86
K	231
Rb	244
Cs	282

State the reason behind the observed trend in the above elements.

3. Answer question numbers 3(a) to 3(d) on the basis of your understanding of the following paragraph and the related studies concepts.

The Tehri dam is the highest dam in India and one of the highest in the World. The Tehri dam withholds a reservoir of capacity 4.0 km^3 and surface area 52 km^2. It is used for irrigation, municipal water supply and the generation of 1000 MW of hydro electricity.

The Tehri Dam has been the object of protests. Environment activist Shri Sunder Lal Bahuguna led the "Anti Tehri Dam Movement" from 1980s to 2014. The protest was against the displacement of town inhabitants and environmental consequences of the weak ecosystem. The relocation of more than 1,00,000 people from the area has led to protracted legal battles over resettlement rights and ultimately resulted in the delayed completion of the project.

(a) How is hydropower harnessed?

(b) Define 1 MW.

(c) Mention two disadvantages of constructing Tehri Dam.

(d) What happens when water from great heights is made to fall on blades of turbine?

4. Questions numbers 4(a) to 4(d) are based on table given below, Study the table in which the levels of Thyroid Stimulating Hormone (TSH) in women are given and answer the questions that follow on the basis of understanding of the following paragraph and the related studied concepts.

Age Range	Normal (mU/L)	Low (mU/L)
18 - 29 years	0.4 - 2.34 mU/L	< 0.4 mU/L
30 - 49 years	0.4 - 4.0 mU/L	< 0.4 mU/L
50 - 79 years	0.46 -4.68 mU/L	< 0.46 mU/L

Women are at greater risk for developing abnormal TSH levels during menstruation, while giving birth and after going through menopause.

Around 5% of women in the United States have some kind of thyroid problem compared to 3% of men. Despite claims that high TSH increases your risk for heart disease, a 2013 study found no link between high TSH and heart diseases. But a 2017 study showed that older women are especially at risk for developing thyroid cancer if they have high TSH levels along with thyroid nodules.

(a) A 35 year old woman has TSH level 6.03 mU/L. What change should she bring in her diet to control this level? **[1 Mark]**

(b) When do women face a greater risk of abnormal TSH level? **[1 Mark]**

(c) State the consequence of low TSH level. **[1 Mark]**

(d) Name the mineral that is responsible for synthesis of hormone secreted by thyroid gland. **[1 Mark]**

5. The sky appears dark to passengers flying at very high altitudes mainly because :

(a) Scatterings of light is not enough at such heights.

(b) There is no atmosphere at great heights.

(c) The size of molecules is smaller than the wavelength of visible light.

(d) The light gets scattered towards the earth.

6. A cylindrical conductor of length 'l' and uniform area of cross section 'A' has resistance 'R'. The area of cross section of another conductor of same material and same resistance but of length '$2l$' is

(a) $\frac{A}{2}$ (b) $\frac{3A}{2}$

(c) 2A (d) 3A

7. The maximum resistance which can be made using four resistors each of resistance $\frac{1}{2}$ Ω is

(a) 2Ω (b) 1 Ω

(c) 2.5 Ω (d) S Ω

8. A diagram of traditional water harvesting system is given below :

The statement which defines the system and its parts is

(a) This is an ideal setting of the Khadin system and A = Catchment area; B = Saline area & C = Shallow dugwell

(b) This is an ideal setting of the Shallow dugwell system and A = Catchment area; B = Saline area and C = Khadin

(c) This is an ideal setting of Catchment area and A = Khadin, B = Saline are and C = Shallow dugwell

(d) This is showing Saline area and A = Catchment area; B = Khadin and C = Shallow dugwell

OR

The major ill effect of mono culture practice in forests is on the

(a) biodiversity which faces large destruction

(b) local people whose basic needs can no longer be met from such forests

(c) industries

(d) forest department

9. Several factories were pouring their wastes in rivers A and B. Water samples were collected from these two rivers. It was observed that sample collected from river A was acidic while that of river B was basic. The factories located near A and B are

(a) Soaps and detergents factories near A and alcohol distillery near B.

(b) Soaps and detergents factories near B and alcohol distillery near A.

(c) Lead storage battery manufacturing factories near A and soaps and detergents factories near B.

(d) Lead storage battery manufacturing factories near B and soaps and detergents factories near A.

10. In which of the following the identity of initial substance remains unchanged?

(a) Curdling of milk

(b) Formation of crystals by process of crystallisation

(c) Fermentation of grapes

(d) Digestion of food

11. An aqueous solution 'A' turns phenolphthalein solution pink. On addition of an aqueous solution 'B' to 'A', the pink colour disappears. The following statement is true for solution 'A' and 'B'.

(a) A is strongly basic and B is a weak base.
(b) A is strongly acidic and B is a weak acid.
(c) A has pH greater than 7 and B has pH less than 7.
(d) A has pH less than 7 and B has pH greater than 7.

12. An element 'X' is forming an acidic oxide. Its position in modern periodic table will be
(a) Group 1 and Period 3
(b) Group 2 and Period 3
(c) Group 13 and Period 3
(d) Group 16 and Period 3

OR

Consider the following statements about an element 'X' with number of protons 13.
(A) It forms amphoteric oxide
(B) Its valency is three
(C) The formula of its chloride is XCl_3
The correct statements(s) is/are
(a) only (A) (b) only (B)
(c) (A) and (C) (d) (A), (B) and (C)

Direction : For question numbers 13 and 14, two statements are given-one labelled Assertion (A) and the other labelled Reason (R). Select the correct answer to these questions from the codes (a), (b), (c) and (d) as given below :
(a) Both (A) and (R) are true and (R) is correct explanation of the assertion.
(b) Both (A) and (R) are true but (R) is not the correct explanation of the assertion.
(c) (A) is true but (R) is false.
(d) (A) is false but (R) is true.

13. Assertion (A) : Following are the members of a homologous series :
CH_3OH, $CH_3\ CH_2OH$, $CH_3CH_2CH_2OH$
Reason (R) : A series of compounds with same functional group but differing by $-CH_2-$ unit is called a homologous series.

14. Assertion (A) : Alloys are commonly used in electrical heating devices like electric iron and heater.
Reason (R) : Resistivity of an alloy is generally higher than that of its constituent metals but the alloys have low melting points than their constituent metals.

SECTION - B

15. Mention with reason the colour changes observed when :.
(i) silver chloride is exposed to sunlight.
(ii) copper powder is strongly heated in the presence of oxygen.
(iii) a piece of zinc is dropped in copper sulphate solution.

16. Complete and balance the following chemical equations :
(i) $NaOH(aq) + Zn(s) \rightarrow$
(ii) $CaCO_3(aq) + H_2O(l) + CO_2(g) \rightarrow$
(iii) $HCl(aq) + H_2O(l) \rightarrow$

OR

During electrolysis of brine, a gas 'G' is liberated at anode. When this gas 'G' is passed through slaked lime, a compound 'C' is formed, which is used for disinfecting drinking water.
(i) Write formula of 'G' and 'C'.
(ii) State the chemical equation involved
(iii) What is common name of compound 'C'? Give its chemical name.

17. Study the data of the following three categories A, B and C.

Category	Name of the element	Atomic Mass
A	Li Na K	7 23 39
B	N P As	14 31 74
C	B Al Ga	10.8 27 69.7

(i) From the given three categories A, B and C, Pick the one which forms Dobereiner's Triads.
(ii) Why did Mendeleev placed elements of category A, B and C in three different groups?
(iii) Is Newland law of octaves applicable to all the three categories?
Give reason to justify your answer.

18. (a) From the following group of organisms create a food chain which is the most advantageous for Human beings in terms of energy.

Hawk, Rat, Cereal plant,
Goat, Snake, Human Being

(b) State the possible disadvantage if the cereal plant is growing in soil rich in pesticides.
(c) Construct a food web using the organisms mentioned above.

OR

(a) Write two harmful effects of using plastic bags on the environment. Suggest alternatives to the usage of plastic bags.
(b) List any two practices that can be followed to dispose off the waste produced in our homes.

19. (a) State the role played by the following in the process of digestion.

(i) Enzyme trypsin

(ii) Enzyme lipase

(b) List two functions of finger like projections present in the small intestine.

20. (a) Classify the following as homologous or analogous pairs :

(i) Broccoli and Cabbage

(ii) Ginger and Raddish

(iii) Fore limbs of birds and lizard

(iv) Wings of a bat and Wings of a bird

(b) State the main feature that categories a given pair of organs as homologous or analogous.

21. A green stemmed rose plant denoted by GG and a brown stemmed rose plant denoted by gg are allowed to undergo a cross with each other.

(a) List your observations regarding

(i) Colour of stem in their F_1 progeny

(ii) Percentage of brown stemmed plants in F_2 progeny if F_1 plants are self pollinated.

(iii) Ratio of GG and Gg in the F_2 progency.

(b) Based on the findings of this cross, what conclusion can be drawn?

22. The diagram given below shows an object O and its image I.

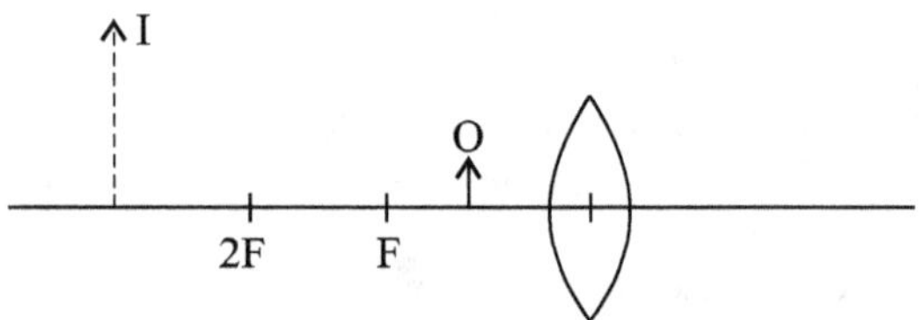

Without actually drawing the ray diagram, state the following :

(i) Type of lens (Converging/Diverging)

(ii) Name two optical instruments where such an image is obtained.

(iii) List three characteristics of the image formed if this lens is replaced by a concave mirror of focal length 'f' and an object is placed at a distance 'f/2' in front of the mirror.

23. Give reasons for the following :

(i) There is either a convergence or a divergence of magnetic field lines near the ends of a current carrying straight solenoid.

(ii) The current carrying solenoid when suspended freely rests along a particular direction.

(iii) The burnt out fuse should be replaced by another fuse of identical rating.

24. (a) With the help of labelled ray diagram show the path followed by a narrow beam of monochromatic light when it passes through a glass prism.

(b) What would happen if this beam is replaced by a narrow beam of white light?

OR

(a) A person is suffering from both myopia and hypermetropia.

(i) What kind of lenses can correct this defect?

(ii) How are these lenses prepared?

(b) A person needs a lens of power + 3D for correcting his near vision and –3D for correcting his distant vision. Calculate the focal lengths of the lenses required to correct these defects.

SECTION - C

25. Write balanced chemical equations to explain what happens, when

(i) Mercuric oxide is heated.

(ii) Mixture of cuprous oxide and cuprous sulphide is heated.

(iii) Aluminium is reacted with manganese dioxide.

(iv) Ferric oxide is reduced with aluminium.

(v) Zinc carbonate undergoes calcination.

OR

(i) By the transfer of electrons, illustrate the formation of bond in magnesium chloride and identify the ions present in this compound.

(ii) Ionic compounds are solids. Give reasons.

(iii) With the help of a labelled diagram show the experimental set up of action of steam on a metal.

26. (a) Compare soaps and detergents on the basic of their composition and cleansing action in hard water.

(b) What happens when ethanol is treated with sodium metal ? State the behaviour of ethanol in this reaction.

(c) Draw the structure of cyclohexane.

(d) Name the following compound.

```
        H
        |
H – C – C – H
    ||  |
    O   H
```

27. (a) Write the correct sequence of steps followed during journey of oxygen rich blood from lungs to various organs of human body.

(b) What happens when the system of blood vessels develop a leak?

28. (a) Draw a diagram showing germination of pollen on stigma of a flower and mark on it the following organs/parts :

(i) Pollen Grain
(ii) Pollen tube
(iii) Stigma
(iv) Female germ cell

(b) State the significance of pollen tube.

(c) Name the parts of flower that develop after fertilization into

(i) Seed
(ii) Fruit

OR

(a) "Use of a condom is beneficial for both the sexes involved in a sexual act." Justify this statement giving two reasons.

(b) How do oral contraceptive help in avoiding pregnancies?

(c) What is sex selective abortion? How does it affect a healthy society?
(State any one consequence)

29. (a) For the combination of resistors shown in the following figure, find the equivalent resistance between M & N.

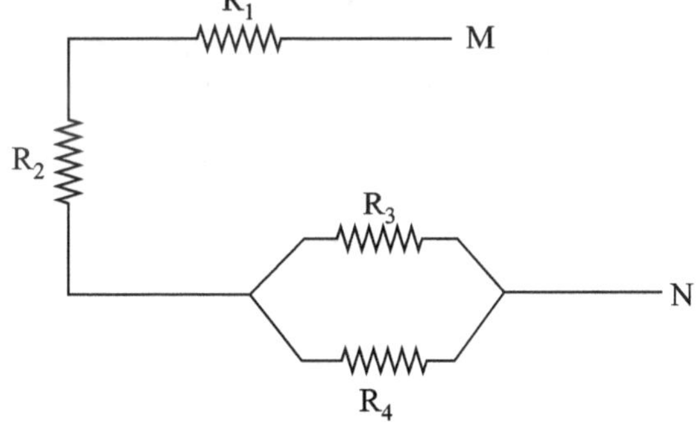

(b) State Joule's law of heating.

(c) Why we need a 5 A fuse for an electric iron which consumes 1 kW power at 220 V?

(d) Why is it impracticable to connect an electric bulb and an electric heater in series?

30. (a) A security mirror used in a big showroom has radius of curvature 5m. If a customer is standing at a distance of 20 m from the cash counter, find the position, nature and size of the image formed in the security mirror.

(b) Neha visited a dentist in his clinic. She observed that the dentist was holding an instrument fitted with a mirror. State the nature of this mirror and reason for its use in the instrument used by dentist.

OR

Rishi went to a palmist to show his palm.
The palmist used a special lens for this purpose.

(i) State the nature of the lens and reason for its use.
(ii) Where should the palmist place/hold the lens so as to have a real and magnified images of an object?
(iii) If the focal length of this lens is 10 cm and the lens is held at a distance of 5 cm from the palm, use lens formula to find the position and size of the image.

Solutions

1. A covalent bond is formed by sharing of electrons from both the participating atoms. **(1 Mark)**

2. Electropositivity is the measure of the ability of elements (mainly metals) to donate electrons to form positive ions. **(1 Mark)**

OR

The atomic size (atomic radii) increases while going down the group because new shells are being added at each step. **(1 Mark)**

3. (a) Water is collected in a reservoir behind the dam. The stored water is released to turn a turbine in order to produce electricity. **(1 Mark)**
   (b) A megawatt is a unit for measuring power. i.e., 1 MW = 1000000 W. **(1 Mark)**
   (c) Construction of Tehri Dam has resulted in large scale destruction of biodiversity in catchment area and large scale displacement of people. **(1 Mark)**
   (d) Blades of turbine move and convert kinetic energy of water into electric energy. **(1 Mark)**

4. (a) By maintaing the level of omega-3 to omega-6 fatty acids as well as diet rich in protein helps in controlling the level of TSH. **(1 Mark)**
   (b) During menstruation, child birth and menopause. **(1 Mark)**
   (c) Low TSH level can result in hyperthyroidism which causes drastic weight loss and weakness. **(1 Mark)**
   (d) Iodine. **(1 Mark)**

Thyroid stimulating hormone is a pituitary hormone which stimulates the thyroid gland to secrete thyroxin hormone that is responsible for the regulation of carbohydrates, proteins and fat metabolism.

5. (a) Scattering of light is not enough at such heights. **(1 Mark)**

6. (c) Resistance of conductor, $R = \rho \frac{l}{A}$

Resistance of another conductor $R' = \rho \frac{2l}{A'}$

[Here, A′ = area of cross-section of another conductor]

According to Question

$R = R'$

$\therefore \rho \frac{l}{A} = \rho \frac{2l}{A'}$

$\Rightarrow A' = 2A$ **(1 Mark)**

Resistivity (ρ) of the material is independent of length and area of cross-section of the material. It depends upon the nature of the material and temperature of the conductor.

7. (a) To get the maximum resistance, all four resistors should be connected in series,

$\therefore R = \frac{1}{2}\Omega + \frac{1}{2}\Omega + \frac{1}{2}\Omega + \frac{1}{2}\Omega = 2\Omega$ **(1 Mark)**

The total resistance in series combination is more than greatest individual resistance in the circuit.

8. (a) This is an ideal setting of the Khadin system and A = Catchment area; B = Saline area & C = Shallow dugwell. **(1 Mark)**

OR,

(a) Biodiversity which faces large destruction. **(1 Mark)**

9. (b) Soaps and detergents factories near B and alcohol distillery near A. **(1 Mark)**

10. (b) Formation of crystals by process of crystallization. **(1 Mark)**

11. (c) Aqueous solution of A is basic while that of B is acidic. Therefore A has pH greater than 7 and B has pH less than 7. **(1 Mark)**

Working range of pH of phenolphthalein = 8.2 – 9.0

Basic solution turns phenolphthalein solution pink while in acidic solution it remain colourless.

12. (d) Elements of group 16 and period 3 are non metals. Non metals generally form acidic oxides. Elements of group 1 and 2 form basic oxides while elements of group 13 form amphoteric oxides. **(1 Mark)**

OR

(d) Element X has 13 protons therefore number of electrons also equal to 13. Therefore statement A, B, C are correct statements. **(1 Mark)**

13. (a) CH_3OH, CH_3CH_2OH, $CH_3CH_2CH_2OH$ belongs to same homologous series with – OH functional group and each member is differ by $-CH_2-$ unit. **(1 Mark)**

14. (c) Alloys are used in electrical heating device because they have high resistivity or resistance as compared to pure metals and high melting point. **(1 Mark)**

Heating element of electrical heating device made up of alloys do not burn (or oxidize) easily even at high temperature.

SECTION - B

15. (i) Photo decomposition of silver chloride takes place which results in formation of silver and colour changing to grey. **(1 Mark)**

$$2AgCl \rightarrow 2Ag + Cl_2$$

(ii) Copper undergoes oxidation and black coloured copper oxide is formed. **(1 Mark)**

$$2Cu + O_2 \rightarrow 2CuO$$

(iii) Zinc displaces copper from its solution as Zn is relatively and is more active than Cu and forms Zn^{2+} in solution colour of the solution changes from blue to colourless.

$Zn\ (s) + CuSO_4\ (aq.) \rightarrow Cu\ (s) + ZnSO_4\ (aq.)$ **(1 Mark)**

Zinc is placed above copper in the reactivity series therefore zinc is able to displace copper from its solution. Reverse of this reaction is not possible.

16. (i) $2NaOH\ (aq.) + Zn\ (s) \rightarrow Na_2ZnO_2 + H_2$ **(1 Mark)**

(ii) $CaCO_3\ (s) + H_2O\ (l.) + CO_2\ (g) \rightarrow Ca(HCO_3)_2$ **(1 Mark)**

(iii) $HCl\ (aq.) + H_2O\ (l) \rightarrow H_3O^+ + Cl^-$ **(1 Mark)**

OR

(i) 'G' is Chlorine (Cl) and 'C' is bleaching powder Ca(OCl)Cl. **(1 Mark)**

(ii) Chemical equation:-

$Ca(OH)_2 + Cl_2 \rightarrow Ca(OCl)Cl + H_2O$ **(1 Mark)**

(iii) Common name is bleaching powder and chemical name is calcium oxychloride. **(1 Mark)**

Electrolysis of aqueous solution of NaCl (brine) liberate chlorine gas at anode and hydrogen gas at cathode.

17. (i) Dobereiner's Triads is **A**. **(1 Mark)**

(ii) Mendeleev placed elements of category A,B and C in three different groups because they have different physical and chemical properties. **(1 Mark)**

(iii) No, Newland's Law of octaves is not applicable for all three categories.

Because the **law of octaves** states that every eighth element has similar properties when the elements are arranged in the increasing order of their atomic masses. **(1 Mark)**

18. (a) Cereal plant → Goat → Human beings; Cereal plant → Human beings **(1 Mark)**

This chain is most advantageous for food purposes.

(b) The cereal plant which is growing in soil rich in pesticides may cause detrimental effects on human as well as animals. It also causes harm to the environment. Use of chemical pesticides also harms the fertility of soil and reduction in crop yield. **(1 Mark)**

(c)

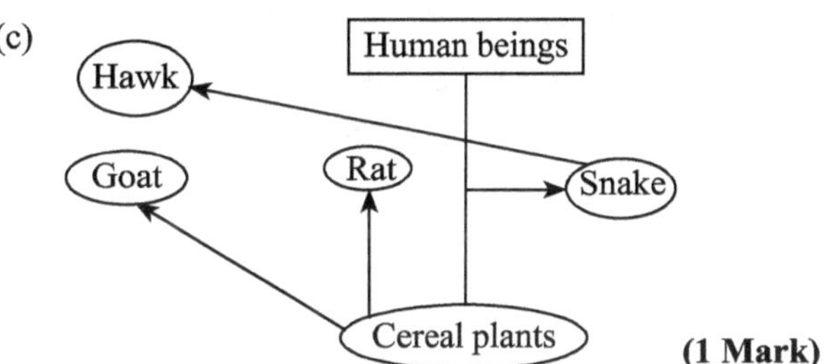

(1 Mark)

A food chain is a linear sequence of organisms through which nutrients and energy can pass on from one organism to another from lower to higher trophic level in an ecological system.

OR

(a) Harmful effects- (i) It causes land, water and air pollution. (ii) Plastic bags when consumed along with food by animals, cause harm to their life.

Suggestions- Jute bags are a good old alternative to plastic bags and the other alternatives are paper bags, cotton bags, etc. **(2 Marks)**

(b) (i) Two practices are- (1) Composting and Vermicomposting (this method is useful for the disposal of biodegradable waste).

(ii) By following the 3R rule recycle, reduce and reuse. **(1 Mark)**

19. (a) The role played by-

(i) Enzyme trypsin breaks down the protein into peptides and peptide into amino acids. (i.e., trypsin involved in the digestion of protein.)

(ii) Enzyme lipase breaks emulsified fats into fatty acids and glycerol.

(i.e., lipase for digestion of fats) **(2 Marks)**

(b) Finger like projections are called villi.

(i) Increase the surface area for absorption of nutrients from digested food.

(ii) They also increases the surface area of intestinal walls. **(1 Mark)**

20. (a) (i) Homologous

(ii) Analogous pair

(iii) Homologous pair

(iv) Analogous pair. **(1 Mark)**

(b) (i) In broccoli and cabbage, both are belonging to cruciferous vegetables. So, this pair is homologous.

(ii) In ginger and raddish, both have different origin & i.e. have different ancestry.

(iii) In forelimbs of birds and lizard, both are belong to the same group of vertebrates.

(iv) In wings of a bat and a bird, the structural dissimilarities (bat & bird wings were not inherited from a common ancestor with wings.) **(2 Marks)**

Homologous organs refers to the different organisms have similar structure but different functions whereas analogous organs refers to the different organism having similar functions but different structures.

21. (a) (i) By the Punnett Square for F_1 progeny-

So, all plants of F_1 generation will have green stem.

GG/gg	G	G
g	Gg	Gg
g	Gg	Gg

(1 Mark)

(ii) By the Punnett Square for F_2 progeny-

Here, GG,Gg & Gg= green stem (75% out of 100%) and gg= brown stem (100-75=25%)

So, 25% plants in F_2 generation will have brown stem(gg).

Gg/Gg	G	g
G	GG	Gg
g	Gg	gg

(1 Mark)

(iii) In the 2nd table, the ratio of GG and Gg is 1:2.

(b) Conclusion from this cross:- Every individual possesses a pair of alleles for a particular trait. During gamete formation, a gamete receives only one trait from the alleles. A particular trait can be dominant or recessive in a particular generation. **(1 Mark)**

22. (i) Converging **(1 Mark)**

(ii) Simple microscope and Telescope **(1 Mark)**

(iii) If lens is replaced by concave mirror and object is placed at f/2

(a) Reflected rays are divergent, therefore image A_1B_1 is formed behind the mirror.

(b) Image is virtual and erect.

(c) Size of image A_1B_1 is larger than object AB. (see the fig.)

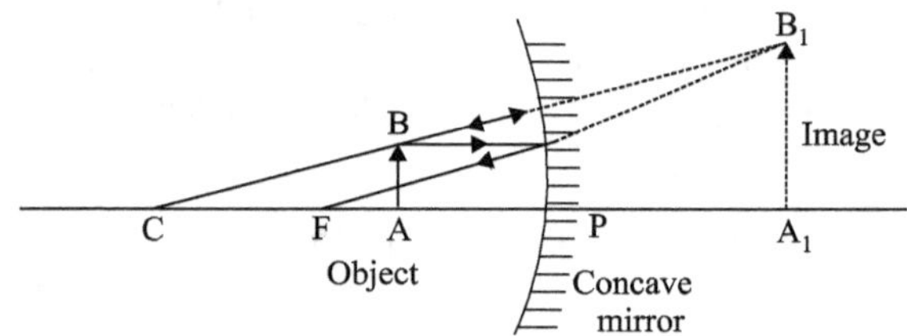

(1 Mark)

23. (i) One end of current carrying solenoid behaves as a magnetic north pole, while the other behaves as the south pole. Like in bar magnet, the field lines emerge from one end and merge into another. So, there is either a convergence at S-pole or a divergence from N-pole of magnetic field lines near the ends of solenoid. **(1 Mark)**

(ii) A current carrying solenoid behaves like a bar magnet. We know that a freely suspended bar magnet aligns itself in the north-south direction. Hence, it rests along north-south direction when suspended freely. **(1 Mark)**

(iii) Fuse of lower rating will blow off immediately (and require frequent replacements). Fuse of higher rating will not break the circuit, even in case of higher load. So, burnt out fuse should be replaced by another fuse of identical rating for electrical safety. **(1 Mark)**

24. (a) Ray diagram of path of monochromatic light when it passes through a prism.

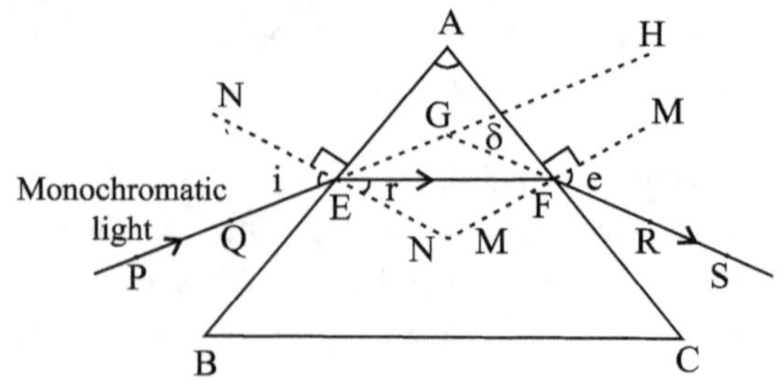

PE – Incident ray $\angle i$ – Angle of incidence
EF – Refracted ray $\angle r$ – Angle of refraction
FS – Emergent ray $\angle e$ – Angle of emergence
$\angle A$ – Angle of the prism $\angle \delta$ – Angle of deviation

(2 Marks)

(b) When a narrow beam of white light passes through a prism, it emerges as a spectrum of all components (VIBGYOR) of white light. (see the fig.)

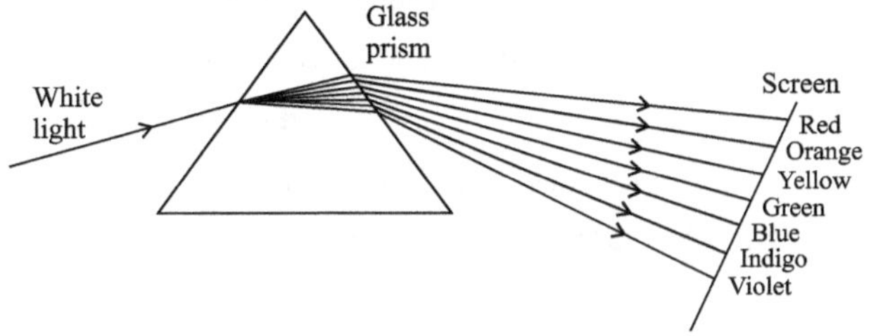

(1 Mark)

Note

The different component colours (VIBGYOR) of the white light have different wavelengths. The wavelength of violet light is smaller than that of red light. As, wavelength vary inversely with refractive index, so refractive index of material of prism is maximum for violet colour and minimum for red colour. This cause violet colour to bend more than red colour.

OR

(a) (i) Bifocal lenses are used to correct the defect when a person suffers from both the defects of vision myopia and hypermetropia. **(1 Mark)**

(ii) Bifocal lens is made by using two lenses in one eyepiece. Convex lens of appropriate focal length is positioned below while concave lens of appropriate focal length is positioned above.

(1 Mark)

(b) We know that, Power of lens(P) = 1/f
Or, f = 1/P
So, focal length (f) of lens for near vision = 1/3 = +0.33m
And focal length of lens for distant vision = −1/3 = −0.33m **(1 Mark)**

SECTION - C

25. (i) Mercuric oxide decomposes to mercury and oxygen gas on heating.

$2HgO \rightarrow 2Hg + O_2$ **(1 Mark)**

(ii) When cuprous oxide is heated with cuprous sulphide, copper metal is obtained.

$2Cu_2O + Cu_2S \rightarrow 6Cu + SO_2$ **(1 Mark)**

(iii) When manganese dioxide reacts with aluminium then it results into the formation of aluminium trioxide and manganese. **(1 Mark)**

$$4Al + 3MnO_2 \rightarrow 2Al_2O_3 + 3Mn$$

(iv) When Ferric oxide is heated with aluminium, iron metal is obtained. **(1 Mark)**

$$Fe_2O_3 + Al \rightarrow 2Fe + Al_2O_3$$

(v) When zinc carbonate is heated in calcination process it converted to zinc oxide then it can be easily converted to metal by heating with e. **(1 Mark)**

$$ZnCO_3 \rightarrow ZnO + CO_2$$

OR

(i) Bond of Magnesium chloride-

$Mg \longrightarrow Mg^{2+} + 2e^-$

2, 8, 2 2, 8

$Cl + e^- \longrightarrow Cl^-$

2, 8, 7 (2, 8, 8)

$Mg \overset{x}{\underset{x}{}} + 2\,\ddot{\underset{..}{Cl}}: \longrightarrow [Mg^{2+}] [\overset{..}{\underset{..}{_x Cl}}:^-]_2$

In $MgCl_2$, Cation is Magnesium (Mg^{2+})

Anion is Chloride (Cl^-). **(2 Marks)**

(ii) The crystal structure of ionic compounds is strong and rigid. It takes a lot of energy to break all those ionic bonds. As a result, ionic compounds are solids with high melting and boiling points.

The strong bonds between their oppositely charged ions lock them into place in the crystal form.

(1 Mark)

Note

Ionic bonds are stronger bonds than covalent bonds due to electrostatic attraction between oppositely charged ions.

(iii) Experimental set-up:-

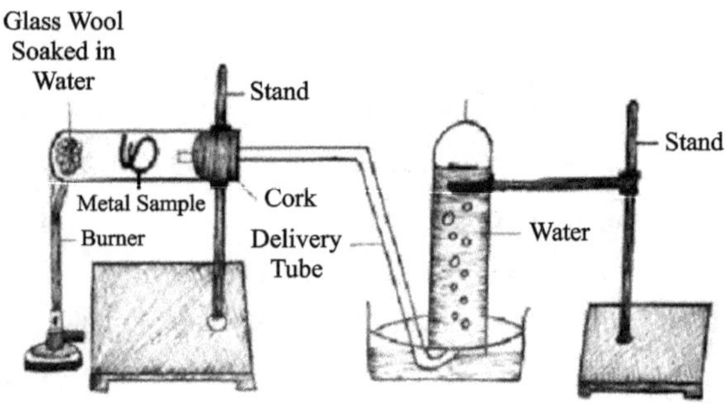

(2 Marks)

26 (a) The Difference between the soaps and detergents-

Composition	**Soaps** are sodium (Na) or Potassium (K) salts of some long chain carboxylic acids.	**Detergents** are ammonium or sulphonated salts of long chains of carboxylic acids.
Cleansing action	Produces scum in hard water which affects it's cleansing action.	Hard water does not affects it's cleansing action.

(2 Marks)

(b) If a small piece of sodium is dropped into some ethanol, it reacts steadily to give off bubbles of hydrogen gas and leaves a colourless solution of sodium ethoxide (CH_3CH_2ONa).

$2CH_3CH_2OH + 2Na \rightarrow 2CH_3CH_2ONa + H_2$

Ethanol behaves as mild acid in the reaction and liberate Hydrogen gas. **(1 Mark)**

(c) Structure of cyclohexane-

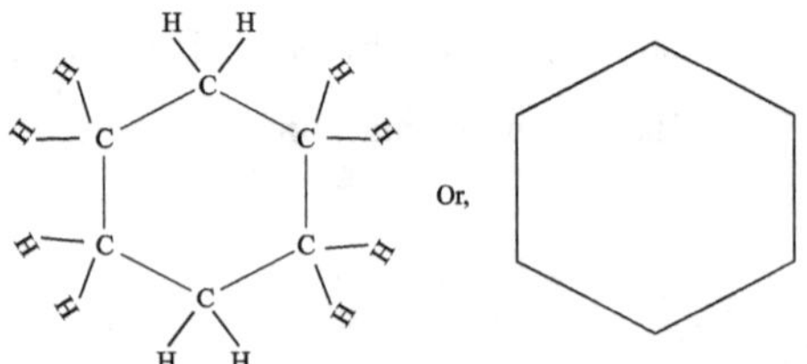

(1 Mark)

(d) Acetaldehyde (IUPAC- Ethanal) **(1 Mark)**

27. (a) Firstly, the left auricles recieve oxygenated blood through pulmonary vein and transfer this oxygenated blood to the left ventricles and is transfered to different parts of the body through aorta. (Lungs → Pulmonary veins → Left atrium → Left ventricle → Aorta → Body parts). **(3 Marks)**

(b) When blood vessels or the circulatory tubes are damaged or injured and get punctured, blood can leak into the surrounding tissues leading to accumulation of blood in the surrounding tissues. This condition is referred to as hematoma and is caused when a capillary, vein or artery is subjected to trauma. **(2 Marks)**

Note

Circulatory system in humans is made up of blood vessels routed either away from and towards the heart. It carries oxygen, nutrients to the different parts of the body & remove carbon dioxide from different parts of the body.

OR

28 (a) Germination of pollen on stigma of a flower:-

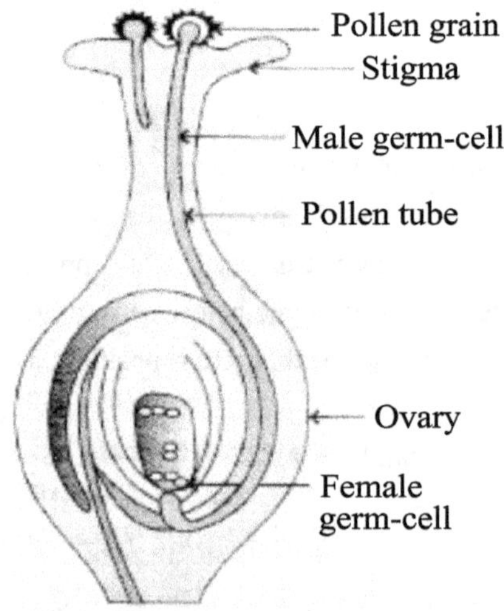

(2 Marks)

(b) A pollen tube is a tubular structure produced by the male gametophyte of seed plants when it germinates. Pollen tubes elongation is an integral stage in the plant life cycle. The pollen tube acts helps in the transportation of the male gamete cells from the pollen grain-either from the stigma (in flowering plants) to the ovules at the base of the pistil or directly through ovule tissue in some gymnosperms. In maize, this single cell can grow longer than 30 cm to transverse the length of the pistil. **(2 Marks)**

(c) (i) Seed - Ovules

(ii) Fruit – Ovary **(1 Mark)**

OR

(a) Use of condom helps in preventing STDs (sexually transmitted diseases) to both partners, it also helps in preventing unwanted pregnancy. **(2 Marks)**

(b) Oral contraceptives contain hormones which prevent ovulation in females. Thus, they help in preventing pregnancy. **(1 Mark)**

(c) Abortion of female foetus to obey the social custom of preference to a male child can be termed as sex selective abortion. This effects the gender ratio which is against women. It also results in mental and physical torture of the girl child and her mother. **(2 Marks)**

29. (a) In the given figure, R_3 and R_4 are connected in parallel.

So, according to the figure the expression for the equivalent resistance of the resistors connected:

$R_{MN} = R_1 + R_2 + [1/R_3 + 1/R_4]$ **(1½ Marks)**

(b) Joule's heating law states the heating effect of current as heat energy released by a conductor when current passes through it. If the conductor is having resistance 'R' and current 'i' passes through it for time 't' then heat produced, $H \propto i^2 Rt$

The mathematical expression of heat energy, $H = i^2 \times R \times t$. **(1½ Marks)**

(c) Power (P) = 1 kW = 1000 W

Voltage (V) = 220 V

So, electric current (i) = P/V = 1000/220 = 4.5 A ≈ 5A

Here, rating of fuse wire is 5A, so we need it. **(1 Mark)**

(d) As we know that, in a series circuit the current is constant throughout the electric circuit. Thus, it is obviously impracticable to connect an electric bulb and an electric heater in series, because they need currents of widely different values to operate properly. **(1 Mark)**

30. (a) For security mirror (convex mirror)

Object distance (u) = –20 m

and focal length(f) = radius of curvature/2 = 5/2 = 2.5 m

Using mirror formula

$1/v + 1/u = 1/f$

$\Rightarrow$ $1/v + 1/(-20) = 1/2.5$

$\Rightarrow$ $1/v = 1/2.5 + 1/20 = 9/20$

$\therefore$ Image distance, v = 20/9 **(1 Mark)**

Here, Image distance (v) is positive hence image formed on the other side of mirror as object.

Nature of image: Virtual and erect. **(1 Mark)**

Size of the image formed in the security mirror.

Magnification, $m = -v/u = \frac{h_i}{h_o}$ [h_i & h_o = size of image & object respectively]

So, $h_i/h_o = (20/9)/20 = 1/9$

Magnification will be 1/9th of size of customer. Hence, image should be smaller than object (customer). **(1 Mark)**

Convex mirror is also used as rear view mirror in vehicles because it has a wider field of view.

(b) Dentists use concave mirror because when object is placed between focus (F) and pole (P) of concave mirror then a virtual, erect and enlarged image is formed behind the mirror. It helps the doctor to see a larger image of tooth. **(2 Mark)**

OR

(i) Palmists use convex lens because it produces enlarged, virtual and erect image when object is placed between focus(F_1) and optical center(O) of convex lens (see fig.) **(1 Mark)**

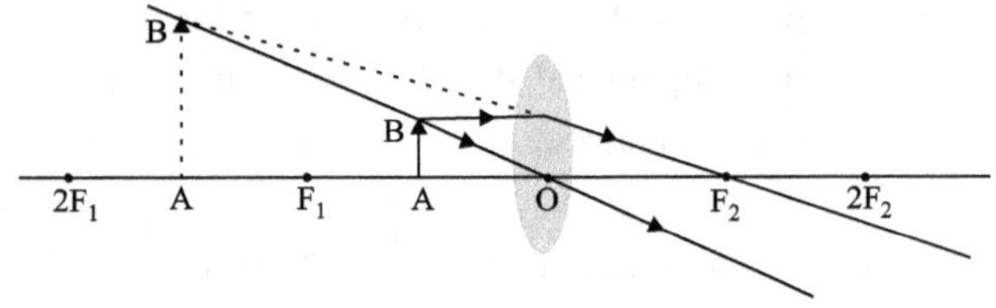

(1 Mark)

(ii) If the palmist wants real and magnified image, he should put object between F and 2F (see in fig.). But in that case he will have to use a screen to see the image.

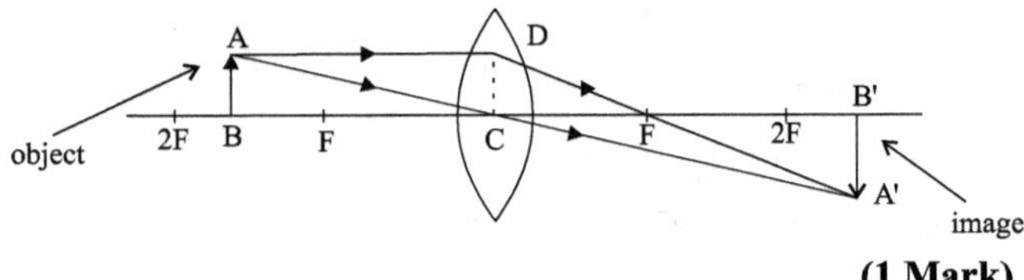

(1 Mark)

(iii) Given, f = 10 cm, u = –5 cm

Using lens formula: $1/v - 1/u = 1/f$

$\Rightarrow \quad 1/v - 1/(-5) = 1/10$

$\Rightarrow \quad 1/v = 1/10 - 1/5 = -1/10$

Image is formed at 10 cm on the same side of lens (as object). It is erect and virtual. **(1 Mark)**

Magnification, $m = v/u = (-10)/(-5) = 2$

i.e., Image is twice as big as object or, image is magnified two times. **(1 Mark)**

Convex lens gives positive magnification for virtual image and negative magnification for real image.

Delhi 2020

CBSE Board Solved Paper

Time Allowed : 3 Hours ***Maximum Marks : 80***

General Instructions: *Read the following instructions very carefully and strictly follow them:*

(i) Question paper comprises **three** sections – **A, B** and **C**. There are **30** questions in the question paper. All questions are compulsory.

(ii) **Section A** – Question no. 1 to 14 – all questions or part there of are of one mark each. These questions comprises multiple choice questions (MCQ), very short answer (VSA) and Assertion-Reason type questions. Answer to these questions should be given in **one word** or **one sentence**.

(iii) **Section B** – Question no. 15 to 24 are short answer type questions, carrying 3 marks each. Answer to these questions should not exceed 50 to 60 words.

(iv) **Section C** – Question no. 25 to 30 are long answer type questions, carrying 5 marks each. Answer to these questions should not exceed 80 to 90 words.

(v) Answer should be brief and to the point. Also the above mentioned word limit be adhered to as far as possible.

(vi) There is no overall choice in the question paper. However, an internal choice has been provided in some questions in each Section. Only one of the choices in such questions have to be attempted.

SECTION - A

1. Name a cyclic unsaturated carbon compound.

2. The change in magnetic field lines in a coil is the cause of induced electric current in it. Name the underlying phenomenon.

Answer question numbers 3(a) to 3(d) and 4(a) to 4(d) on the basis of your understanding of the following paragraphs and the related studied concepts.

3. The growing size of the human population is a cause of concern for all people. The rate of birth and death in a given population will determine its size. Reproduction is the process by which organisms increase their population. The process of sexual maturation for reproduction is gradual and takes place while general body growth is still going on. Some degree of sexual maturation does not necessarily mean that the mind or body is ready for sexual acts or for having and bringing up children. Various contraceptive devices are being used by human beings to control the size of population.

(a) List two common signs of sexual maturation in boys and girls.

(b) What is the result of reckless female foeticide?

(c) Which contraceptive method changes the hormonal balance of the body?

(d) Write two factors that determine the size of a population.

4. Human body is made up of five important components, of which water is the main component. Food as well as potable water are essential for every human being. The food is obtained from plants through agriculture. Pesticides are being used extensively for a high yield in the fields. These pesticides are absorbed by the plants from the soil along with water and minerals and from the water bodies these pesticides are taken up by the aquatic animals and plants. As these chemicals are not biodegradable, they get accumulated progressively at each trophic level. The maximum concentration of these chemicals gets accumulated in our bodies and greatly affects the health of our mind and body.

(a) Why is the maximum concentration of pesticides found in human beings?

(b) Give one method which could be applied to reduce our intake of pesticides through food to some extent.

(c) Various steps in a food chain represent:

(a) Food web (b) Trophic level

(c) Ecosystem (d) Biomagnification

(d) With regard to various food chains operating in an ecosystem, man is a:

(a) Consumer (b) Producer

(c) Producer and consumer

(d) Producer and decomposer

5. Calcium oxide reacts vigorously with water to produce slaked lime.

$CaO(s) + H_2O(l) \rightarrow Ca(OH)_2(aq)$

This reaction can be classified as:

(A) Combination reaction

(B) Exothermic reaction

(C) Endothermic reaction

(D) Oxidation reaction

Which of the following is a correct option?

(a) (A) and (C) (b) (C) and (D)

(c) (A), (C) and (D) (d) (A) and (B)

OR

When hydrogen sulphide gas is passed through a blue solution of copper sulphate, a black precipitate of copper sulphide is obtained and the sulphuric acid so formed remains in the solution. The reaction is an example of a:

(a) Combination reaction

(b) Displacement reaction

(c) Decomposition reaction

(d) Double displacement reaction

6. In a double displacement reaction such as the reaction between sodium sulphate solution and barium chloride solution:

(A) exchange of atoms takes place

(B) exchange of ions takes place

(C) a precipitate is produced

(D) an insoluble salt is produced

The correct option is:

(a) (B) and (D) (b) (A) and (C)

(c) only (B) (d) (B), (C) and (D)

7. Baking soda is a mixture of:

(a) Sodium carbonate and acetic acid

(b) Sodium carbonate and tartaric acid

(c) Sodium hydrogen carbonate and tartaric acid

(d) Sodium hydrogen carbonate and acetic acid

8. The chemical formula for plaster of Paris is:

(a) $CaSO_4 . 2H_2O$ (b) $CaSO_4 . H_2O$

(c) $CaSO_4 . H_2O$ (d) $2CaSO_4 . H_2O$

9. The laws of reflection hold true for:

(a) plane mirrors only

(b) concave mirrors only

(c) convex mirrors only

(d) all reflecting surfaces

OR

When an object is kept within the focus of a concave mirror, an enlarged image is formed behind the mirror. This image is:

(a) real (b) inverted

(c) virtual and inverted

(d) virtual and erect

10. At the time of short circuit, the electric current in the circuit:

(a) vary continuously

(b) does not change

(c) reduces substantially

(d) increases heavily

OR

Two bulbs of 100 W and 40 W are connected in series. The current through the 100 W bulb is 1 A. The current through the 40 W bulb will be:

(a) 0.4 A (b) 0.6 A

(c) 0.8 A (d) 1A

11. Which one of the following is responsible for the sustenance of under ground water?

(a) Loss of vegetation cover

(b) Diversion for high water demanding crops

(c) Pollution from urban wastes

(d) Afforestation

12. Incomplete combustion of coal and petroleum:

(A) increases air pollution.

(B) increases efficiency of machines.

(C) reduces global warming.

(D) produce poisonous gases.

The correct option is:

(a) (A) and (B) (b) (A) and (D)

(c) (B) and (C) (d) (C) and (D)

For question numbers 13 and 14, two statements are given – one labelled Assertion (A) and the other labelled Reason (R). Select the correct answer to these questions from the codes (a), (b), (c) and (d) as given below:

(a) Both A and R are true and R is correct explanation of the Assertion.

(b) Both A and R are true but is not the correct explanation of the Assertion.

(c) A is true but R is false.

(d) A is false but R is true.

13. **Assertion (A):** Esterification is a process in which a sweet smelling substance is produced.

Reason (R): When esters react with sodium hydroxide an alcohol and sodium salt of carboxylic acid are obtained.

14. **Assertion (A):** In the process of nuclear fission, the amount of nuclear energy generated by the fission of an atom of uranium is so tremendous that it produces 10 million times the energy produced by the combustion of an atom of carbon from coal.

Reason (R): The nucleus of a heavy atom such as uranium, when bombarded with low energy neutrons, splits apart into lighter nuclei. The mass difference between the original nucleus and the product nuclei gets converted to tremendous energy.

SECTION - B

15. 1 g of copper powder was taken in a China dish and heated. What change takes place on heating? When hydrogen gas is passed over this heated substance, a visible change is seen in it. Give the chemical equations of reactions, the name and the color of the products formed in each case.

16. List the important products of the Chlor-alkali process. Write one important use of each.

OR

How is washing soda prepared from sodium carbonate? Give its chemical equation. State the type of this salt. Name the type of hardness of water which can be removed by it?

17. 3 mL of ethanol is taken in a test tube and warmed gently in a water bath. A 5% solution of alkaline potassium permanganate is added first drop by drop to this solution, then in excess.

(i) How is 5% solution of $KMnO_4$ prepared?

(ii) State the role of alkaline potassium permanganate in this reaction. What happens on adding it in excess?

(iii) Write chemical equation of this reaction.

18. A squirrel is in a scary situation. Its body has to prepare for either fighting or running away. State the immediate changes that take place in its body so that the squirrel is able to either fight or run?

OR

Why is chemical communication better than electrical impulses as a means of communication between cells in a multi-cellular organism?

19. Define the term pollination. Differentiate between self pollination and cross pollination. What is the significance of pollination?

20. What are homologous structures? Give an example. Is it necessary that homologous structures always have a common ancestor. Justify your answer.

21. Why is Tyndall effect shown by colloidal particles? State four instances of observing the Tyndall effect.

OR

Differentiate between a glass slab and a glass prism. What happens when a narrow beam of (i) a monochromatic light, and (ii) white light passes through (a) glass slab and (b) glass prism?

22. Draw a labelled diagram to show (i) reddish appearance of the sun at the sunrise or the sunset and (ii) white appearance of the sun at the noon when it is overhead.

23. A V-I graph for a nichrome wire is given below. What do you infer from this graph? Draw a labelled circuit diagram to obtain such a graph.

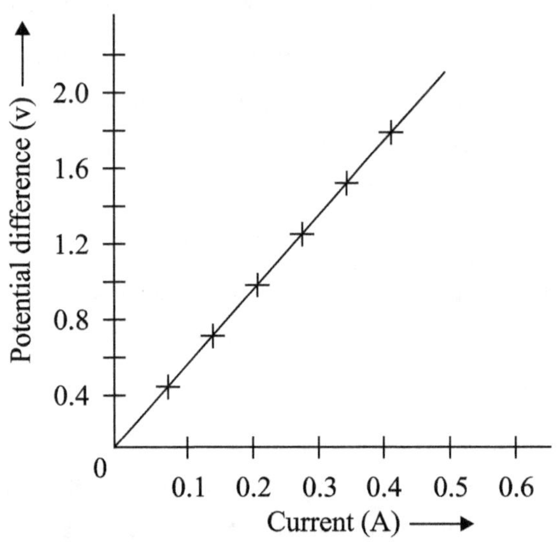

24. (a) Write the mathematical expression for Joule's law of heating.

(b) Compute the heat generated while transferring 96000 coulomb of charge in two hours through a potential difference of 40 V.

SECTION - C

25. Carbon cannot reduce the oxides of sodium, magnesium and aluminium to their respective metals. Why? Where are these metals placed in the reactivity series? How are these metals obtained from their ores? Take an example to explain the process of extraction along with chemical equations.

26. The position of certain elements in the Modern Periodic Table are shown below.

Group →	1	2	3 to 12	13	14	15	16	17	18
↓Period									
1	G								H
2	A			I			B		C
3		D			E				F

Using the above table answer the following questions giving reasons in each case:

(i) Which element will form only covalent compounds?

(ii) Which element is a non-metal with valency 2?

(iii) Which element is a metal with valency 2?

(iv) Out of H, C and F which has largest atomic size?

(v) To which family does H, C and F belong?

OR

Define atomic size. Give its unit of measurement. In the modern periodic table what trend is observed in the atomic radius in a group and a period and why is it so?

27. (a) Why is there a difference in the rate of breathing between aquatic organisms and terrestrial organisms? Explain.

(b) Draw a diagram of human respiratory system and label – pharynx, trachea, lungs, diaphragm and alveolar sac on it.

OR

(a) Name the organs that form the excretory system in human beings.

(b) Describe in brief how urine is produced in human body.

28. (a) What is the law of dominance of traits ? Explain with an example.

(b) Why are the traits acquired during the life time of an individual not inherited? Explain.

29. Draw a ray diagram in each of the following cases to show the formation of image, when the object is placed:

(i) between optical centre and principal focus of a convex lens.

(ii) anywhere in front of a concave lens.

(iii) at 2F of a convex lens.

State the signs and values of magnifications in the above mentioned cases (i) and (ii).

OR

An object 4.0 cm in size, is placed 25.0 cm in front of a concave mirror of focal length 15.0 cm.

(i) At what distance from the mirror should a screen be placed in order to obtain a sharp image?

(ii) Find the size of the image.

(iii) Draw a ray diagram to show the formation of image in this case.

30. (a) What is an electromagnet? List any two uses.

(b) Draw a labelled diagram to show how an electromagnet is made.

(c) State the purpose of soft iron core used in making an electromagnet.

(d) List two ways of increasing the strength of an electromagnet if the material of the electromagnet is fixed.

Solutions

SECTION - A

1. Benzene is a cyclic unsaturated carbon compound. **(1 Mark)**

2. Electromagnetic induction **(1 Mark)**

3. (a) The two common signs of sexual maturation in boys and girls are:
   - Appearance of facial hair growth and hair in genital area and armpits
   - Release of hormones (growth and sex). **(1 Mark)**

   (b) The reckless female foeticide is the forceful abortion of female foeticides. It is illegal practice and because of this child sex ratio is declining at an alarming rate in the society. **(1 Mark)**

   (c) Oral contraceptives which is commonly called 'birth control pills'. The pills works by changing the hormonal balance of the body so that eggs are not released and fertilisation cannot occur. **(1 Mark)**

   (d) The rate of birth and death in a given population will determine the size of the population and because of an expanding population that makes it harder to improve everybody's standard of living. **(1 Mark)**

Contraception aims for prevention of pregnancy as it prevents the meeting of egg and sperm and stops formation of egg.

4. (a) The maximum concentration of pesticides is found in humans because of biomagnification. As, large amount of fishes are consumed by humans. A human belongs to higher trophic level. The toxic substance that can be accumulated by an organism cannot be metabolised or excreted and passed on from on to the next trophic level. **(1 Mark)**

Biomagnification refers to the increase in concentration of the toxicant at successive trophic levels.

   (b) Methods by which one can reduce the intake of pesticides through food to some extent are as follows:
   - Avoid using chemical pesticides
   - Consumption of organic food
   - Always consume washed fruits and vegetables.

   (1 Mark)

   (c) Option (b) is correct. Various steps in a food chain represent trophic level. Producers in a food chain represents first trophic level, herbivores or primary consumers represents second trophic level, and carnivores or secondary consumers represents third trophic levels. **(1 Mark)**

   (d) Option (a) is correct. With regard to various food chains operating in an ecosystem, man is a consumer. As, humans are placed on the top of the food chain because commonly they are omnivores as they eat both organisms and products that are obtained from organisms. **(1 Mark)**

Food chain is a linear sequence organisms in a food web that represents the flow of energy from one organism to another in an ecosystem.

5. (d) Calcium oxide react with water to form calcium hydroxide with the evolution of heat therefore it is a type of combination reaction and exothermic. **(1 Mark)**

OR

(d) $H_2S(g) + CuSO_4(aq) \longrightarrow CuS\downarrow + H_2SO_4(aq)$ **(1 Mark)**

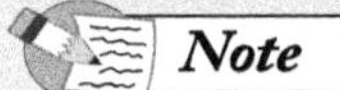

Double displacement reactions are the reactions in which the reactant ions exchange place to form product. Generally precipitate is formed as the product of double displacement reaction.

6. (d) Exchange of ions take place in double displacement reaction that results into the formation of precipitate which is a insoluble salt. **(1 Mark)**

7. (c) Baking powder is a mixture of sodium hydrogen carbonate and tartaric acid. **(1 Mark)**

Baking soda is sodium hydrogen carbonate while baking powder is a mixture of sodium hydrogen carbonate (baking soda) and a mild acid (tartaric acid).

8. (d) The formula of plaster of Paris is $CaSO_4 \cdot \frac{1}{2}H_2O$. **(1 Mark)**

9. (d) All reflecting surfaces obey the laws of reflection. **(1 Mark)**

OR

Concave mirror form virtual and erect image when an object is kept within its focus. **(1 Mark)**

10. (d) At the time of short circuit, the electric current in the circuit increases heavily. **(1 Mark)**

OR

As the bulbs of 100W and 40W are connected in series, so same current will flow through them. i.e., 1A. **(1 Mark)**

Short circuit occur when a very low resistance electrical path is created e.g., live and neutral wires come in contact with each other. In this case, resistance of a circuit decreases to a very small value and hence increases the current heavily.

11. (d) Afforestation is responsible for the sustenance of underground water. Sustenance of the ground water means the maintenance of ground water which is possible by the process of afforestation. Afforestation is responsible for more entrapment of ground water. **(1 Mark)**

Afforestation is the process of planting trees and plant. Afforestation is important for the maintenance of biodiversity.

12. (b) Incomplete combustion of coal and petroleum results in increasing air pollution. Coal and petroleum on incomplete combustion produce carbon monoxide which is a poisonous gas. Hence, correct option is (b). **(1 Mark)**

13. (b) Esterification is a process in which ester is formed from alcohol and carboxylic acid in presence of an acid. **(1 Mark)**

$$\underset{\text{Easter}}{CH_3COOC_2H_5} + NaOH \rightarrow C_2H_5OH + \underset{\text{Na-salt of acetic acid}}{CH_3COONa}$$

This reaction is known as saponification.

Esters are sweet smelling compounds and are used as a constituent of perfumes. Naturally occurring fats and oils are fatty acid esters of glycerol.

14. (a) In nuclear fission, unstable heavy nuclei splits into two or more lighter nuclei.

During this process, the mass difference between the original nucleus and the product nuclei get converted into energy. This energy is 10 million times the energy produced by the combustion of an atoms of carbon from coal. Hence, both assertion and Reason is correct. **(1 Mark)**

SECTION - B

15. When copper powder is heated in a china dish it gets oxidised and converted to copper (II) oxide which is black in colour. When Hydrogen gas is passed over this heated substance black coloured copper oxide further reduced to copper and colour changes to brown. **(2 Marks)**

$$2Cu + O_2 \xrightarrow{\text{Heat}} 2CuO \text{ (Black)}$$

$$CuO + H_2 \xrightarrow{\text{Heat}} \underset{\text{(Brown)}}{Cu} + H_2O$$

(1 Mark)

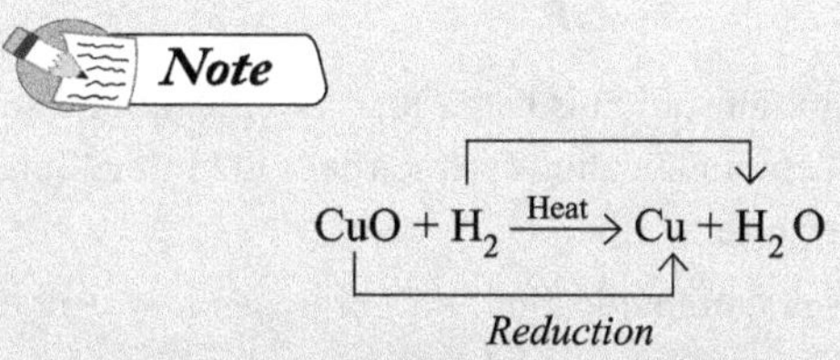

$$CuO + H_2 \xrightarrow{\text{Heat}} Cu + H_2O$$

Reduction

Oxidation : gain of oxygen or loss of Hydrogen

Reduction : loss of oxygen or gain of Hydrogen

Oxidising agent : reduces itself and oxidises other substance.

Reducing agent : oxidises itself and reduces other substance.

16. Important products of chlor–alkali process are chlorine, sodium hydroxide and hydrogen gas.

Use of chlorine: Chlorine is used as disinfectant in water treatment plant and swimming pools. It is also used in the preparation of PVC and pesticides. **(1 Mark)**

Use of sodium hydroxide: Sodium hydroxide is used in preparation of soaps and detergents. **(1 Mark)**

Use of hydrogen gas: Hydrogen gas is used for the preparation of ammonia for fertilizers. **(1 Mark)**

OR

Sodium carbonate undergoes hydration process to give washing soda. ($Na_2CO_3.10H_2O$). **(1 Mark)**

$$\underset{\text{Sodium carbonate}}{Na_2CO_3} + 10H_2O \longrightarrow \underset{\text{Sodium carbonate decahydrate (Washing soda)}}{Na_2CO_3.10H_2O}$$ **(1 Mark)**

Washing soda is a basic salt and it is used for removing permanent hardness of water. **(1 Mark)**

17. (a) 5% solution of $KMnO_4$ is prepared by dissolving 5g of $KMnO_4$ in 100 mL of water. **(1 Mark)**

(b) alkaline potassium permagnate act as oxidising agent in the reaction. **(1 Mark)**

(c) $CH_3CH_2OH + \text{alk. } KMnO_4 \longrightarrow CH_3COOH$

(1 Mark)

18. The immediate change that takes place in the body of squirrel for either fighting or to run involves:

- The sympathetic nervous system is activated by hypothalamus and also releases adrenaline from the adrenal gland.
- The adrenaline causes an increase in heart-pumping rate as well as breathing rate.
- The blood pressure and pupilary dilation increases and
- Activities of digestive and reproductive system suppresses in this moment. **(3 Marks)**

OR

Chemical communication is better than electrical impulses as a means of communication between cells in multicellular organisms because:

- It involves communication via hormones and it does not require any specialized tissue like nervous tissues for signalling.
- Electrical communication is limited for those regions that are connected with nerves whereas chemical coordination can take place throughout the body.
- Chemical communication can be done steadily and persistently whereas nervous coordination can be done only at specific intervals. **(3 Marks)**

When a nerve impulse reaches the end of an axon, it releases a chemical called neurotransmitters and the neurotransmitters travel across the synapse between the axon and the dendrite of the next neuron.

19. The process of transfer of pollen grains from anthers to the stigma of the same flower is called pollination.

For example: Rice, tomatoes, wheat and so on

There are two types of pollination such as self-pollination and cross-pollination:

(i) Self-pollination: Type of pollination which involves the transfer of pollen grain from anther to the stigma of same flower.

For example: Rice, tomatoes, wheat and so on

(ii) Cross-pollination: Type of pollination which involves the transfer of pollen grain from anther to the stigma of different flower.

For example: Apple, pumpkin, daffodils and so on.

Importance of pollination:

Pollination is important because pollination promotes the production of fruits and seeds. Seeds are sown for production of more plants. **(3 Marks)**

20. The homologous organs are the type of organs have similar structures but perform different functions.

For example: Wings of birds or bat and flippers of a whale.

Yes, homologous structures are inherited from a common ancestor. **(3 Marks)**

21. Tyndall effect is due to the scattering of light from the surface of colloidal particles. **(1 Mark)**

The Tyndall effect can be observed.

(i) When a fine beam of light enters a room through a small hole.

(ii) When sunlight passes through the canopy of a dense forest.

(iii) When visible beams of headlights in fog the light is scattered.

(iv) When a beam of light is directed at the glass of milk, the light is scattered. **(½ × 4 = 2 Marks)**

OR

Glass slab	Glass prism
(i) Glass slab is a transparent plate in which both reflecting surface are parallel to each other.	(i) Prism is a transparent plate in which both reflecting surface are at an angle.
(ii) In glass slab, the direction of incident ray and the emergent ray of light are parallel to each other.	(ii) In glass prism, the direction of the incident ray and the emergent ray of light is not parallel to each other.

(½ × 2 = 1 Mark)

(i) (a) When a narrow beam of monochromatic light passes through a glass slab, it deviates from the actual path but the direction of incident ray and the emergent ray of light are parallel to each other. **(½ Mark)**

(b) When a narrow beam of monochromatic light passes through a glass prism, it has deviated from the actual path but the direction of incident ray and emergent ray of light are not parallel to each other. **(½ Mark)**

(ii) (a) When a narrow beam of white light passes through a glass slab, the splitting of white light into its constituent colour does not occur. The direction of incident ray and the emergent ray of light are parallel to each other. **(½ Mark)**

(ii) (b) When a narrow beam of white light passes through a glass prism, the splitting of white light into its constituent seven colours occurs. Also, the direction of the incident ray and emergent ray of light is not parallel to each other. **(½ Mark)**

22. (i) Diagram to show, reddish appearance of the sun at the sunrise or the sunset.

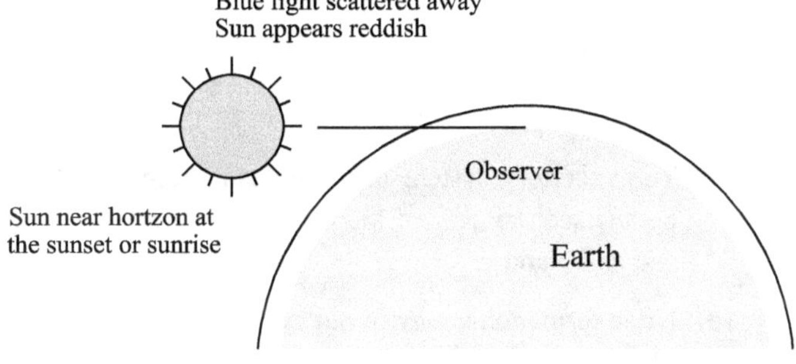

(1½ Mark)

(ii) Diagram to show, white appearance of the sun at the noon when it is overhead.

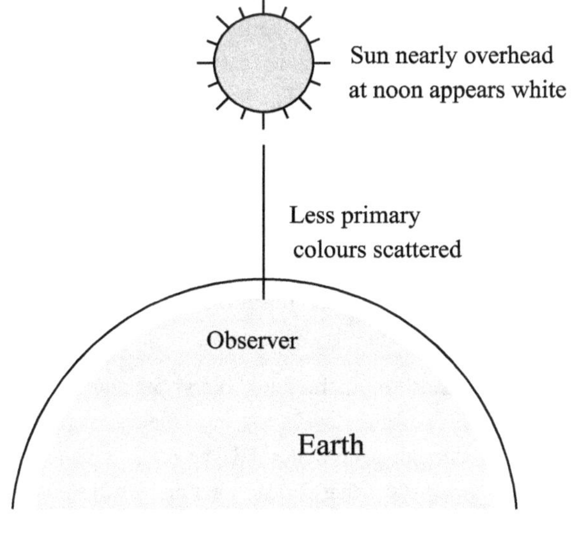

(1½ Mark)

Note

According to Rayleigh law of scattering, the amount of scattered light $\propto \frac{1}{\lambda^4}$*. Here,* λ *= wavelength of light*

Scattering of light decreases with increase in wavelength.

23. The graph shows that potential difference is directly proportional to current i.e., $V \propto I$. **(1 Mark)**

Circuit diagram to obtain the graph:

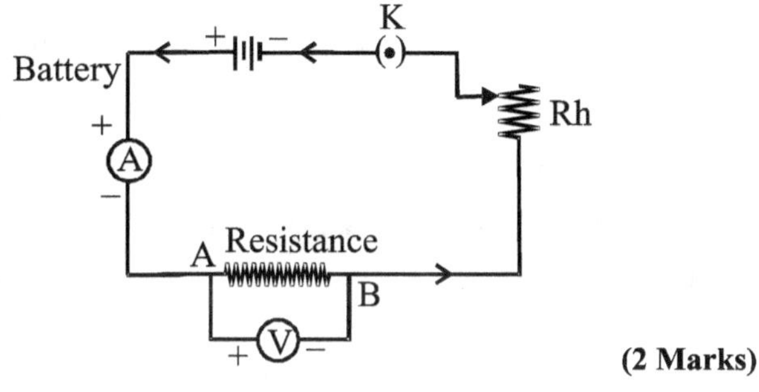

(2 Marks)

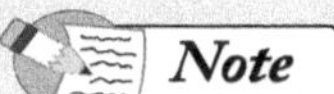

Note

To obtain such V-I graph, physical conditions (i.e., temperature, pressure etc.) should remain constant. It represent Ohm's law.

24. (a) The mathematical expression for Joule's law of heating is

$H \propto I^2Rt$ **(1 Mark)**

where, H = heat produced, I = current flowing

R = resistance and t = time taken

(b) Given,

Charge, Q = 96000 C,

Time, t = 2 h

Potential difference, V = 40 V

Heat generated, H = VIt **(1 Mark)**

$$= V \times \frac{Q}{t} \times t$$

$$= 40 \times 96000 = 3840000 \text{ J}$$ **(1 Mark)**

SECTION - C

25. Carbon cannot reduce the oxides of sodium, magnesium and aluminum because these metals have more affinity for oxygen than carbon. These metals are placed at top most position in the reactivity series because they are very reactive. These metals are obtained by electrolytic reduction. For example sodium is obtained by the electrolysis of its molten chloride. The metal is deposited at cathode and chlorine is liberated at anode. **(3 Marks)**

At cathode $Na^+ + e^- \longrightarrow Na$

At anode $2Cl^- \longrightarrow Cl_2 + 2e^-$ **(2 Marks)**

26. (a) Elements B and E will form only covalent compounds. **(1 Mark)**

(b) Element B is a non metal with valency 2. **(1 Mark)**

(c) Element D is a metal with valency 2. **(1 Mark)**

(d) Element F has largest size among H, C, F. **(1 Mark)**

(e) H, C, F belongs to noble gas family. **(1 Mark)**

OR

The distance between the nucleus and the outermost shell of an isolated atom is known as atomic size or atomic radius. The unit of measurement of atomic size is picometre, 1 pm = 10^{-12}m. **(2 Marks)**

Trend in a group: In the modern periodic table atomic size increases down the group. This is because new shells are being added as we go down the group. This increases the distance between the outermost electrons and the nucleus. **(1½ Marks)**

Trend in a period: In the modern periodic table atomic size decreases on moving left to right in the period. This is due to an increase in nuclear charge which tends to pull the electrons closer to the nucleus and reduces the size of the atom. **(1½ Marks)**

27. (a) Aquatic organisms such as fishes obtain oxygen from water which is present in dissolved state through gills. Since, the amount of dissolved oxygen present in water is low as compared to in the air. The breathing rate in aquatic organisms is much faster because of the availability of low oxygen level in the aquatic environment than that of in terrestrial organisms. **(3 Marks)**

(b) **Diagrammatic representation of human respiratory system:**

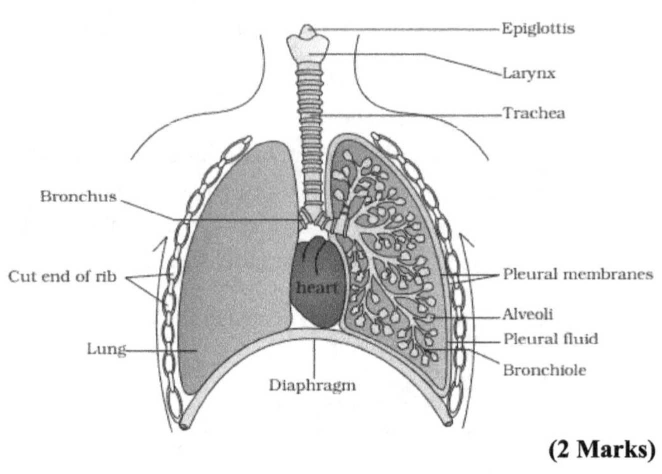

(2 Marks)

OR

(a) The excretory system in the human beings involves organs such as pair of kidney, pair of ureter, urethra and gall bladder. **(2 Marks)**

(b) Urine formation is carried out by the excretory system. The nephrons play an important role in the process of urine formation. The steps involved in urine formation are as follows:

- Each nephron consists of glomerulus, which serves as site for blood filtration. The glomerulus is a network of capillaries that are surrounded by a cuplike structure called glomerular capsule or Bowman's capsule.
- As, the blood flows through the glomerulus, the blood pressure increases results in secretion of water and solutes from the capillaries into the capsule through a filtration membrane.
- The glomerular filtration is the first step in Urine formation.
- Inside the glomerulus, blood pressure transports the fluid from capillaries into the glomerular capsule through a specialized layer of cells called filtration membrane that allows water and small solutes to pass. It also blocks blood cells and large proteins. Those components remain in the bloodstream. The filtrate flows from the glomerular capsule into the nephron.
- Thus the resulting filtrate contains waste, body requires other essential substances such as glucose, amino acids and smaller proteins as well as essential ions.

- Waste ions and hydrogen ions pass from the capillaries into the renal tubule and this process is called secretion. The secreted ions combine with the remaining filtrate and become urine.
- The urine flows out of the nephron tubules and then transported into a collecting duct. Then it passes out of the kidney and down to the bladder. **(3 Marks)**

Note

Urine is waste in the form of liquid and consists of water, salt, electrolyte such as potassium and phosphorus and other chemicals such as urea and uric acid.

28. (a) Mendal's law of dominance states that characters are controlled by discrete units called factors and factors occur in pairs. In a dissimilar pair of factors one member of the pair dominates (dominant) the other (recessive).

Diagrammatic representation of a genetic cross:

Parents:	TT		X	tt
Gametes:	T T			t t
F1 generation:	Tt	Tt	Tt	Tt
Self-crossing results	(Tt) X (Tt)			
Parents:	Tt		X	Tt
Gametes:		T t		T t
F2 generation:	Tt	Tt	Tt	tt

Phenotypic ratio: 3: 1

Genotypic ratio: 1:2:1 **(3 Marks)**

Note

The law of dominance is used to explain the expression of only one of the parental characters in a monohybrid cross.

(b) Acquired traits are inherited during the lifetime cannot be inherited in the successive generation as the changes do not reflect in the DNA of the germ cells instead they occur in the somatic cells. As, any mutations in the germ cells can result in the new traits being acquired by the successive generation. **(2 Marks)**

29. (i) Ray diagram when the object is placed between optical centre and principal focus of a convex lens. **(1 Mark)**

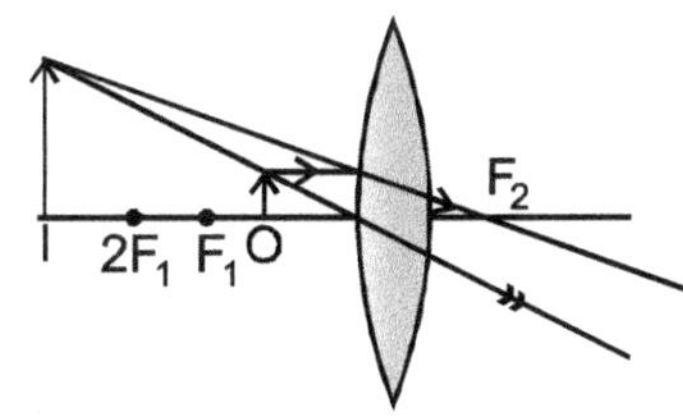

Magnification $m = \dfrac{\text{height of image}}{\text{height of object}}$ $m > 1$ **(1 Mark)**

(ii) Ray diagram when the object is placed anywhere in front of a concave lens. **(1 Mark)**

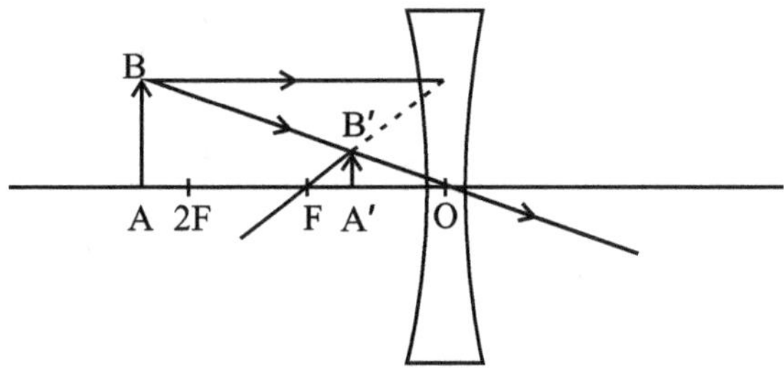

Magnification m, $= \dfrac{\text{height of image}}{\text{height of object}} = <$ **(1 Mark)**

(iii) Ray diagram when object is placed at 2F of a convex lens.

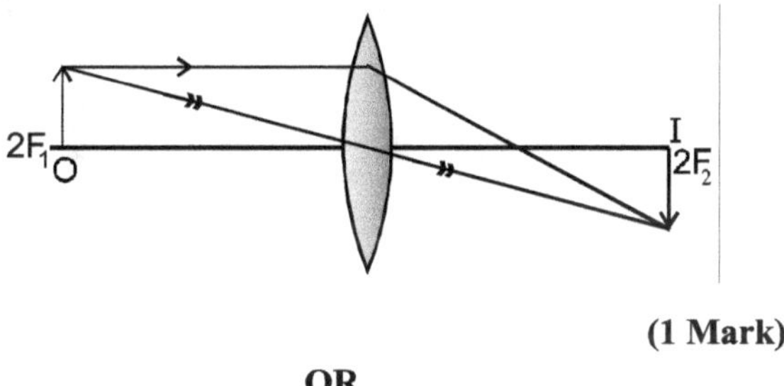

(1 Mark)

OR

Given,

Size of the object, $h_o = 4$ cm

Distance of the object, u = –25 cm

Focal length of concave mirror, f = –15 cm

Using mirror formula

$$\frac{1}{v} + \frac{1}{u} = \frac{1}{f}$$ **(1 Mark)**

$$\Rightarrow \frac{1}{v} - \frac{1}{25} = \frac{1}{-15}$$

$$\Rightarrow \frac{1}{v} = \frac{-1}{15} + \frac{1}{25} = \frac{(-5+3)}{75}$$

$$\Rightarrow v = \frac{-75}{2} = -37.5 \text{ cm}$$ **(1 Mark)**

(i) As the sign of v is negative, so the image should be in front of the mirror. The screen should be placed in front of the mirror at a distance of 37.5 cm. **(1 Mark)**

(ii) Magnification, $m = \dfrac{v}{u} = \dfrac{h_i}{h_o}$ **(1 Mark)**

$$\Rightarrow \frac{(37.5)}{25} = \frac{h_i}{4}$$

$$\Rightarrow h_i = \frac{37.5 \times 4}{25} = 6$$

$\therefore$ Size of the image, $h_i = 6$ cm **(½ Mark)**

(iii) Ray diagram to show the formation of image

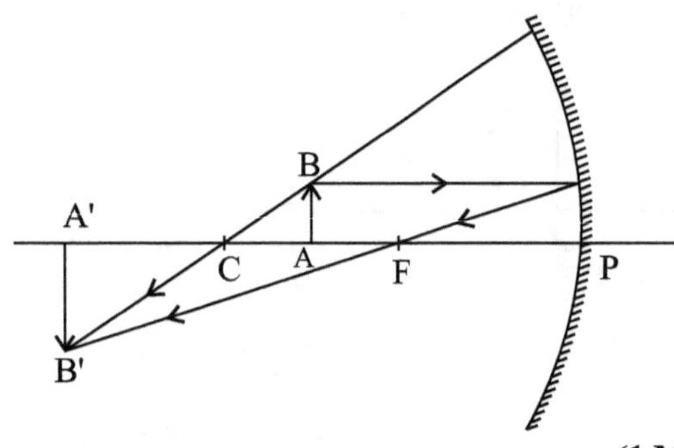

(1 Mark)

30. (a) An electromagnet is a soft iron piece converted into a magnet when a current is passed in the wire wound around the iron piece. **(1 Mark)**

Uses of Electromagnet

(i) in electric bell

(ii) in motors and generators. **(1 Mark)**

(b) Labelled diagram to show how an electron-agent is made **(½ + ½ = 1 Mark)**

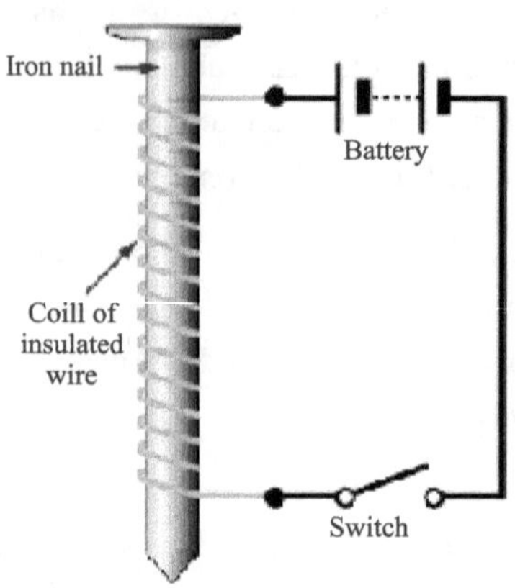

(1 Mark)

(c) The soft iron inside the coil makes the magnetic field stronger. Also, soft iron loses its magnetism as soon as the current stops flowing. **(1 Mark)**

(d) We can increase the strength of an electromagnet by

(i) increasing the current flowing through the coil and

(ii) increasing number of turns would around the soft iron core. **(1 Mark)**

Maglev trains using powerful electromagnets to develop high speed. Maglev is the short form of magnetic levitation.

All India 2019

CBSE Board Solved Paper

Time Allowed : 3 Hours **_Maximum Marks : 80_**

General Instructions:

I. The question paper comprises five sections, **A, B, C, D** and **E**. You are to attempt all the sections.

II. All questions are compulsory.

III. Internal choice is given in sections **B, C, D** and **E**.

IV. Question numbers **1** and **2** in Section **A** are **one** mark questions. They are to be answered in one word or in one sentence.

V. Question numbers **3** to **5** in Section **B** are **two** marks questions. These are to be answered in about **30** words each.

VI. Question numbers **6** to **15** in Section **C** are **three** marks questions. These are to be answered in about **50** words each.

VII. Question numbers **16** to **21** in Section **D** are **five** marks questions. These are to be answered in about **70** words each.

VIII. Question numbers **22** to **27** in Section **E** are based on practical skills. Each question is a **two** marks question. These are to be answered in brief.

SECTION - A

1. Name two industries based on forest produce.

2. Why are the heating elements of electric toasters and electric irons made of an alloy rather than a pure metal ?

SECTION -B

3. Write the molecular formula of ethene and draw its electron dot structure.

4. Give reasons :

(a) Platinum, gold and silver are used to make jewellery.

(b) Metals like sodium and potassium are stored under oil.

OR

Silver articles become black when kept in open for some time, whereas copper vessels lose their shiny brown surfaces and gain a green coat when kept in open. Name the substances present in air with which these metals react and write the name of the products formed.

5. The absolute refractive index of Ruby is 1·7. Find the speed of light in Ruby. The speed of light in vacuum is 3×10^8 m/g

SECTION - C

6. On heating blue coloured powder of copper (II) nitrate in a boiling tube, black copper oxide, O_2 and a brown gas X is formed.

(a) Identify the type of reaction and the gas X.

(b) Write balanced chemical equation of the reaction.

(c) Write the pH range of aqueous solution of the gas X.

7. (a) While diluting an acid, why is it recommended that the acid should be added to water and not water to the acid?

(b) Dry hydrogen chloride gas does not change the colour of dry litmus paper. Why ?

OR

How is sodium hydroxide manufactured in industries ? Name the process. In this process a gas X is formed as by-product. This gas reacts with lime water to give a compound Y, which is used as a bleaching agent in the chemical industry. Identify X and Y and write the chemical equation of the reactions involved.

8. What are amphoteric oxides ? Give an example. Write balanced chemical equations to justify your answer.

9. What is a homologous series of carbon compounds ? Give an example and list its three characteristics.

10. List in tabular form three distinguishing features between autotrophic nutrition and heterotrophic nutrition.

11. What is transpiration ? List its two functions.

OR

(a) What is translocation ? Why is it essential for plants?

(b) Where do the substances in plants reach as a result of translocation ?

12. What is carpel ? Write the function of its various parts.

13. A student holding a mirror in his hand, directed the reflecting surface of the mirror towards the Sun. He then directed the reflected light on to a sheet of paper held close to the mirror.

(a) What should he do to burn the paper ?

(b) Which type of mirror does he have ?

(c) Will he be able to determine the approximate value of focal length of this mirror from this activity ? Give reason and draw ray diagram to justify your answer in this case.

OR

A 10 cm tall object is placed perpendicular to the principal axis of a convex lens of focal length 12 cm. The distance of the object from the lens is 18 cm. Find the nature, position and size of the image formed.

14. What are solar cells ? Explain the structure of solar panel. List two principal advantages associated with solar cells.

15. Write the essential function performed by ozone at the higher levels of the Earth's atmosphere ? How is it produced? Name the synthetic chemicals mainly responsible for the drop of amount of ozone in the atmosphere. How can the use of these chemicals be reduced ?

SECTION - D

16. (a) List any three observations which posed a challenge to Mendeleev's Periodic Law.

(b) How does the metallic character of elements vary on moving from

(i) left to right in a period,

(ii) from top to bottom in a group of the Modern Periodic Table ? Give reason for your answer.

OR

The electrons in the atoms of four elements A, B, C and D are distributed in three shells having 1, 3, 5 and 7 electrons respectively in their outermost shells. Write the group numbers in which these elements are placed in the Modern Periodic Table. Write the electronic configuration of the atoms of B and D and the molecular formula of the compound formed when B and D combine.

17. (a) Why is the use of iodised salt advisable ? Name the disease caused due to deficiency of iodine in our diet and state its one symptom.

(b) How do nerve impulses travel in the body ? Explain.

OR

What is hydrotropism? Design an experiment to demonstrate this phenomenon.

18. (a) What are homologous structures ? Give an example.

(b) "The sex of a newborn child is a matter of chance and none of the parents may be considered responsible for it." Justify this statement with the help of a flow chart showing sex-determination in human beings.

19. When do we consider a person to be myopic or hypermetropic? List two causes of hypermetropia. Explain using ray diagrams how the defect associated with hypermetropic eye can be corrected.

20. (a) How will you infer with the help of an experiment that the same current flows through every part of a circuit containing three resistors in series connected to a battery ?

(b) Consider the given circuit and find the current flowing in the circuit and potential difference across the 15 Ω resistor when the circuit is closed.

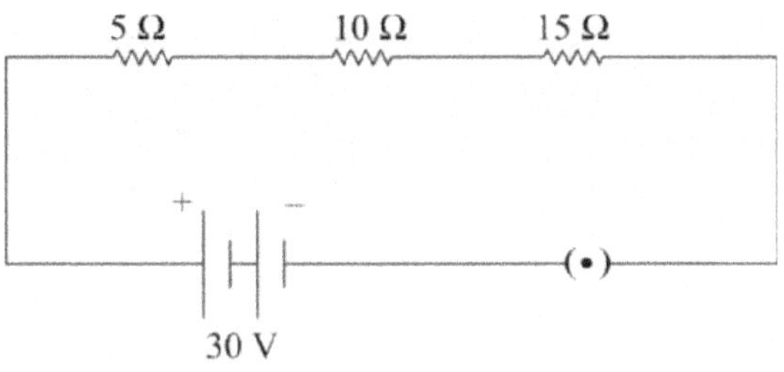

5 Ω 10 Ω 15 Ω

+ –

(•)

30 V

OR

(a) Three resistors R_1, R_2 and R_3 are connected in parallel and the combination is connected to a battery, ammeter, voltmeter and key. Draw suitable circuit diagram and obtain an expression for the equivalent resistance of the combination of the resistors.

(b) Calculate the equivalent resistance of the following network :

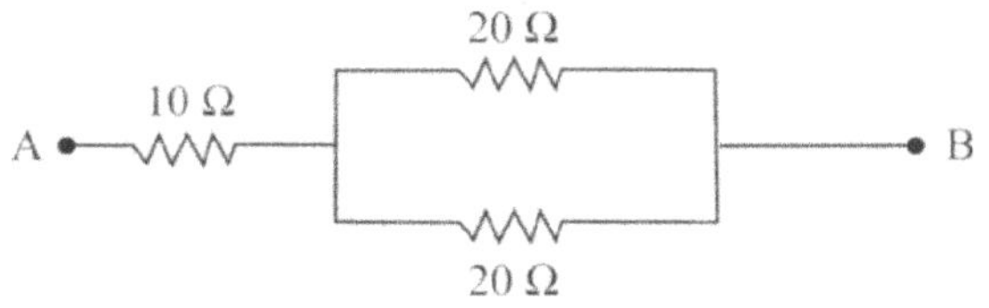

20 Ω

10 Ω

A B

20 Ω

21. Draw the pattern of magnetic field lines produced around a current carrying straight conductor passing perpendicularly through a horizontal cardboard. State and apply right-hand thumb rule to mark the direction of the field lines. How will the strength of the magnetic field change when the point where magnetic field is to be determined is moved away from the straight conductor ? Give reason to justify your answer.

SECTION - E

22. A teacher provided acetic acid, water, lemon juice, aqueous solution of sodium hydrogen carbonate and sodium hydroxide to students in the school laboratory to determine the pH values of these substances using pH papers. One of the students reported the pH values of the given substances as 3, 12, 4, 8 and 14 respectively. Which one of these values is not correct ? Write its correct value stating the reason.

OR

What would a student report nearly after 30 minutes of placing duly cleaned strips of aluminium, copper, iron and zinc in freshly prepared iron sulphate solution taken in four beakers ?

23. What is observed when a pinch of sodium hydrogen carbonate is added to 2 mL of acetic acid taken in a test tube ? Write chemical equation for the reaction involved in this case.

24. List in proper sequence four steps of obtaining germinating dicot seeds.

OR

After examining a prepared slide under the high power of a compound microscope, a student concludes that the given slide shows the various stages of binary fission in a unicellular organism. Write two observations on the basis of which such a conclusion may be drawn.

25. List four precautions which a student should observe while preparing a temporary mount of a leaf peel to show stomata in his school laboratory.

26. Draw the path of a ray of light when it enters one of the faces of a glass slab at an angle of nearly 45°. Label on it (i) angle of refraction, (ii) angle of emergence and (iii) lateral displacement.

OR

A student traces the path of a ray of light through a glass prism as shown in the diagram, but leaves it incomplete and unlabelled. Redraw and complete the diagram. Also label on $\angle i$, $\angle e$, $\angle r$, and $\angle D$.

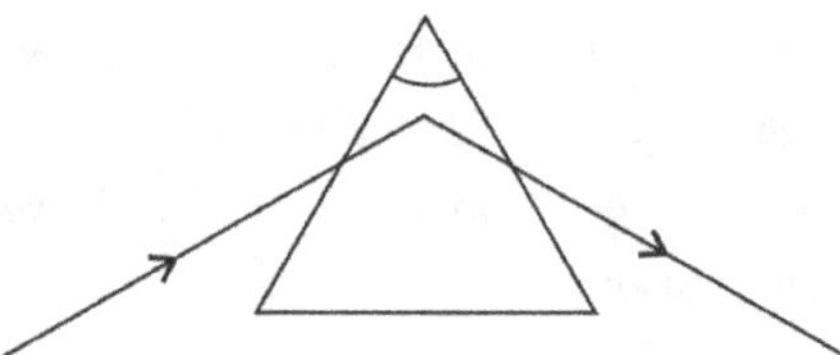

27. The current flowing through a resistor connected in a circuit and the potential difference developed across its ends are as shown in the diagram by milliammeter and voltmeter readings respectively :

(a) What are the least counts of these meters ?

(b) What is the resistance of the resistor ?

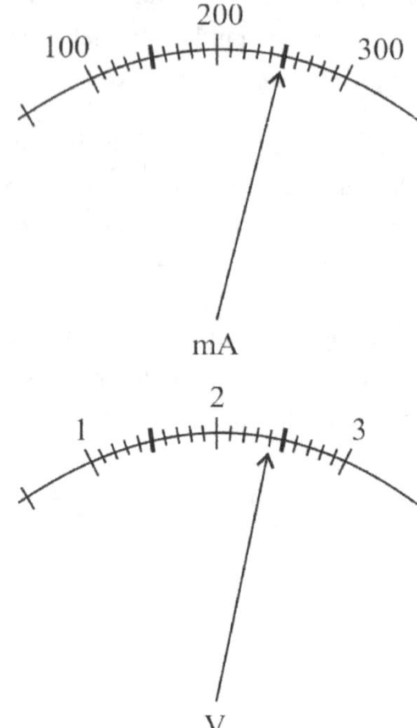

Solutions

SECTION - A

1. A few industries based on forest produce are rubber, paper, sports goods, mining, timber and pharmaceutical. **(1 Mark)**

2. Heating elements of electric toasters and electric irons made of an alloy rather than pure metal because
   (i) Alloys have higher value of resistivity.
   (ii) Alloys do not oxidise easily at high temperatures. **(1 Mark)**

SECTION - B

3. Molecular formula of ethene is C_2H_4. **(1 Mark)**
   Electron dot structure:

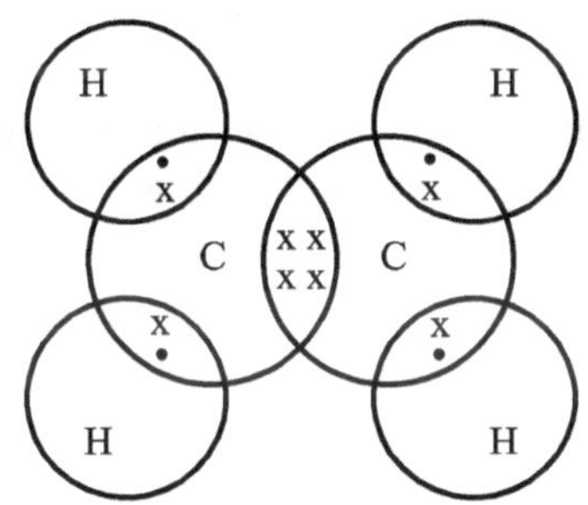

(1 Mark)

4. (a) Platinum, gold and silver rarely react with oxygen and have shining appearance therefore they are used to make jewellery. **(1 Mark)**
   (b) Sodium and potassium are reactive metals therefore they are stored under oil. **(1 Mark)**

OR

Silver articles become black after some time when exposed to air because it react with sulphur in the air and form coating of silver sulphide. **(1 Mark)**

$$4Ag + O_2 \rightarrow Ag_2O\downarrow$$

$$Ag_2O + H_2S \rightarrow \underset{\text{(Black)}}{Ag_2S}\downarrow + H_2O$$

Copper reacts with moist carbon dioxide present in air and gains a green coat of copper carbonate. **(1 Mark)**

$$2\,Cu + H_2O + O_2 + CO_2 \longrightarrow \underbrace{Cu(OH)_2 + CuCO_3}_{\text{green}}$$

5. Given,
   Refractive index of ruby, $\mu = 1.7$
   Speed of light in vacuum, $c = 3 \times 10^8$ m/s
   Refractive index, $\mu = \frac{c}{v}$ **(1 Mark)**
   Here, v = speed of light in ruby
   $\therefore v = \frac{c}{\mu} = \frac{3 \times 10^8}{1.7} = 1.76 \times 10^8$ m/s **(1 Mark)**

Refractive index is a measure of how much speed of light changes when it enter the medium from air. Refractive index is the property of medium.

SECTION - C

6. (a) The reaction is decomposition reaction and the gas X is NO_2. **(1 Mark)**
   (b) $2\,Cu(NO_3)_2(s) \longrightarrow \underset{\text{Black}}{2CuO(s)} + \underset{\text{Brown}}{4NO_2(g)} + O_2(g)$
   (c) Aqueous solution of NO_2 gas is acidic therefore it has pH range 3–4. **(1 Mark)**

7. (a) The process of dilution of an acid is highly exothermic reaction and huge amount of energy is released. When acid is added to water, amount of energy which is released is absorbed by water. But if water is added to acid, it may results into spill of acid due to large amount of energy released which may cause accident. **(2 Marks)**
   (b) Dry hydrogen chloride gas is a covalent compound and will not dissociate into H^+ and Cl^- ions.
   $HCl\,(aq) \rightleftharpoons H^+\,(aq) + Cl^-\,(aq)$
   In absence of water H^+ ion is not produced. Thus, do not give litmus test. **(1 Mark)**

OR

Sodium hydroxide manufactured in industries by chlor-alkali process. In this process electricity is passed through an aqueous solution of sodium chloride, it decomposed to form sodium hydroxide, chlorine gas and hydrogen gas. Gas X is chlorine gas which react with lime water to produce bleaching powder (Y).

Chlor alkali process:

$$2\,NaCl\,(aq) + 2H_2O\,(l) \longrightarrow 2NaOH\,(aq) + \underset{\text{'X'}}{Cl_2(g)} + H_2(g)$$

$$\underset{\text{Lime water}}{Ca(OH)_2} + \underset{\text{'X'}}{Cl_2} \longrightarrow \underset{\text{'Y'}}{(CaOCl)Cl} + H_2O$$

(3 Marks)

8. Amphoteric oxides are the oxides which react with both acids as well as bases to produce salts and water. For example Aluminum oxides reacts with both acids as well as bases.

$Al_2O_3 + 6HCl \longrightarrow 2AlCl_3 + 3H_2O$ **(1 + 1 = 2 Marks)**

$Al_2O_3 + 2NaOH \longrightarrow 2NaAlO_2 + H_2O$ **(1 Mark)**

In the periodic table elements of group 1 and group 2 generally form basic oxides while metalloids (Al, Si, Ge, As, Sb) form amphoteric oxides. Non metals generally form acidic oxides.

9. Homologous series of carbon compounds is the series of compounds having same general formula and having same functional group but the successive compounds in the homologous series differ by $-CH_2-$ unit.

For example homologous series for alkene

General formula: C_nH_{2n}

$n = 2$, C_2H_4	Ethene
$n = 3$, C_3H_6	Propene
$n = 4$, C_4H_8	Butene
$n = 5$, C_5H_{10}	Pentene

(1½ Marks)

Characteristics:

(i) Melting and boiling point increases with increasing molecular mass.

(ii) All the members are differ by $-CH_2-$ unit.

(iii) All the members show nearly same chemical properties that are exhibit by double bond in alkenes.

(½ + ½ + ½ = 1½ Marks)

10. The difference between autotrophic nutrition and heterotrophic nutrition are as follows:

Autotrophic nutrition	Heterotrophic nutrition
(i) Autotrophic nutrition means that the organism prepares their own food and is not dependent on other organisms.	(i) Heterotrophic nutrition means that organism does not prepare its own food and dependent on other organism for food.
(ii) Food is prepared in the presence of carbon dioxide, water and sunlight.	(ii) Food is not prepared in the presence of carbon dioxide, water and sunlight.
(iii) Green plants and autotrophic bacteria have autotrophic mode of nutrition.	(iii) All higher animals, humans and fungi have heterotrophic mode of nutrition.

(3 Marks)

11. Transpiration is defined as the process of evaporation of excess water from the stomata of the leaves of plants. It performs following functions such as:

- The process of transpiration is important for upward movement of water in plants.
- Transpiration also helps in the regulation of temperature of plant. **(3 Marks)**

Stomata are small pores that are surrounded by specialized parenchymatic cells called guard cells. It facilitates the gaseous exchange in the leaves of the plant through photosynthesis. The opening and closing of the pore is a function of the guard cells.

OR

(i) Translocation is defined as the process of movement of material (food and water) from the leaves and roots to different parts of the plant. Plants synthesis their food in the form of sugar (glucose) and they can be stored in the leaves in the form of starch. Food is transported to the different parts of the plant through phloem and water is transported to the different parts of the plant through xylem. Xylem and phloem are vascular tissue in the plants.

Translocation plays an essential role in the transportation of food and water to the different parts of the plant.

(ii) With the help of translocation, food prepared by the process of photosynthesis is transported to different parts of plant such as stem, root and other storage regions of the plant. **(3 Marks)**

Photosynthesis is a biochemical process in which green plants synthesise their own food in the presence of sunlight, carbon dioxide and water. This process involves the conversion of light energy into chemical energy.

12. Carpel is located in the centre of a flower and is the female reproductive part. It is made of three parts. The swollen bottom part is called ovary, middle elongated part is called style and the terminal part which may be sticky is the stigma.

The ovary contains ovules and each ovule has an egg cell. **(3 Marks)**

Stigma : Sticky in nature so that the pollen grains get attached to it easily.

Style : It helps in providing stigma height so that it can receive pollen grains.

Ovary : It is the part containing the ovule. On maturity the ovule becomes a seed and the ovary when matured becomes a fruit.

The male germ-cell is produced by pollen grain that fuses with the female present in the ovule and the fusion of germ-cells with ovule results in the formation of zygote which is capable of growing into a new plant.

13. (a) To burn the paper, student should move (adjust) the mirror in such a way that paper is positioned at the focus of the mirror. **(1 Mark)**

(b) He has concave mirror. **(1 Mark)**

(c) Yes, approximate value of focal length can be measured from this activity as paper will start burning when it is kept at the focus of the mirror.

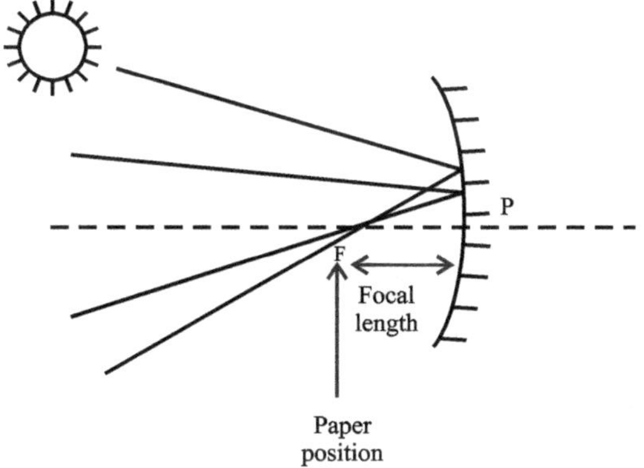

(1 Mark)

OR

Given,

Distance of object from the lens, $u = -18$ cm

Focal length of convex lens, f = 12 cm

Height of the object, $h_o = 10$ cm

Using lens formula

$$\frac{1}{v} - \frac{1}{u} = \frac{1}{f}$$

$$\Rightarrow \frac{1}{v} = \frac{1}{f} + \frac{1}{u}$$

$$\Rightarrow \frac{1}{v} = \frac{1}{12} + \frac{1}{(-18)}$$

$$\Rightarrow \frac{1}{v} = \frac{3-2}{36} = \frac{1}{36}$$

$\Rightarrow v = 36$ cm **(1 Mark)**

Magnification, $m = \frac{h_i}{h_o} = \frac{v}{u}$

$$\Rightarrow \frac{36}{-18} = \frac{h_i}{10}$$

$\Rightarrow h_i = -20$ cm (size of the image) **(1 Mark)**

Nature of the image = Real and inverted **(1 Mark)**

14. Solar cell is a device which convert solar energy directly into electric energy in DC form. **(1 Mark)**

Solar panels is an arrangement of large number of solar cells joined together in a definite pattern to provide greater power at higher voltage. **(1 Mark)**

Advantages of solar cells.

(i) Solar cells are pollution free and cause no green house gases to be emitted after installation.

(ii) Solar cells are used to provide electricity to remote, inaccessible placed where normal electricity transmission lines not exist. **(½ × 2 = 1 Mark)**

A solar cell develops a voltage of 0.5 - 1V *and can produce* 0.7 W *of electricity. Silver is used for connecting solar cells to each other.*

15. Ozone layer play an essential role in the prevention of the entry of harmful UV radiations on the earth. Ozone (O_3) is produced by reaction of oxygen molecules with free radicle of oxygen in the presence of solar radiation.

Chlorofluorocarbons (CFCs) are synthetic chemicals that are responsible for ozone layer depletion.

Emission of CFCs can be prevented by reducing the use of AC, fridge and perfumes. **(3 Marks)**

Note

Ozone is found in the upper part of the atmosphere called stratosphere and it acts as a shield for absorbing harmful ultraviolet radiation coming from the sun.

SECTION - D

16. (a) Three observations which posed a challenge to Mendeleev's Periodic law are :

(i) Position of hydrogen in the periodic table:

Hydrogen resembles alkali metals as hydrogen also combine with oxygen and sulphur to form compounds having same formulae. Hydrogen also resemble halogens and combine with metals and non metals forming covalent compound.

(ii) Position of isotopes in the Mendeleev's periodic table posed a challenge to Mendeleev's law.

(iii) In Mendeleev's periodic table atomic masses do not increase in a regular manner in going from one element to the next. **(3 Marks)**

(b) (i) Metallic character decreases on going from left to right in the periodic table due to increase in effective nuclear charge. **(1 Mark)**

(ii) Metallic character increases on going from top to bottom in a group due to decrease in effective nuclear charge. **(1 Mark)**

Note

As the effective nuclear charge acting on the valence shell electrons increases across a period, the tendency to lose electrons will decrease therefore metallic character decreases.

Down the group, the effective nuclear charge experienced by valence electrons decreases because the outermost electrons are farther away from the nucleus therefore they can be lost easily hence metallic character increases down the group.

OR

Elements	A	B	C	D	
outer most shell electrons	1	3	5	7	(given)
Group Number	gp.1	gp.13	gp.15	gp.17	**(1 Mark)**

Electronic configuration : B (2, 8, 3) **(1 Mark)**

: D (2, 8, 7) **(1 Mark)**

3 ╲╱ 1

B ╱╲ D

Molecular formula of the compound is BD_3. **(2 Marks)**

Note

Valency of element B is 3 and valency of element D is 1. Valency is the number of electrons that are lost or gain or shared to attain noble gas configuration. Element D require only 1 electron to complete its octet therefore it exhibit valency – 1.

17. (a) Iodine is an important element required for the thyroid gland for the synthesis of thyroxin hormone. Thyroxin hormone regulates the carbohydrate, protein and fat metabolism in the body and also provides balance for growth.

Diet deficient in iodine leads to cause goitre disease and its symptoms involves swollen neck and enlargement of thyroid gland.

Hence, doctor advised for intake of iodized salt in order to prevent goitre disease. **(3 Marks)**

(b) The nerve impulse travels from dendrite to cell body and then along the axon to its end. At the end of the axon, the electrical impulse sets off the release of some chemicals. These chemicals cross the gap, or synapse and start a similar electrical impulse in a dendrite of the next neuron. **(2 Marks)**

Note

The chemical synapse is a gap between two neurons where information passes chemically in the form of neurotransmitter molecules.

OR

Hydrotropism is the process of growth or movement of roots towards the source of water.

Experimental explanation of hydrotropism is as follows:

Take a plant (pea seedling) in a nude jar filled with sand. Now place a porous pot filled with water in the wide jar. Roots of the plant will grow towards water and bend towards the water source showing hydroponics.

Diagrammatic representation of hydrotropism in plants:

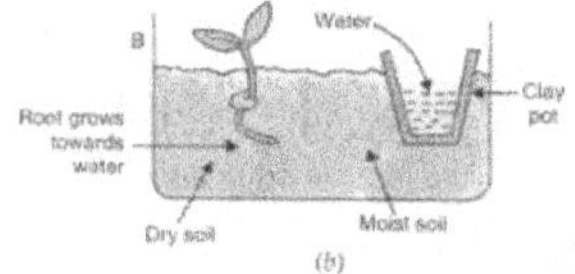

(5 Marks)

18. (a) The homologous organs are the type of organs have similar structures but perform different functions.

For example: Wings of birds or bat and flippers of a whale.

(2 Marks)

Note

Homologous structures are inherited from a common ancestor.

(b) In human beings, the females have two X chromosomes and the males have one X and Y chromosome. So, the females are XX and males are XY. At the time of mating, large number of sperms is ejaculated from the male reproductive organ into the female reproductive organ. Then the sperm travel towards the fallopian tubes where only one sperm meets with the egg. The process of fusion of the sperm and ovum is called fertilisation. The sperm has either X and Y chromosome and egg has only X chromosome.

So, if sperm carrying Y chromosome fuses with egg, the child will be male and if sperm carrying X chromosome fuses with the egg the child will be female. There is an equal chance of fusion of either X and Y chromosome with the egg. Hence, it is proved that sex of the new born child not determined by mother and none of the parent is responsible for it.

Genetic cross represents sex determination in humans:

Parents: XY (male) X XX (female)

Offsprings: XX XX XY XY

50% offsprings are male and 50% offsprings are female.

(3 Marks)

19. We consider a person myopic when he is able to see nearby objects but cannot see far off objects distinctly. **(1 Mark)**

We consider a person hypermetropic when he is able to see far off objects clearly but cannot see nearby object clearly.

This defect arises either because: **(1 Mark)**

(i) the focal length of the eye lens is too flat or inflexible or

(ii) the eyeball has become too short **(½ × 2 = 1 Mark)**

Correction of Hypermetropia:

(i) This defect can be corrected by using a convex lens of appropriate power.

(ii) Eye-glasses with converging lenses provide the additional focusing power required for forming the image on the retina. **(½ × 2 = 1 Mark)**

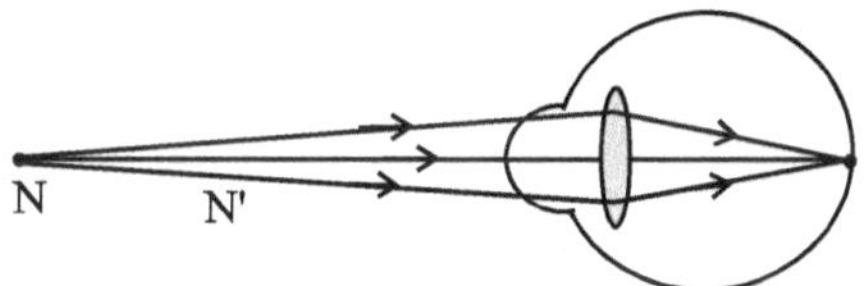

(A) Near point of a Hypermetropic eye

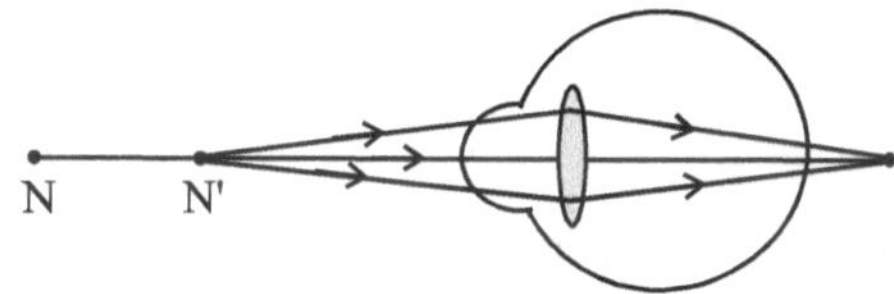

(B) Hypermetropic eye

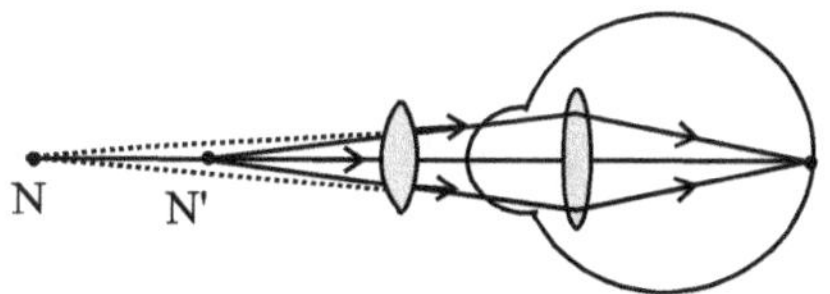

(C) Correction for Hypermetropic eye **(1 Mark)**

20. (a)

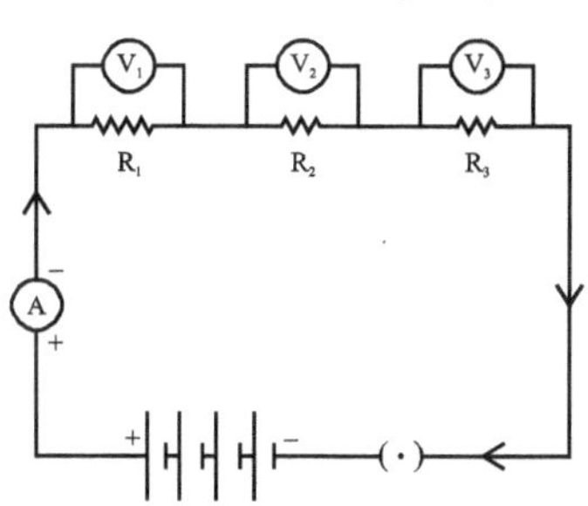

(1 Mark)

Make the circuit as shown in the figure. Note the reading of the voltmeter let us say they are V_1, V_2 and V_3 respectively. From Ohm's law

$i_1 = \frac{V_1}{R_1}$, $i_2 = \frac{V_2}{R_2}$, $i_3 = \frac{V_3}{R_3}$, **(1 Mark)**

We will find that $i_1 = i_2 = i_3$

Hence, same current flows in every part of the circuit.

(1 Mark)

(b) Let R_1, R_2 and R_3 be the resistance of three resistors connected in series.

$R_1 = 5\ \Omega, R_2 = 10\ \Omega, R_3 = 15\ \Omega.$

Net Resistance, $R = R_1 + R_2 + R_3$

$\Rightarrow R = 5\ \Omega + 10\ \Omega + 15\ \Omega$

$\Rightarrow R = 30\ \Omega$ **(½ Mark)**

Current in the circuit, $I = \frac{V}{R}$

$\Rightarrow I = \frac{30\ V}{30\ \Omega} = 1\ A$ **(½ Mark)**

Potential drop across 15 Ω resistor

$V_3 = IR_3$

$\Rightarrow V_3 = 1 \times 15 = 15\ V$ **(1 Mark)**

OR

(a) Let the three resistances R_1, R_2 and R_3 be connected in parallel across the two ends A and B. This combination is connected to a battery of 'V' volt which supplies a current 'I'. Since these three resistances are across the same points A and B i.e. why they have same PD i.e. 'V' volt.

But the current gets divided into I_1, I_2 and I_3 through R_1, R_2 and R_3 respectively.

According to Ohm's law,

$V = IR \Rightarrow I = \frac{V}{R}$

Current I_1, (flowing through R_1) $= \frac{V}{R_1}$

Current I_2, (flowing through R_2) $= \frac{V}{R_2}$

Current I_3 (flowing through R_3) $= \frac{V}{R_3}$ **(1 Mark)**

Since, $I = I_1 + I_2 + I_3$

Therefore, $I = \frac{V}{R}$

$$\frac{V}{R} = \frac{V}{R_1} + \frac{V}{R_2} + \frac{V}{R_3}$$

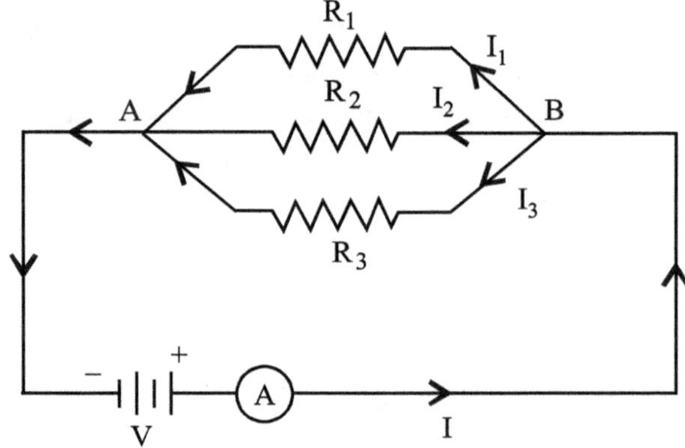

$$\frac{V}{R} = V\left[\frac{1}{R_1} + \frac{1}{R_2} + \frac{1}{R_3}\right]$$

$$\frac{I}{R} = \frac{I}{R_1} + \frac{I}{R_2} + \frac{I}{R_3}$$ **(1 Mark)**

If two or more resistances are connected in parallel, then the reciprocal of total resistance is equal to sum of reciprocals of individual resistance.

(b) In the given circuit, two resistors of 20 Ω connected in parallel. So, their equivalent resistance is

$\frac{1}{R} = \frac{1}{20\ \Omega} + \frac{1}{20\ \Omega}$

$\Rightarrow \frac{1}{R} = \frac{1}{10\ \Omega}$

$\Rightarrow R = 10\ \Omega$ **(1 Mark)**

This combination is in series with a resistor of 10 Ω.

Net equivalent Resistance,

$R' = R + 10\ \Omega$

$= 10\ \Omega + 10\ \Omega$

$= 20\ \Omega$ **(1 Mark)**

21. (i)

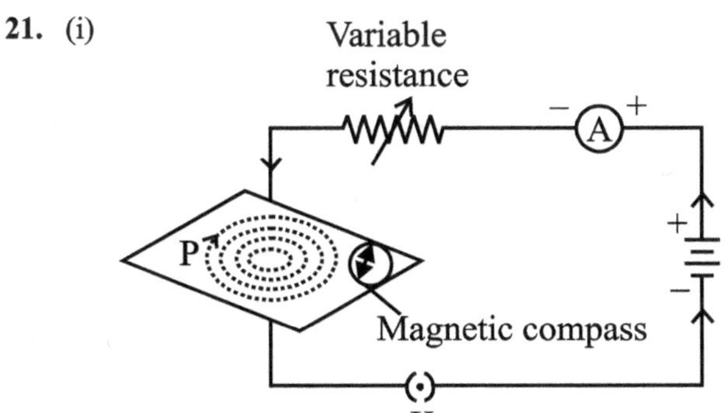

(ii)

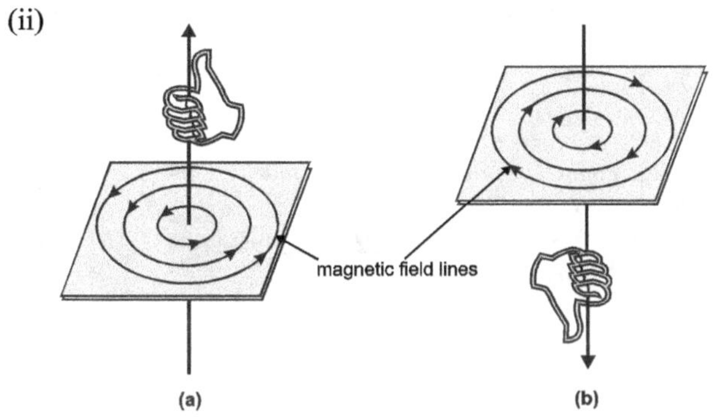

Direction of magnetic field easily found by applying the Right hand Thumb Rule. According to this rule, If we hold the current carrying conductor in right hand such that thumb is stretched along the direction of current, then fingers will warp around the wire in the direction of magnetic field. **(1 Mark)**

(iii) The strength of magnetic filed decreases as the point where magnetic field is to be determined is moved away from the straight conductor. **(1 Mark)**

SECTION - E

22. pH value given for water is not correct. It should not be 12, the correct pH value for pure water should be 7. Pure water is neutral. **(2 Marks)**

OR

Aluminium and zinc will able to displace iron from iron sulphate solution while copper is less reactive than iron will not give any reaction.

$Cu + FeSO_4 \longrightarrow$ no reaction

$Fe + FeSO_4 \longrightarrow$ no reaction

$Zn + FeSO_4 \longrightarrow Fe \downarrow + ZnSO_4$

$Al + FeSO_4 \longrightarrow Fe \downarrow + Al_2 (SO_4)_3$ **(2 Marks)**

23. $NaHCO_3 + CH_3\,COOH \longrightarrow CH_3\,COONa + CO_2 + H_2O$ **(1 Mark)**

Brisk effervescence of CO_2 gas is observed. **(1 Mark)**

24. The four steps involved in the obtaining germinating dicot seeds are as follows:

- **Imbition:** It is a seed' or plant's absorption of water process which involves swelling in some plant cells and organs. Seeds undergo imbition swelling which is exposed to water.
- **Respiration:** Oxygen is required by the germinating seed during aerobic respiration. Cellular respiration is required for the growth and development of seed.
- **Effect of light:** Light promotes seed germination.
- **Mobilizing of reserve food:** The process of germination is shortly followed by the mobilization of food reserves from the seed storage organs such as endosperm that provides essential energy for growth and development of seed. **(3 Marks)**

A seed is an embryonic plant which is enclosed in a protective outer covering called ***seed coat****.*

OR

The two conclusions drawn from observation of students are as follows:

- Elongation of the nucleus because of karyokinesis
- Appearance of constriction due to the division of the cytoplasm. **(2 Marks)**

Many bacteria and protozoa split into two equal halves during cell division and in Amoeba, the splitting of the two cells during division can take place in any plane and is referred to as binary fission.

25. Following are the precautions taken by student while preparing a temporary mount of a leaf peel to show stomata are

- Cut the peel to a proper size and avoid folding it.
- Always place the peel at the centre of the slide and hold the side at the edge.
- Do not over-stain or under strain the peel.
- Remove excess stain and glycerin with a blotting paper.

(2 Marks)

26.

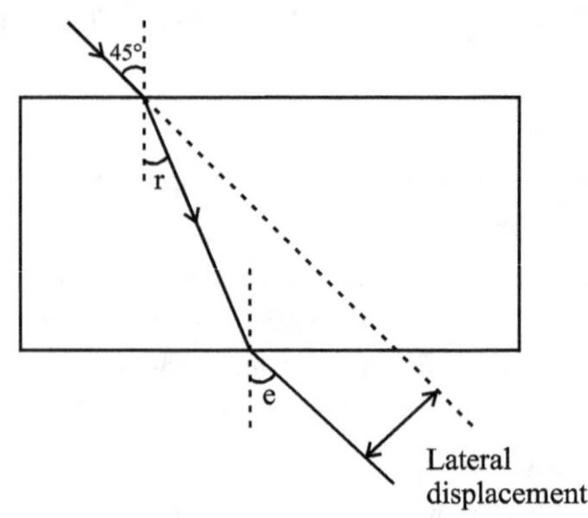

(2 Marks)

OR

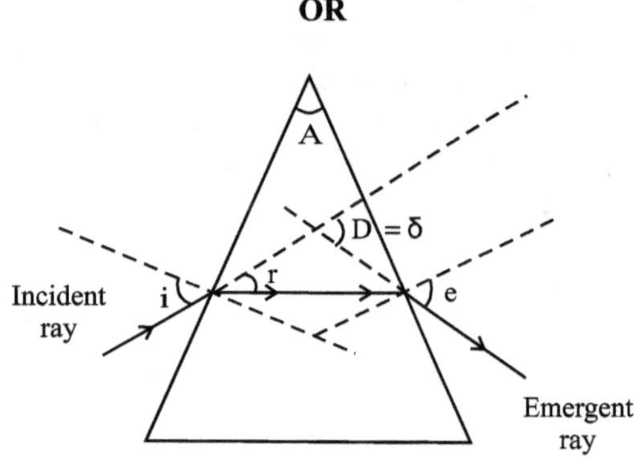

(2 Marks)

When a ray of light is perpendicular to the refracting surface it will not show any deviation. In this case, angle of incidence and angle of deviation both are zero.

27. (a) Least counts of meters are 10 mA and 0.1V **(1 Mark)**

(b) Given,

Voltage, V = 2.4 Volt

Current, I = 250 mA

Using Ohm's law

V = IR $\frac{2.4\text{V}}{250\text{ mA}}$

$\Rightarrow R = \frac{V}{I} =$ **(½ Mark)**

$\Rightarrow R = \frac{2.4}{0.25\text{ A}} = 9.6\ \Omega$ **(½ Mark)**

Least count is the smallest value that can be measured by an instrument

$$\textit{Least count} = \frac{\textit{Value measured in n divisions}}{n}$$

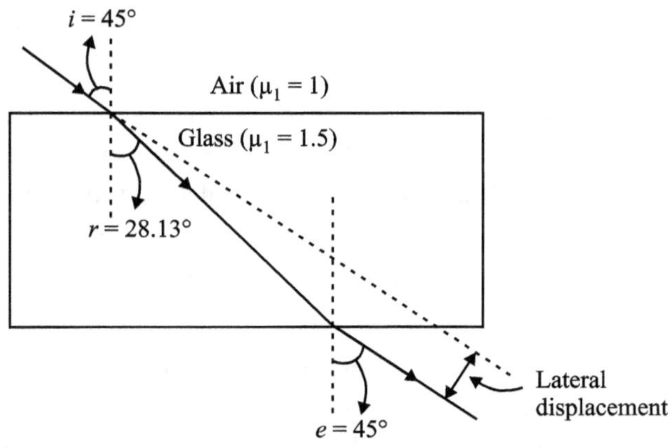

Delhi 2019

CBSE Board Solved Paper

Time Allowed : 3 Hours ***Maximum Marks : 80***

General Instructions:

(i) The question paper comprises **five** sections, **A, B, C, D** and **E.** You are to attempt all the sections.

(ii) All questions are compulsory.

(iii) Internal choice is given in sections, **B, C, D** and **E.**

(iv) Question members **1** and **2** in Section **A** are **one** mark questions. They are to be answered in **one** word or in one sentence.

(v) Question numbers **3** to **5** in Section **B** are **two**-marks questions. These are to be answered in about **30** words each.

(vi) Question numbers **6** to **15** in Section **C** are **three**-marks questions. These are to be answered in about **50** words each.

(vii) Question numbers **16** to **21** in Section **D** are **five**-marks questions. These are to be answered in about **70** words each.

(viii) Question numbers **22** to **27** in Section **E** are based on practical skills. Each question is a **two** marks question. These are to be answered in brief.

SECTION - A

1. If you could use any source of energy for heating your food which one would you prefer? State one reason for your choice.

2. Write the function of voltmeter in an electric circuit.

SECTION - B

3. What happens to the image distance in the normal human eye when we decrease the distance of an object, say 10 m to 1 m ? Justify your answer.

4. List two different functions performed by pancreas in our body.

5. How it can be proved that the basic structure of the Modern Periodic Table is based on the electronic configuration of atoms of different elements?

OR

The electronic configuration of an element is 2, 8, 4. State its:

(a) group and period in the Modern Periodic Table.

(b) name and write its one physical property.

SECTION - C

6. How can we help in reducing the problem of waste disposal? Suggest any three methods.

OR

Define an ecosystem. Draw a block diagram to show the flow of energy in an ecosystem.

7. List three advantages each of :

(i) exploiting resources with short term aims, and

(ii) using a long term perspective in managing our natural resources.

8. What is a rainbow? Draw a labelled diagram to show the formation of a rainbow.

9. Nervous and hormonal systems together perform the function of control and coordination in human beings. Justify this statement with the help of an example.

10. Trace the sequence of events which occur when a bright light is focused on your eyes.

11. What is photosynthesis? Explain its mechanism.

12. Name the plant Mendel used for his experiment. What type of progeny was obtained by Mendel in F_1 and F_2 generations when he crossed the tall and short plants? Write the ratio he obtained in F_2 generation plants.

OR

List two differences between acquired traits and inherited traits by giving an example of each.

13. 2 g of silver chloride is taken in a china dish and the china dish is placed in sunlight for sometime. What will be your observation in this case ? Write the chemical reaction involved in the form of a balanced chemical equation. Identify the type of chemical reaction.

OR

Identify the type of reactions taking place in each of the following cases and write the balanced chemical equation for the reactions.

(a) Zinc reacts with silver nitrate to produce zinc nitrate and silver.

(b) Potassium iodide reacts with lead nitrate to produce potassium nitrate and lead iodide.

14. Based on the group valency of elements write the molecular formula of the following compounds giving justification for each:

(i) Oxide of first group elements.

(ii) Halide of the elements of group thirteen, and

(iii) Compound formed when an element, A of group 2 combines with an element, B of group seventeen.

15. Explain the following:

(a) Sodium chloride is an ionic compound which does not conduct electricity in solid state where as it does conduct electricity in molten state well as in aqueous solution.

(b) Reactivity of aluminium decrease if it is dipped in nitric acid.

(c) Metals like calcium and magnesium are never found in their free state in nature.

SECTION - D

16. (a) With the help of a suitable circuit diagram prove that the reciprocal of the equivalent resistance of a group of resistances joined in parallel is equal to the sum of the reciprocals of the individual resistances.

(b) In an electric circuit two resistors of 12 Ω each are joined in parallel to a 6 V battery. Find the current drawn from the battery.

OR

An electric lamp of resistance 20 Ω and a conductor of resistance 4 Ω are connected to a 6 V battery as shown in the circuit. Calculate :

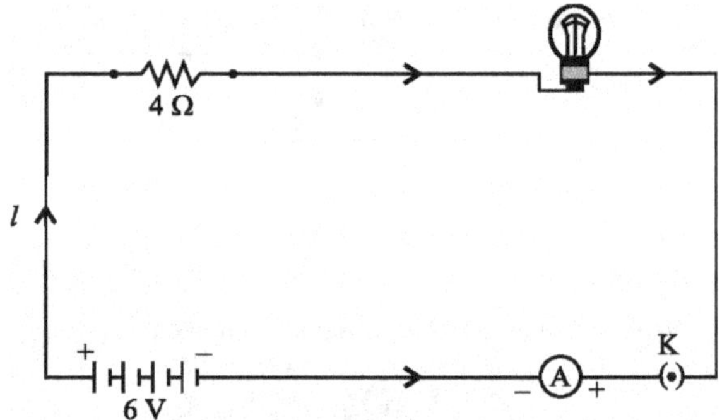

(a) the total resistance of the circuit,

(b) the current through the circuit,

(c) the potential difference across the (i) electric lamp and (ii) conductor, and

(d) power of the lamp.

17. (a) Draw magnetic field lines produced around a current carrying straight conductor passing through a cardboard. Name, state and apply the rule to mark the direction of these field lines.

(b) How will the strength of the magnetic field change when the point where magnetic field is to be determined is moved away from the straight wire carrying constant current? Justify your answer.

18. An object is placed at a distance of 60 cm from a concave lens of focal length 30 cm.

(i) Use lens formula to find the distance of the image from the lens.

(ii) List four characteristics of the image (nature, position, size, erect/inverted) formed by the lens in this case.

(iii) Draw ray diagram to justify your answer of part (ii).

19. Define pollination. Explain the different types of pollination. List two agents of pollination. How does suitable pollination lead to fertilization?

OR

(a) Identify the given diagram. Name the parts 1 to 5.

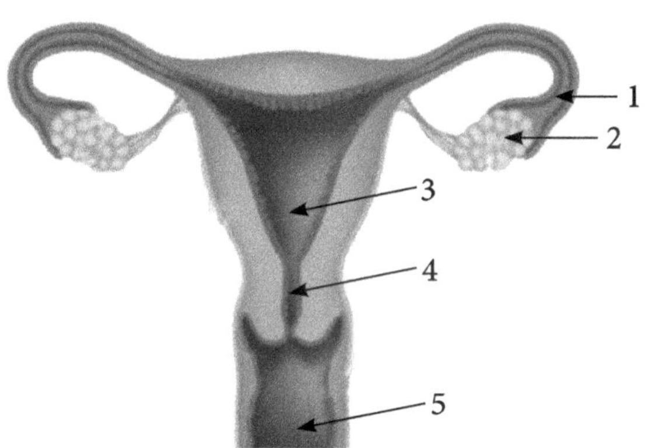

(b) What is contraception? List three advantages of adopting contraceptive measures.

20. Write the chemical formula and name of the compound which is the active ingredient of all alcoholic drinks. List its two uses. Write chemical equation and name of the product formed when this compound reacts with -

(i) sodium metal

(ii) hot concentrated sulphuric acid

OR

What is methane? Draw its electron dot structure. Name the type of bonds formed in this compound. Why are such compounds?

(i) Poor conductors of electricity and

(ii) Have low melting and boiling points? What happens when this compound burns in oxygen?

21. Write the main difference between an acid and a base. With the help of suitable examples explain the term neutralization and the formation of-

(i) acidic,

(ii) basic and

(iii) neutral salts.

SECTION - E

22. In the experimental set up to show that "CO_2 is given out during respiration", name the substance taken in the small test tube kept in the conical flask. State its function and the consequence of its use.

23. A student is observing the temporary mount of a leaf peel under a microscope. Draw labelled diagram of the structure of stomata as seen under the microscope.

OR

Draw a labelled diagram in proper sequence to show budding in hydra.

24. List four precautions which a student should observe while determining the focal length of the given convex lens by obtaining image of a distant object on a screen.

25. While studying the dependence of potential difference (V) across a resistor on the current (I) passing through it, in order to determine the resistance of the resistor, a student took 5 readings for different values of current and plotted a graph between V and I. He got a straight line graph passing through the origin. What does the straight line signify? Write the method of determining resistance of the resistor using this graph.

OR

What would you suggest to a student if while performing an experiment he finds that the pointer/needle of the ammeter and voltmeter do not coincide with the zero marks on the scales when circuit is open? No extra ammeter/voltmeter is available in the laboratory.

26. In three test tubes A, B and C, three different liquids namely, distilled water, underground water and distilled water in which a pinch of calcium sulphate is dissolved, respectively are taken. Equal amount of soap solution is added to each test tube and the contents are shaken. In which test tube will the length of the foam (lather) be longest ? Justify your answer.

27. Blue litmus solution is added to two test tubes A and B containing dilute HCl and NaOH solution respectively. In which test tube a colour change will be observed? State the colour change and give its reason.

OR

What is observed when 2 mL of dilute hydrochloric acid is added to 1 g of sodium carbonate taken in a clean and dry test tube? Write chemical equation for the reaction involved.

Solutions

SECTION - A

1. We will use natural gas for heating and cooking food because it is a clean source of energy. It does not produce huge amount of smoke on burning. **(1 Mark)**

2. Voltmeter is an instrument used for measuring electrical potential difference between two points in an electric circuit. **(1 Mark)**

A voltmeter is always connected in parallel with a device to measure its voltage.

SECTION - B

3. Human eye has ability to adjust focal length of its lens using ciliary muscles. When object is moved from 10 m to 1 m from eye, our eyes change its focal length so as to form image on retina itself. **(2 Marks)**

4. Pancreas produces two important hormones such as - glucagon & insulin.
   (a) **Insulin** hormone is secreted by beta cells of pancrease and is involved in the regulation of blood sugar level in the body. As, in the body, insulin hormone lowers the blood sugar level.
   (b) **Glucagon** hormone is secreted by alpha cells of pancreas and is responsible for increasing the blood sugar level in the body. **(2 Marks)**

Pancrease is a composite gland which acts as both exocrine and endocrine gland.

5. The modern periodic table is based on the electronic configuration of the atom. It can be proved by taking the example of chlorine. Electronic configuration of Cl (17) is 2, 8, 7 which suggest that its outer shell has 7 electrons and it belong to group 17 of the periodic table. **(2 Marks)**

Group number of any element is given by the formula (10 + no. of electron in outermost shell)

OR

(a) Given element belongs to group 14 and period 3 of the periodic table. **(1 Mark)**

(b) Given element is silicon (14) with electronic configuration 2, 8, 4. Silicon is a semiconductor. **(1 Mark)**

SECTION - C

6. We can reduce the problem of waste disposal by following methods:-
   - By minimizing the use of disposable items and promoting the use of recycled articles.
   - Before dumping, select and separate biodegradable and non-biodegradable wastes.
   - Recycling of non-biodegradable waste material. **(3 Marks)**

OR

An ecosystem is defined as a complex relationship between all the living (plants, animals & microorganisms) and non-living things (sun, water, climate) which tends to interact with each other. Ecosystem is responsible for the maintainance of the natural balance of the earth.

(2 Marks)

Diagrammatic representation of the flow of energy in an ecosystem:

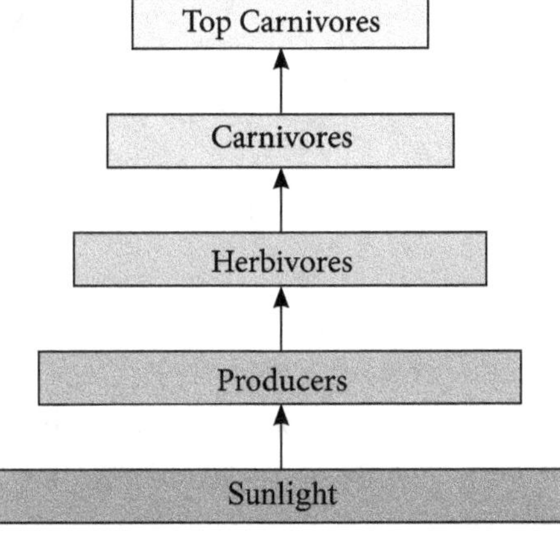

(1 Mark)

Fig. Diagram showing flow of energy in an ecosystem

7. (i) The three advantages for exploitting resources with short term aim are as follows:
   - It immediately fulfils the basic human needs.

- It promotes fast industrilization and development of large number of resources are available for use. **(1½ Mark)**
- Provides comfort to humans.

(ii) Long term perspective in managing our natural resources are always better than that of short-term approach because

The advantages of long-term approach in managing our natural resources are as follows :

(i) Long-term perspective helps in the conservation of natural resources and also protects the environment.

(ii) Long-term perspective for managing our natural resources serves as an integral part of the sustainable development.

(iii) This approach also provide benefits to our future generation by conserving natural resources.

(1½ Mark)

8. A rainbow is a natural spectrum of sunlight in the form of bows appearing in the sky when the sun shines on rain drops. **(1 Mark)**

It is formed by dispersion of sunlight by tiny droplets presents in the atmosphere. Water droplets act as small prisms. They refract and disperse the sunlight, then reflect it internally and finally refract it again when it comes out of the raindrop. **(1 Mark)**

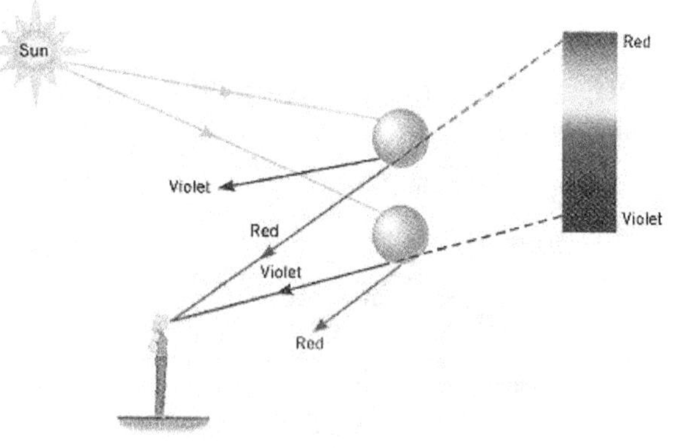

(1 Mark)

Fig. Rainbow formation

9. Nervous system is responsible for passing the sensory information from receptor to effector organ and generate response.

The sensory neurons transmits the sensory information from sensory receptors to spinal cord and brain. The neurons receives the information in the form of nerve impulse & is transmitted to the motor neurons. The motor neuron transmit the information to the effector organs such as muscles and glands.

The nerve impulse stimulates the release or suppression of hormones for the activity of effector organs. So, the secretion of hormone is under the control of nervous system. **(3 Marks)**

Note

Hormones are the chemical substances that are secreted by endocrine glands directly into the bloodstream. They serves as a messenger that controls and coordinate the different functions of the body.

10. When bright light is focussed on our eyes, receptor cell receives the message and pass it to the sensory neurons. They carry the message to the spinal cord which transports the message to brain. The brain reverts back the message by motor neurons which contracts the pupil. **(2 Marks)**

The sequence of events which occur is

Receptor → Sensory neuron → Brain → Motor neuron → Eye → Eye muscle contracts. **(1 Mark)**

11. Photosynthesis is defined as the process of conversion of light energy into chemical energy. In this process, green plants synthesise their own food in the presence of sunlight, carbon dioxide and water. They synthesise their food in the form of glucose and oxygen is released and can be stored in leaves in the form of starch.

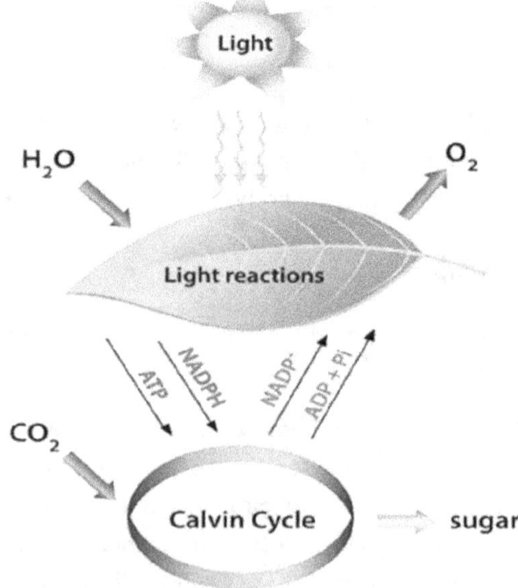

(i) Absorption of light energy by chlorophyll.

(ii) Conversion of light energy to chemical energy and splitting of water molecules into hydrogen and oxygen.

(iii) Reduction of carbon dioxide to carbohydrates.

(3 Marks)

12. Mendel uses pea plant *Pisum sativum* for his experiment. **(1 Mark)**

In F_1 generation, all the progenies obtained are tall as, when he crossed homozygous tall & dwarf pea plants.

Parents	TT	×	tt
	(male tall)		(female dwarf)
Gametes	(T) (T)	×	(t) (t)
F_1 generation	Tt Tt		Tt Tt

All the progenies are tall

- In the F_2 generation, self-crossing is done.

Parents	Tt	×	Tt
	(male)		(female)
Gametes	(T) (t)	×	(T) (t)
F_2 generation	TT Tt		Tt tt

Phenotypic ratio 3:1 (3 tall & 1 dwarf)

Genotypic ratio 1 : 2 : 1 (one pure homozygours tall, two heterozygous tall, one dwarf) **(2 Marks)**

OR

Difference between acquired traits and inherited traits.

Acquired trait	Inherited trait
(i) Acquired traits cannot be passed on from one generation to another generation.	(i) Inherited traits can be passed on from one generation to another generation.
(ii) Acquired traits or characteristics are because of the change in somatic cells.	(ii) Inherited traits or characterstics are because of the change in genes.
e.g. Low in weight due to starvation, if a mouse's tail gets cut, the cut tail is an acquired trait.	e.g. Brown eyes, curly hairs.

(3 Marks)

13. When silver chloride is kept in sunlight in a china dish we observe that white color of silver chloride changes into grey which is due to the formation of silver in solid state. **(1 Mark)**

$$2AgCl(s) \xrightarrow{\text{Sunlight}} 2Ag(s) + Cl_2(g)$$ **(1 Mark)**

The above reaction is a type of decomposition reaction. In this reaction silver chloride decomposes in presence of sunlight into silver and chlorine gas. **(1 Mark)**

Decomposition reaction in presence of light is known as photodecomposition reaction while in presence of heat it is known as thermal decomposition reaction.

OR

(a) displacement reaction **(½ Mark)**

$Zn + 2AgNO_3 \longrightarrow Zn(NO_3)_2 + 2Ag$ **(1 Mark)**

(b) double displacement reaction **(½ Mark)**

$$\underset{\text{Lead nitrate}}{Pb(NO_3)_2\,(aq)} + \underset{\text{Potassium iodide}}{2KI(aq)} \longrightarrow \underset{\text{Lead iodide (Yellow ppt.)}}{PbI_2(s)} + \underset{\text{Potassium nitrate}}{2KNO_3(aq)}$$

(1 Mark)

14. (i) Group valency of first group elements is 1 and oxygen is divalent therefore molecular formula of their oxide should be M_2O. **(1 Mark)**

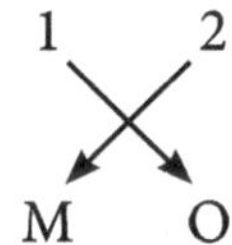

(ii) Group valency of group thirteen element is 3 and chlorine is mono valent therefore molecular formula of their chloride should be MCl_3. **(1 Mark)**

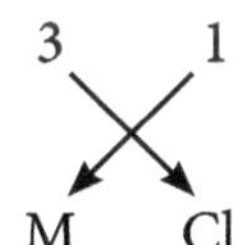

(iii) Element A belongs to group 2 therefore it should be divalent. Element B belongs to group seventeen and it shows valency 1. **(1 Mark)**

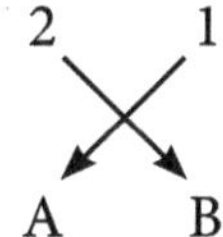

Therefore molecular formula should be AB_2.

15. (a) Sodium chloride is an ionic compound which does not conduct electricity in solid state because in solid state ions are packed in crystal structure. As a result ions are not free in solid state to conduct electricity. Whereas in molten state and in aqueous solution sodium chloride is dissociated as Na^+ and Cl^-. Because of the presence of these ions conduction of electricity become possible in molten state. **(1 Mark)**

(b) Nitric acid is strong oxidizing agent therefore when aluminium is dipped in nitric acid it oxidizes aluminium to aluminium oxide. Formation of passive layer of aluminium oxide decreases the reactivity of aluminium. **(1 Mark)**

(c) Metals like calcium and magnesium are highly reactive metals therefore they never found in free state in nature. They always found in combined state. **(1 Mark)**

Reactive metals occupy top most positions in the reactivity series.

SECTION - D

16. (a) Let there are n resistances, each of value R_1, R_2 ...... R_n respectively, are connected in parallel to a battery of voltage V. The equivalent resistance is defined by

$$R_{eq} = \frac{V}{i}$$

$$\Rightarrow i = \frac{}{eq}$$ **(1 Mark)**

As all the resistors are connected in parallel, So voltage across them is same. The current is divided into $i_1, i_2, i_3, ... i_n$

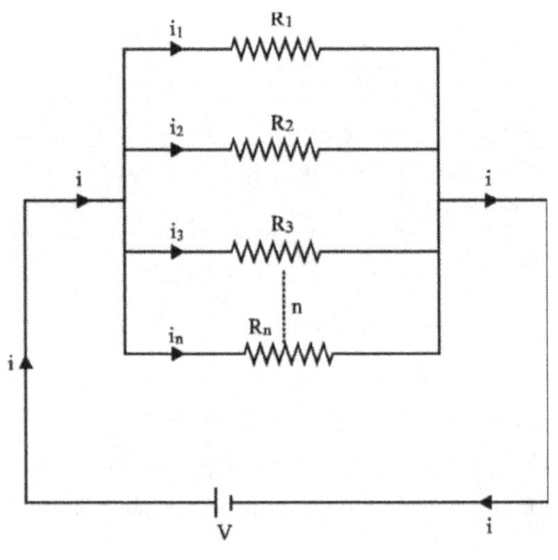

(1 Mark)

Net current, $i = i_1 + i_2 + i_3 + ... + i_n$

$$\frac{V}{R_{eq}} = \frac{V}{R_1} + \frac{V}{R_2} + \frac{V}{R_3} .... + \frac{V}{R_n}$$

$$\Rightarrow \frac{V}{R_{eq}} = V\left(\frac{1}{R_1} + \frac{1}{R_2} + \frac{1}{R_3} + ... \frac{1}{R_n}\right)$$

$$\Rightarrow \frac{1}{R_{eq}} = \frac{1}{R_1} + \frac{1}{R_2} + \frac{1}{R_3} + ... \frac{1}{R_n}$$ **(1 Mark)**

Thus, the reciprocal of the equivalent resistance of a group of resistances joined in parallel is equal to the sum of the reciprocals of the individual resistances.

(b) Given,

Voltage of the battery, V = 6V

Resistance of resistors, R = 12 Ω

Using

$$\frac{1}{R'} = \frac{1}{R} + \frac{1}{R}$$

$$\Rightarrow \frac{1}{R'} = \frac{1}{12} + \frac{1}{12} = \frac{2}{12}$$

$\Rightarrow R' = 6\ \Omega$ **(1 Mark)**

Current drawn from the battery, $I = \frac{V}{R'}$ **(1 Mark)**

$$\Rightarrow I = \frac{6V}{6\Omega} = 1A$$

The equivalent resistance Req in parallel comination is less than each of the resistances.

OR

(a) As electric lamp of resistance 20 Ω and a conductor of resistance 4 Ω are connected in series,

∴ Equivalent resistance, $R = R_1 + R_2$

$\Rightarrow R = 20\ \Omega + 4\ \Omega = 24\ \Omega$ **(1 Mark)**

(b) Voltage of the battery, V = 6V

Current through the circuit, I = — Ω

$$\Rightarrow I = \frac{6V}{24\Omega} = \frac{1}{4}A$$

$\Rightarrow I = 0.25A$ **(1 Mark)**

(c) On applying ohm's law to the electric lamp and resistor separately, we get potential difference across the electric lamp

$V_1 = IR_1$

$\Rightarrow V_1 = 0.25A \times 20\ \Omega = 5V$ **(1 Mark)**

and across the conductor

$V_2 = IR_2 = 0.25A \times 4\,\Omega = 1V$ **(1 Mark)**

(d) Power of the lamp, $P = \frac{V_1^2}{R_1}$

$\Rightarrow P = \frac{(5)^2}{20} = \frac{25}{20}$

$\Rightarrow P = 1.25$ W **(1 Mark)**

17. (a) Right hand thumb rule will be used to find out the direction of magnetic field lines. If we hold the current carrying conductor in the right hand such that the thumb points in the direction of current, then the fingers encircle the wire will be in the direction of magnetic lines of force. **(2 Marks)**

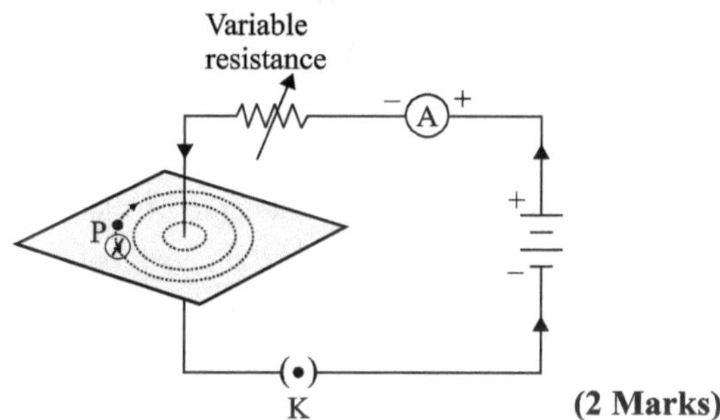

(2 Marks)

(b) The strength of magnetic field decreases when the point where magnetic field is to be determined is moved away from the straight wire carrying constant current. The strength of the magnetic field is inversely proportional to the distance from the origin, So as the distance increases, the magnetic field strength decreases. **(1 Mark)**

18. Given,

Object distance, u = – 60 cm

Focal length of the concave lens, f = – 30 cm

Using lens formula

$$\frac{1}{v} - \frac{1}{u} = \frac{1}{f}$$

$$\Rightarrow \frac{1}{v} - \frac{1}{(-60)} = \frac{1}{(-30)}$$ **(1 Mark)**

$$\Rightarrow \frac{1}{v} = \frac{-1}{30} - \frac{1}{60} = \frac{-3}{60}$$

$\Rightarrow$ v = – 20 cm **(1 Mark)**

Thus, the image will be formed at a distance of 20 cm infront of the lens.

(ii) The characteristics of the image are

(a) Nature of the image is virtual.

(b) Image is erect

(c) Size of the image is diminished

(d) The image is formed at a distance of 20 cm from the optical center of the concave lens on the same side of the object. **(½×4=2 Marks)**

(iii)

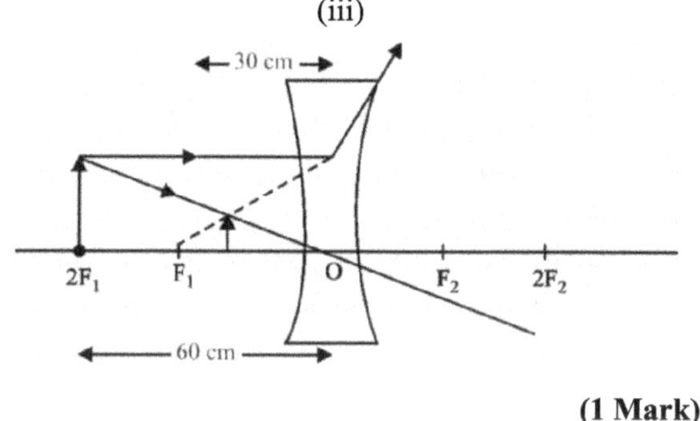

(1 Mark)

Note

For any position of the object, the image formed by a concave lens is always virtual, erect and diminished.

19. Pollination is the transfer of pollen grain from anthers to the stigma of a pistil. **(1 Mark)**

There are two types of pollination such as:-

(i) Self-pollination:- Type of pollination, which involves the transfer of pollen grain from anther to the stigma of same flower.

For e.g. rice, tomatoes, wheat and so on.

(ii) Cross-pollination:- Type of pollination, which involves the transfer of pollen grain from anther to the stigma of different flower.

For e.g. apple, pumpkin, daffodils and so on. **(1 Mark)**

The two agents of pollination are wind and insects.

Pollination by wind is called anemophily. For example: Grasses

Pollination by insects is called entomophily. For example: Rose **(1 Mark)**

During pollination, the compatible pollen grain is landed on the stigma of female flower and forms pollen tube. The pollen tube reaches to the (ovary) egg results in the fertilisation. After fertilisation zygotes is formed which further divides to form embryo within the ovule. The ovule is developed into a tough coat is converted into seed which further forms fruit. **(2 Marks)**

Or

(a) In the given diagram, **(2 Marks)**

1. Fallopian tube
2. Ovary
3. Uterus
4. Cerevix
5. Vagina.

(b) Contraception is defined as the prevention of pregnancy by using artificial methods such as using contraceptive pills, surgical method (tubectomy and vasecotomy).

The three advantages of contraception are as follows:

(i) Contraception helps in the prevention of unwanted pregnancies.

(ii) It controls the birth rate & maintains the population size.

(iii) It prevents the transmission of sexually transmitted diseases. **(3 Marks)**

20. Ethyl alcohol is the active ingredient of all alcoholic drinks. **(1 Mark)**

Chemical formula: CH_3CH_2OH

Uses: 1. Ethyl alcohol is used in medicines,cough syrups and tonics.

2. It is used in the manufacture of varnishes and perfumes. **(2 Marks)**

(i) When ethyl alcohol react with sodium metal sodium ethanoate and hydrogen gas are produced.

$2C_2H_5OH + 2\,Na \longrightarrow \underset{\text{Sodium ethanate}}{2\,C_2H_5ONa} + H_2$ **(1Mark)**

(ii) ethyl alcohol react with concentrated sulphuric acid to form ethene.

$CH_3CH_2OH \xrightarrow[443\,K]{H_2SO_4} \underset{\text{Ethane}}{CH_2 = CH_2} + H_2O$ **(1 Mark)**

Or

Methane is the first member of alkane homologus series with general formula C_nH_{2n+2}. When n = 1, the formula become CH_4 which is the molecular formula of methane. Carbon atom form four covalent bond with four hydrogen atoms by sharing of one electron each. **(2 Marks)**

Electron dot structure: **(1 Mark)**

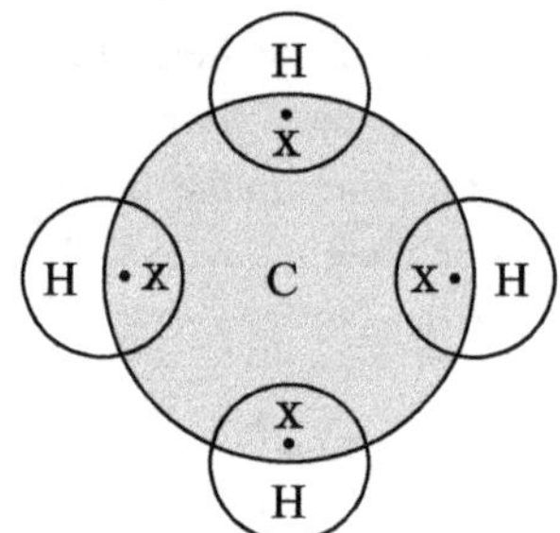

(i) Methane is poor conductor of electricity because all the four C-H bonds are covalent bond therefore electrons are not free for conduction. It makes methane a poor conductor of electricity. **(1 Mark)**

(ii) Methane molecule has four covalent bonds which are weaker than ionic bonds. Therefore it has low melting and boiling point. **(1 Mark)**

when methane reacts with oxygen :

$CH_4 + 2O_2 \longrightarrow CO_2 + 2H_2O$

21. The main difference between acid and base is that acids give hydrogen ions in aqueous solution while bases give hydroxyl ions in aqueous solution. When acid and base react together it results into the formation of salt and water, the reaction is known as neutralization reaction. **(2 Marks)**

$\underset{\text{Acid}}{HCl} + \underset{\text{Base}}{NH_4OH} \longrightarrow \underset{\text{Salt}}{NH_4Cl} + \underset{\text{Water}}{H_2O}$

(i) Formation of acidic salt **(1 Mark)**

$HCl + NH_4OH \longrightarrow NH_4Cl + H_2O$

When strong acid reacts with weak base it results into the formation of acidic salt. For example hydrochloric acid is strong acid and it react with ammonium hydroxide (weak base) to form ammonium chloride which is a acidic salt.

(ii) Formation of basic salt **(1 Mark)**

$CH_3COOH + NaOH \longrightarrow CH_3COONa + H_2O$

When weak acid reacts with strong base it results into the formation of basic salt. For example acetic acid (weak acid) reacts with sodium hydroxide (strong base) to form sodium acetate which is a basic salt.

(iii) Formation of neutral salt **(1 Mark)**

$CH_3COOH + NH_4OH \longrightarrow CH_3COONH_4 + H_2O$

When weak acid reacts with weak base or strong acid react with strong base it results into the formation of neutral salt. For example when acetic acid (weak acid) react with ammonium hydroxide (weak base) it form ammonium acetate which is a neutral salt.

SECTION - E

22. In this experiment, CO_2 is given out during respiration KOH (Pottassium hydroxide) solutions or pellets are taken in a test tube & placed in a conical flask. KOH absorbs CO_2 and prevents it from being utilized by the plant for the process of photosynthesis. **(2 Marks)**

23. **Diagrammatic representation of the structure of stomata under the microscope.** **(2 Marks)**

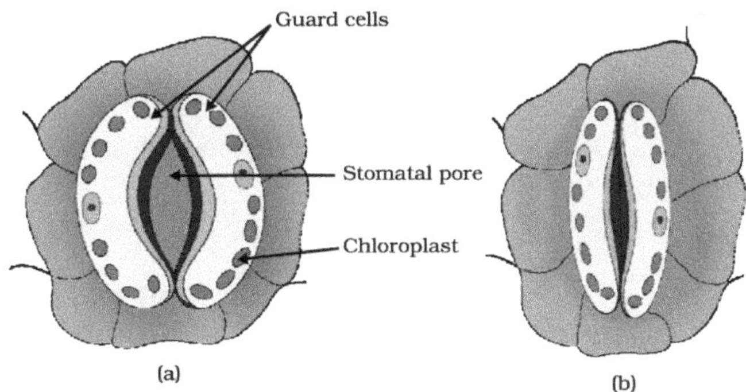

Fig. (a) Open and (b) Closed stomatal pore

Stomata in leaves of the plants are small openings that are responsible for gaseous exchange in leaves for photosynthesis. (CO_2 & O_2)

Or

Diagrammatic representation of the sequence of budding in *Hydra*.

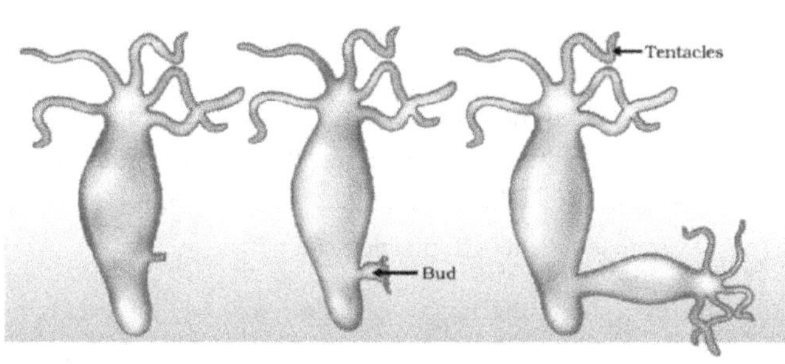

(2 Marks)

Budding is a type of asexual reproduction in which a new organism is formed from an outgrowth or bud produced by parent cell.

24. Following are the precautions while determining the focal length of a convex lens.

(a) Lens should be fix vertically in the lens holder.

(b) The image of the distant object should be well defined and sharp.

(c) The base of the lens and white screen should be in a line with the measuring scale.

(d) There should not be any obstacle in the path of convex lens. **(½×4=2 Marks)**

25. The straight line obtained verifies Ohm's law.

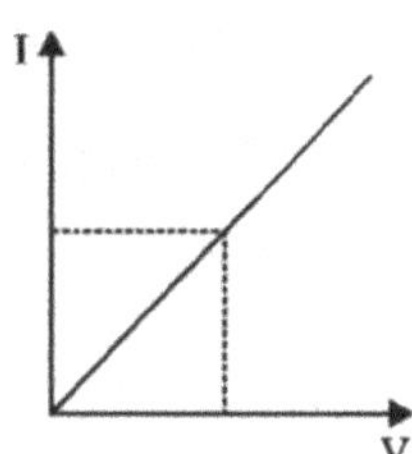

$$\text{Slope of the graph} = \frac{\Delta I}{\Delta V} = \frac{1}{R}$$

$$\Rightarrow R = \frac{1}{\text{Slope of the graph}} = \frac{\Delta V}{\Delta I}$$

In this way, resistance can be determined. **(2 Marks)**

For Ohm's law to be valid, physical conditions of the conductor like temperature, pressure, etc. should remain same.

Or

This is called the zero error of the scale of voltmeter or ammeter. If there is a zero error, then error is subtracted from the value which obtained when the circuit is closed. Otherwise he/she will not get true

26. In test tube A the length of lather will be longest with soap solution. Distill water does not contain salts of calcium and magnesium which causes hardness of water. Test tube B and C contain calcium sulphate therefore soap solution is unable to form lather in test tube B and C as calcium and magnesium sulphate cause permanent hardness in water. **(2 Marks)**

27. Colour change is observed in test tube A as it contain acid. Acid turn blue litmus solution to red. **(2 Marks)**

Or

When hydrochloric acid react with sodium carbonate it results into the formation of sodium chloride salt and water with the evolution of carbondioxide gas.

$$Na_2CO_3 + 2HCl \longrightarrow 2NaCl + CO_2 + H_2O$$

(2 Marks)

All India 2018

CBSE Board Solved Paper

Time Allowed : 3 Hours *Maximum Marks : 80*

General Instructions:

Read the following instructions very carefully and strictly follow them :

(i) The question paper comprises **two** sections, A and B. You are to attempt both the sections.

(ii) All questions are **compulsory**.

(iii) All questions of Section-A and B are to be attempted separately.

(iv) There is an internal choice in three questions of **three** marks each, two questions of **five** marks each in section A and in one question of **two** marks in section B.

(v) Question numbers **1** and **2** in Section-A are **one** mark question. They are to be answered in **one** word or in one sentence.

(vi) Question numbers **3** to **5** in Section- A are **two** marks questions. These are to be answered in **30** words each.

(vii) Question numbers **6** to **15** in Section-A are **three** marks questions. These are to be answered in about **50** words each.

(viii) Question numbers **16** to **21** in Section-A are **five** marks questions. These are to be answered in **70** words each.

(ix) Question numbers **22** to **27** in Section- B are based on practical skills. Each question is a **two** marks question. These are to be answered in brief.

SECTION - A

1. Write the energy conversion that takes place in a hydropower plant.

2. A Mendelian experiment consisted of breeding pea plants bearing violet flowers with pea plants bearing white flowers. What will be the result in F_1 progeny?

3. (a) Name one gustatory receptor and one olfactory receptor present in human beings.

(b) Write a and b in the given flow chart of neuron through which information travels as an electrical impulse.

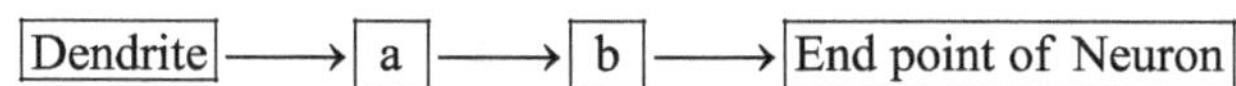

4. If the image formed by a spherical mirror for all positions of the object placed in front of it is always erect and diminished, what type of mirror is it? Draw a labelled ray diagram to support your answer.

5. A compound 'X' on heating with excess conc. sulphuric acid at 443 K gives an unsaturated compound 'Y'. 'X' also reacts with sodium metal to evolve a colourless gas 'Z'. Identify 'X', 'Y' and 'Z'. Write the equation of the chemical reaction of formation of 'Y' and also write the role of sulphuric acid in the reaction.

6. State the laws of refraction of light. Explain the term 'absolute refractive index of a medium' and write an expression to relate it with the speed of light in vacuum.

OR

What is meant by power of a lens? Write its SI unit. A student uses a lens of focal length 40 cm and another of –20 cm. Write the nature and power of each lens.

7. Write one main difference between asexual and sexual mode of reproduction. Which species is likely to have comparatively better chance of survial – the one reproducing asexually or the one reproducing sexually? Give reason to justify your answer.

8. Show how would you join three resistors, each of resistance 9 Ω so that the equivalent resistance of the combination is

(i) 13.5 Ω,

(ii) 6 Ω?

OR

(a) Write Joule's law of heating.

(b) Two lamps, one rated 100 W; 220 V, and the other 60 W; 220 V, are connected in parallel to electric mains supply. Find the current drawn by two bulbs from the line, if the supply voltage is 220V.

9. Name the hormones secreted by the following endocrine glands and specify one function of each :

(a) Thyroid

(b) Pituitary

(c) Pancreas

10. 2 mL of sodium hydroxide solution is added to a few pieces of granulated zinc metal taken in a test tube. When the contents are warmed, a gas evolves which is bubbled through a soap solution before testing. Write the equation of the chemical reaction involved and the test to detect the gas. Name the gas which will be evolved when the same metal reacts with dilute solution of a strong acid.

OR

The pH of a salt used to make tasty and crispy pakoras is 14. Identify the salt and write a chemical equation for its formation. List its two uses.

11. (a) Why are most carbon compounds poor conductors of electricity?

(b) Write the name and structure of a saturated compound in which the carbon atoms are arranged in a ring. Give the number of single bonds present in this compound.

12. Decomposition reactions require energy either in the form of heat or light or electricity for breaking down the reactants. Write one equation each for decomposition reactions where energy is supplied in the form of heat, light and electricity.

13. What is a dam? Why do we seek to build large dams? While building large dams, which three main problem should particularly be addressed to maintain peace among local people? Mention them.

14. Student in a school listened to the news read in the morning assembly that the mountain of garbage in Delhi, suddenly exploded and various vehicles got buried under it. Several people were also injured and there was traffic jam all around. In the brain storming session the teacher also discussed this issue and asked the students to find out a solution to the problem of garbage. Finally they arrived at two main points – one is self management of the garbage we produce and the second is to generate less garbage at individual level.

(a) Suggest two measures to manage the garbage we produce.

(b) As an individual, what can we do to generate the least garbage? Give two points.

(c) List two values the teacher instilled in his students in this episode.

15. (a) List the factors on which the resistance of a conductor in the shape of a wire depends.

(b) Why are metals good conductors of electricity whereas glass is a bad conductor of electricity? Give reason.

(c) Why are alloys commonly used in electrical heating devices? Give reason.

16. (a) State Fleming's left hand rule.

(b) Write the principle of working of an electric motor.

(c) Explain the function of the following parts of an electric motor.

(i) Armature

(ii) Brushes

(iii) Split ring

17. (a) Write the function of following parts in human female reproductive system :

(i) Ovary

(ii) Oviduct

(iii) Uterus

(b) Describe in brief the structure and function of placenta.

18. (a) Write the steps involved in the extraction of pure metals in the middle of the activity series from their carbonate ores.

(b) How is copper extracted from its sulphide ore? Explain the various steps supported by chemical equations.

(c) Draw labelled diagram for the electrolytic refining of copper.

19. (a) Mention any two components of blood.

(b) Trace the movement of oxygenated blood in the body.

(c) Write the functions of valves present in between atria and ventricles.

(d) Write one structural difference between the composition of artery and veins.

OR

(a) Define excretion.

(b) Name the basic filtration unit present in the kidney.

(c) Draw excretory system in human beings and label the following organs of excretory system which perform following functions :

(i) form urine.

(ii) is a long tube which collects urine from kidney.

(iii) store urine until it is passed out.

20. (a) The modern periodic table has been evolved through the early attempts of Dobereiner, Newland and Mendeleev. List one advantage and one limitation of all the three attempts.

(b) Name the scientists who first of all showed that atomic number of an element is a more fundamental property than its atomic mass.

(c) State Modern periodic law.

21. (a) A student is unable to see clearly the words written on the blackboard placed at a distance of approximately 3 m from him. Name the defect of vision the boy is suffering from. State the possible causes of this defect and explain the method of correcting it.

(b) Why do stars twinkle? Explain.

OR

(a) Write the function of each of the following parts of human eye :

(i) Cornea

(ii) Iris

(iii) Crystalline lens

(iv) Ciliary muscles

(b) Why does the sun appear reddish early in the morning? Will this phenomenon be observed by an astronaut on the Moon? Give reason to justify your answer.

SECTION - B

22. Name the process by which an *Amoeba* reproduces. Draw the various stages of its reproduction in a proper sequence.

OR

A student is viewing under a microscope a permanent slide showing various stages of asexual reproduction by budding in *Yeast*. Draw diagrams of what he observes (in proper sequence).

23. An object of height 4.0 cm is placed at a distance of 30 cm from the optical centre 'O' of a convex lens of focal length 20 cm. Draw a ray diagram to find the position and size of the image formed. Mark optical centre 'O' and principal focus 'F' on the diagram. Also find the approximate ratio of size of the image to the size of the object.

24. A student added few pieces of aluminium metal to two test tubes A and B containing aqueous solutions of iron sulphate and copper sulphate. In the second part of her experiment, she added iron metal to another test tubes C and D containing aqueous solution of aluminium sulphate and copper sulphate.

In which test tube or test tubes will she observe colour change? On the basis of this experiment, state which one is the most reactive metal and why?

25. What is observed when a solution of sodium sulphate is added to a solution of barium chloride taken in a test tube? Write equation for the chemical reaction involved and name the type of reaction in this case.

26. The value of current (I) flowing through a given resistor of resistance (R), for the corresponding values of potential difference (V) across the resistor are as given below :

V (Volts)	0.5	1.0	1.5	2.0	2.5	3.0	4.0	5.0
I (amperes)	0.1	0.2	0.3	0.4	0.5	0.6	0.8	1.0

Plot a graph between current (I) and potential difference (V) and determine the resistance (R) of the resistor.

27. List the steps of preparation of temporary mount of a leaf peel to observe stomata.

Solutions

1. In hydropower plant, kinetic, potential, mechanical energy of water converts into electrical energy. **(1 Mark)**

2. Genetic cross:-

Parents WW (Violet) × ww(white)

gametes W W w w

F_1 generation

	W	W
w	Ww	Ww
w	Ww	Ww

All the progeny obtained in F_1 generation are violet as violet flower is dominant over white flower. **(1 Mark)**

3. (a) Olfactory receptors are responsible for smell and are present in nose. Gustatory receptors provide the sense of taste and are present in tongue.

(b) a-Cellbody; b-Axon. The information travels as an electrical impulse from the dendrite to the cell body and then along the axon to its end. **(2 Marks)**

4. Convex mirror. It forms an image smaller than that of the object. **(1 Mark)**

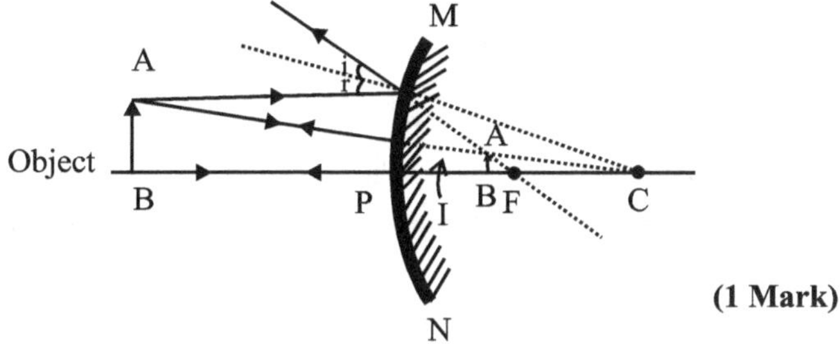

(1 Mark)

5. $CH_3CH_2OH + H_2SO_4(conc.) \xrightarrow{443\ K} CH_2 = CH_2 + H_2O$

'X' 'Y'

(½ + ½ Mark)

$2CH_3CH_2OH + 2Na \longrightarrow 2CH_3CH_2ONa + H_2$

'Z'

(½ Mark)

Role of sulphuric acid (H_2SO_4): acts as a dehydrating agent. **(½ Mark)**

Dehydrating agents are the chemical compound which abstract the water molecules from the reactant during the chemical reactions. Examples are conc. sulphuric acid, concentrated phosphoric acid, hot aluminium oxide.

6. **Laws of refraction of light:**

(i) The incident ray, the refracted ray and the normal at the point of incidence all lies in the same plane for the two given mediums.

(ii) The ratio of sine of angle of incidence (*i.e.*, sin *i*) to the sine of angle of refraction (*i.e.*, sin *r*) is always constant for the light of given colour and for the given pair of media.

Mathematically, $\frac{\sin i}{\sin r} = \text{constant} = n$

(2 × 1 = 2 Marks)

The constant '*n*' is called refractive index of the second medium with respect to the first medium.

Absolute refractive index of a medium is defined as the ratio of the velocity of light in a vacuum to the velocity of light in the medium.

Absolute refractive index of the medium is given by

$$n = \frac{\text{Speed of light in vacuum (c)}}{\text{Speed of light in medium } (v)}$$ **(1 Mark)**

Refractive index of a medium is that characteristic which decides speed of light in it. It is a scalar, unitless and dimensionless quantity.

OR

The power of a lens is defined as the reciprocal of its focal length (f) expressed in metres. SI unit of power is dioptre. **(1 Mark)**

Focal length of lens is positive 40 cm hence lens is convex and the lens of focal length negative 20cm is concave lens. **(1 Mark)**

Power of lens of focal length (f = 40 cm)

$$= \frac{1}{\frac{40}{100}} = 2.5 \text{ dioptre}$$ **(½ Mark)**

Power of lens of focal length (f = – 20cm)

$$= \frac{1}{\frac{-20}{100}} = -5 \text{ dioptre}$$ **(½ Mark)**

7. The difference between asexual and sexual reproduction is that in asexual reproduction only one parent is involved, whereas in the sexual mode of reproduction two parents are involved.

The organism reproducing sexually have a better chances of survival than asexually because it incorporates variations and promote diversity of characters in an offspring due to combinations of genes and thus the offspring are better adapted to the environment and they survive for a longer period of time. **(3 Marks)**

Note

The process of asexual reproduction involves fusion of male gametes haploid) with female gamete (haploid) results in the formation of zygote (diploid).

8. (i) For getting a resistance of 13.5 Ω, the two resistors should be connected in parallel and one in series with them.

The equivalent resistance of the two resistors in parallel, R_p is given by

$$\frac{1}{R_p} = \frac{1}{9} + \frac{1}{9} = \frac{2}{9} \Rightarrow R_p = 4.5\,\Omega$$ **(½ Mark)**

Now, the equivalent resistance of R_p and 9 Ω in series is given by

(½ Mark)

$R = R_p + 9 = 4.5 + 9 = 13.5\,\Omega.$ **(½ Mark)**

(ii) To get a resistance of 6 Ω, two resistors should be connected in series and one in parallel to them.

The equivalent resistance of the two resistors in series is given by

$$R_s = 9\,\Omega + 9\,\Omega = 18\,\Omega$$ **(½ Mark)**

Now, the equivalent resistance of R_s and 9 Ω in parallel is given by

(½ Mark)

$$\frac{1}{R} = \frac{1}{R_s} + \frac{1}{9}$$

$$= \frac{1}{18} + \frac{1}{9}$$

$$= \frac{1+2}{18} = \frac{3}{18} = \frac{1}{6}$$ **(½ Mark)**

$R = 6\Omega$

Note

Decoration of lights in festivals is an example of series grouping whereas all household appliances are connected in parallel grouping.

OR

(a) **Joule's Law of Heating:** It states that the amount of heat produced in a conductor is

directly proportional to the square of current passing through it, i.e., $H \propto I^2$ .... (i)

directly proportional to the resistance of conductor, i.e., $H \propto R$ .... (ii)

directly proportional to the time for which current passed, i.e., $H \propto t$ .... (iii)

Combining (i), (ii) and (iii). $H \propto I^2 Rt$.

Here, constant of proportionality is 1.

$\therefore\; H = I^2Rt$ joule **(1½ Marks)**

(b) We know that, P = VI

$$\Rightarrow I = \frac{P}{V}$$ **(½ Mark)**

Hence, current in I lamp = $I_1 = \frac{P_1}{V} = \frac{100}{220} = 0.45A$

(½ Mark)

Similarly, current in II lamp = $I_2 = \frac{P_2}{V} = \frac{60}{220} = 0.27A$

(½ Mark)

9. (a) Thyroid gland secretes thyroxin hormone which regulates carbohydrate, protein and fat metabolism so as to provide the proper balance for growth development of the body such as our breathing, heart rate, temperature, etc.

(b) Pituitary gland secretes growth hormone. It regulates growth and development of body. Hyper-secretion may cause gigantism and hypo-secretion may cause dwarfism

(c) Pancreas secretes insulin. It helps in regulating blood sugar level in body. **(3 Marks)**

Note

(a) Iodine is an important element which is required for the synthesis of thyroxin hormone deficiency of iodine in the diet leads to cause goitre.

(c) Pancreas also secrete glucogon hormone from the alpha cells of the pancreas. This hormone increase the blood sugar level.

10. Reaction involved is

$$2NaOH + Zn \xrightarrow{\Delta} Na_2ZnO_2 + H_2$$ **(1 Mark)**

Hydrogen can be tested by bringing burning matchstick. It burns with pop sound. **(1 Mark)**

$$2HCl\,(dil.) + Zn \longrightarrow ZnCl_2 + H_2$$ **(1 Mark)**

Note

Hydrogen gas is not evolved when a metal reacts with nitric acid because nitric acid is a strong oxidising agent. It oxidized H_2 to produce water and itself get reduced to any of the nitrogen oxides. But Mg and Mn react with very dil. HNO_3 to evolve H_2 gas.

OR

The salt used to make crispy pakoras is $NaHCO_3$.

(1 Mark)

Preparation:

$$NaCl + H_2O + CO_2 + NH_3 \longrightarrow NH_4Cl + NaHCO_3$$

(1 Mark)

Uses: $NaHCO_3$ is used

(1) for making baking powder

(2) in antacids **(1 Mark)**

11. (a) Carbon compounds are poor conductors of electricity because most of the carbon compounds are covalent. **(1 Mark)**

(b) Cyclohexane

(1 Mark)

Number of single bonds are 18. **(1 Mark)**

Note

Generally carbon compounds are poor conductor of electricity because they are covalent compounds. Electrons are not free for conduction of electricity in the covalent compound. Exception is graphite which is an allotrope of carbon. Graphite is also a covalent compound but it is a good conductor of electricity. Presence of free electron in graphite impart conduction of electricity in graphite.

12. (1) $\underset{\text{Ferroussulphate}}{2FeSO_4(s)} \xrightarrow{\text{Heat}} \underset{\text{Ferricoxide}}{Fe_2O_3(s)} + SO_2(g) + SO_3(g)$

(1 Mark)

(2) $2AgCl(s) \xrightarrow{\text{Sunlight}} 2Ag(s) + Cl_2(g)$ **(1 Mark)**

(3) $2H_2O(l) \xrightarrow{\text{electricity}} 2H_2(g) + O_2(g)$ **(1 Mark)**

13. A dam is built to control water through placement of a blockage of earth, rock and/or concrete across a stream or river. Large dams can ensure the storage of adequate water not just for irrigation, but also for generating electricity. Criticisms about large dams address three problems in particular are: **(1 ½ Mark)**

(i) **Social problems** because they displace large number of peasants and tribals without adequate compensation or rehabilitation.

(ii) **Economic problems** because they swallow up huge amounts of public money without the generation of proportionate benefits.

(iii) **Environmental problems** because they contribute enormously to deforestation and the loss of biological diversity. **(½ × 3 = 1½ Marks)**

14. (a) It can be used to landfill and some garbage can be used for making fertilizers and manure. **(1 Mark)**

(b) To generate least garbage we should simply use things again and again (i.e. reuse strategy). For e.g. instead of throwing away used envelopes, we can reverse it and use it again. The bottles in which we buy various food-items like jam or pickle can be used for storing things in the kitchen. In addition, we should reduce the use of non-biodegradable substances like polythene etc. **(1 Mark)**

(c) Two values the teacher instilled in his students are: Concern for community health, personal health and awareness about environment. **(1 Mark)**

15. (a) Resistance of a conductor depends upon

(i) nature of material (resistivity ρ)

(ii) length of wire (l) i.e., $R \propto l$

(iii) area of cross section of wire (A) i.e., $R \propto \frac{1}{A}$

(1 Mark)

(b) Metals are good conductors of electricity as there are free electrons to conduct whereas there are no free electrons in glass hence bad conductor of electricity. **(1 Mark)**

(c) Alloys have high resistivity in comparison to pure metals. Also alloys do not oxidise readily at high temperatures but pure metals do. Therefore, alloys are used for making coils of electric heating devices rather than a pure metal. **(1 Mark)**

16. (a) **Fleming's left-hand rule :** It states that if thumb, forefinger, and middle finger of left hand are stretched in such a way that they are mutually perpendicular to each other, and if the forefinger points in the direction of magnetic field and the middle finger points in the direction of current, then the thumb will point in the direction of motion or the force acting on the conductor. **(1 Mark)**

(b) An electric motor works on the principle that when a rectangular coil is placed in a magnetic field and a current is passed through it, a force acts on the coil which rotates it continuously. **(1 Mark)**

(c) Function of parts of an electric motor :

(i) Armature:- Armature refers to rotating coils which enhances the power of the motor.

(ii) Brushes:- Brushes allow the easy conduction of charge between coil and external circuit.

(iii) Split ring:- In electric motor, split ring acts as commutator i.e., it reverses the direction of flow of current through a circuit. **(1 × 3 = 3 Marks)**

Note

Fleming's left hand rule is also used to find the direction of force on charged particle.

Here, first finger (indicates) → Direction of magnetic field

Middle finger → Direction of motion of positive charge

Thumb → Direction of force

17. (a)

(i) The ovaries have two main reproductive functions in the body. They produce oocytes (eggs) for fertilization and they produce the reproductive hormones, oestrogen and progesterone.

(ii) Oviduct (fallopian tube) helps in transport of ova from ovary to the uterus and providing the necessary environment for fertilization and for initial development of the fertilized egg or zygote.

(iii) The uterus plays on essential role in human reproduction as it is a site where implantation takes place and also provides nourishment to the fertilized ovum. It also provides mechanical protection to help prevent damage to the fetus. **(3 Marks)**

Uterus helps in pushing out the baby during birth (parturition) through muscle contraction.

(b) The embryo gets nutrition from the mother's blood with the help of a special tissue called placenta. This is a disc which is embedded in the uterine wall. It contains villi on the embryo's side of the tissue. On the mother's side are blood spaces, which surround the villi. This provides a large surface area for glucose and oxygen to pass from the mother to the embryo. The developing embryo will also generate waste substances which can be removed by transferring them into the mother's blood through the placenta. The development of the child inside the mother's body takes approximately nine months. **(2 Marks)**

Placenta also acts as an endocrine tissue produces pregnancy hormones.

18. (a)

Ores → Concentraction of Ore → Metals of medium reactivity →

→ Carbonate Ore → Calcination

→ Sulphide Ore → Roasting

→ Oxides of metals → Reduction of metals oxides → Purification of metal

(1 ½ Marks)

(b) Copper is found as Cu_2S in nature and can be obtained from its ore just by heating in air.

Step - 1 is the heating of sulphide ore of copper in the presence of excess of air. This process in known as roasting.

$$2Cu_2S + 3O_2(g) \xrightarrow{\Delta} 2Cu_2O(s) + 2SO_2(g)$$

Step - 2 is the self reduction of copper.

$$2Cu_2O + Cu_2S \xrightarrow{\Delta} 6Cu(s) + SO_2(g)$$ **(2 Marks)**

(c) **(1 ½ Mark)**

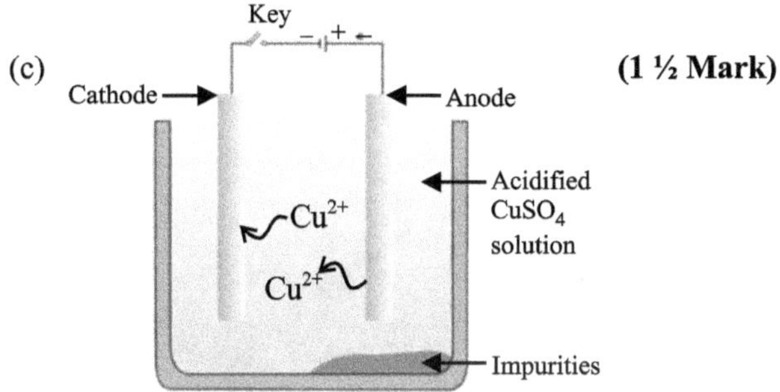

19. (a) Blood consists of a fluid medium called plasma in which the cells (R.B.C, W.B.C and platelets) are suspended. **(1 Mark)**

(b) Oxygenated-blood comes from the lungs to the thin-walled upper chamber of the heart on the left, called left atrium. Then, the left atrium through pulmonary vein left atrium pumps blood into the left ventricle though mitral valve left ventricle pumps oxygenated blood to different parts of the body though aorta. **(2 Marks)**

Aorta is the largest artery in the human body and valves prevent the backward flow of blood during atrial and or ventricular contraction.

(1) (c) Valves ensure that blood does not flow backwards when the atria or ventricles contract. **(1 Mark)**

(2) It regulates the blood pressure.

(d) Arteries have thick, elastic, muscular walls whereas veins have thin walls with few elastic fibers. Arteries do not need valves as the blood is flowing at such a high pressure that it cannot go backwards. **(1 Mark)**

OR

(a) The biological process involved in the removal of harmful metabolic wastes from the body is called excretion. **(1 Mark)**

(b) Nephron is the basic filtration unit present in the kidney. **(1 Mark)**

Diagrammatic representation of excretory system in human being.

(c)

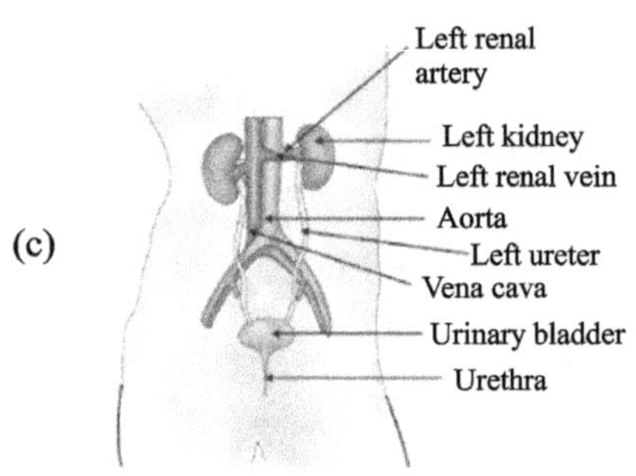

(i) Kidney

(ii) Ureter

(iii) Bladder **(3 Marks)**

20. (a) **Dobereiner** :

Advantage : He gave idea of classification of elements in order of increasing atomic masses in the form of triads. **(½ Mark)**

Disadvantage : He could arrange only a few elements in triads. **(½ Mark)**

Newland :

Advantage : He arranged known elements in order of increasing atomic mass and encouraged other chemist to correlate the properties of elements with their atomic masses. **(½ Mark)**

Disadvantage : Newland could arrange elements only upto calcium. **(½ Mark)**

Mendeleev:

Advantage : Mendeleev's periodic table had some blank spaces in it. These vacant spaces were for elements that were yet to be discovered. **(½ Mark)**

Disadvantage : Atomic masses irregularly arranged **(½ Mark)**

(b) Henry Moseley **(1 Mark)**

(c) The properties of the elements are periodic functions of their atomic numbers. **(1 Mark)**

21. (a) **Myopia or short-sightedness:** Myopia is inability of an eye in viewing long distance objects. The image in this case falls before the retina due to long size of eyeball or eye lens is too spherical. For every myopic eye, there exists a far point beyond which clear image cannot be seen. **(1 Mark)**

The short-sightedness is corrected by using a concave lens which diverges and shifts the image to the retina. **(1 Mark)**

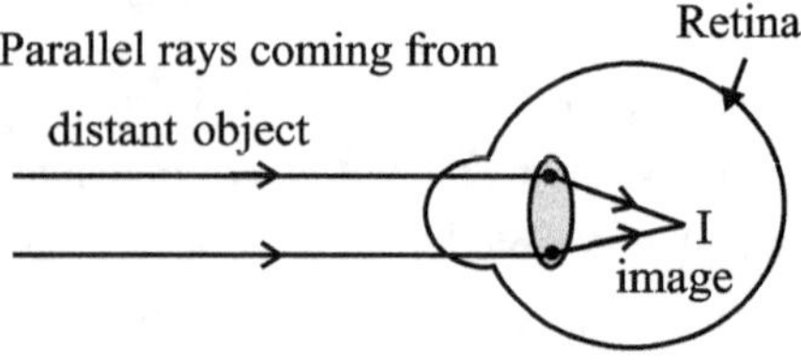

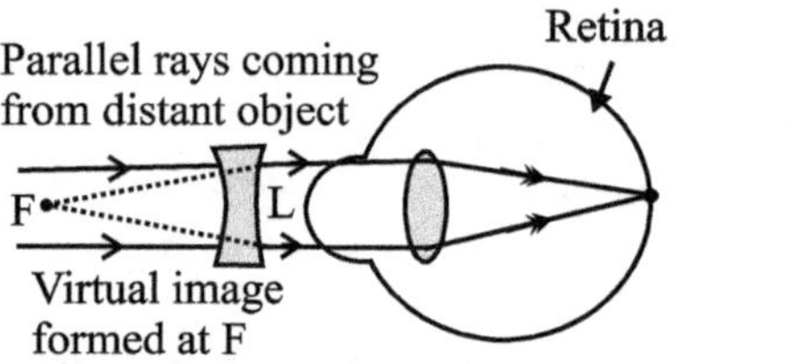

(1 Mark)

Note

If defected far point is at a distance d from eye then focal length of used lens f = –d = –(defected far point)

A person can see upto distance x, wants to see distance y so focal length of lens, $f = \frac{xy}{x-y}$

Power of the lens, $P = \frac{x-y}{xy}$

(b) Stars twinkle when we see them from the Earth's surface because we are viewing them through thick layers of turbulent (moving) air in the Earth's atmosphere. Stars (except the Sun) appear as tiny dots in the sky; as their light travels through the many layers of the Earth's atmosphere, the light of the star is bent (refracted) many times and in random directions (light is bent when it hits a change in density like a pocket of cold air or hot air). This random refraction or atmospheric refraction results in the twinkling of star. **(2 Marks)**

OR

(a) (i) **Cornea** – Refracts the rays of light falling on the eye.

(ii) **Iris** – Controls the size of the pupil.

(iii) **Crystalline lens** – Focuses the image of the object on the retina.

(iv) **Ciliary muscles** – Holds the eye lens and adjusts its focal length. **(½ × 4 = 2 Marks)**

(b) In the morning, the sun lies close to the horizon and hence, light has to travel longer distance. Blue light have shorter wavelength, so, it scatters more. Therefore the red light which have longer wavelength reaches upto the eye of observer and the sun appears reddish. **(2 Marks)**

This phenomenon is not observed by astronaut on the moon as there is no atmosphere. **(1 Mark)**

SECTION - B

22. *Amoeba* reproduce by the process of binary fission. Binary fission is a type of asexual reproductions in which a cell divides into two halves and each rapidly grows into an adult for e.g. *Paramecium*. **(2 Marks)**

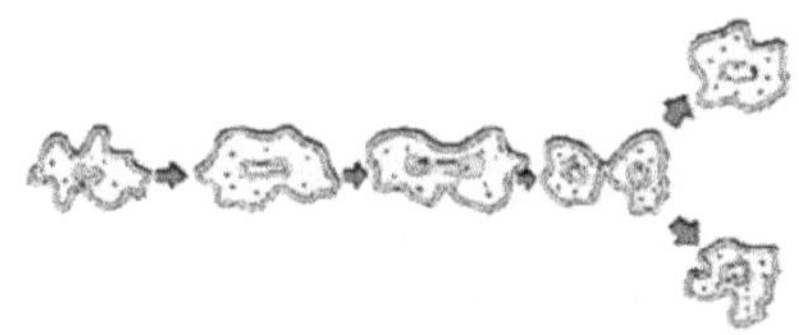

Fig. Binary fission in *Amoeba*

A type of reproduction in which offsprings are produced by a single parent with or without the involvement of gamete formation on and is called asexual reproduction.

OR

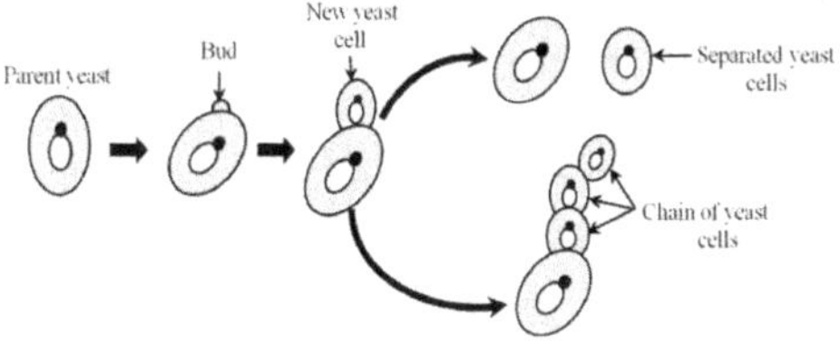

Fig. Budding in *Yeast* **(2 Marks)**

In yeast, the division is unequal and small buds are produced that remain attached initially to the parent cell which eventually gets separated and mature into new Yeast organisms (cells). This process is called budding.

23. Ray diagram to find the position and size of the image formed.

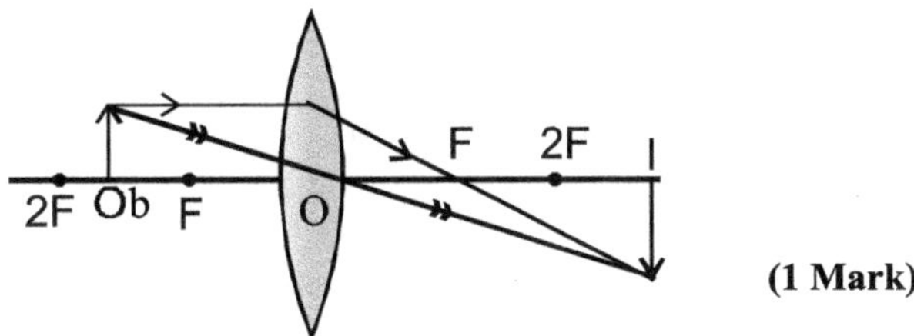

(1 Mark)

Here, focal length, f = 20 cm, u = –30cm, h_0= 4cm

Using, lens formula, $\frac{1}{f} = \frac{1}{v} - \frac{1}{u}$

$$\Rightarrow \frac{1}{20} = \frac{1}{v} - \frac{1}{(-30)}$$

$$\Rightarrow \frac{1}{v} = \frac{1}{20} - \frac{1}{30}$$

∴ Image distance, v = 60cm **(½ Mark)**

The image formed is real and inverted.

The ratio of size of the image to the size of the object

$$\frac{h_1}{h_0} = \frac{v}{u} = \frac{60}{30} = 2:1$$ **(½ Mark)**

24. A - $FeSO_4$ C - $Al_2(SO_4)_3$

B - $CuSO_4$ D - $CuSO_4$

(A) $\underset{\text{Green}}{3FeSO_4} + 2Al \longrightarrow \underset{\text{White}}{Al_2(SO_4)_3} + 3Fe$

(B) $\underset{\text{Blue}}{3CuSO_4} + 2Al \longrightarrow \underset{\text{White}}{Al_2(SO_4)_3} + Cu$

(C) $\underset{\text{White}}{Al_2(SO_4)_3} + Fe \longrightarrow$ No reaction

(D) $\underset{\text{Blue}}{CuSO_4} + Fe \longrightarrow \underset{\text{Green}}{FeSO_4} + Cu$

Color change occurs in test tube A, B and D, no color change will be observed in test tube (C) becauase there is no reaction.

Al is most reactive because it displaces copper, zinc and iron from their sulphate salts. **(2 Marks)**

25. When a solution of sodium sulphate is added to a solution of barium chloride a white insoluble substance is formed.

$$Na_2SO_4(aq) + BaCl_2(aq) \longrightarrow \underset{\text{white ppt.}}{BaSO_4(s)\downarrow} + 2NaCl(aq)$$

This is a double displacement reaction. **(2 Marks)**

26. Graph between current (I) and potential difference (V)

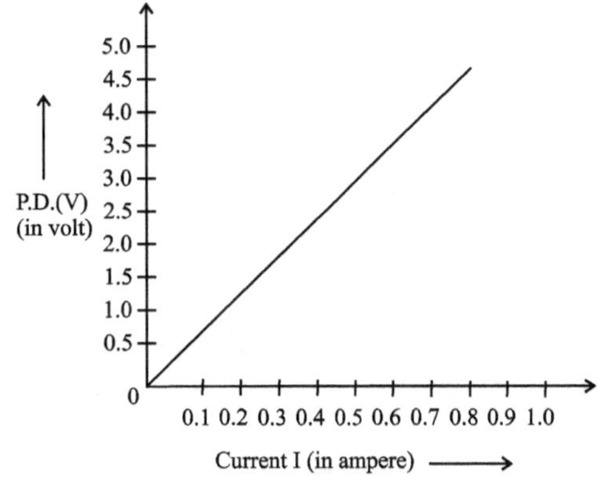

Resistance of the resistor, $R = \frac{V_2 - V_1}{I_2 - I_1}$ **(1 Mark)**

or, $R = \frac{5-4}{1.0-0.8} = \frac{1}{0.2} = 5\Omega$ **(1 Mark)**

The graph between V and I for a metallic conductor is a straight line. At different temperatures V-I curves are different.

27. Following are the steps of preparation of temporary mount of a leaf peel to observe stomata.

(i) Remove a healthy leaf from the potted plant.

(ii) Remove a part of the peel from the lower surface of the leaf. You can do this by folding the leaf over and gently pulling the peel apart using forceps. Keep the peel in a watch glass containing water.

(iii) Put a few drops of safranin stain in a watch glass.

(iv) After 2-3 minutes take out the peel and place it on a clean glass slide.

(v) Put a drop of glycerine over the peel and place a clean coverslip gently over it with the help of a needle.

(vi) Remove the excess stain and glycerine with the help of blotting paper.

(vii) Observe the slide under the low-power and high-power magnifications of the compound microscope.

(2 Marks)

All India 2017

CBSE Board Solved Paper

Time Allowed : 3 Hours ***Maximum Marks : 80***

General Instructions:

(i) The question paper comprises **two Sections, A and B**. You are to attempt both the sections.

(ii) **All** questions are **compulsory.**

(iii) There is no choice in any of the questions.

(iv) **All** questions of **Section-A** and **all** questions of **Section-B** are to be attempted separately.

(v) Question numbers **1** to **3** in **Section-A** are **one** mark questions. These are to be answered in **one word** or in **one sentence.**

(vi) Question numbers **4** to **6** in **Section-A** are **two** marks questions. These are to be answered in about **30 words** each.

(vii) Question numbers **7** to **18** in **Section-A** are **three** marks questions. These are to be answered in about **70 words** each.

(viii) Question numbers **19** to **24** in **Section-A** are **five** marks questions. These are to be answered in about **70 words** each.

(ix) Question numbers **25** to **33** in **Section-B** are multiple choice questions based on practical skills. Each question is a **one** mark question. You are to select one most appropriate response out of the four provided to you.

(x) Question numbers **34** to **36** in **Section-B** are two marks questions based on practical skills. These are to be answered in brief.

SECTION - A

1. Write the molecular formula of the 2nd and 3rd member of the homologous series whose first member is methane.

2. When a cell reproduces, what happen to its DNA?

3. In the following food chain, 100 J of energy is available to the lion. How much energy was available to the producer?

Plant $\longrightarrow$ Deer $\longrightarrow$ Lion

4. An object is placed at a distance of 30 cm from a concave lens of focal length 15 cm. List four characteristics (nature, position, etc.) of the image formed by the lens.

5. State two advantages of conserving
(i) forests, and (ii) wild–life.

6. Explain two main advantages associated with water harvesting at the community level.

7. Write the structural formula of ethanol. What happens when it is heated with excess of conc. H_2SO_4 at 433 K? Write the chemical equation for the reaction stating the role of conc. H_2SO_4 in this reaction.

8. Distinguish between esterification and saponification reactions with the help of the chemical equations for each. State one use of each (i) esters, and (ii) saponification process.

9. Write the number of periods and groups in the Modern Periodic Table. How does the metallic character of element vary on moving (i) from left to right in a period, and (ii) down a group? Give reason to justify your answer.

10. Na, Mg and Al are the elements of the 3rd period of the Modern Periodic Table having group number 1, 2 and 13 respectively. Which one of these elements has the (i) highest valency, (ii) largest atomic radius, and (iii) maximum chemical reactivity? Justify your answer stating the reason for each.

11. Reproduction is one of the most important characteristics of living beings. Give three reasons in support of the statement.

12. What is vegetative propagation? State two advantages and two disadvantages of this method.

13. List three techniques that have been developed to prevent pregnancy. Which one of these techniques is not meant for males? How does the use of these techiques have a direct impact on the health and prosperity of a family?

14. How did Mendel explain that is it possible that a trait is inherited but not expressed in an organism?

15. "Evolution and classification of organisms are interlinked." Give reasons to justify this statement.

16. If the image formed by a lens for all position of an object placed in front of it is always erect and diminished, what is the nature of this lens? Draw a ray diagram to justify your answer. It the numerical value of the power of this lens of 10 D, what is its focal length in the Cartesian system?

17. State the cause of dispersion of white light by a glass prism. How did Newton, using two identical glass prisms, show that white light is made of seven colours? Draw a ray diagram to show the path of a narrow beam of white light, thought a combination of two identical prisms arranged together in inverted position with respect to each other, when it is allowed to fall obliquely on one of the face of the first prism of the combination.

18. (a) Water is an elixir of life, a very important natural resource. Your Science teacher wants you to prepare a plan for a formative assessment activity, "how to save water, the vital natural resource". Write any two ways that you will suggest to bring awareness in your neighborhood, on 'how to save water'.

(b) Name and explain any one way by which the underground, on 'how to save water'.

19. Why are certian compounds called hydrocarbons? Write the general formula for homologous series of alkanes, alkenes and alkynes and also draw the structure of the first member of each series. Write the name of the reaction that converts alkenes into alkanes and also write a chemical equation to show the necessary conditions for the reaction to occur.

20. (a) Write the functions of each of the following parts in a human female reproductive system:

(i) Ovary

(ii) Uterus

(iii) Fallopian tube

21. With the help of one example for each, distinguish between the acquired traits and the inherited traits. Why are the traits/experiences acquired during the entire lifetime of an individual not inherited in the next generation? Explain the reason of thus fact with an example.

22. Analyse the following observation table showing variaton of image-distance (v) with object-distance (u) in case of a convex lens and answer the question that follow without doing any calculation:

S. No.	Ojects distance u (cm)	Image distance v(cm)
1	-100	+ 25
2	-60	+ 30
3	-40	+ 40
4	-30	+ 60
5	-25	+ 100
6	-15	+ 120

(i) What is the focal length of the convex lens? Give reason to justify your answer.

(ii) Write the serial number of the observation which is not correct. On what basis have you arrived at this conclusion?

(iii) Select an appropriate scale and draw a ray diagram for the observation at S.No.2. Also find the approximate value of magnification.

23. (i) If the image formed by a mirror for all positions of the objects placed in front of it is always diminished, erect and virtual, state the type of the mirror and also draw a ray diagram to justify your answer. Write one use such mirror are put to and why?

(ii) Define the radius of curvature of spherical mirrors. Find the nature and focal length of a spherical mirror whose radius of curvature is + 24 cm.

24. (a) A student suffering from myopia is not able to see distinctly the objects placed beyond 5 m. List two possible reasons due to which this defect of vision may have arisen. With the help of rays diagrams, explain

(i) why the student is unable to see distinctly the objects placed beyond 5 m from his eyes.

(ii) The type of the corrective lens used to restore proper vision and how this defect is corrected by the use of this lens.

(b) If, in this case, the numerical value of the focal length of the corrective lens is 5 m, find the power of the lens as per the new Cartesian sign convention.

SECTION - B

25. When you add a few drops of acetic acid to a test-tube containing sodium bicarbonate powder, which one of the following is your observation?

(a) No reaction takes place

(b) A coloureless gas with pungent smell is released with brisk effervescence

(c) A brown coloureless gas is released with brisk effervescence

(d) Formation of bubbles of a colourless and odourless gas

26. While studying the saponification reaction, what do you observe when you mix an equal amount of colourless vegetable oil and 20% aqueous solution of NaOH in a beaker?

(a) The colour of the mixture has become dark brown.

(b) A brisk effervescence is taking place in the beaker

(c) The outer surface of the beaker has become hot

(d) The outer surface of the beaker has become cold

27. A student requires hard water for an experiment in his laboratory which is not available in the neighbouring area. In the laboratory there are some salts, which when dissolved in distilled water can convert it into hard water. Select from the following groups of salts, a group, each salt of which when dissolved in distilled water will make it hard.

(a) Sodium chloride, Potassium chloride

(b) Sodium sulphate, Potassium sulphate

(c) Sodium sulphate, Calcium sulphate

(d) Calcium sulphate, Calcium chloride

28. To perform an experiment to identify the different parts of an embryo of a dicot seed, first of all require a dicot seed. Select dicot seeds from following groups:

Wheat, Gram, Maize, Pea, Barley, Ground-nut

(a) Wheat, Gram and Pea

(b) Gram, pea and Ground-nut

(c) Maize, Pea and Barley

(d) Gram, Maize and Ground-nut

29. The following vegetables are kept in a basket:

Potato, Tomato, Radish, Brinjal, Carrot, Bottle-gourd

Which two of these vegetable correctly represent the homologous structures?

(a) Carrot and Tomato

(b) Potato and Brinjal

(c) Radish and Carrot

(d) Radish and Bottle-gourd

30. Study the given ray diagrams and select the correct statement from the following:

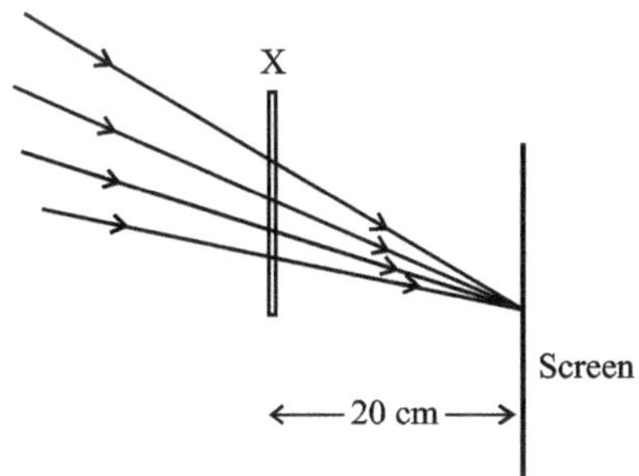

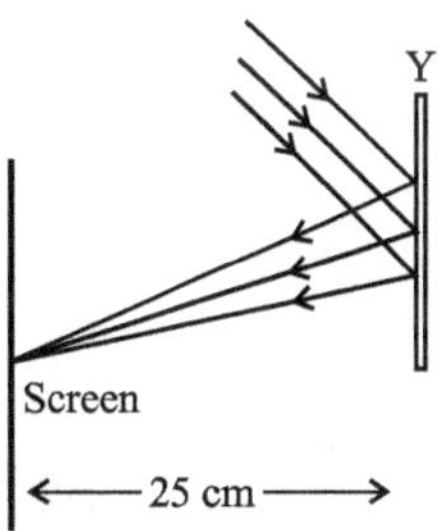

(a) Device X is a concave mirror and device Y is a convex lens, whose focal lengths are 20 cm and 25 cm respectively.

(b) Device X is a convex lens and device Y is a concave mirror, whose focal lengths are 10 cm and 25 cm respectively.

(c) Device X is a concave lens and device Y is a convex mirror, whose focal lengths are 20 cm and 25 cm respectively.

(d) Device X is a convex lens and device Y is a concave mirror, whose focal lengths are 20 m and 25 cm respectively.

31. A student obtaines a blurred image of a distant object on a screen using a convex lens. To obtain a distinct image on the screen he should move the lens

(a) away from the screen

(b) towords the screen

(c) to a position very far away from the screen

(d) either towards or away from the screen depending upon the position of the object.

32. A student very cautiously traces the path of a ray through a glass slab for different values of the angle of incidence ($\angle i$). He then measures the corresponding value of the angle of refraction ($\angle r$) and the angle of emergence ($\angle e$) for every value of the angle of incidence. On analysing these measurements of angles, his conclusion would be

(a) $\angle i > \angle r > \angle e$ (b) $\angle i = \angle e > \angle r$

(c) $\angle i < \angle r > \angle e$ (d) $\angle i = \angle e < \angle r$

33. Study the following ray diagram:

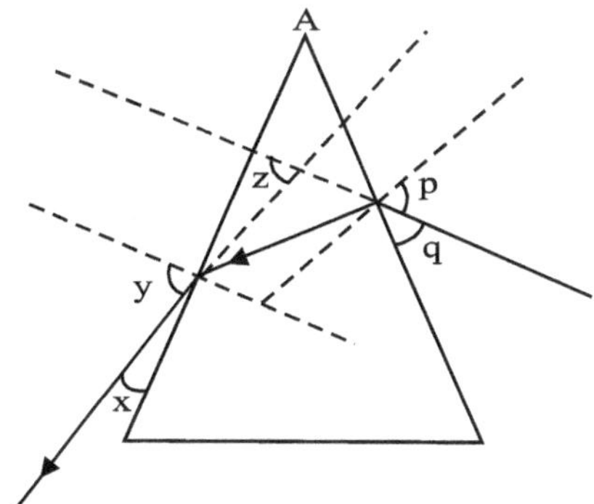

In this diagram, the angle of incidence, the angle of emergence and the angle of deviation respectively have been represented by

(a) y, p, z (b) x, q, z

(c) p, y, z (d) p, z, y

34. Mention the essential material (chemicals) used to prepare soap in the laboratory. Describe in brief the test of determining the nature (acidic/alkaline) of the reaction mixture of saponification reaction.

35. Draw in sequence (showing the four stages), the process of binary fission in *Amoeba*.

36. A student focuses the image of a candle frame, placed at about 2 m from a convex lens of focal length 10 cm, on a screen. After that he move gradually the flame towards the lens and each time focuses its image on the screen.

(i) In which direction does he move the lens of focus the flame on the screen?

(ii) What happens to the size of the image of the flame on the screen?

(iii) What difference is seen in the intensity (brightness) of the images of the flame on the screen?

(iv) What is seen on the screen when the flame is very close (at about 5 cm) to the lens?

Solutions

SECTION - A

1. Ethance (C_2H_6) and Propane (C_3H_8). **(1 Mark)**

In the homologous series of alkanes, members show similar chemical properties and they have trends in physical properties. For example as the chain length increases, boiling point also increases. In the homologous series the alkanes show isomerism.

2. When a cell reproduces, its DNA is copied or replicated and passed on to the offsprings or the next generation. DNA carries hereditary information which is passed from one generation to next generation. **(1 Mark)**

DNA is Deoxyribonucleic acid that has double helical structure and carries genetic information for the growth, development, proper functioning and reproduction of all known organisms and many viruses.

3. 10000 J **(1 Mark)**

4. Using lens formula, $\frac{1}{f} = \frac{1}{v} - \frac{1}{u}$

$$\Rightarrow \frac{1}{-15} = \frac{1}{v} - \frac{1}{-30}$$

$$\Rightarrow \frac{1}{v} = -\frac{1}{10} \quad \therefore \quad v = -10 \text{ cm}$$

The four characteristics of the image formed by the concave lens are–

(i) Image will be in between focus and optical centre

(ii) Formed infront of the lens

(iii) Smaller than the size of the object

(iv) Virtual and erect **(½ × 4 = 2 Marks)**

5. Two advantages for conservation of forests include:

(i) Forests keeps balance between abiotic and biotic factors of the environment.

(ii) They are the source of various products in the form of food, medicines wood and raw materials of different industries.

Two advantage of Wild life Conservation include:

(i) Protection of biodiversity.

(ii) It maintaining balance in the will help in ecosystem. **(2 Marks)**

6. Two main advantages of water harvesting at the community level include:

(i) Water evaporation does not occur, rather it percolates into the ground. Therefore, result in the recharging of wells.

(ii) water storage provides moisture to the vegetation within the area. **(2 Marks)**

7. Structural formula of ethanol

$$H-\underset{H}{\overset{H}{\underset{|}{\overset{|}{C}}}}-\underset{H}{\overset{H}{\underset{|}{\overset{|}{C}}}}-OH$$ **(1 Mark)**

H_2SO_4 behaves as a dehydrating agent **(1 Mark)**

$$\underset{\text{Ethanol}}{CH_3CH_2OH} \xrightarrow[443K]{H_2SO_4} \underset{\text{Ethene}}{CH_2 = CH_2} + H_2O$$

(1 Mark)

8. Esterification is a process in which a carboxylic acid react with an alcohol to form ester in presence of an acid.

$$RCOOH + R'OH \xrightarrow{H^+} \underset{\text{Ester}}{RCOOR'} + H_2O$$ **(1 Mark)**

In saponification, as ester reacts with a strong base or an acid to give alcohol and sodium salt of carboxylic acid or carboxylic acid.

$$RCOOR' + NaOH \longrightarrow RCOONa + R'OH$$ **(1 Mark)**

(i) Esters are used as a constituent of perfumes, essential oils, food flavourings etc. **(½ Mark)**

(ii) Saponification process is used in the manufacturing of soap used as cleansing agent. **(½ Mark)**

Saponification process is the reverse reaction of esterification process.

$$\textit{Acid + Alcohol} \underset{OH^- \text{ Saponification}}{\overset{\text{Esterification } H^+}{\rightleftharpoons}} \textit{Ester + water}$$

9. There are 7 periods and 18 groups present in the periodic table. **(1 Mark)**

Variation of metallic character:

(i) From left to right in a period the metallic character of elements decreases due to decreases in atomic size therefore electrons are not released easily. **(1 Mark)**

(ii) Down in a group, the metallic character increases due to increase in atomic size therefore the electrons can be removed easily. **(1 Mark)**

10. (i) Na: 2, 8, 1
Valency = 1
for, Mg: 2, 8, 2
Valency = 2
Al : 2, 8, 3
Valency = 3

Al has the highest valency because it can share all the three electrons present in the outermost shell. **(1 Mark)**

(ii) Na has the largest atomic radius in given elements because atomic radius decreases across the period due to increases in number of electrons and nuclear charge which tends to pull the electrons closer to the nucleus. **(1 Mark)**

(iii) Na has the maximum chemical reactivity as it contains only one electron in its valence shell so can loose it easily to form cation in comparison to Mg and Al. **(1 Mark)**

11. Reproduction is an important characteristics of living beings because it enables them to produce offspring and continuity of the population. Living beings transfer their genetic information to the next generation. Through reproduction, it ensures continuity of existence of organisms on earth. **(3 Marks)**

12. Vegetative propagation is a type of asexual reproduction where plant progeny are formed from (parts of the plants) such as roots, steam, leaves and buds. For example; eye of potato etc.

Advantages:

(i) Offsprings are genetically similar to their parents and therefore useful traits can be preserved.

(ii) It is quick and economical method.

Disadvatages:

(i) No introduction of new characters in progeny hence no genetic variation.

(ii) The disease of the parent plant is passed on to the offsprings. **(3 Marks)**

Note

Plants raised by vegetative propagation can bear flowers and fruits earlier than those produced from seeds. This method make possible the propagation of plants such as banana, orange, rose and jasmine that have lost the capacity to produce seeds.

13. Three techniques that have been developed to prevent pregnancy are:

(i) Mechanical method: Physical barriers such as condoms, diaphragm and cervical caps are used to prevent entry of sperms in females.

(ii) Chemical methods are comprised of drugs such as oral pills and vaginal pills which are used by females.

(iii) Surgical methods include vasectomy in males and tubectomy in females.

Chemical techniques are not developed for males.

The use of techiques helps in controlling population explosion which provide better living conditions.

Using these techniques helps in keeping proper gap between siblings and better health to other as well as children. **(3 Marks)**

Note

There are several natural methods that work on the principle of avoiding chances of ovum and sperms meeting the natural methods are periodic abstinence, withdrawl or coitus interrupts and lactational amenorrhea.

14. Mendel crossed a homozygous tall pea plant and a short pea plant and progeny produced from them till the first (F_1) generation plants were all tall.

But after crossing F_1 generation plants, the second

(F_2) generation plants were not all tall, instead, one quarter of them were short. Thus it indicate that both the tallness and shortness traits were inherited in the F_1 plants but only the tallness trait was expressed.

This shows that both traits were inherited but not expressed in an organism. **(3 Marks)**

15. Every organism shows inherent tendency for genetic variations which plays an important role in the origin of new species and is the basis for evolution. The more characteristics two species have in common, the more closely they are related. Classification of organisms into different groups is based on the similarities and dissimilarities of characteristics. Therefore, classification of species involves evolutionary relationship between organism. Thus it justifies that evolution and classification of organisms are interlinked. **(3 Marks)**

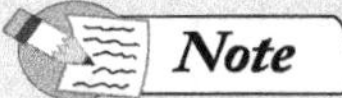

Evolution refers to the change in the characteristics of a species over several generations and relies on the process of natural selection.

16. If the image formed by a lens for all positions of the object in front of it is always virtual, erect and diminished, the lens is concave.

- When object is at infinity object is formed at focus F_1.

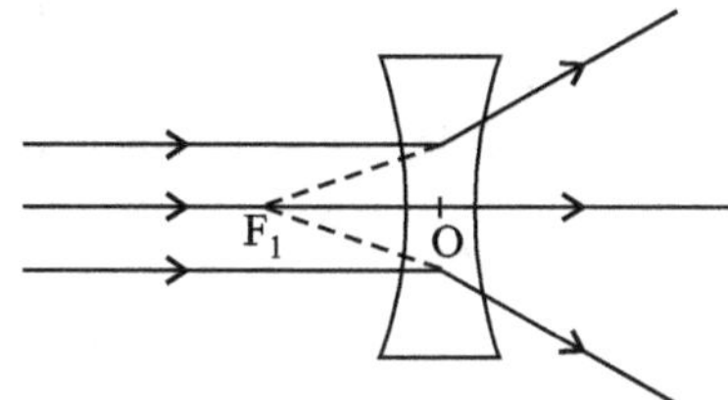

(1 Mark)

- When object is between infinity and optical centre (O) of lens - image is formed between focus and optical centre of lens.

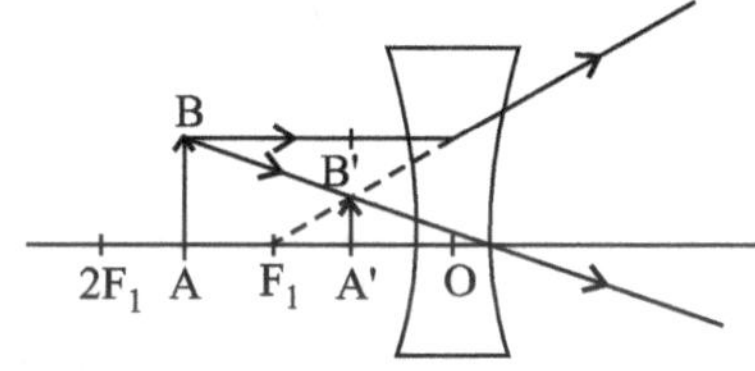

(1 Mark)

Power of the lens, $P = \dfrac{1}{f\,(in\ m)}$

$\Rightarrow\ 10 = \dfrac{-1}{f}\ \Rightarrow\ f = \dfrac{-1}{10}$

$\therefore$ Focal length, $f = -0.1$ m **(1 Mark)**

The ability of a lens to diverage or converge the rays of light passing through it is called power of the lens. If the lens converges the rays parallel to principal axis its power is positive and if it diverges the rays power of the lens is negative.

Pconvex ⟶ Positive, Pconcave ⟶ Negative.

17. Light is formed of different colours which travel at their own speed inside a prism. Due to which the light bends the through different angles with respect to the incident ray, as they pass through a prism. The red light bends the least while the violet most causing dispersion this can be explained by the fact that light of different colours having different wavelengths has different velocities while travelling in a medium $v_m = n\lambda_m$. **(1 Mark)**

Newton showed that the reverse of dispersion of light is also possible. If we kept two prisms close to each other one in erect position and the other in an inverted position, the light get dispersed when passes through the first prism. The second prism receives all the seven coloured rays from first prism and combines into original while light *i.e.*, recombine the different colours of spectrum and hence gives white light. This proves that white light is made of seven constituents colours (VIBGYOR).

(1 Mark)

Ray diagram:

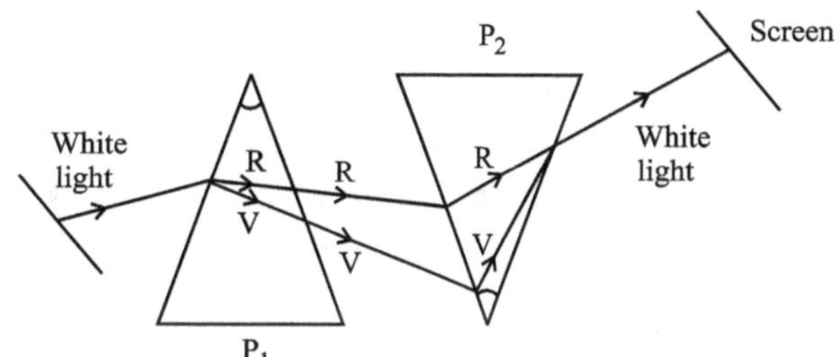

(Dispering Prism) (Recombination Prism)

(1 Mark)

18. (a) Two ways to bring awareness on "how to save water" are:–

(i) By organising a demonstration of the households practices to minimize the wastage of water.

(ii) By organising every week every for year to create awareness (poster competitions on "how to save water") **(2 Marks)**

(b) Rainwater harvesting is the better way by which the underground water table does not go down further. In this we can collect rainwater and store it in the form of pits and lakes ensuring that the water seeps through the soil and recharges the aquifers.

(1 Mark)

19. Hydrocarbons are those compounds which are formed from carbon and hydrogen. **(1 Mark)**

Formula for Homologous series of alkanes, alkenes and alkynes:

	Series	General Formula	Structur of the first member
(i)	Alkane	C_nH_{2n+2}	$H-\underset{H}{\overset{H}{\vert}}\!\!\!\!C\!\!\!\!\underset{\vert}{}-H$ (H–C(H)(H)–H)
(ii)	Alkene	C_nH_{2n}	H–C(H)=C(H)–H
(iii)	Alkyne	C_nH_{2n-2}	$H-C\equiv C-H$

(3 Marks)

Hydrogenation converts alkenes into alkane.

$$CH_2 = CH_2 + H_2 \xrightarrow{Pt/Pd/Ni} CH_3 - CH_3$$

Alkene reacts with dihydrogen in the presence of catalysts like Pt, Pd or Ni to given alkane. **(1 Mark)**

Hydrogenation reactions are extensively used to create commercial goods. Hydrogenation is used in food industry to make a large variety of goods like spreads from liquid oil. This process also incresases the chemical stability of products and yield semi-solid products like margarine.

20. (a) **Functions of ovary are :**

(i) Ovaries are the female sex organs that produces the female Primary gametes (ovum).

(ii) Secretion of female sex hormones such as estrogen which helps in the development of secondary sexual characteristics in females.

Functions of uterus are:

(i) It provides space where embryo gets implanted and develops into foetus.

(ii) The wall of the uterus provides safety and nutrition to the developing foetus.

Functions of fallopian tube are:

(i) It is the site where fertilization takes places in females.

(ii) It helps in the transfer of fertilised eggs from ovary to the uterus for implantation. **(5 Marks)**

The uterus is supported by ligaments attached to the pelvic wall and the wall of the uterus that has three layers of tissue such as endometrium myometrium and perimetrium.

21. Acquired traits are the characters that are acquired by the individual during its lifetime. These traits cannot be inherited to progeny for example, if a athlete develops large muscles due to his training program that does not mean it will be passed on to his offspring.

Inherited traits are the characters which are inherited by the progeny from their parents. These traits are expressed in the offspring and further on to the next generation. various are: examples skin colour eye colour and shape.

Acquired traits occur due to change in the lifestyles, injury, loss of body parts or disuse of some body parts. These changes occur in the somatic cells, not involving germ cells and genetic materials. Therefore, these traits are not transferred or inherited in the next generation. Example, low weight of a starving beetle. **(5 Marks)**

22. (a) The focal length of the convex lens can be calculated from S.No. 3 as when an object is placed at a distance from the convex lens its image is formed on the other side of the lens at the same distance from the lens. So, the radius of curvature is 40 cm. Thus, focal length is half the radius of curvature (f = R/2)

i.e., $f = \frac{R}{2} = +20$ cm. **(1 Mark)**

(b) S. No. 6 is incorrect as the objects distance is between focus and pole and this always forms virtual and erect image of object so image distance is negative but the image distance given is positive (+ 120 cm). **(1 Mark)**

(c)

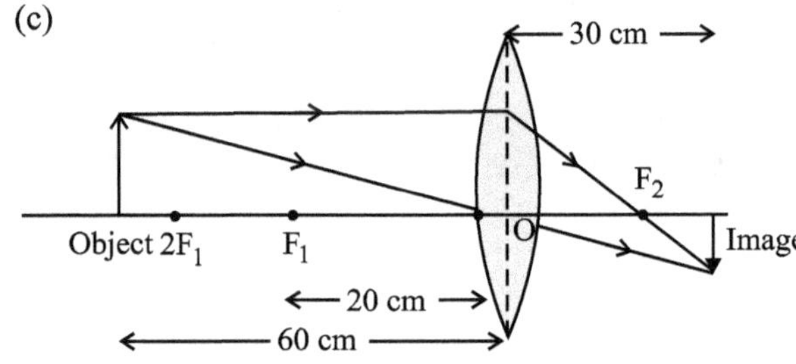

(2 Marks)

Approximate vale of magnification for object distance $u = -60$ cm and image distance $v = +30$ cm is i.e. , $m = \frac{v}{u} = \frac{30}{60} = 0.5$. **(1 Mark)**

Image formed by convex lens may be real or virtual, may be inverted or erect, may be smaller, larger, or equal in size of object. But image formed by concave lens is always virtual, erect and smaller than the size of the object.

23. (a) A convex mirror forms an erect, diminished and virtual image for all the positions of the object placed at infinity or between infinity and pole, in front of it. **(1 Mark)**

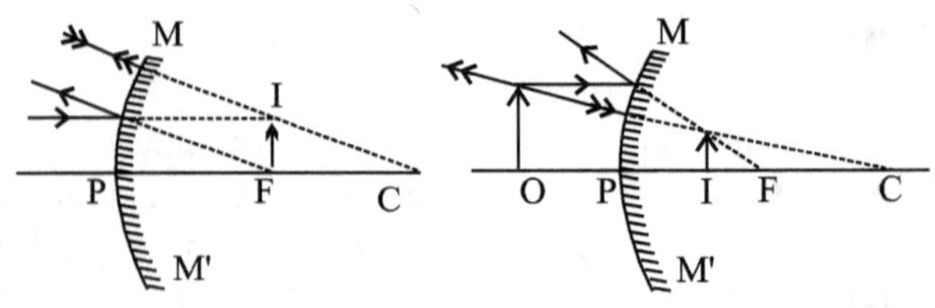

(1 Mark)

Convex mirror is commonly used as rear-view mirrors in vehicles as they always give an erect and diminished image. So that covers a wide field of view. **(1 Marks)**

(b) The radius of the sphere of which the reflecting surface or spherical mirror forms a part is called the radius of curvature of the mirror.

Focal length, $f = \frac{R}{2}$

As the radius of curvature is positive, so the mirror is convex. **(1 Mark)**

So, $f = \frac{24}{2} = 12$ cm **(1 Mark)**

Thus, the focal length of the convex mirror is 12 cm.

24. (a) The student is unable to see distinctly the objects placed beyond 5 cm from his eyes as he is suffering from myopia i.e., near-sightedness where a person can see near by objects clearly but cannot see distant objects distinictly. **(1 Mark)**

(i) This defect arises due to

(1) reduced radii of curvature of lens.

(2) increase in distance between eye lens and retina. **(1 Mark)**

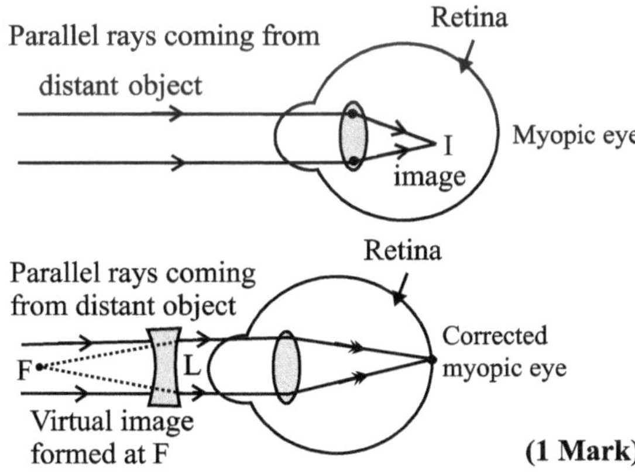

(1 Mark)

(i) The student is unable to see distinctly the objects placed beyond 5 m from his eyes because the image of distant object is formed before retina instead of retina.

(ii) Concave lens can be used to diverge the light rays before they enter the eye as the corrective lens to restore proper vision. A concave lens of suitable focal length will bring the image back on the retina and thus the defect is corrected. **(1 Mark)**

(b) Given, $u = -\infty$ and $v = -5$ m

Using lens formula, $\frac{1}{f} = \frac{1}{v} - \frac{1}{u}$

$$\Rightarrow \frac{1}{f} = \frac{1}{-5} - \frac{1}{-\infty}$$

$$\Rightarrow \frac{1}{f} = \frac{1}{-5} - 0$$

$$\Rightarrow f = -5\text{m}$$

Power of the lens, $P = \frac{1}{f} = \frac{1}{(-5)} = -0.2$ D **(1 Mark)**

SECTION - B

25. (d) Formation of bubbles of a colourless and odourless gas (CO_2). **(1 Mark)**

$$CH_3COOH + NaHCO_3 \longrightarrow CH_3COONa + CO_2 \uparrow + H_2O$$

26. (c) The outer surface of the beaker has become hot. Saponification is an exothermic reaction. **(1 Mark)**

27. (d) Calcium sulphate, calcium chloride. **(1 Mark)**

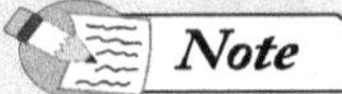

Note

Permanent hardness of water is caused by chloride and sulphate salt of calcium and magnesium while temporary hardness is caused by the carbonate and bicarbonate salt of calcium and magnesium.

28. (b) Gram, pea and Groundnut **(1 Mark)**

Note

Plants with the seed having two cotyledons are called as dicots, and such plants are called dicotyledons.

29. (c) Radish and carrot **(1 Mark)**

Note

Homologous organs share common ancestory as they have similar structures but perform different functions.

30. (d) Device X is a convex or, converging lens and device Y is a concave mirror, whose focal lengths are 20 cm and 25 cm respectively. **(1 Mark)**

31. (d) Either towards or away from the screen depending upon the position of the object. **(1 Mark)**

32. (b) $\angle i = \angle e > \angle r$ **(1 Mark)**

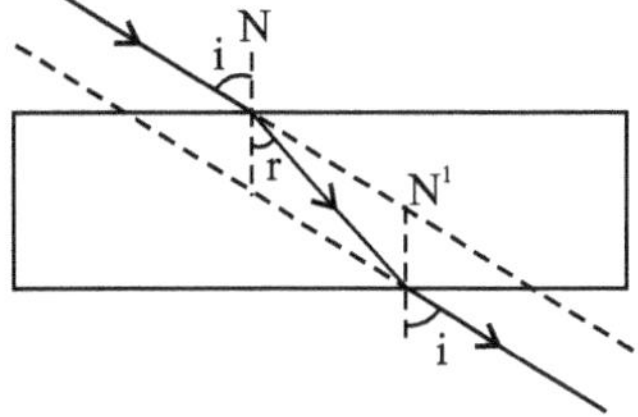

33. (a) p, y, z **(1 Mark)**

34. Raw materials for preparation of soap in the laboratory are fat, oils and sodium hydroxide.

Test to determine the nature of the reaction mixture of saponification process: When a small quantity of NaCl is added to a soap solution and stirred with a glass rod, a suspension gets precipitated as solid. When it is tested with red litmus paper its colour changes to blue. This shows that suspension is alkaline in nature. **(2 Marks)**

35. Binary fission in *Amoeba* is shown as :–

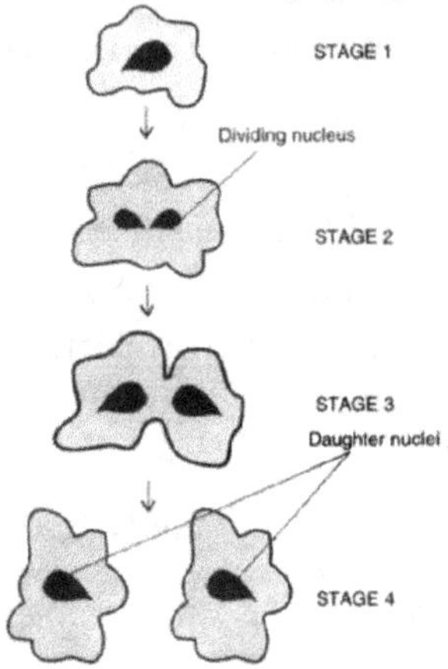

(2 Marks)

Binary fission is a type of asexual reproduction in which parental identity is lost. It involves the formation of two identical daughter cells from a parent single cell.

36. (i) He moves the lens away from the screen to focus the image.

(ii) Size of the image increases

(iii) The intensity of image decreases as the flame moves towards the lends.

(iv) Image is not formed on the screen as the image formed is virtual. **(½ × 4 = 2 Marks)**

2016-2017

Solved Paper Term I

Time Allowed : 3 Hours ***Maximum Marks : 90***

General Instructions:

(i) The question paper comprises **two Sections, A and B**. You are to attempt both the sections.

(ii) **All** questions are **compulsory**.

(iii) There is no choice in any of the questions.

(iv) **All** questions of **Section-A** and **all** questions of **Section-B** are to be attempted separately.

(v) Question numbers **1** to **3** in **Section-A** are **one** mark questions. These are to be answered in **one word** or in **one sentence**.

(vi) Question numbers **4** to **6** in **Section-A** are **two** marks questions. These are to be answered in about **30 words** each.

(vii) Question numbers **7** to **18** in **Section-A** are **three** marks questions. These are to be answered in about **70 words** each.

(viii) Question numbers **19** to **24** in **Section-A** are **five** marks questions. These are to be answered in about **70 words** each.

(ix) Question numbers **25** to **33** in **Section-B** are multiple choice questions based on practical skills. Each question is a one mark question. You are to select one most appropriate response out of the four provided to you.

(x) Question numbers **34** to **36** in **Section-B** are two marks questions based on practical skills. These are to be answered in brief.

SECTION-A

1. Can a double displacement reaction take place when the products are highly soluble or highly ionized?

2. What precautions should be taken to avoid the overloading of domestic electric circuits?

3. Define coordination.

4. How is electricity generated by a hydro electric power plant? Explain.

5. Give advantages of solar energy over conventional fuel.

6. The resistance of a wire of 0.01 cm radius is 10Ω. If the resistivity of the material of the wire is 50×10^{-8} ohm meter, find the length of the wire.

7. Give reasons for the following :

(a) Metals are regarded as electropositive elements.

(b) When a piece of Copper metal is added to a solution of zinc sulphate, no change takes place, but the blue colour of copper sulphate fades away when a piece of zinc is placed in its solution.

8. Name three forms in which energy from ocean is made available for use. What are OTEC power plants ? How do they operate ?

9. Explain with the help of experiment the formation of induced current.

10. Ajay, a student of chemistry, was performing chemical reaction between sodium thiosulphate and HCl. He found that time required to appear turbidity increases when concentration of HCl or sodium thiosulphates or both decreases.

Answer the following questions based on the above information:

(a) Mention the reason for appearance of turbidity.

(b) Write the chemical reaction involved.

(c) Mention the values associated with above experiment.

11. What is the difference between a direct current and an alternating current? How many times does AC used in India change direction in one second?

Why is a generator armature harder to rotate when it is connected to a circuit and supplying electric current?

12. Write combination reactions that occur when the metal barium reacts with the following non-metals.

(a) hydrogen (b) sulfur

(c) nitrogen

13. (a) Name the chief ore of iron. Write its formula.

(b) How is an iron ore concentrated ? Describe it briefly.

14. For making cake, baking powder is taken. If at home your mother uses baking soda instead of baking powder in cake.

(a) how will it affect the taste of the cake and why?

(b) how can baking soda be converted into baking powder?

(c) what is the role of tartaric acid added to baking soda?

15. Why is tungsten metal selected for making filaments of incandescent lamp bulbs?

Compare the power used in the 2Ω resistor in each of the following circuits :

(a) a 6V battery in series with 1Ω and 2Ω resistors and

(b) a 4V battery in parallel with 12Ω and 2Ω resistors.

16. There are 5 rooms in a house. Each room has a 100W bulb and a 40W tube light. If every day the bulb is used for 1 hour and tube light is used for 5 hours in each room then what will be the cost of total electric energy consumed in 30 days when 1 unit of electric energy costs ₹ 2.5.

17. Draw a diagram of the human brain and mention its functions.

18. Name the three kinds of blood vessels of human circulatory system. Write the function of each.

19. Give the full form of GH. Name the gland that secretes it. Mention its any two functions. Name the hormone that inhibits the secretion of GH. Name the disorder that is caused due to the failure of secretion of GH.

20. Derive a formula for the equivalent resistance for the three resistances connected in parallel.

21. (a) What is an electromagnet ?

(b) List any of its two uses.

(c) What is the purpose of the soft iron core used in making an electromagnet ?

22. (a) A metal carbonate X on reacting with an acid gives a gas which when passed through a solution Y gives the carbonate back. On the other hand, a gas G that is obtained at anode during electrolysis of brine is passed on dry Y, it gives a compound Z, used for disinfecting drinking water. Identity X, Y, G and Z.

(b) Write the chemical formula of plaster of paris.

23. Explain the following

(a) Reactivity of Al decreases if it is dipped in HNO_3

(b) Carbon cannot reduce the oxides of Na or Mg

(c) NaCl is not a conductor of electricity in solid state whereas it does conduct electricity in aqueous solution as well as in molten state

(d) Iron articles are galvanised

(e) Metals like Na, K, Ca and Mg are never found in their free state in nature.

24. (a) Explain why photosynthesis is considered the most important process in the biosphere.

(b) Differentiate between autotrophs and heterotrophs.

SECTION - B

25. A dilute solution of sodium carbonate was added to two test tubes – one containing dil. HCl (*A*) and the other containing dilute NaOH (*B*). The correct observation was

(a) a brown coloured gas liberated in test tube *A*

(b) a brown coloured gas liberated in test tube *B*

(c) a colourless gas liberated in test tube *A*

(d) a colourless gas liberated in test tube *B*

26. Take about 1.0g $CaCO_3$ in a test tube. Heat it over a flame, when a colourless gas comes out. The reaction is called a

(a) decomposition reaction

(b) displacement reaction

(c) double decomposition reaction

(d) double displacement reaction

27. Observe the experimental setup carefully and give correct order of reactivity of these metals with dil. HCl :

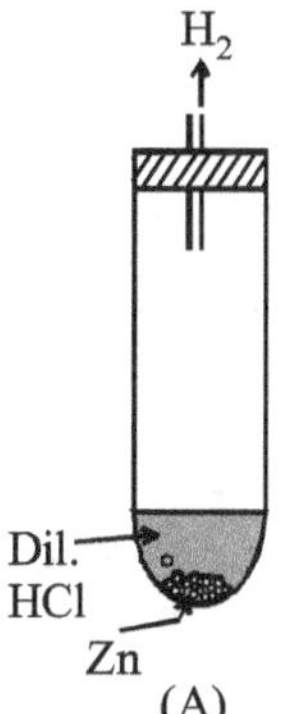

(A)

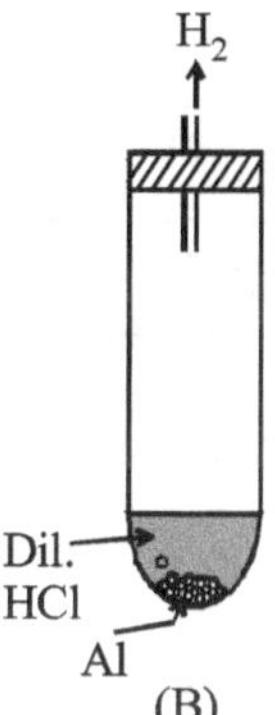

(B)

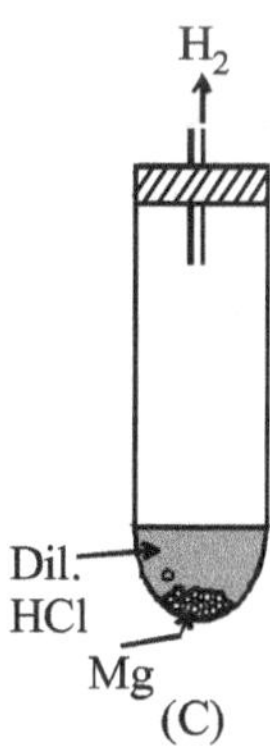

(C)

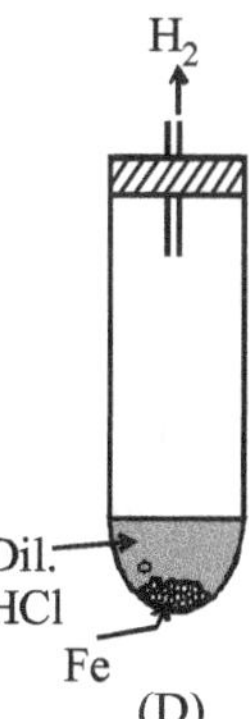

(D)

(a) C>B>A>D

(b) C>A>B>D

(c) D>B>A>C

(d) D>A>B>C

28. Which one observations is correct according to effect of acids and bases on some indicators

	Test Sample	Red litmus	Blue litums	Phenol-phthalein	Methyl orange
I	Dil. HCl	No effect	Turn red	No effect	Turn red
II	Dil H_2SO_4	Turn blue	No effect	Turn pink	Turn red
III	$Ca(OH)_2$	No effect	Turn red	Turn pink	Turn red
IV	$Mg(OH)_2$	Turn blue	Turn red	No effect	No effect

(a) I observation is correct

(b) II observation is correct

(c) III observation is correct

(d) IV observation is correct

29. What happens when a solution of an acid is mixed with a solution of a base in a test tube ?

(i) The temperature of the solution increases

(ii) The temperature of the solution decreases

(iii) The temperature of the solution remains the same

(iv) Salt formation takes place

(a) (i) only

(b) (i) and (iii)

(c) (ii) and (iii)

(d) (i) and (iv)

30. In the experiment on finding the equivalent resistance of two resistors, connected in series, the ammeter is correctly connected in :

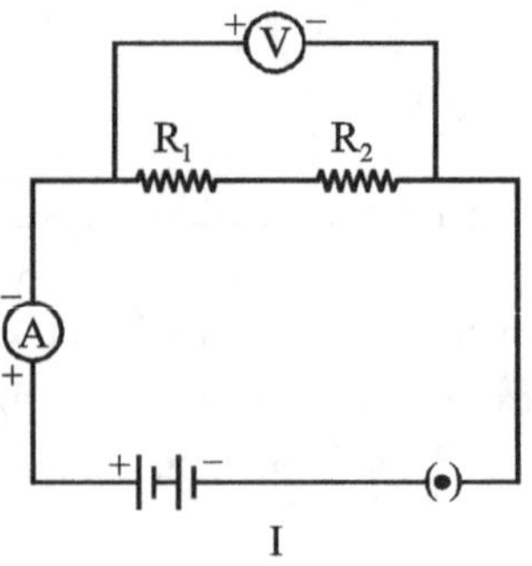

I

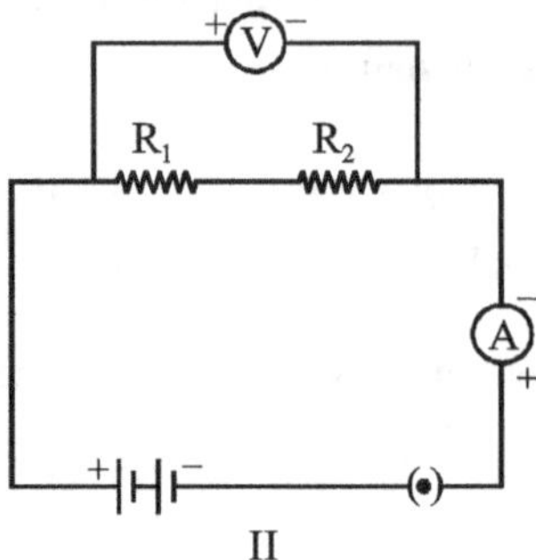

II

(a) circuit (I) only.

(b) circuit (II) only

(c) both circuits (I) and (II)

(d) neither of the two circuits.

31. While performing the experiment on studying the dependence of current (I) on the potential difference (V) across a resistor, four students set up the circuit as shown

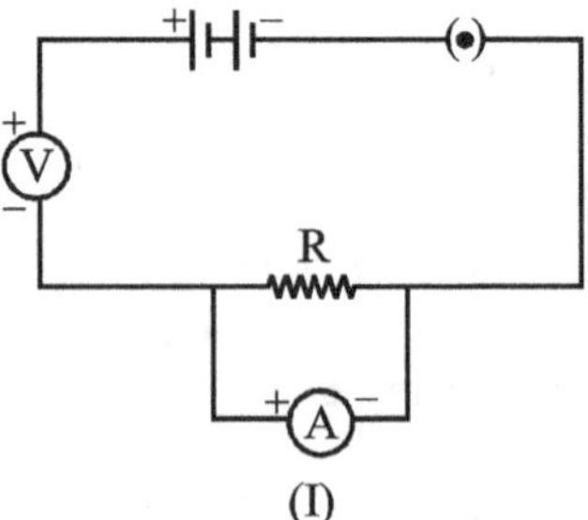

(I)

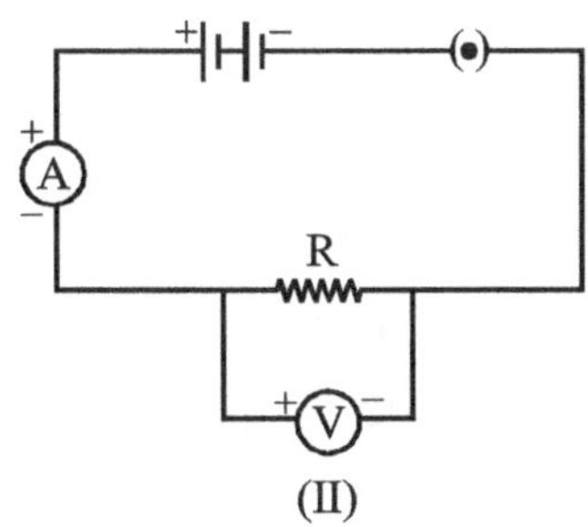

(II)

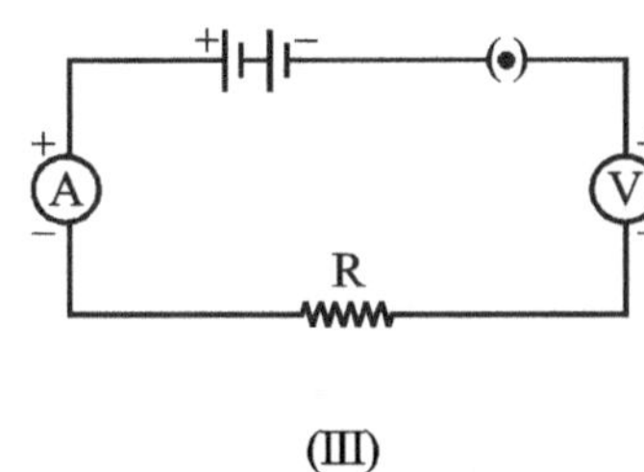

(III)

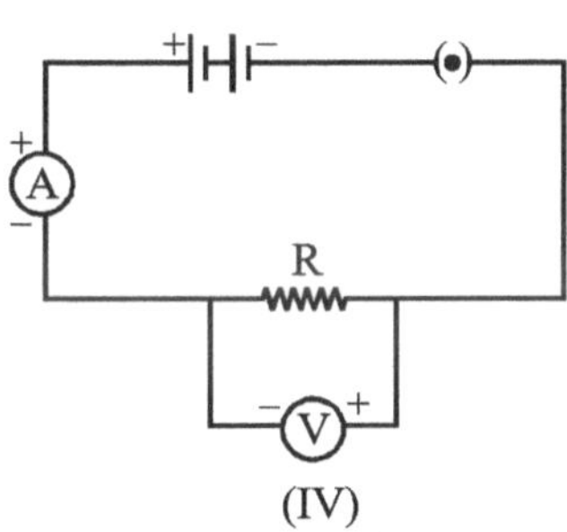

(IV)

The correct setup is

(a) I

(b) II

(c) III

(d) IV

32. Given alongside is a sketch of a leaf partially covered with black paper and which is to be used in the experiment to show that light is compulsory for the process of photosynthesis. At the end of the experiment, which one of the leaf parts labelled I, II and III will become black when dipped in iodine solution?

(a) I only (b) II only

(c) I and III (d) II and III.

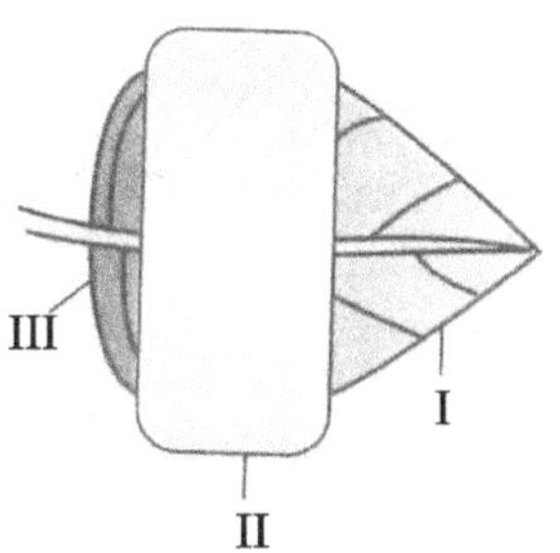

33. Which region of the human digestive system releases bile juice?

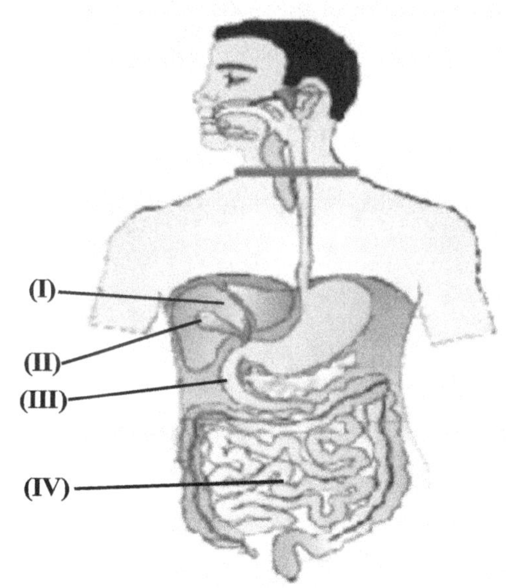

(a) I

(b) II

(c) III

(d) IV

34. A student adds a spoon full of powered sodium hydrogen carbonate to a flask containing ethanoic acid. List two main observations, he must note in is notebook, about the reaction that takes place.

35. In the circuit shown in the figure: Find the power supplied by the battery. What is the potential difference across 4Ω resistance?

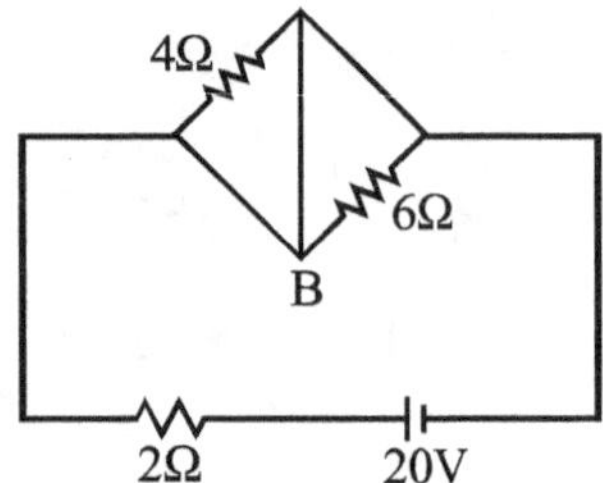

36. In the following sketch of stomatal apparatus, parts I, II, III and IV were labelled differently by four students. Name the labelling I, II, III and IV.

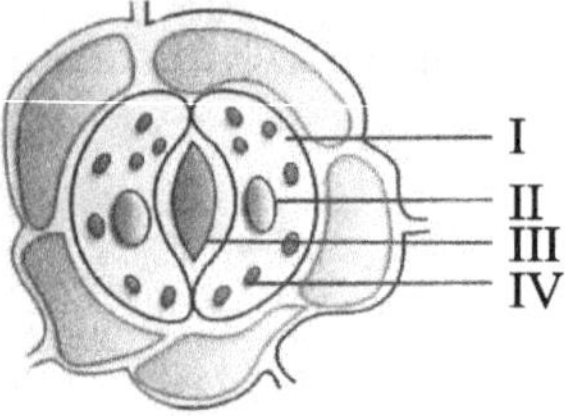

Solutions

SECTION-A

1. No, double displacement reaction takes place when there is formation of a sparingly soluble salt. **(1 mark)**

2. (i) We can avoid overloading by not connecting too many appliances to a single socket.

   (ii) We must avoid uses of too many appliances in our houses. **(1 mark)**

3. Coordination is the working together of various agents of the body of an organism in a proper manner to produce an appropriate reaction to a stimulus. **(1 mark)**

4. Water stored behind the dams, possesses potential energy. When the iron gates of the dam are opened, the water flows down and its energy gets converted into kinetic energy and falls on the turbine and rotates its blades. The turbine inturns rotates the crankshaft which generates electricity with the help of generator. **(2 marks)**

5. (i) Renewable source of energy.

   (ii) Free of cost.

   (iii) Eco-friendly. **(2 marks)**

6. Given, Radius (r)= 0.01 cm = 0.01×10^{-2} m.

   Resistivity (ρ) = $50 \times 10^{-8} \Omega$ m.

   Resistance (R) = 10Ω

   As we know, $\left[\because A = \pi r^2\right]$

   $$R = \rho\frac{l}{A} = \rho\frac{l}{\pi r^2}$$

   $$\Rightarrow l = \frac{R\pi r^2}{\rho}$$

   $$= \frac{10 \times 3.14 \times 0.01 \times 10^{-2} \times 0.01 \times 10^{-2}}{50 \times 10^{-8}}$$

   $$= \frac{314 \times 10^{-4}}{50 \times 10^{-8} \times 10^{5}}$$

   $$\text{Length} = \frac{6.28 \times 10^{-4}}{10^{-3}} = 0.628 \text{ m.}$$ **(2 marks)**

7. (a) It is because metals can lose electrons easily to form positive ions, therefore, regarded as electropositive elements. **(1 mark)**

   (b) It is because copper is less reactive than Zn, therefore, it cannot displace Zn from $ZnSO_4$ solution.

   $Cu + ZnSO_4 \longrightarrow$ No reaction

   But when Zn is dipped in copper sulphate solution, it displaces copper from $CuSO_4$ to form $ZnSO_4$ which is colourless. Reddish brown copper metal gets precipitated because Zn is more reactive than Cu.

   $$\underset{\text{Zinc}}{Zn} + \underset{\text{(Blue)}}{CuSO_4} \longrightarrow \underset{\text{(Colourless)}}{ZnSO_4} + \underset{\text{Copper}}{Cu}$$ **(2 marks)**

Metals which are high in the reactivity series displaces metal which are at lower position in the reactivity series from its salt solution.

8. Three forms of oceanic energy are

   (a) Sea wave energy

   (b) Tidal energy

   (c) Ocean thermal energy. **(1 mark)**

   OTEC power plant. The plants which are used to harness ocean thermal energy is called OTEC power plant. **(½ mark)**

Working of OTEC power plant. A temperature difference between warm surface water heated by sun and colder water at deeper level upto 1000 m is 20°C or more is required to operate OTEC plant.

In the OTEC system, the warm surface water is used to boil a liquid like ammonia. The vapour of liquid is then used to rotate the turbine of a generator. The cold water from the deeper level is used to convert the ammonia vapour again into liquid. **(1½ marks)**

9. When straight conductor moves in a magnetic field, current is generated in the conductor. This field, current is

generated in the conductor. This phenomenon of production of electric current is know as Electro Magnetic Induction and the current so obtained is called induced current. An experiment to show the formation of induced current.

Take a coil which has *n* no. of turns. The two ends of the coil are attached to a sensitive galvanometer. Now take a bar magnet and try to move it towards coil, the galvanometer shows a deflection in a particular direction which indicates that the current is flowing through the circuit. Now move this magnet away from the coil and again the galvanometer shows deflection but in the opposite direction which confirms that the current is being produced in the circuit due to the motion of magnet with respect to the coil. The same effect can be observed if the coil moves towards and away from the magnet and there is no deflection in the galvanometer if both coil and magnet are stationary. So this experiment shows that the motion of magnet with respect to coil (vice versa) produces an induced potential difference. [Electro motive force (EMF)] This EMF produces an induced current in the coil.

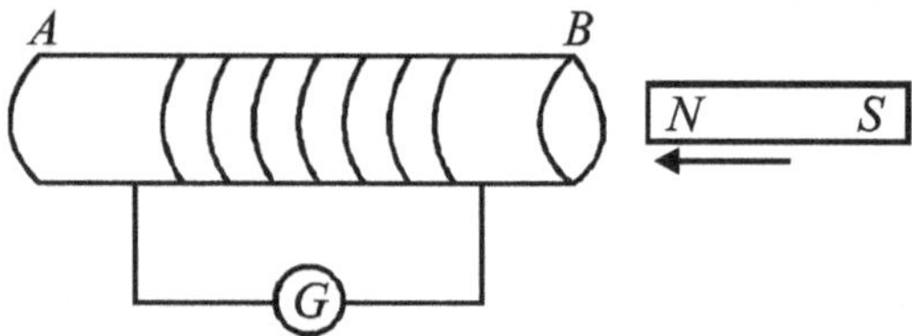

(3 marks)

The magnitude of current induced in the coil can be increased.

(a) by winding the coil on a soft iron core

(b) by increasing the number of turns in the coil.

(c) by increasing the speed of magnet

(d) by increasing the strength of magnet

10. (a) In the reaction between sodium thiosulphate and HCl, sulphur is formed in the solid state. As the reaction proceeds, more sulphur is formed. This is visible in the form of a turbidity. **(1 mark)**

(b) HCl + Sodium thiosulphate → Sodium chloride + Sulphur dioxide + Sulphur + Water.

$$HCl\ (aq) + Na_2S_2O_3\ (aq) \rightarrow NaCl\ (aq) + SO_2\ (g) + S(s) + H_2O\ (l)$$

(1 mark)

(c) Critical thinking and problem analysis.

(1 mark)

11. Direct current always flows in one direction but the alternating current reverses its direction periodically. **(1 mark)**

The frequency of AC in India is 50 Hz and in each cycle it alters direction twice. Therefore AC changes direction 2 × 50 = 100 times in one second. **(1 mark)**

When a circuit is connected to the armature of a generator and a current is supplied through it, the current establishes its own magnetic field which oppose the magnetic field producing it. Therefore, it is harder to rotate the armature in this case. **(1 mark)**

12. (a) $Ba(s) + H_2(g) \longrightarrow BaH_2(s)$ **(1 mark)**

(b) $8Ba(s) + S_8(g) \longrightarrow 8BaS(s)$ **(1 mark)**

(c) $3Ba(s) + N_2(g) \longrightarrow Ba_3N_2(s)$ **(1 mark)**

13. (a) Haematite is chief ore of iron. Its formula is $Fe_2O_3 . xH_2O$. **(½ + ½ = 1 mark)**

(b) It is concentrated by hydraulic washing. The ore is washed with stream of water under high pressure. Lighter impurities are washed away whereas heavier minerals are left behind. **(2 marks)**

14. (a) Baking soda is sodium hydrogen carbonate. On heating, it is converted into sodium carbonate which is bitter in taste

$$2NaHCO_3 \rightarrow \underset{\text{Sodium carbonate}}{Na_2CO_3} + CO_2 + H_2O$$

(1 mark)

(b) Baking soda can be converted into baking powder by the addition of appropriate amount of tartaric acid to it. **(1 mark)**

(c) The tartaric acid is used to neutralise sodium carbonate and cake will not taste bitter. **(1 mark)**

15. Tungsten metal has high resistivity and high melting point. **(1 mark)**

(a) Equivalent resistance of 1Ω and 2Ω in series,

$R = 1\Omega + 1\Omega = 3\Omega$

Potential difference, $V = 6V$,

Current, $I = \frac{V}{R} = \frac{6}{3} = 2A$

Current in series circuit is same.

$\therefore$ current in 2Ω resistor $= 2A$

Power in 2Ω resistor, $P = I^2R = 2^2 \times 2 = 8W$ **(1 mark)**

(b) Potential difference across 2Ω

resistor $= 4V$

Power, $P' = \frac{V^2}{R} = \frac{4^2}{2} = 8W$ **(1 mark)**

16. Energy used every day in 5 bulbs $= 5 \times 100 \times 1$ Wh $= 500$ Wh

Energy used everyday in 5 tube lights $= 5 \times 40 \times 5$ Wh $= 1000$ Wh

Total energy used everyday by bulb and tube light $= (500 + 1000)$ Wh $= 1500$ Wh

Total energy used in 30 day $= 1500 \times 30$ Wh $= 45000$ Wh $= \frac{45000}{1000}$ KWh $= 45$ KWh (unit)

Cost of the total energy used $= 45 \times 2.50$ ₹ $=$ ₹ 112.50

(3 mark)

17.

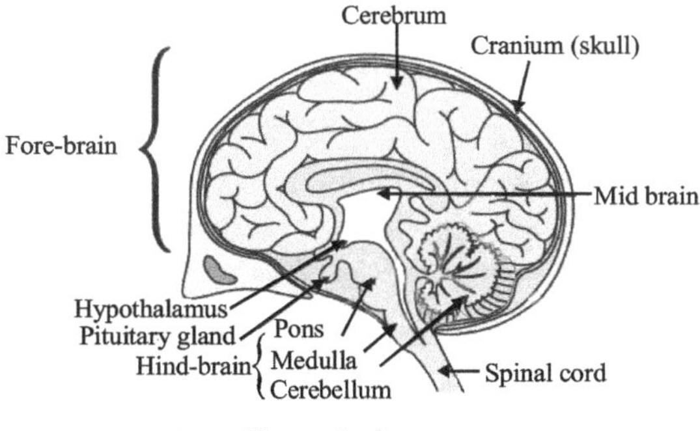

Human brain

(1 mark)

The various functions of brain are as follows :

(i) It receives the sensory messages from the various sense organs.

(ii) It stores information for the future use on the basis of past experiences.

(iii) It correlates various stimuli from different sense organs in its association. **(2 marks)**

The human brain is one of the largest and most complex organ in the human body. It is made up of many specialized areas that work together and cerepral cortex is the outermost protective layer of the brain cells.

18. There are three types of blood vessels of different sizes involved in blood circulation, viz., arteries, veins and capillaries, which are all connected to form a continuous closed system.

(i) Arteries are wide and thick-walled vessels that carry oxygenated blood from the heart to different organs of the body.

(ii) Veins are thin walled, having valves that carry deoxygenated blood from different organs to the heart.

(iii) Capillaries are extremely narrow and thin-walled blood vessels. These walls are permeable, so that water and dissolved substances pass in and out, exchanging oxygen, carbon dioxide, dissolved nutrients and excretory products across the tissues.

(1+1+1=3 marks)

Blood vessels are defined as vessels found in the human or animal body in which the blood circulation takes place.

19. Growth hormone (GH) is secreted by the pituitary gland. It plays an important role in maintaining normal body structure and metabolism. **(2 marks)**

Functions :

(i) It stimulates body growth by stimulating the retention of proteins and calcium in the body.

(ii) It also stimulates synthesis and deposition of proteins in the tissues. **(2 marks)**

Somatostatin inhibits the secretion of GH. Dwarfism is caused due to the failure of secretion of GH.

(1 mark)

20. To find out the total resistance of the circuit when three resistances are connected in parallel:

Let the three resistances R_1, R_2 and R_3 be connected in parallel across the two ends A and B. This combination is connected to a battery of 'V' volt which supplies a current 'I'. Since these three resistances are across the same points A and B i.e. why they have same PD i.e. 'V' volt.

But the current gets divided into I_1, I_2 and I_3 through R_1, R_2 and R_3 respectively.

According to Ohm's law,

$$V = IR \Rightarrow I = \frac{V}{R}$$

$$\text{Current } I_1, \text{(flowing through } R_1) = \frac{V}{R_1}$$

$$\text{Current } I_2, \text{(flowing through } R_2) = \frac{V}{R_2}$$

$$\text{Current } I_3 \text{ (flowing through } R_3) = \frac{V}{R_3}$$

Since, $I = I_1 + I_2 + I_3$

Therefore, $I = \frac{V}{R}$

$$\frac{V}{R} = \frac{V}{R_1} + \frac{V}{R_2} + \frac{V}{R_3}$$

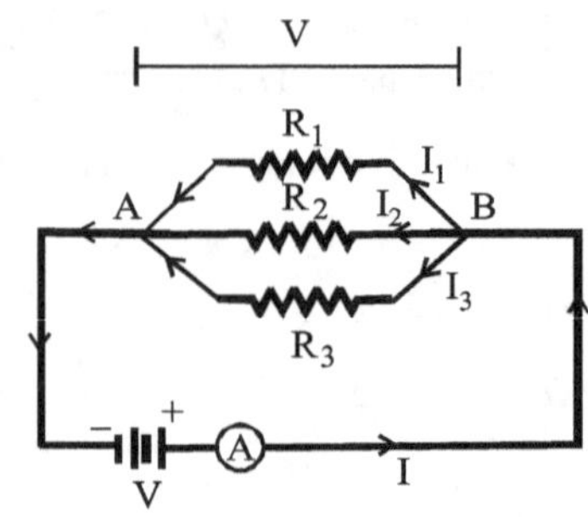

$$\Rightarrow \frac{V}{R} = V\left[\frac{1}{R_1} + \frac{1}{R_2} + \frac{1}{R_3}\right]$$

$$\Rightarrow \frac{1}{R} = \frac{1}{R_1} + \frac{1}{R_2} + \frac{1}{R_3}$$ **(5 marks)**

When a number of resistance are connected in parallel then their combined resistance is less than the smallest individual resistance.

21. (a) Magnetising a Material. When a material, like soft iron, is placed inside a coil carrying current (may be a solenoid), it will get magnetised. Once the current is put-off, the magnetic field will also be lost. Such magnets are called electromagnets. **(2 marks)**

(b) Two uses of electromagnet.

(i) In electric bells.

(ii) For sorting scrap metal. **(1 mark)**

(c) The purpose of soft iron core used in making an electromagnet is that (a) it is temporarily magnetised (b) it retains magnetism as long as current flow is maintained. (c) it will ensure an uniform and stronger field. **(2 marks)**

An electromagnet works on the magnetic effect of current.

22. (a) The gas evolved at anode during electrolysis of brine is chlorine (*G*) When chlorine gas is passed through dry $Ca(OH)_2$ (*Y*) produces bleaching powder (*Z*) used for disinfecting drinking water.

$$Ca(OH)_2 + Cl_2 \rightarrow CaOCl_2 + H_2O$$

Slaked lime — Bleaching powder

Since *Y* and *Z* are calcium salts, therefore *X* is also a calcium salt and is calcium carbonate.

$$CaCO_3 + 2HCl \rightarrow CaCl_2 + CO_2 + H_2O$$

$$Ca(OH)_2 + CO_2 \rightarrow CaCO_3 + H_2O$$

(1+1+1+1=4 marks)

(b) The chemical formula of plaster of paris is $CaSO_4.\frac{1}{2}H_2O$. **(1 mark)**

Note

Calcium carbonate when reacted with hydrochloric acid produces carbon dioxide gas which when passed through slakedlime gives back calcium carbonate.

23. (a) Due to the formation of a layer of oxide i.e., Al_2O_3 **(1 mark)**

(b) Na or Mg are more reactive metals as compared to carbon. **(1 mark)**

(c) In solid NaCl, the movement of ions is not possible due to its rigid structure but in aqueous solution or molten state, the ions can move freely. **(1 mark)**

(d) To protect from corrosion. **(1 mark)**

(e) They are highly reactive. **(1 mark)**

24. (a) Photosynthesis is considered the most important process in the biosphere because :

(i) It is the only known process which converts light energy into chemical energy for utilisation by all living organisms.

(ii) It manufactures organic food. All heterotrophs are dependent on the organic food prepared by the green plants by photosynthesis.

(iii) A number of plant products of economic importance such as timber, fibres, resins, alkaloids, gums, tannins, oils, rubber, cork, etc. are produced by photosynthesis.

(iv) Coal, natural gas and petroleum are products of photosynthetic organisms that lived in the past on this earth.

(v) It maintains the concentration of atmospheric carbon dioxide and oxygen. **(3 marks)**

(b)

Autotrophs	**Heterotrophs**
1. They can make their own food from raw materials in presence of sunlight.	1. They cannot make their own food.
2. They take in simple inorganic substances and change it into complex organic food. *e.g.*, all green plants.	2. They take in complexed food and break it into simple food *e.g.*, all animals and fungi and non-green plants.

(2 marks)

SECTION - B

25. (c) $Na_2CO_3 + 2HCl \rightarrow 2NaCl + H_2O + CO_2\uparrow$ (colourless) **(1 mark)**

26. (a) $CaCO_3 \xrightarrow{\Delta} CaO + CO_2\uparrow$ **(1 mark)**

27. (a) C > B > A > D is the correct order because this is the order of reactivity of these metals with dil HCl. **(1 mark)**

28. (a) Blue litmus turns red in acidic medium. Phenolphtholein turns pink in mild basic medium ~ pH 8.5. Methylorange turns red in acidic medium. **(1 mark)**

29. (d) $HCl + NaOH \longrightarrow NaCl + H_2O + Heat$ **(1 mark)**

Acid-base neutralization reaction is an exothermic process.

30. (a) In case II ammeter is connected in opposite direction. **(1 mark)**

31. (b) In this ammeter is connected in series and Voltmeter in parallel. **(1 mark)**

32. (c) **(1 mark)**

33. **(a)** The label I represents liver. It is the liver that releases bile, which is then stored in gall bladder. **(1 mark)**

34. **(c)** Two observations are:

(i) A colourless and odourless gas is evolved accompanied by brisk effervescence.

(ii) When the gas is bubbled through lime water, it becomes milky. **(2 marks)**

35. 4Ω and 6Ω resistances are short circuited. Therefore, no current will flow through these two resistances. Current passing through the battery is $I = (20/2) = 10A$.

This is also the current passing in wire AB from B to A.

Power supplied by the battery.

$P = EI = (20)(10) = 200$ Watt **(1 mark)**

Potential difference across 4Ω resistance

= Potential difference across 6Ω resistance

$= 0$ **(1 mark)**

36. **(b)** I - Cytoplasm, II - Nucleus

III - Stoma IV - Chloroplast **(2 marks)**

2015-2016

Solved Paper Term – I

Time Allowed : 3 Hours **_Maximum Marks : 90_**

General Instructions:

(i) Question paper comprises of two sections, A and B. You are to attempt both the sections.

(ii) All questions are compulsory.

(iii) All questions of section A and all questions of section B are to be attempted separately.

(iv) Question numbers **1** to **3** in section A are one mark each, to be answered in one word or one sentence.

(v) Question numbers **4** to **6** are two marks each, to be answered in about 30 words.

(vi) Question numbers **7** to **18** are three marks each, to be answered in about 50 words.

(vii) Question numbers **19** to **24** are five marks each, to be answered in about 70 words.

(viii) Question numbers **25** to **33** in section B are MCQ based on practical skills. Each question is a one mark question.

(ix) Question number **34** to **36** in section B are question based on practicalskill. Each Question is of two marks.

SECTION - A

1. What happens to the force between two electric charges, if the distance between them is

(a) halved, (b) doubled?

2. What happens chemically when quicklime is added to water?

3. What is a neurotransmitter?

4. The waste materials collected from a market complex are scrap paper, thermocol, vegetable wastes, tin, cans and glass bottles. Which of these can be used for producing biogas? Mention three advantages of converting these into biogas rather than burning them?

5. A family consumes 14.5 kg of LPG in 30 days. Calculate the average energy consumed per day, if the calorific value of LPG is 55 kJ/g?

6. How is electricity generated by a hydro electric power plant? Explain.

7. Explain Maxwell's right hand thumb rule?

8. Explain what causes the wind to blow in equatorial regions. What is wind energy?

9. Kangana is a model by profession. She visited Tokyo, capital city of Japan with her mother. There they wanted to visit a nearby town. They bought tickets for a railway train between the two cities. Kangana's mother refused to board the train when she came to know that the train does not have wheels. This created a problem. It was necessary for her to board the train and reach the other city where she had to shoot and film. Seeing her mother in quandary Kangana talked to her mother by giving her complete details of how the train will move. This convinced her mother. Then they boarded the train and reached the destination safely.

(a) Which value do you think is shown by Kangana?

(b) Name such type of train which does not require wheels? How does it move?

10. (a) State one difference between.

(i) Combination and decomposition reaction.

(ii) Displacement and double displacement reaction

(b) Balance the following chemical equation:

$$Pb(NO_3)_2(s) \xrightarrow{\text{Heat}} PbO(s) + NO_2(g) + O_2(g)$$

11. Why don't two magnetic lines of force intersect each other?

List three sources of magnetic fields.

12. Represent each of the following word equations with a balanced chemical equation.

(a) Disilane gas (Si_2H_6) undergoes combustion to form solid silicon dioxide and water.

(b) Solid aluminium hydride is formed by a combination reaction of its two elements.

(c) When solid calcium bisulfite is heated, it decomposes to solid calcium oxide, sulfur dioxide gas, and water.

13. (a) Name a non-metallic element which conducts electricity.

(b) Give reasons for the following :

(i) Metals conduct electricity.

(ii) Reaction of nitric acid with metals generally does not evolve hydrogen gas.

14. (a) Why should curd and sour substances not be kept in brass and copper vessels ?

(b) Why does distilled water not conduct electricity, whereas rain water does ?

15. Explain the following.

(a) Why is the tungsten used almost exclusively for filament of electric lamps?

(b) An electric heater of resistance 8Ω draws 15A from the service mains in 2hrs. Calculate the rate at which heat is developed in the heater.

16. (a) Specific resistance of copper, silver and constant are 1.18×10^{-6} Ω cm, 1×10^{-6} Ω cm and 48×10^{-6} Ω cm respectively. Which is the best electrical conductor and why?

(b) A cell of e.m.f 2V and internal resistance 0.1 Ω is connected to a 3.9 Ω external resistance. What will be the p.d across the terminals of the cell?

(c) A uniform wire of resistance 20 Ω is cut into two equal parts. These parts are how connected in parallel. What will be the resistance of the combination?

17. (a) Name the components of circulatory system.

(b) What is the advantage of having four chambered heart?

18. Why is the use of iodised salt advisable?

19. (a) Name two hormones secreted by pancreas.

(b) Why are some patients of diabetes treated by giving injections of insulin?

20. Give two reasons why are the conductors (filament) of electrical heating devices made of an alloy rather than a pure metal.

A wire having resistance of 16Ω is drawn to triple of its length. Calculate its new resistance. What is the effect on its resistivity.

21. A straight conductor passes vertically through a cardboard sprinkled with iron filings. Show the setting of the iron filings when a weak current is passed in the downward direction. What changes occur if,

(a) the strength of the current is increased.

(b) the single conductor is replaced by several parallel conductors with current flowing in the same direction.

22. (a) Write balanced acid–base neutralization reactions that would lead to formation of the following salts or acid salts.

(i) $CaBr_2$

(ii) $Sr(ClO_2)_2$

(iii) $Ba(HS)_2$

(iv) Li_2S

(b) Why does dry HCl gas not change the colour of the dry litmus paper ?

23. (a) Why is an ionic bond also called an electrovalent bond ?

(b) What is an alloy ? Name the constituents of 22-carat gold. Why is 24-carat gold converted to 22-carat gold?

(c) Why do ionic compounds have high melting points ?

24. Describe and explain the variation in blood pressure throughout an individual's circulatory system during a single heartbeat.

SECTION - B

25. Observe the following experimental set-up

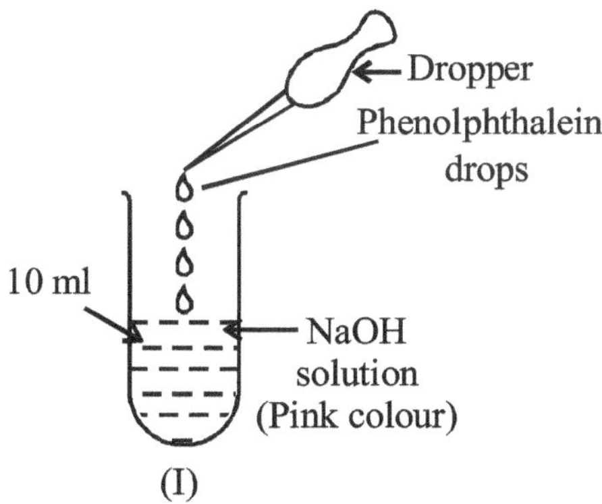

(I)

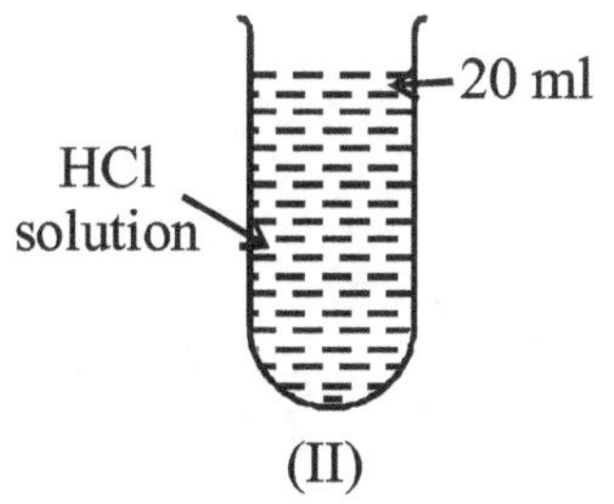

(II)

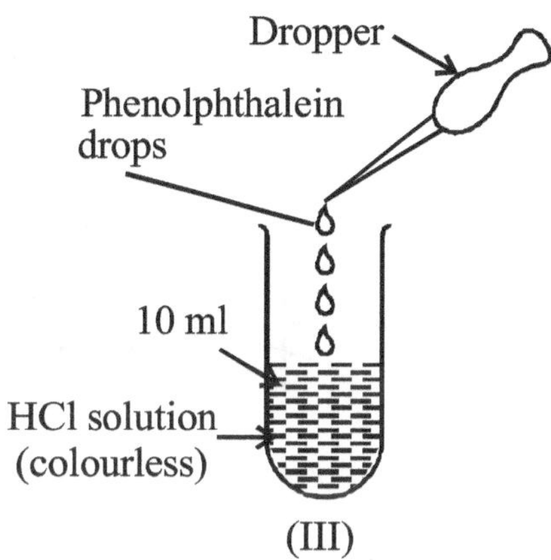

(III)

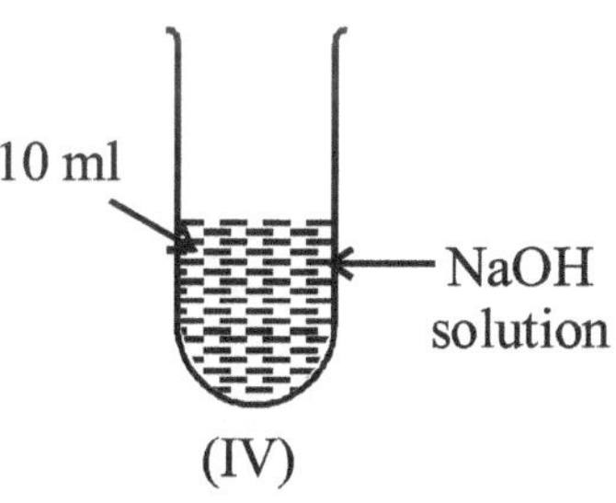

(IV)

Statement – I : When (I) test tube and (II) test tube containing NaOH & HCl solution respectively are mixed together completely the colour of the solution changed to colourless.

Statement -II : When test tube (III) & (IV) are mixed together completely, the resultant solution remains colourless.

(a) Only (I) is correct

(b) Only (II) is correct

(c) Both (I) and (II) are correct

(d) None of these

26. Observe the experimental setup carefully

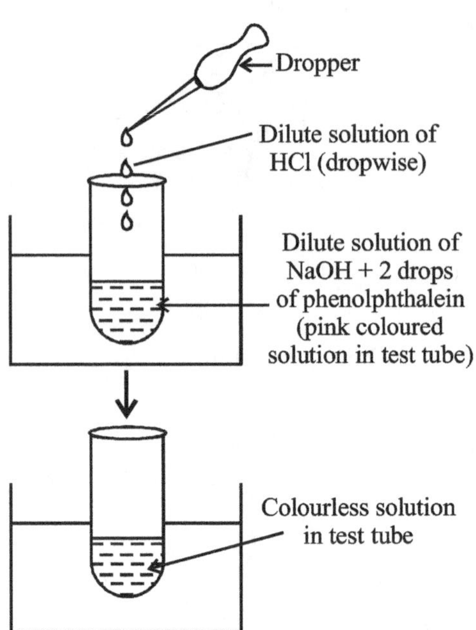

Which type of reaction is this ?

(a) Isomerisation

(b) Neutralisation

(c) Saponification

(d) Both (b) and (c)

27. Four students studied reactions of Zinc and Na_2CO_3 with dil HCl and dil NaOH solution and presented their result as follows. The ' ' represents evolution of a gas where as 'x' represents no reaction.

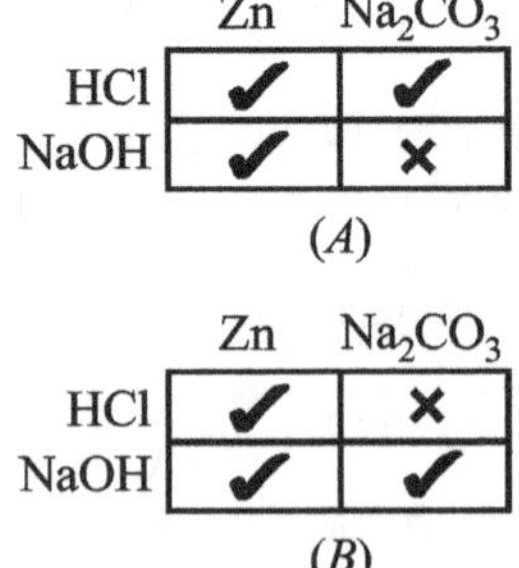

	Zn	Na_2CO_3
HCl	✔	✔
NaOH	✔	✕

(*A*)

	Zn	Na_2CO_3
HCl	✔	✕
NaOH	✔	✔

(*B*)

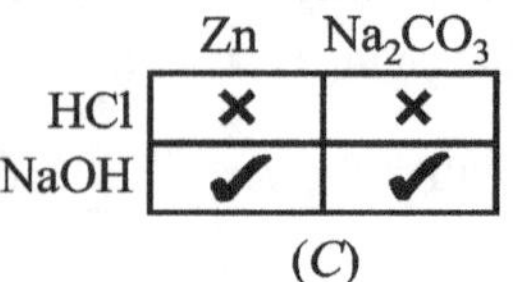

	Zn	Na_2CO_3
HCl	✕	✕
NaOH	✔	✔

(*C*)

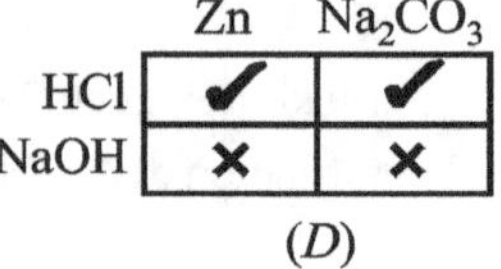

	Zn	Na_2CO_3
HCl	✔	✔
NaOH	✕	✕

(*D*)

The right set of observation is that of student

(a) A (b) B

(c) C (d) D

28. The colour of pH paper when put in distilled water changed to green. Now some common salt is added to water and pH paper is tested in this solution. The colour of pH paper in this case is likely to be

(a) green

(b) yellow

(c) red

(d) blue

29. Observe this experiment carefully :

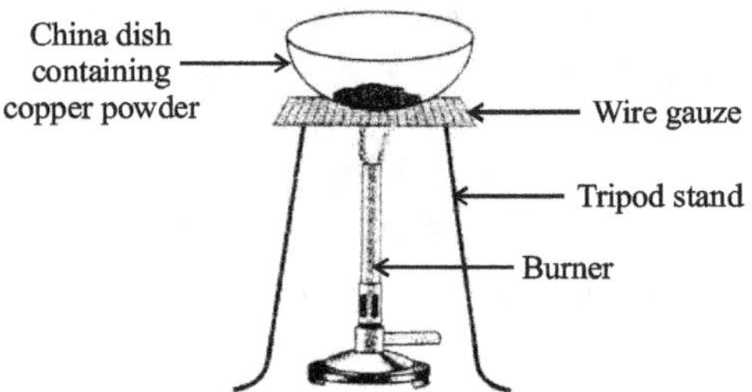

In above experiment copper powder turned to black coloured product on heating. It is due to the reason that:

(a) Copper has absorbed heat

(b) Copper (II) oxide is formed

(c) Copper (I) oxide is formed

(d) Both (a) and (c) are correct

30. A constant current flows in a horizontal wire in the plane of the paper from east to west as shown in Fig. The direction of magnetic field at a point will be North to South

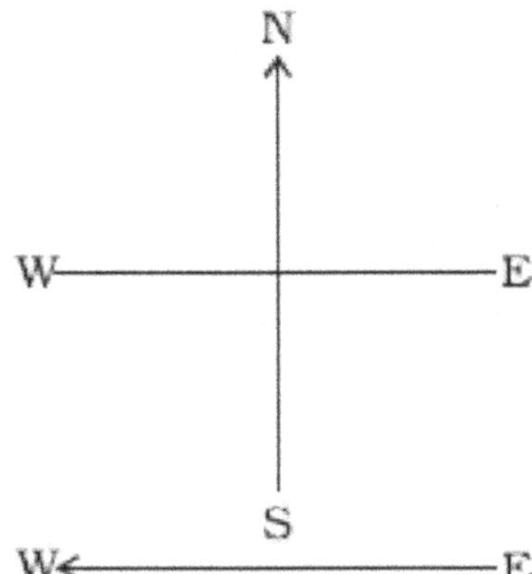

(a) directly above the wire

(b) directly below the wire

(c) at a point located in the plane of the paper, on the north side of the wire

(d) at a point located in the plane of the paper, on the south side of the wire

31. In the arrangement shown in Fig., there are two coils wound on a non-conducting cylindrical rod.

Initially the key is not inserted. Then the key is inserted and later removed. Then

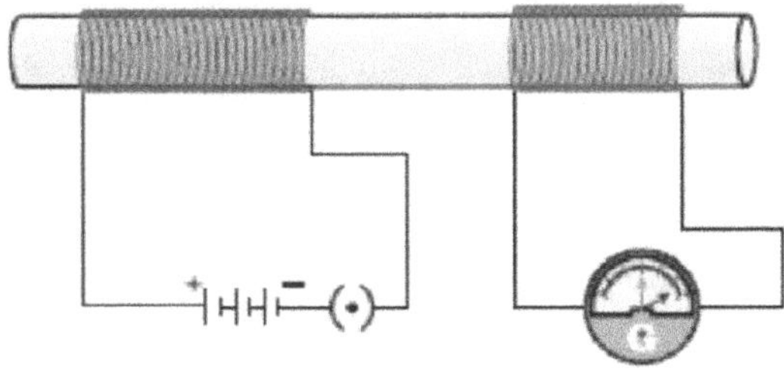

(a) the deflection in the galvanometer remains zero throughout

(b) there is a momentary deflection in the galvanometer but it dies out shortly and there is no effect when the key is removed

(c) there are momentary galvanometer deflections that die out shortly; the deflections are in the same direction

(d) there are momentary galvanometer deflections that die out shortly; the deflections are in opposite directions

32. What is the correct sequence for nutrition in *Amoeba*?

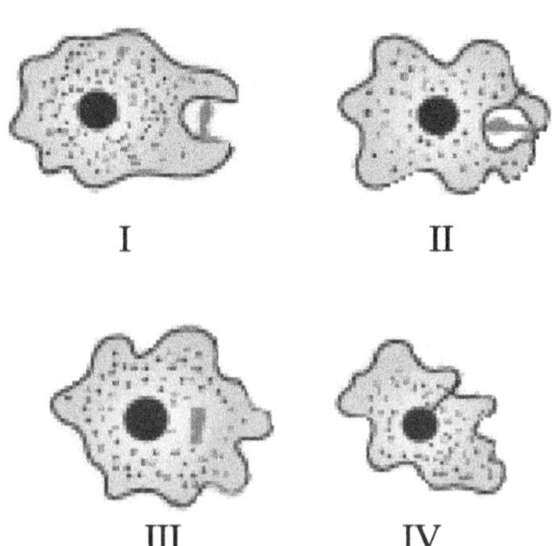

(a) (I), (III), (IV), (II) (b) (IV), (I), (II), (III)

(c) (II), (III), (IV), (I) (d) (III), (IV), (II), (I)

33. Which of the following diagram correctly shows pseudopodia in *Amoeba*?

(a) (b)

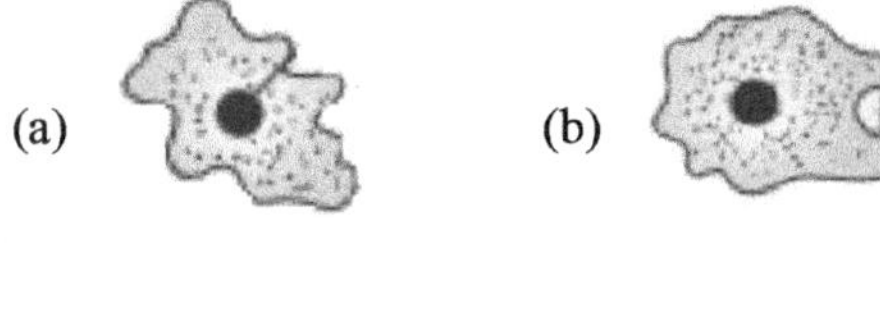

(c)

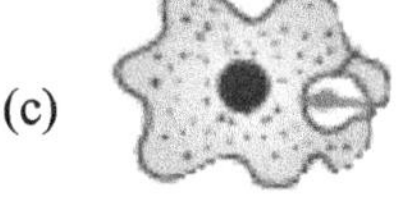

(d)

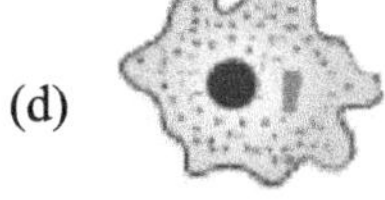

34. A student added zinc granules to copper sulphate solution taken in a test tube. Write the observation and chemical reaction behind this.

35. Six equal resistors of 1Ω each are connected to form a hexagon ABCDEF as shown. If the current enters at A and leaves at D, find the resistance offered by the combination

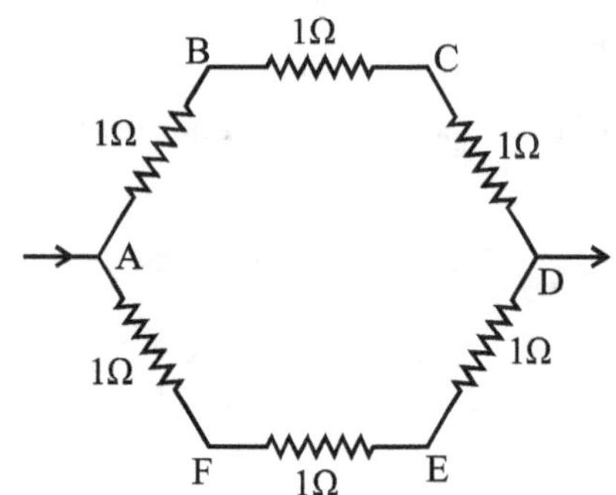

36. In the given figure, label I represents _________ while label II represents _________.

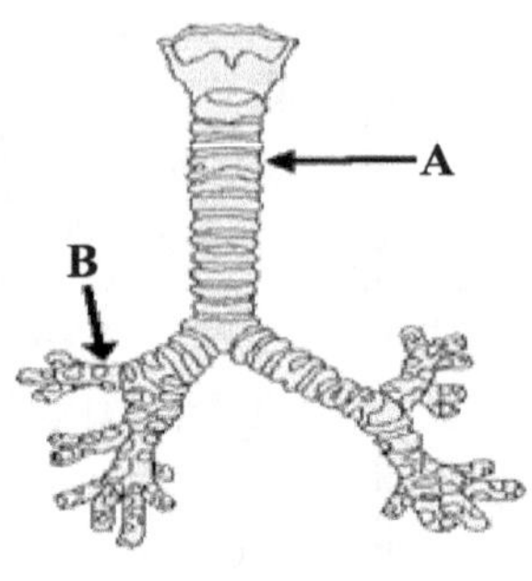

Solutions

1. (i) It becomes four times (½ + ½ = 1 mark)

(ii) It becomes one fourth.

2. Quicklime reacts with water to produce slaked lime. In this process, large amounts of heat is released.

$$\underset{\substack{\text{Calcium oxide} \\ \text{(Quick lime)}}}{CaO(s)} + H_2O(l) \longrightarrow \underset{\substack{\text{Calcium hydroxide} \\ \text{(Slaked lime)}}}{Ca(OH)_2(aq)} + \text{Heat}$$

(1 mark)

3. Neurotransmitter is a chemical extruded by an axon terminal for passage of impulse to the next neuron, muscle, gland or organ. **(1 mark)**

4. Scrap paper and vegetable wastes can be used to produce biogas. **(1 mark)**

Advantages of converting biomass into biogas:-

(i) Biogas has high calorific value than biomass.

(ii) Biogas does not produce any smoke.

(iii) Biogas does not leave any residue.

(iv) By obtaining biogas from biomass, the left over residue can be used by farmers as manure.

(1 mark)

5. Here,

Mass of LPG consumed, m = 14.5 kg = 14500 g

Calorific value of LPG, c = 55 kJ/g

No. of days of consumption, n = 30 days

Total energy consumed, Q = mc

Putting values, we get Q = 14500 × 55 kJ

= 797500 kJ.

$$\text{Average consumption per day} = \frac{Q}{n} = \frac{797500}{30}$$

= 26583.3 kJ

Average energy consumed per day = 26583.3 kJ.

(2 marks)

6. Water stored behind the dams, possesses potential energy. When the iron gates of the dam are opened, the water flows down and its energy gets converted into kinetic energy and falls on the turbine and rotates its blades. The turbine inturns rotates the crankshaft which generates electricity with the help of generator.

(1 mark)

7. According to this rule if we imagine that we are holding a wire carrying current and thumb is stretched in the direction of current then the direction in which fingers will be wrapped gives the direction of magnetic lines of force. It means if the current is flowing in the upward direction then the direction of magnetic lines of force will be anticlockwise and if current is flowing in the downward direction then the direction of magnetic lines of force will be clockwise.

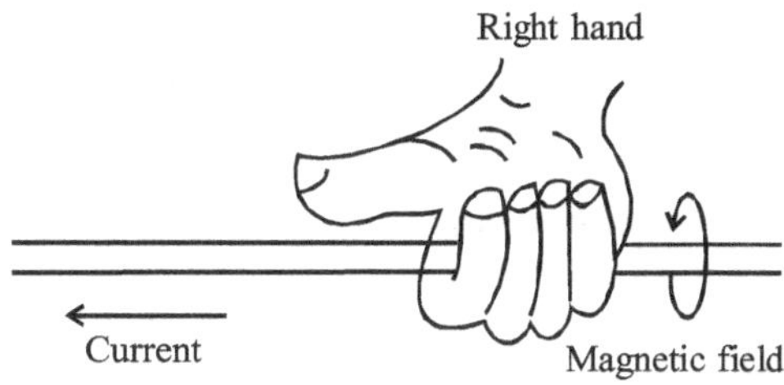

(3 marks)

8. Solar energy is responsible for wind to blow. The intensity of sun-rays is much more stronger near the equator of the earth than in the polar region. Due to more intense heat, the air near the surface of the earth in equatorial regions become quite hot. The hot air being lighter rises upward

and cooler air from the polar region of earth starts flowing which causes wind to blow from the high pressure to low pressure region. So wind blows to equatorial regions. The energy possessed by this wind is called wind energy. **(2+1= 3 marks)**

9. **(a)** Concern for her mother, good use of fundamentals learnt, responsibility. **(1 mark)**

(b) Train is called Maglev (Magnetic Levitation). To move such type of train instead of wheels, electromagnets are mounted on the magnetic levitation vehicle, and a series of propulsion coils are placed along the side of the track. The polarity of the magnets on the vehicle remains constant. An electrical signal is passed through the coils such that each magnet on the vehicle "sees" a coil with opposite polarity ahead of it and a coil with the same polarity behind it. As a result, the vehicle experiences an attractive force from the coil a head of it and a requlsive force from the coil behind it, both forces pushing the vehicle in the forward direction. This propels the train which does not require wheels.

(2 marks)

10. **(a)** (i) Combination reactions are generally exothermic whereas decomposition reaction are endothermic. **(1 mark)**

$$2Cu + O_2 \longrightarrow 2CuO$$

(ii) In a displacement reaction one element displaces another element from its compound, whereas in double displacement reaction two different atoms or group of atoms are exchanged. **(1 mark)**

$$Na_2SO_4 + BaCl_2 \longrightarrow BaSO_4 + 2NaCl$$

(b) $2Pb(NO_3)_2(s) \xrightarrow{\text{Heat}} 2PbO(s) + 4NO_2(g) + O_2(g)$

(1 mark)

11. Two magnetic lines of force never intersect each other. If the lines intersect, then at the point of intersection there would be two directions (the needle would point towards two directions) for the same magnetic field, which is not possible. **(1½ marks)**

(a) Natural and artificial magnets.

(b) Electromagnets

(c) A current carrying conductor produces magnetic field. **(1½ marks)**

12. **(a)** $2Si_2H_6(g)+7O_2(g) \longrightarrow 4SiO_2(s)+6H_2O(l)$

(1 mark)

(b) $2Al(s)+3H_2(g) \longrightarrow 2AlH_3(s)$ **(1 mark)**

(c) $Ca(HSO_3)_2(s) \longrightarrow CaO(s)+2SO_2(s)+H_2O(l)$ **(1 mark)**

13. **(a)** Carbon in the form of graphite conducts electricity, used as electrodes in electrolytic cells and dry cells.

(1 mark)

(b) (i) Metals conduct electricity due to presence of free electrons which can easily move. **(½ mark)**

(ii) It is because nitric acid is good oxidising agent and it oxidises H_2 to H_2O. **(1 mark)**

Note

Generally non metals are bad conductor of electricity. However graphite which is an allotrope of carbon is a good conductor of electricity due to presence of free electrons.

14. **(a)** This is because curd and other sour substances contain acids which can react with the metal of the vessel to form poisonous metal compounds with evolution of H_2 which can cause food poisoning and harmful for our health. **(1 mark)**

(b) Distilled water does not conduct electricity because it does not contain any ionic compound like acids, bases or salts, dissolved in it. Rain water, while falling to the earth through the atmosphere, dissolves acidic gases like CO_2, SO_2 etc. from the air thus forms acids like carbonic acid (H_2CO_3), sulphurous acid (H_2SO_3) etc. These acids provides hydrogen ions (H^+) to rain water. So, due to presence of these acids, the rain water conducts electricity. **(2 marks)**

Material or compounds which have free electrons or ions conduct electricity for example glucose solution do not conduct electricity because glucose do not produce free ions on dissociation.

15. **(a)** Tungsten has very high melting point (3380°C). So it can't melt upto a high temperature. This is the reason why tungsten is used almost exclusively for filament of electric lamps. **(1 mark)**

(b) $P = \frac{E}{t} = \frac{I^2Rt}{t} = I^2R = 15 \times 15 \times 8$

$= 1800$ W.

So, heat is developed at a rate of 1800J/sec.

(2 marks)

16. **(a)** The specific resistance of silver is least. So it is the best conductor as the conductivity is the reciprocal of specific resistance.

We can use resistivity values to compare the resistances of two or more substances. A good conductor of electicity should have low resistivity and poor conductor of electricity will have a high resistivity.

(1 mark)

(b) $V = E - Ir = 2 - I \times 0.1$

Also $I = \frac{E}{R+r} = \frac{2}{3.9+0.1} = \frac{2}{4} = \frac{1}{2} = 0.5$ A.

$\therefore \quad V = 2 - 0.5 \times 0.1 = 2 - 0.05 = 1.95$ V **(1 mark)**

(c) $\because \quad R \propto \ell$

$\therefore$ Resistance of each part is 10 Ω.

$\therefore \quad R_{eq} = \frac{10 \times 10}{10+10} = \frac{100}{20} = 5\ \Omega$. **(1 mark)**

17. **(a)** Circulatory system consists of blood vessels, a pumping heart, blood and lymph. **(1 mark)**

(b) Four chambered heart ensures complete separation of oxygenated and deoxygenated bloods. Only oxygenated blood is pumped out to supply all parts of the body. It is received by left auricle from lungs and pumped out by left ventricle. The blood returns to heart after deoxygenation. It is received by right auricle and pumped out by right ventricle to lungs for oxygenation. The mechanism is useful to animals with high energy needs (due to thermoregulation and higher activity) such as birds and mammals.

(2 marks)

The heart is a muscular organ that plays an essential role in transportation of oxygen nutrients to the different parts of the body through blood.

18. Iodine is essential for synthesis of hormone thyroxine in thyroid gland. Thyroxine controls basal metabolic rate, physical activity, body temperature, heart beat, mental, physical and sexual development. **(2 marks)**

Deficiency of thyroxine disturbs metabolic, physical and mental activities besides causing disorders of simple goitre, cretinism and myxedema. Therefore, it is always advisable to take iodised salt so that there is no deficiency of iodine.

(1 mark)

19. **(a)** Insulin and Glucagon **(1 + 1 = 2 marks)**

(b) Diabetes mellitus is of two types, insulin dependent and insulin independent. In insulin dependent diabetes, pancreas is unable to produce required quantity of insulin. As a result blood sugar continues to rise and part of sugar is excreted through urine resulting in diabetes. This is kept under check by regular injection of insulin. Availability of insulin will help the cells to take up glucose while liver and muscles are induced to store excess of glucose as glycogen. **(3 marks)**

Hormones are chemical messengers that are secreted directly into the blood stream and are transported to different organs and tissues to perform specific function in the body.

20. (i) alloy has high resistivity.

(ii) alloy does not burn (oxidise) easily (i.e. high melting point). **(2 marks)**

$R_1 = 16\ \Omega$ $R_2 = ?$

$\ell_1 = \ell$ $\ell_2 = 3\ell$

Let initial area $A_1 = A$ & final area is A_2

We know that the volume of metal remains constant.

$A_1\ \ell_1 = A_2\ \ell_2$

$A.\ell = A_2.3\ell$

$A_2 = A/3$

$$R_1 = \rho\frac{\ell_1}{A_1}$$

$$R_2 = \rho\frac{\ell_2}{A_2} \Rightarrow \frac{R_1}{R_2} = \frac{\ell_1.A_2}{\ell_2.A_1}$$

$$\frac{R_1}{R_2} = \frac{\ell \times A}{3\ell \times A \times 3} = \frac{1}{9}$$

$R_2 = 9R_1 = 9 \times 16 = 144\Omega$

There is no change in resistivity. **(3 marks)**

Resistivity of a substance does not depend on its length or thickness. It depends on the nature of the substance and temperature.

21. Figure shows the setting of the iron filings.

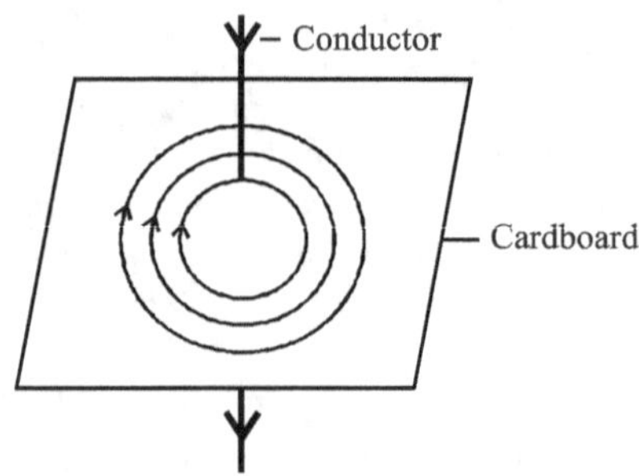

(2 marks)

(a) The shape of distribution of iron filings remains unchanged but they get arranged upto a larger distance from the conductor when the strength of current is increased. This is because on increasing the strength of current, the strength of the magnetic field is increased and it is effective upto a larger distance from the conductor. **(2 marks)**

(b) Magnetic field strength is increased so the iron filings get arranged upto a larger distance. **(1 mark)**

The magnitude of magnetic field produced by a straight conductor is inversely proportional to the distance of that point from the wire.

22. **(a)** (i) $2HBr + Ca(OH)_2 \longrightarrow CaBr_2 + 2H_2O$

(1 mark)

(ii) $2HClO_2 + Sr(OH)_2 \longrightarrow Sr(ClO_2)_2 + 2H_2O$

(1 mark)

(iii) $2H_2S + Ba(OH)_2 \longrightarrow Ba(HS)_2 + 2H_2O$

(1 mark)

(iv) $H_2S + 2LiOH \longrightarrow Li_2S + 2H_2O$

(1 mark)

(b) Dry HCl gas does not change the colour of dry litmus paper because it has no hydrogen ions (H^+) in it. Dry HCl is a covalent compound.

(1 mark)

23. (a) An ionic bond is also called an electrovalent bond because of the involvement of electrostatic forces of attraction between oppositely charged ions in the formation of this bond. **(1 mark)**

(b) Alloy is homogeneous mixture of two or more metals. One of them can be non-metal also.

(1 mark)

22 carat gold contains $\frac{22}{24} \times 100 = 90.66\%$ gold and remaining copper. **(1 mark)**

It is because 24 carat gold (pure gold) is too soft to make ornaments. **(1 mark)**

(c) The ionic compounds are made up of positive and negative ions. There is a strong force of attraction between the oppositly charged ions, therefore a lot of energy is required to break this force of attraction and melt this ionic compound. That is why ionic compounds have high melting points.

(1 mark)

Ionic compounds have crystalline structure. They have strong electrostatic attraction. Hence ionic compounds have high melting and boiling point.

24. The highest blood pressure (approximately 120 mm Hg) occurs when the left ventricle contracts, pumping blood into arteries to be carried throughout the body. When this ventricle relaxes and refills, the pressure drops to about 80 mm Hg. Sphygmomanometer used for measuring blood pressure.

Blood pumped from the right ventricle goes to the lungs. Since it has a shorter distance to travel, less pressure needs to be generated: 25 mm Hg drops to 8 mm during relaxation. As the blood passes into capillaries, friction drag lowers the pressure to 35 mm Hg. Pressure of blood leaving the smaller-diameter capillaries drops to 10mm Hg. Resistance to blood flow is increased when the diameter of a vessel is decreased, slowing down the blood flow. Blood that must travel uphill to return to the heart depends on skeletal muscles to push it upward against gravity. Valves in the veins keep it from flowing backward. The consistent decrease in blood pressure throughout the human circulatory system is necessary to allow the blood to complete a circuit of the circulatory system by always flowing from a region of higher blood pressure to a region of lower blood pressure.

(5 marks)

Blood is a body fluid found in humans and other animals that delivers oxygen and other necessary substances such nutrients to the cells and facilitates the removal of carbon dioxide and other metabolic waste out of the body.

25. (c) Neutralisation reaction results into formation of salt and water which are neutral.

$$NaOH + HCl \longrightarrow NaCl + H_2O$$

Phenolphthalein is colourless in acidic and neutral medium. **(1 mark)**

26. (b) $HCl + NaOH \longrightarrow NaCl + H_2O$

Neutralization reaction. **(1 mark)**

27. (a) $Zn + 2\,HCl \longrightarrow ZnCl_2 + H_2\uparrow$

$Na_2CO_3 + 2\,HCl \longrightarrow 2NaCl + H_2O + CO_2\uparrow$

$Zn + 2\,NaOH + 2H_2O \longrightarrow Na_2[Zn(OH)_4] + H_2\uparrow$

(1 mark)

28. (a) NaCl solution in water is neutral i.e., pH = 7. The colour of pH paper will be the same as that of distilled water as NaCl is a salt of strong acid and strong base. **(1 mark)**

29. (b) $2Cu + O_2 \longrightarrow \underset{\text{Black}}{2CuO}\downarrow$ **(1 mark)**

30. **(b)** By right hand rule. **(1 mark)**

31. **(d)** Current in induced for short time when key is inserted and then becomes zero after when key is removed then current is induced in opposite direction.

(1 mark)

32. **(b)**

(1 mark)

33. **(b)** *Amoeba* takes in food using temporary finger like extension (Pseudopodia) of the cell surface which fuse over the food particle forming a food-vacuole.

(1 mark)

34. **(c)** The displacement reaction that occurs is the colour of zinc granules changes to brownish black.

$$Zn(s) + CuSO_4(aq) \rightarrow ZnSO_4(aq) + \underset{\text{(Brownish black)}}{Cu(s)}$$

(2 marks)

35. **(d)** $\frac{1}{R} = \frac{1}{3} + \frac{1}{3}$

$R = \frac{3}{2} = 1.5\Omega$ **(2 marks)**

36. **(d)** The label A represents trachea while label B represents bronchiole. **(2 marks)**

Delhi 2016

CBSE Board Solved Paper

Time Allowed : 3 Hours ***Maximum Marks : 80***

General Instructions:

(i) The question paper comprises **two Sections, A and B**. You are to attempt both the sections.

(ii) **All** questions are **compulsory.**

(iii) There is no choice in any of the questions.

(iv) **All** questions of **Section-A** and **all** questions of **Section-B** are to be attempted separately.

(v) Question numbers **1** to **3** in **Section-A** are **one** mark questions. These are to be answered in **one word** or in **one sentence.**

(vi) Question numbers **4** to **6** in **Section-A** are **two** marks questions. These are to be answered in about **30 words** each.

(vii) Question numbers **7** to **18** in **Section-A** are **three** marks questions. These are to be answered in about **70 words** each.

(viii) Question numbers **19** to **24** in **Section-A** are **five** marks questions. These are to be answered in about **70 words** each.

(ix) Question numbers **25** to **33** in **Section-B** are multiple choice questions based on practical skills. Each question is a **one** mark question. You are to select one most appropriate response out of the four provided to you.

(x) Question numbers **34** to **36** in **Section-B** are two marks questions based on practical skills. These are to be answered in brief.

SECTION - A

1. Write the next homologue of each of the following: (i) C_2H_4 (ii) C_4H_6

2. Name the part of *Bryophyllum* where the buds are produced for vegetative propagation.

3. List two natural ecosystems.

4. State two positions in which a concave mirror produces a magnified image of a given object. List two differences between the two images.

5. List four advantages of properly managed watershed management.

6. Explain giving example where active involvement of local people lead to efficient management of forest.

7. What are covalent compounds? Why are they different from ionic compounds? List their three characteristic properties.

8. When ethanol reacts with ethanoic acid in the presence of conc. H_2SO_4, a substance with fruity smell is produced. Answer the following:

(i) State the class of compounds to which the fruity smelling compounds belong. Write the chemical equation for the reaction and write the chemical name of the product formed.

(ii) State the role of conc.H_2SO_4 in this reaction.

9. Calcium is an element with atomic number 20. Stating reason answer each of the following questions:

(i) Is calcium a metal or non-metal?

(ii) Will its atomic radius be larger or smaller than that of potassium with atomic number 19?

(iii) Write the formula of its oxide.

10. An element 'M' with electronic configuration (2, 8, 2) combines separately with $(NO_3)^-$, $(SO_4)^{2-}$ and $(PO_4)^{3-}$ radicals. Write the formula of the three compounds so formed. To which group and period of the Modern Periodic Table does the elements 'M' belong? Will 'M' form covalent or ionic compounds? Give reason to justify your answer.

11. How do organisms, whether reproduced asexually or sexually maintain a constant chromosome number through several generations? Explain with the help of suitable example.

12. Name the parts A, B and C shown in the following diagram and state one function of each.

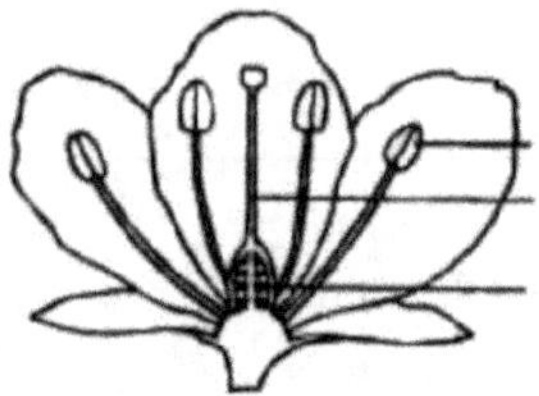

13. Suggest three contraceptive methods to control the size of human population which is essential for the health and prosperity of a country. State the basic principle involved in each.

14. In one of his experiments with pea plants Mendel observed that when a pure tall pea plant is crossed with a pure dwarf pea plant, in the first generation, F_1 only tall plants appear.

(a) What happens to the traits of the dwarf plants in this case?

(b) When the F_1 generation plants were self-fertilised, he observed that in the plants of second generation, F_2 both tall plants and dwarf plants were present. Why it happened? Explain briefly.

15. List three distinguishing features, in tabular form, between acquired traits and the inherited traits.

16. Draw the following diagram, in which a ray of light is incident on a concave/convex mirror, on your answer sheet. Show the path of this ray, after reflection, in each case.

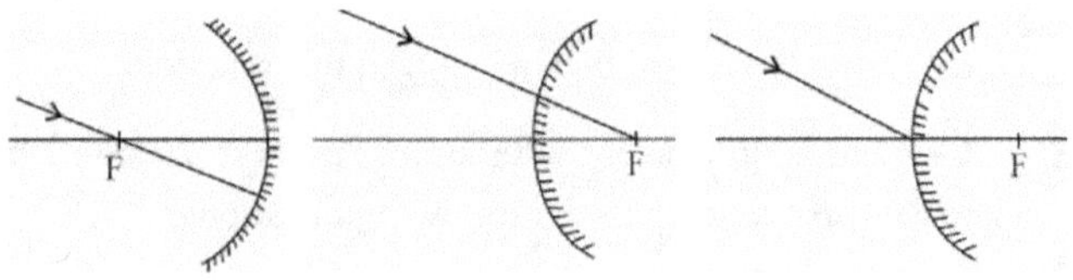

17. Why does the sun appear reddish early in the morning? Will this phenomenon be observed by an observer on the moon? Justify your answer with a reason.

18. Give reason to justify the following:

(a) The existence of decomposers is essential in a biosphere.

(b) Flow of energy in a food chain is unidirectional.

19. (a) Give a chemical test to distinguish between saturated and unsaturated hydrocarbon.

(b) Name the products formed when ethane burns in air. Write the balanced chemical equation for the reaction showing the types of energies liberated.

(c) Why is reaction between methane and chlorine in the presence of sunlight considered a substitution reaction?

20. (a) Write the functions of the following parts in human female reproductive system:

(i) Ovary (ii) Oviduct (iii) Uterus

(b) Describe the structure and function of placenta.

21. What is meant by speciation? List four factors that could lead to speciation. Which of these cannot be a major factor in the speciation of a self-pollinating plant species. Give reason to justify your answer.

22. (a) Define the following terms in the context of spherical mirrors:

(i) Pole (ii) Centre of curvature (iii) Principal axis (iv) Principal focus

(b) Draw ray diagrams to show the principal focus of a :

(i) Concave mirror (ii) Convex mirror

(c) Consider the following diagram in which M is a mirror and P is an object and Q is its magnified image formed by the mirror.

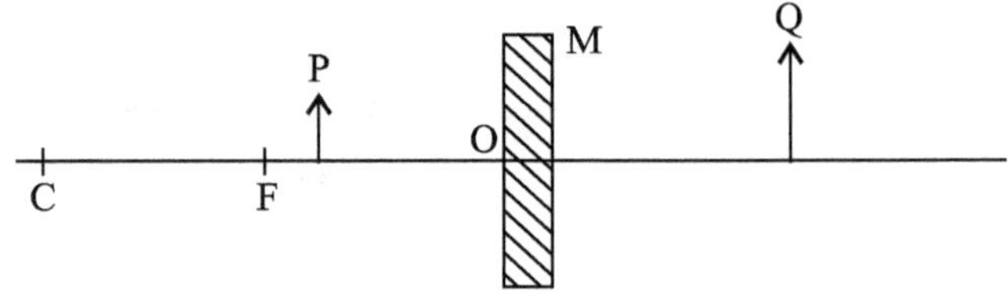

State the type of the mirror M and one characteristic property of the image Q.

23. (a) Draw a ray diagram to show the formation of image by a convex lens when an object is placed in front of the lens between its optical centre and principal focus.

(b) In the above ray diagram mark the object-distance (u) and the image-distance (v) with their proper signs (+ve or –ve as per the new Cartesian sign convention) and state how these distances are related to the focal length (f) of the convex lens in this case.

(c) Find the power of a convex lens which forms a real, and inverted image of magnification –1 of an object placed at a distance of 20 cm from its optical centre.

24. (a) Write the function of each of the following parts of human eye:

Cornea; iris; crystalline lens: ciliary muscles

(b) Millions of people of the developing countries of world are suffering from corneal blindness. These persons can be cured by replacing the defective cornea with the cornea of a donated eye. A charitable society of your city has organised a campaign in your neighbourhood in order to create awareness about this fact. If you are asked to participate in this mission how would you contribute in this noble cause?

(i) State the objective of organising such campaigns.

(ii) List two arguments which you would give to motivate the people to donate their eyes after death.

(iii) List two values which are developed in the persons who actively participate and contribute in such programmes.

SECTION - B

25. Which of the following sets of materials can be used for conducting a saponification reaction for the preparation of soap?

(a) $Ca(OH)_2$ and neem oil

(b) NaOH and neem oil

(c) NaOH and mineral oil

(d) $Ca(OH)_2$ and mineral oil

26. A student takes four test tubes marked P, Q, R and S of 25 mL capacity and fill 10 mL of distilled water in each. He dissolves one spoon full of four different salts in each as - KCl in P, NaCl in Q, $CaCl_2$ in R and $MgCl_2$ in S. He then adds about 2 mL of a sample of soap solution to each of the above test tubes. On shaking the contents of each of the test tubes, he is likely to observe a good amount of lather (foam) in the test tubes marked :

(a) P and Q (b) R and S

(c) P, Q and R (d) P, Q and S

27. Consider the following comments about saponification reactions :

I. Heat is evolved in these reactions

II. For quick precipitation of soap sodium chloride is added to the reaction mixture.

III. Saponification reactions are special kind of neutralization reactions.

IV. Soaps are basic salts of long chain fatty acids.

The correct comments are:

(a) I, II and III (b) II, III and IV

(c) I, II and IV (d) Only I and IV

28. A student has to perform the experiment "To identify the different parts of an embryo of a dicot seed." Select from the following an appropriate group of seeds:

(a) pea, gram, wheat

(b) red kidney bean, maize, gram

(c) maize, wheat, red kidney bean

(d) red kidney bean, pea, gram

29. Which of the following is a correct set of homologous organs?

(a) Forelimbs of frog, bird and lizard

(b) Spine of cactus and thorn of bougainvillea

(c) Wings of bat and wings of butterfly

(d) Wings of a bird and wings of a bat

30. A student obtained a sharp image of a candle flame placed at the distant end of the laboratory table on a screen using a concave mirror to determine its focal length. The teacher suggested him to focus a distant building about 1 km far from the laboratory, for getting more correct value of the focal length. In order to focus the distant building on the same screen the student should slightly move the :

(a) mirror away from the screen

(b) screen away from the mirror

(c) screen towards the mirror

(d) screen towards the building

31. To determine the approximate focal length of the given convex lens by focussing a distant object (say, a sign board), you try to focus the image of the object on a screen. The image you obtain on the screen is always:

(a) erect and laterally inverted

(b) erect and diminished

(c) inverted and diminished

(d) virtual, inverted and diminished

32. Select from the following the best experimental set-up for tracing the path of a ray of light passing through a rectangular glass slab :

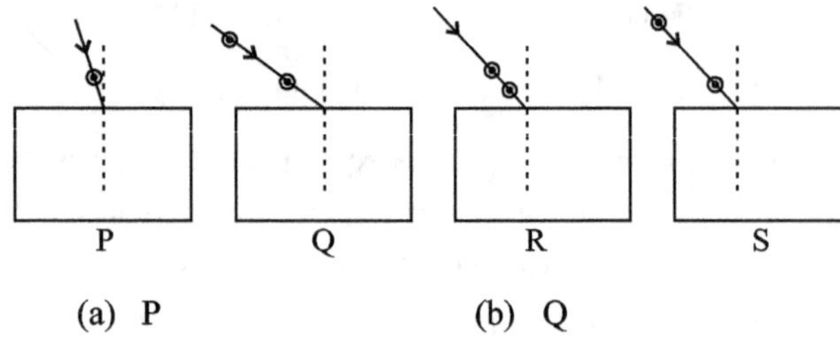

(a) P (b) Q

(c) R (d) S

33. Study the following figure in which a student has marked the angle of incidence ($\angle i$), angle of refraction ($\angle r$), angle of emergence ($\angle e$), angle of prism ($\angle A$) and the angle of deviation ($\angle D$).

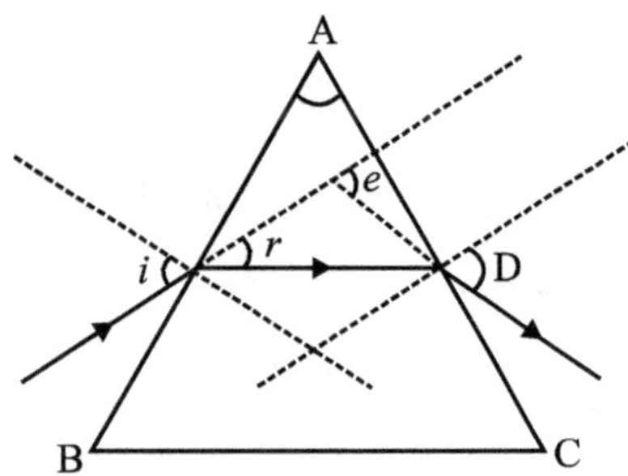

The correctly marked angles are:

(a) $\angle A$ and $\angle i$ (b) $\angle A$, $\angle i$ and $\angle r$

(c) $\angle A$, $\angle i$, $\angle e$ and $\angle D$ (d) $\angle A$, $\angle i$, $\angle r$ and $\angle D$

34. What do you observe when you drop a few drops of acetic acid to a test tube containing :

(i) phenolphthalein

(ii) distilled water

(iii) universal indicator

(iv) sodium hydrogen carbonate powder

35. Draw a labelled diagram to show that particular stage of binary fission in *Amoeba* in which its nucleus elongates and divide into two and a constriction appears in its cell membrane.

36. A student focuses the image of a well illuminated distant object on a screen using a convex lens. After that he gradually moves the object towards the lens and each time focuses its image on the screen by adjusting the lens.

(i) In which direction-towards the screen or away from the screen, does he move the lens?

(ii) What happens to the size of the image-does it decrease or increase?

(iii) What happens to the image on the screen when he moves the object very close to the lens?

Solutions

SECTION - A

1. (i) Next homologue of alkene series is C_3H_6.

(½ Mark)

(ii) Next homologue of alkyne series is C_5H_8.

(½ Mark)

General formula for alkane series is C_nH_{2n+2} where n = 1, 2, 3, 4....

General formula for alkene series is C_nH_{2n} where n = 2, 3, 4 .....

General formula for alkyne series is C_nH_{2n-2} where n = 2, 3, 4.....

2. Bud is the part of *Bryophyllum* where the buds are produced for vegetative propagation. Buds produced in the notches along the leaf margin of *Bryophyllum* fall on the soil and develop into new plants. **(1 Mark)**

3. The natural ecosystem is a biological environment created by nature rather than being created by man. Some of them include,

(a) **Terrestrial ecosystem :** It is a type of ecosystem that exists on land. Examples include desert, forest, etc.

(b) **Aquatic ecosystem :** It is a type of ecosystem that exists in the water bodies. Examples include river, pond, etc. **(1 Mark)**

4. (i) A concave mirror produces a magnified image of given object when object is placed

(a) between its pole and focus

(b) between the focus and centre of curvature

(1 Mark)

(ii) Two differences are in case of (a) the image is virtual and erect and in case of (b) the image is real and inverted. **(1 Mark)**

5. Advantages of watershed management are as follows:

(i) Mitigates drought and floods.

(ii) Increase the life of the dams and reservoirs downstream.

(iii) Increase the biomass production and thereby the income of the watershed community.

(iv) Helps in maintaining ecological balance by scientific conservation of soil and water. **(2 Marks)**

6. The examples when the active involvement of local people led to efficient management of forest are as follows:

Bishnoi community in Rajasthan: They worked traditionally for the conservation of forests.

Amrita Devi Bishnoi sacrificed her life along with 363 others for the protection of 'Khejri' trees in Khejrali village near Jodhpur in Rajasthan.

The Chipko Andolan or 'Hug the trees Movement' was the result of a grassroot level effort of the local people to protect the forests. The movement originated from an incident in a remote village called Reni in Garhwal in the Himalayas during the early 1970s. The local people hugged the trees and prevented the contractors from felling the trees. **(2 Marks)**

7. Covalent compounds are formed by the mutual sharing of electrons. Ionic compounds are formed by the complete gain or loss of electrons therefore they are different from the covalent compounds which are formed by the sharing of electrons. **(½ + 1 = 1½ Marks)**

Characteristics of covalent compound:

(i) Covalent compounds have low melting and boiling points. **(½ Mark)**

(ii) Covalent compounds are poor conductor of electricity. **(½ Mark)**

(iii) Covalent compounds are soluble in non-poplar solvents like kerosene, petrol etc. **(½ Mark)**

In an ionic bond, bonding involves a metal and non-metal, whereas in the covalent compounds, bonding is between non-metals.

8. (i) Esters the compounds which have fruity small.

(1 Mark)

$$\underset{\text{Ethanol}}{CH_3CH_2OH} + \underset{\text{Ethanoic acid}}{CH_3COOH} \xrightarrow{\text{Conc. } H_2SO_4} \underset{\text{Ethylethanoate}}{CH_3COOCH_2CH_3} + H_2O$$

(1 Mark)

(ii) Conc. H_2SO_4 acts as catalytic agent in the reaction. **(1 Mark)**

9. (i) Ca : 20 (2, 8, 8, 2) Calcium is a metal. **(1 Mark)**

(ii) Calcium has smaller size than potassium. **(1 Mark)**

(iii) 2 ╲╱ 2

Ca ↙ ↘ O

Molecular formula : CaO **(1 Mark)**

Note

Electronic configuration of $_{20}Ca$ is (2, 8, 8, 2) and it belongs to group 2 and period 4. As it belongs to group 2 therefore it is a metal. In the periodic table it comes after K in the same period. On moving from left to right in the period in the periodic table size decrease. Therefore size of calcium is smaller than potassium.

10. Valency of element 'M' is 2.

2 ╲╱ 1

M ↙ ↘ (NO_3^-)

Molecular formula: $M(NO_3)_2$ **(½ Mark)**

2 ╲╱ 2

M ↙ ↘ SO_4^{2-}

Molecular formula: M SO_4 **(½ Mark)**

2 ╲╱ 3

M ↙ ↘ PO_4^{3-}

Molecular formula: $M_3(PO_4)_2$ **(½ Mark)**

Element 'M' belongs to group 2 and period 3 of the periodic table. **(½ Mark)**

Element 'M' will form ionic compounds because its valency is +2, and it can easily give up two valence electron to complete the octet (i.e., 2, 8). Thus it will form ionic compounds. **(1 Mark)**

11. The maintenance of chromosome is an important phenomenon when an organism is reproducing either asexually or sexually. The mechanism is different in different organisms:

In case of asexual reproduction, the whole set of chromosomes is replicated and transferred to the next generation. For example, asexual reproduction in *Amoeba* by binary fission.

In case of sexual reproduction, the chromosome number is halved by the process of meiosis for the formation of gametes. The haploid male and female gametes are fuse to form zygote and are diploid. In this way, organisms produced by sexual reproduction maintain the original chromosome number.

For example: In case of human beings there are 46 chromosomes in normal cells but at the time gamete formation, the chromosome number is reduced to halve such as 23 in male and 23 in female gamete by the process of meiosis. At the time of reproduction, the haploid male and female gametes are fuse to form a diploid zygote having 46 chromosomes (23+23). **(3 Marks)**

Note

Meiosis is a process in which a single cell divides twice to produce four cells containing half the original number of chromosome. This is also called reductional division because it ensures that all organisms produced by sexual reproduction contain the correct number of chromosomes.

12. In the given figure, the labelled parts represents:

A- Anther

B- Style

C- Ovary

Function of these parts are as follows:

Anther: The anther is an important structure in the reproduction of flowering plants and produces pollen grain.

Style: Style is a tube-like structure that connects the stigma and the ovary.

Ovary: Ovary is the enlarged basal portion of the pistil and the female organ of a flower. It contains ovules which develop into seeds after fertilisation. **(3 Marks)**

Note

The flower is a modified shoot, meant for sexual reproduction.

13. The three contraceptive methods to control the size of human population.

Oral pills: Oral pills change the hormone balance so that eggs are not released and fertilisation cannot occur.

Mechanical method: In this method, the fertilisation is prevented by using barriers such as condom.

Surgical methods: This method involves the surgical removal of vas deferens in males and fallopian tube in females to block the entry of sperm into the female reproductive system.

The removal of vas deferens is called vasectomy in males and in female's removal of fallopian tube called tubectomy. **(3 Marks)**

Natural methods are also used as contraceptive methods which work on the principle of avoiding the chances of ovum and sperms meeting.

14. (a) The dwarf trait is recessive that is it can only be expressed when present in homozygous condition. The cross produces heterozygous and thus the dominant allele for tallness masks the dwarf allele. Hence, the dwarf trait cannot be expressed.

(b) In the F_2 generation, the traits are segregated according to the law of segregation in which the two alleles segregate independently during gamete formation. The two gametes are produced in equal proportions.

Genetic cross:

Parents:	TT (tall)	X	tt	(dwarf)
Gametes:	T	T	t	t
F1 generation:	Tt	Tt	tt	tt
Selfing F1 :	Tt	X	Tt	
Gametes:	T	t	T	t
F2 generation:	TT	Tt	Tt	tt

Phenotypic ratio is 3:1

Genotypic ratio is 1:2:1

Law of dominance states that one of the pairs of inherited traits will be dominant and the others recessive unless both the factors are recessive.

15. Difference between acquired trait and inherited trait:

	Acquired trait		**Inherited trait**
(i)	Acquired traits cannot be passed on from one generation to another generation.	(i)	Inherited traits can be passed on from one generation to another generation.
(ii)	Acquired traits or characteristics are because of the change in somatic cells.	(ii)	Inherited traits or characteristics are because of the change in the genes.
(iii)	For example: Low in wieight due to starvation if a mouse tail gets cut, tail is an acquired trait.	(iii)	For example: Brown eyes and curly hairs.

(3 Marks)

16.

Incident ray

F

reflected ray

(1 Mark)

Incident ray

reflected ray

F

(1 Mark)

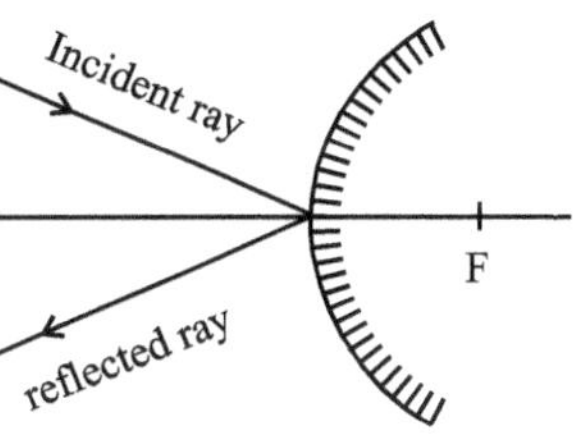

(1 Mark)

17. In the morning, the sun is nearer to the horizon. Blue light have shorter wavelength, so , it scatters more. Therefore the red light which have longer wavelength reaches upto the eye of observer and the sun appears reddish.

(2 Marks)

No, this phenomenon will not occur on the Moon as there is no atmosphere on its surface to scatter light. **(1 Mark)**

18. (a) Decomposers break down complex organic substances (dead remains and waste products of organism) into simpler inorganic substances that can be absorbed by the plants. They are essential for the proper functioning of an ecosystem.

- Decomposers plays an important role in the cycling of materials in the biosphere.
- By decomposing dead bodies of plants and animals they help in cleaning the environment they replenish the soil naturally. **(1 ½ Marks)**

(b) In the ecosystem, flow of energy from one trophic level to the next trophic level of the food chain. Energy flows from producers such as green plants to the consumers. It does not flow from the last consumer to the producer the energy captured by the autotrophs does not go back to the solar input.

Hence, the flow of energy in a food chain is unidirectional. **(1 ½ Mark)**

19. (a) **Bromine water test:** Unsaturated hydrocarbons decolourise the brown colour of bromine water while saturated hydrocarbons donot decolourise bromine water. **(1 Mark)**

(b) $2CH_3 - CH_3 + 7O_2 \longrightarrow 4CO_2 + 6H_2O + \text{energy}$

(1 Mark)

Carbon dioxide gas and water are is formed when ethane is burnt in air. **(1 Mark)**

(c) The reaction between methane and chlorine in the presence of sunlight considered as substitution reaction because chlorine radical generated in sunlight substitute hydrogen atom in methane. In stepwise manner all the hydrogen atoms are replaced by chlorine atom in the reaction. **(2 Marks)**

Mechanism:

$$Cl - Cl \xrightarrow{\text{Sunlight}} \dot{C}l + \dot{C}l$$

$$CH_4 \xrightarrow{\dot{C}l} CH_3Cl + HCl$$

$$CH_3Cl \xrightarrow{\dot{C}l} CH_2Cl_2 + HCl$$

$$CH_2Cl_2 \xrightarrow{\dot{C}l} CHCl_3 + HCl$$

$$CHCl_3 \xrightarrow{\dot{C}l} CCl_4 + HCl$$

20. (a) (i) **Ovary:** Ovaries are the main female reproductive part in the body that produces oocytes or eggs for fertilisation and also secretes two hormones such as oestrogen and progesterone.

(ii) **Oviduct:** It is also called fallopian tube. It is site where the sperm and egg meets and carry out the process of fertilisation. It provides the suitable environment for fertilisation and transports the fertilised ova in the uterus for implantation.

(iii) **Uterus:** The uterus plays an important role in human reproduction as it is a site where the implantation takes place and it also provides nourishment to the fertilized ovum. Uterus exhibits strong contraction during delivery of the baby. **(2½ Marks)**

(b) The embryo gets nutrition from the mother's blood with the help of a special tissue placenta. This a disc which is embedded in the uterine wall. It contains villi on the embryo's side of the tissue. The chorionic villi and uterine tissue combined with each other and jointly form a structural and functional unit between developing embryo (foetus) and maternal body called **placenta.**

The placenta facilitates the supply of oxygen and nutrients to the embryo and also removal of carbon dioxide as well as excretory/ waste materials produced by the embryo. It is connected to the embryo through an umbilical cord that helps in the transport of substances to and from the embryo. **(2½ Marks)**

Placenta also acts as an endocrine tissue and produces several pregnancy hormones such as human chorionic gonadotropin (hCG), human placental lactogen (hPL), estrogens, progestogens.

21. Speciation is the evolutionary process by which populations evolve to become distinct species.

Four factors that lead to speciation are as follows:

(i) Gene flow between the populations of one species is restricted to allow them to diverge.

(ii) A component of the divergence products a complete barrier to inter-breeding called a mating-isolation mechanism

(iii) The initial barrier can be either spatial or temporal

(iv) Climate change also results in isolation of population on the mountain peaks or in remnant lakes or rare migrants may colonize new areas such as Galapagos Islands. **(5 Marks)**

22. (a) (i) **Pole:** Centre of the reflecting surface of the mirror is called pole of the mirror.

(ii) **Centre of curvature:** The centre of the hollow sphere of which the reflecting surface of mirror is a part is called centre of curvature.

(iii) **Principal axis:** Straight-line passing through the pole and the centre of curvature of a spherical mirror is called principal axis.

(iv) **Principal focus:** Incident rays parallel to principal axis, after reflection, either converge to or appear to diverge from a fixed point on the principal axis called principal focus of the spherical mirror. **(½ × 4 = 2 Marks)**

(b) (i)

(1 Mark)

(ii)

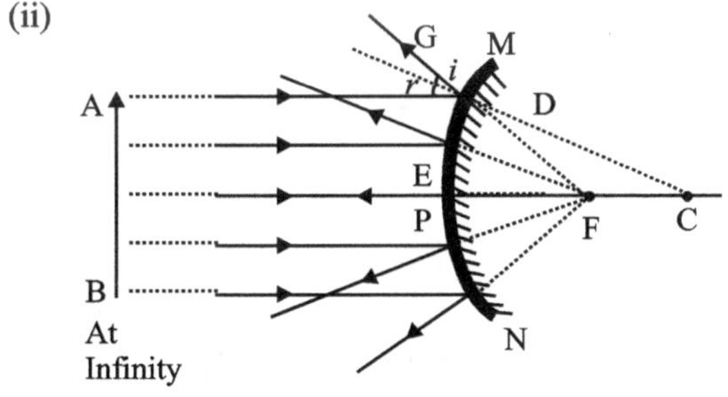

(1 Mark)

(iii) Concave mirror. Image Q is a virtual image

(1 Mark)

23. (i)

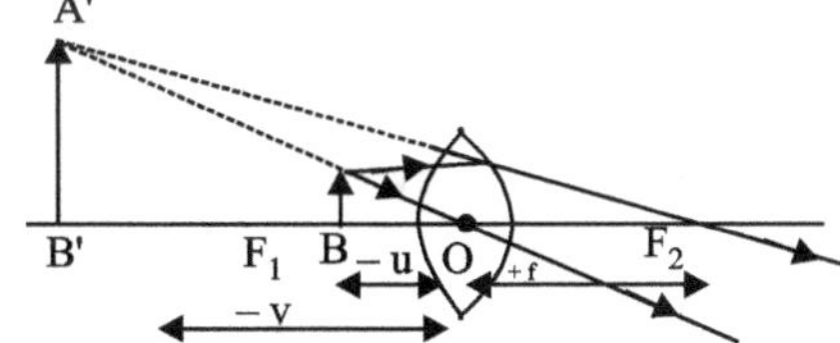

(2 Marks)

(ii) Relation between object distance (u) and image distance (v) and focal length (f) is

$$\frac{1}{f} = \frac{1}{v} - \frac{1}{u}$$ **(1 Mark)**

(iii) $m = -1$; $u = -20$ cm; $v = ?, f = ?$

$$m = \frac{v}{u}$$

$\Rightarrow \quad \therefore \quad v = +20$ cm

thus object is at 2F

i.e., $2f = 20$ cm

$\therefore \quad f = 10$ cm $= 0.1$ m **(1 Mark)**

$$P = \frac{1}{f} = \frac{1}{0.1} = +10 \text{ D}$$ **(1 Mark)**

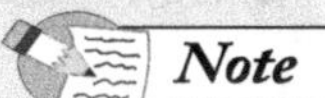

Minimum distance between an object and its real image formed by a convex lens of focal length f is 4f.

24. (a) (i) **Cornea** – Refracts the rays of light falling on the eye.

(ii) **Iris** – Controls the size of the pupil.

(iii) **Crystalline lens** – Focuses the image of the object on the retina.

(iv) **Ciliary muscles** – Holds the eye lens and adjusts its focal length. **(½ × 4 = 2 Marks)**

(b) (i) **Objectives** – To make people aware and realize their duties towards society. **(1 Mark)**

(ii) One person can give sight to two people. We have got the gift of vision, why not pass it on to some body who does not have it. **(1 Mark)**

(iii) Concern for others/Responsible behaviour / Group work/or any other. **(1 Mark)**

SECTION - B

25. (b) Sodium hydroxide and neem oil vegetable oil can be used for saponification reaction. **(1 Mark)**

26. (a) P Q R S

KCl NaCl $CaCl_2$ $MgCl_2$

All contain 10 mL distill water

On adding soap solution in all the four test tubes.

Only P and Q show lather formation with soap. Calcium and magnesium chloride salts causes hardness of water in test tube R and S. **(1 Mark)**

27. (c) I, II and IV are correct statements. Saponification reaction is a type of hydrolysis reaction. **(1 Mark)**

28. Correct option: (d) **(1 Mark)**

Red kidney bean, pea and gram are from a dicot plants.

Dicots have two seeds leaves inside the seed coat and are usually rounded as well as fat because they contain endosperm to feed the embryo plant.

29. Correct option: (a) **(1 Mark)**

Forelimbs of frog, birds and lizard are the homologous organs.

Homologous organs are those organs which have similar structures but different functions.

30. (c) To focus the distant building, which is 1 km from the laboratory, the student should move the screen slightly towards the mirror. It is because the object (building) is at infinity and its image will be formed at the focus. **(1 Mark)**

31. (c) The image formed by lens will be inverted and diminished. **(1 Mark)**

32. (d) S is most suitable setup for tracing a ray of light passing through a rectangular glass slab. **(1 Mark)**

If the incident ray falls normally to the surface of the glass slab then there is no bending of the ray of light. Light goes straight without any deviation.

33. (a) The correctly marked angles in the given figure are the angle of prism (A) and the angle of incidence (i).

(1 Mark)

When angle of incidence increases, angle of deviation decreases, till it becomes minimum at a particular angle of incidence. The minimum value of angle of deviation for a triangular prism is called the angle of minimum deviation. The refracted ray becomes parallel to base of the prism under the minimum deviation position.

34. (i) No colour charge is observed when acetic acid added to the phenolphthalein solution. **(½ Mark)**

(ii) Distill water dilute the acetic acid solution.

(½ Mark)

(iii) Acetic acid turns the colour of the universal indicator to pale orange. **(½ Mark)**

(iv) Effervescence of CO_2 gas are observed when acetic acid added to sodium bicarbonate. **(½ Mark)**

35. Diagrammatic representation of stages of binary fission in *Amoeba* in which its nucleus elongates:

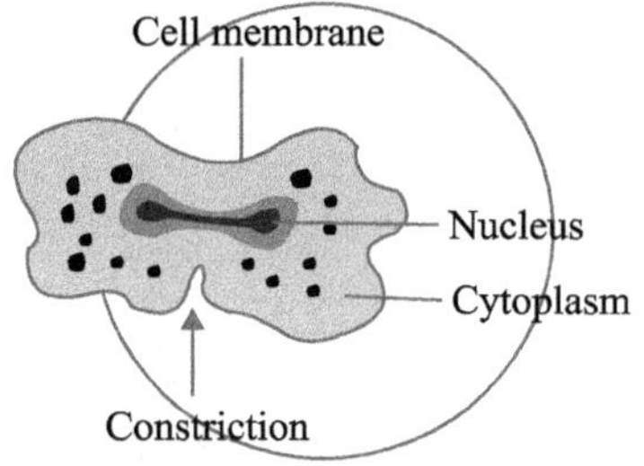

(2 Marks)

Binary fission is a type of asexual reproduction in which a single organism (parent cell) divides into two daughter cells that are identical to their parent.

36. (i) As the object is moved towards the lens, the image distance increases. Thus, the student moves the lens away from the screen to focus the image.

(ii) The size of the image increases when the object is moved towards the lens.

(iii) When the object is moved very close to the lens, no image is formed on the screen. A virtual image is formed behind the object on the same side of the screen. **(2 Marks)**

All India 2015

CBSE Board Solved Paper

Time Allowed : 3 Hours | ***Maximum Marks : 80***

General Instructions:

(i) The question paper comprises of **two** Sections, **A** and **B**. You are to attempt both the sections.

(ii) All questions are compulsory.

(iii) There is no choice in any of the questions.

(iv) All questions of Section-A and all questions of Section-B are to be attempted separately.

(v) Question numbers **1** to **3** in Section-A are **one** mark questions. These are to be answered in **one** word or in **one** sentence.

(vi) Question numbers **4** to **6** in Section-A are **two** marks questions. These are to be answered in about **30** words each.

(vii) Question numbers **7** to **18** in Section-A are **three** marks questions. These are to be answered in about **50** words each.

(viii) Question numbers **19** to **24** in Section-B are **five** marks questions. These are to be answered in about **70** words each.

(ix) Question numbers **25** to **33** in Section-B are multiple choice questions based on practical skills. Each question is a **one** mark question. You are to select **one** most appropriate response out of the **four** provided to you.

(x) Question numbers **34** to **36** in Section-B are **two** marks questions based on practical skills. These are to answered in brief.

SECTION - A

1. Write the number of covalent bonds in the molecule of ethane.

2. Name the life process of an organism that helps in the growth of its population.

3. What will be the amount of energy available to the organisms of the 2nd trophic level of a food chain, if the energy available at the first trophic level is 10,000 joules?

4. The absolute refractive indices of glass and water are 4/3 and 3/2 respectively. If the speed of light in glass is 2×10^8 m/s, calculate the speed of light in (i) vacuum, (ii) water.

5. List two main causes of the pollution of water of the river Ganga. State how pollution and contamination of river water prove harmful for the health of the people of neighbouring areas.

6. What is biodiversity ? What will happen if biodiversity of an area is not preserved ? Mention one effect of it.

7. List two tests for experimentally distinguishing between an alcohol and a carboxylic acid and describe how these tests are performed.

8. Draw the electron-dot structure for ethyne. A mixture of ethyne and oxygen is burnt for welding. In your opinion, why cannot we use a mixture of ethyne and air for this purpose ?

9. Two elements 'P' and 'Q belong to the same period of the modern periodic table and are in Group-1 and Group-2 respectively. Compare their following characteristics in tabular form:

   (a) The number of electrons in their atoms

   (b) The sizes of their atoms

   (c) Their metallic characters

   (d) Their tendencies to lose electrons

   (e) The formula of their oxides

   (f) The formula of their chlorides

10. Taking the example of an element of atomic number 16, explain how the electronic configuration of the atom of an element relates to its position in the modern periodic table and how valency of an element is calculated on the basis of its atomic number.

11. List six specific characteristics of sexual reproduction.

12. What are chromosomes ? Explain how in sexually reproducing organisms the number of chromosomes in the progeny is maintained.

13. List four points of significance of reproductive health in a society. Name any two areas related to reproductive health which have improved over the past 50 years in our country.

14. Explain with an example for each, how the following provides evidences in favour of evolution in organisms :

(a) Homologous organs

(b) Analogous organs

(c) Fossils

15. Explain the following:

(a) Speciation

(b) Natural Selection

16. If the image formed by a mirror for all positions of the object placed in front of it is always erect and diminished, what type of mirror is it? Draw a ray diagram to justify your answer. Where and why do we generally use this type of mirror ?

17. What is meant by scattering of light ? Use this phenomenon to explain why the clear sky appears blue or the sun appears reddish at sunrise.

18. Differentiate between biodegradable and non-biodegradable substances with the help of one example each. List two changes in habit that people must adopt to dispose non-biodegradable waste, for saving the environment.

SECTION - B

19. Both soap and detergent are some type of salts. What is the difference between them ? Describe in brief the cleansing action of soap. Why do soaps not form lather in hard water ? List two problems that arise due to the use of detergents instead of soaps.

20. (a) Name the human male reproductive organ that produces sperms and also secretes a hormone. Write the functions of the secreted hormone.

(b) Name the parts of the human female reproductive system where

(i) fertilisation takes place,

(ii) implantation of the fertilised egg occurs.

Explain how the embryo gets nourishment inside the mother's body.

21. How do Mendel's experiments show that the

(a) traits may be dominant or recessive,

(b) traits are inherited independently?

22. What is meant by power of a lens? Define its S.I. unit. You have two lenses A and B of focal lengths +10 cm and –10 cm respectively. State the nature and power of each lens. Which of the two lenses will form a virtual and magnified image of an object placed 8 cm from the lens ? Draw a ray diagram to justify your answer.

23. One half of a convex lens of focal length 10 cm is covered with a black paper. Can such a lens produce an image of a complete object placed at a distance of 30 cm from the lens ? Draw a ray diagram to justify your answer. A 4 cm tall object is placed perpendicular to the principal axis of a convex lens of focal length 20 cm. The distance of the object from the lens is 15 cm. Find the nature, position and size of the image.

24. Write the importance of ciliary muscles in the human eye. Name the defect of vision that arises due to gradual weakening of the ciliary muscles in old age. What type of lenses are required by the persons suffering from this defect to see the objects clearly ?

Akshay, sitting in the last row in his class, could not see clearly the words written on the blackboard. When the teacher noticed it, he announced if any student sitting in the front row could volunteer to exchange his seat with Akshay. Salman immediately agreed to exchange his seat with Akshay. He could now see the words written on the blackboard clearly. The teacher thought it fit to send the message to Akshay's parents advising them to get his eyesight checked.

In the context of the above event, answer the following questions:

(a) Which defect of vision is Akshay suffering from? Which type of lens is used to correct this defect?

(b) State the values displayed by the teacher and Salman.

(c) In your opinion, in what way can Akshay express his gratitude towards the teacher and Salman ?

25. What do we observe on pouring acetic acid on red and blue litmus papers ?

(a) Red litmus remains red and blue litmus turns red.
(b) Red litmus turns blue and blue litmus remains blue.
(c) Red litmus turns blue and blue litmus turns red.
(d) Red litmus becomes colourless and blue litmus remains blue.

26. While preparing soap a small quantity of common salt is generally added to the reaction mixture of vegetable oil and sodium hydroxide. Which one of the following may be the purpose of adding common salt?

(a) To reduce the basic nature of the soap
(b) To make the soap neutral
(c) To enhance the cleansing power of the soap
(d) To favour the precipitation of the soap

27. A student takes about 4 mL of distilled water in four test tubes marked P, Q, R and S. He then dissolves in each test tube an equal amount of one salt in one test tube, namely sodium sulphate in P, potassium sulphate in Q. calcium sulphate in R and magnesium sulphate in S. After that he adds an equal amount of soap solution in each test tube. On shaking each of these test tubes well, he observes a good amount of lather (foam) in the test tubes marked

(a) P and Q (b) Q and R
(c) P, Q and S (d) P, R and S

28. A student was asked to observe and identify the various parts of an embryo of a red kidney bean seed. He identified the parts and listed them as under:

I. Tegmen II. Testa
III. Cotyledon IV. Radicle
V. Plumule

The correctly identified parts among these are

(a) I, II and III (b) II, III and IV
(c) III, IV and V (d) I, III, IV and V

29. Given below is the list of vegetables available in the market. Select from these the two vegetables having homologous structures :

Potato, sweet potato, ginger, radish, tomato, carrot, okra (Lady's finger)

(a) Potato and sweet potato (b) Radish and carrot
(c) Okra and sweet potato (d) Potato and tomato

30. A student obtains a sharp image of the distant window (W) of the school laboratory on the screen (S) using the given concave mirror (M) to determine its focal length. Which of the following distances should he measure to get the focal length of the mirror ?

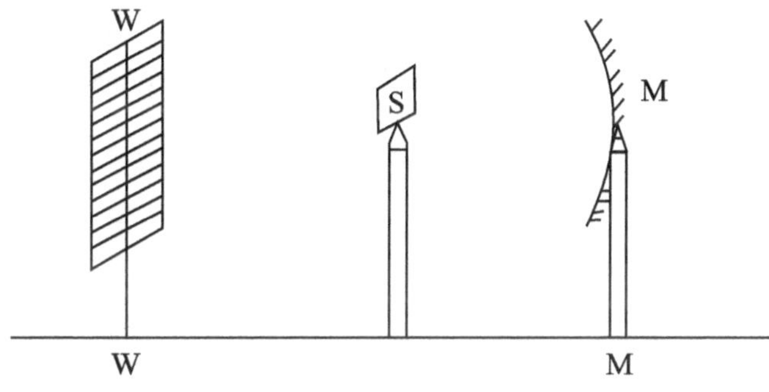

(a) MW (b) MS
(c) SW (d) MW-MS

31. A student used a device (X) to obtain/focus the image of a well illuminated distant building on a screen (S) as shown below in the diagram. Select the correct statement about the device (X).

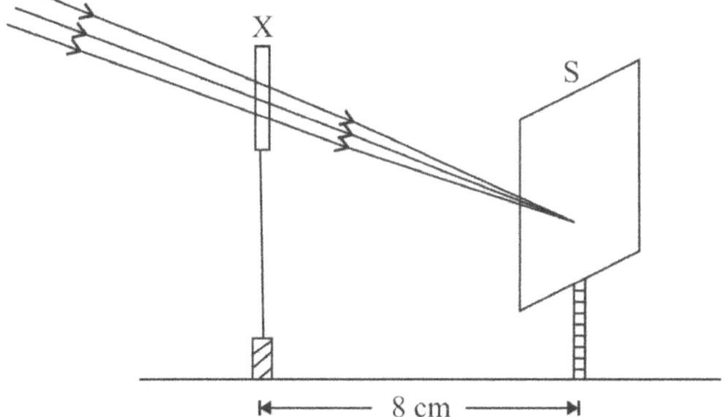

(a) This device is a concave lens of foal length 8 cm.
(b) This device is a convex mirror of focal length 8 cm.
(c) This device is a convex lens of focal length 4 cm.
(d) This device is a convex lens of focal length 8 cm.

32. A student traces the path of a ray of light through a rectangular glass slab for the different values of angle of incidence. He observes all possible precautions at each step of the experiment. At the end of the experiment, on analyzing the measurements, which of the following conclusions is he likely to draw ?

(a) $\angle i = \angle e < \angle r$ (b) $\angle i < e < \angle r$
(c) $\angle i > \angle e > \angle r$ (d) $\angle i = \angle e > \angle r$

33. A student traces the path of a ray of light through a triangular glass prism for different values of angle of incidence. On analysing the ray diagrams, which one of the following conclusions is he likely to draw?

(a) The emergent ray is parallel to the incident ray.
(b) The emergent ray bends at an angle to the direction of the incident ray.
(c) The emergent ray and the refracted ray are at right angles to each other.
(d) The emergent ray is perpendicular to the incident ray.

34. When you add sodium hydrogen carbonate to acetic acid in a test tube, a gas liberates immediately with a brisk effervescence. Name this gas. Describe the method of testing this gas.

35. Students were asked to observe the permanent slides showing different stages of budding in yeast under high power of a microscope.

(a) Which adjustment screw (coarse/fine) were you asked to move to focus the slides?
(b) Draw three diagrams in correct sequence showing budding in yeast.

36. A 4 cm tall object is placed on the principal axis of a convex lens. The distance of the object from the optical centre of the lens is 12 cm and its sharp image is formed at a distance of 24 cm from it on a screen on the other side of the lens. If the object is now moved a little away from the lens, in which way (towards the lens or away from the lens) will he have to move the screen to get a sharp image of the object on it again ? How will the magnification of the image be affected ?

Solutions

SECTION - A

1.

```
    H   H
    |   |
H — C — C — H (Ethane)
    |   |
    H   H
```

Ethane molecule has seven covalent bonds **(1 Mark)**

2. The process of reproduction helps in the population growth of an organism. **(1 Mark)**

Note

Reproduction is defined as a biological process in which an organism gives rise to young one similar to itself.

3. According to 10% rule, the energy transferred to the 2nd trophic level of a food chain will be 10% of the 1st trophic level. Therefore,

Energy in 1st trophic level = 10,000 J

Energy in 2nd trophic level = 10% of 10,000 J

= 1000 J **(1 Mark)**

4. Absolute refractive index of glass

$$\mu_g = \frac{\text{Speed of light in vacuum}}{\text{Speed of light in glass}}$$

$$\Rightarrow \mu_g = \frac{4}{3} = \frac{\text{Speed of light in vacuum}}{2 \times 10^8}$$

$$\Rightarrow \text{Speed of light in vacuum} = \frac{4 \times 2 \times 10^8}{3} \text{ m/s}$$

$= 2.667 \times 10^8$

$\approx 2.7 \times 10^8$ or 3×10^8 m/s **(1 Mark)**

Absolute refractive index of water

$$= \frac{\text{Speed of light in vacuum}}{\text{Speed of light in water}} = \frac{3}{2}$$

$$\therefore \text{ Speed of light in water} = \frac{2.7 \times 10^8}{\frac{3}{2}} = \frac{2 \times 2.7 \times 10^8}{3}$$

$= 1.8 \times 10^8$ m/s **(1 Mark)**

5. The two main causes of the pollution of water of the river Ganga are :

(i) Disposal of untreated sewage and industrial wastes directly into the water.

(ii) Immersion of ashes of dead, dumping of corpses, bathing, washing etc.

Pollution or contamination of river water is very harmful for neighbor regions as it can lead to water borne diseases like typhoid, cholera, jaundice etc. and is also disturbes ecological balance of water body which can also lead to biomagnifications of chemicals. **(2 Marks)**

6. Biodiversity refers to the variety of organisms living in a particular area. If the biodiversity in an area is not preserved it can lead to extinction of vulnerable species. **(2 Marks)**

7. Alcohols and carboxylic acids can be experimentally distinguished by the following tests:

(i) Carboxylic acids on reaction with $NaHCO_3$ gives brisk effervescence of CO_2 and water, whereas alcohol does not gives this reaction. **(1 Mark)**

$$R\text{–}COOH + NaHCO_3 \longrightarrow RCOONa + CO_2 \uparrow + H_2O$$

(½ Mark)

(ii) Alcohol on reaction with sodium metal gives hydrogen gas, whereas carboxylic acid does not gives this reaction. **(1 Mark)**

$$2R\text{–}OH + 2Na \longrightarrow 2R\text{–}ONa + H_2 \uparrow$$ **(½ Mark)**

8. **Ethyne (C_2H_2) :**

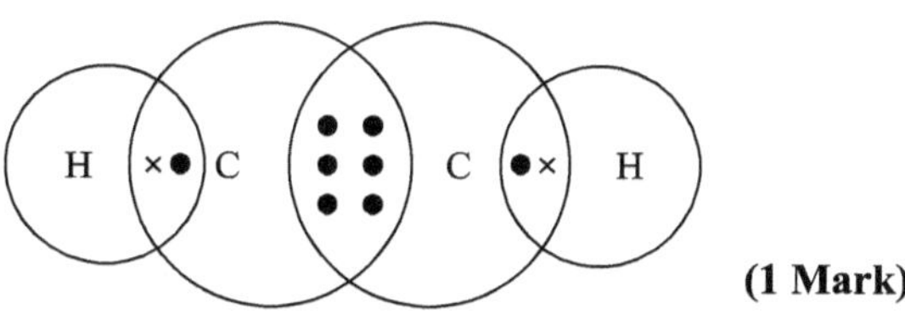

(1 Mark)

Electron Dot Structure

When a mixture of ethyne and oxygen is burnt, it gives clean flame with very high temperature (in 3000ºC). Hence, this mixture is used for welding purpose.

$$2C_2H_2 + 5O_2 \longrightarrow 4CO_2 + 2H_2O + \text{Heat}$$

When a mixture of ethyne and air is burnt, it gives sooty flame due to incomplete combustion and it also does not give very high temperature. Thus, it is not used for welding. **(2 Marks)**

Note

When ethyne is burnt in air, it gives sooty flame due to incomplete combustion. Therefore oxy acetylene flame is used for welding so that it can give clean flame with temperature 3000°C.

9.

	Characteristics	'p' (Group-1); 'Q' (Group-2)	
(a)	The number of electrons	P < Q	**(½ Mark)**
(b)	Size of atom	P > Q	**(½ Mark)**
(c)	Metallic character	P > Q	**(½ Mark)**
(d)	Tendency to lose electrons	P will lose electrons more easily than 'Q'	**(½ Mark)**
(e)	Formula of oxide	P_2O ; QO	**(½ Mark)**
(f)	Formula of chloride	PCl ; QCl_2	**(½ Mark)**

Element P has greater tendency to lose electrons than element Q because of greater atomic size of element P. Greater atomic size results into lesser attraction of nucleus with the outermost electrons. Hence element P can easily lose electrons than element Q.

10. Atomic number of an element = 16

Electronic configuration : 2, 8, 6

Since, the number of shells in the electronic configuration is three, therefore it belongs to the 3rd period. And as the number of electrons in the outermost orbit is six, therefore it belongs to the 16th group. **(2 Marks)**

Valency of the element = (8 – No. of electron in outermost shell)

= 8 – 6 = 2 **(1 Mark)**

11. Characteristics of sexual reproduction are as follows:

1. It involves two organisms of different sexes i.e. male and female.
2. It is a slow process.
3. It involves the process of fertilisation.
4. Both meiosis and mitotic divisions occurs in sexual reproduction. Meiosis occurs after fertilisation.
5. It is responsible for variation in the next generation.
6. It is important for evolution and natural selection.

(3 Marks)

12. Chromosomes are thread-like structures present in the nucleus of the cell. It contains genetic information in the form of DNA.

In sexual reproduction, the male and female gametes are formed by meiosis therefore they contain half a set of chromosomes of each parent. When the two gametes fuse together zygote is formed which has the full set of chromosomes. Hence, the formation of gametes by meiosis helps to maintain the number of chromosomes in the progeny. **(3 Marks)**

Meiosis is a type of cell division which is also called reductional division. In this process, a single cell divides twice to produce four cells that contains half the number of chromosomes from the original number of chromosomes.

13. Significance of reproductive health in a society are :

(i) Sexually transmitted diseases (STDs) such as AIDS, syphilis etc. are prevented.

(ii) Individuals produce offspring having better chances of survival and better health.

(iii) Prevention of population explosion by better sex education and awareness.

(iv) Prevention of unwanted pregnancies and fascilitation in family planning.

Area related to reproductive health which has improved over the past 50 years in our country are

(i) Better sex education and awareness.

(ii) Increased number of medical assistance in deliveries and post natal care. **(3 Marks)**

Sexually Transmitted Diseases (STD's), are usually passed from one infected person to another person through sexual contact.

14. **Homologous organs:** Homologous organs are referred to as the organs/ traits that are inherited by two different organisms but from the same ancestry.

- They are similar in structure but different in function.
- Examples of homologous organs are the forelimbs of bird and that of humans.

Analogous organs: Wings of birds and bats have different structure and components even though they have a common use that is for flying. This analogous characteristic tells that they do not have common origin.

Fossils: Fossils of dinosaurs in rocks above the rocks containing earlier invertebrate fossils suggest the evolutionary process millions of years ago. **(3 Marks)**

15. (a) **Speciation.** The process by which new species develop from existing species due to results of isolation, genetic drift or/and natural selection, is called **as speciation.**

(b) **Natural selection.** It is the process by which individual who are most adaptable and fit are selected by the nature. Their offspring are also better developed and well adapted to the environment.

(3 Marks)

16. Convex mirror always forms image erect and diminished, for all positions of the object placed in front of it.

(1 Mark)

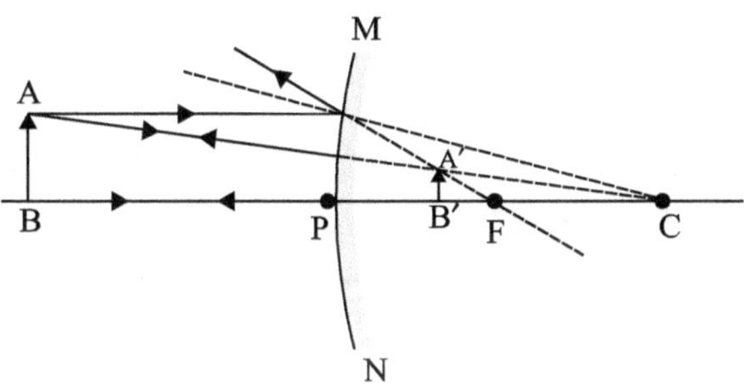

(1 Mark)

Use: Convex mirror are commonly used as rear-view mirrors in vehicles because they always give an erect image. **(1 Mark)**

17. When a beam of light passes through a medium e.g. air, water etc., it gets reflected in all direction. The phenomenon is referred to as scattering of light.

(1 Mark)

The colour of the scattered light depends on the size of the medium particles, fine particles scatter smaller wavelength whereas large particles scatter larger wavelength.

When sunlight passes through the atmosphere, the fine particles in air scatter the shorter wavelength more strongly and so the sky appears blue. **(1 Mark)**

Whereas, during sunrise and sunset, light has to travel larger distance and blue light is more scattered away. Since, the red light is scattered less and they can travel longer distance too, hence the sun appears red. **(1 Mark)**

18. **Biodegradable substances:** Substances that are broken down by biological process are said to be biodegradable.

For example, vegetable peels, human excreta etc.

Non biodegradable substances: Substances that are not broken down by biological process are said to be non-biodegradable.

For example, plastics, polythene etc.

- We can save the environment by recycling and reusing the non biodegradable substances. **(3 Marks)**
- Reducing the use of non-biodegradable wastes.

SECTION - B

19. Soaps are sodium or potassium salt of long chain fatty acids. Detergents are sodium salt of long chain benzene suphonic acids. **(1 Mark)**

Cleansing action of soap:

Soap contain a large hydrocarbon chain which is hydrophobic and a negative charged head which is hydrophillic. When soap is dissolved in water the molecules gather together as clusters called micelles. The hydrocarbon tail attaches itself to oily dirt and ionic head points to the water molecule. When water is agitated, the oily dirt tends to lift off from the dirty surface and dissociates into fragments. **(2 Marks)**

Soap do not form lather because of the presence of calcium and magnesium salt which results into the formation of scum.

Problems with the use of detergent :

(a) detergents are non-biodegradable

(b) detergents are harsh and strongly basic than soap.

(2 Marks)

20. (a) The human male reproductive organ that produces sperms or germ cells is testes. It secretes the hormone, testosterone.

The functions of testosterone are :

(i) Regulation of the formation of germ cells or sperms.

(ii) To bring changes in appearance seen in boys at the time of puberty. **(1½ Marks)**

(b) In human female reproductive system.

(i) Fertilisation of egg takes place in the oviduct or fallopian tube.

(ii) Implantation of fertilised egg i.e. zygote occurs in the uterus. **(1½ Marks)**

The embryo gets nourishment from the mother's blood with the help of a special tissue called placenta. This is a disc embedded in the uterine wall. It contains villi on the embryo's side of tissue and on the mother's side are blood spaces which surround the villi. This provides a large surface area for glucose and oxygen to pass from the mother to the embryo. **(2 Marks)**

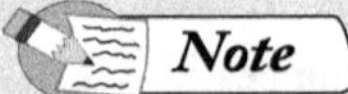

Placenta also acts as an endocrine tissue and produces several pregnancy hormones such as human chorionic gonadotropin (hCG), human placental Lactogen (hPL), estrogens and progestogens.

21. (a) Mendel experimented on garden pea plant with selection of seven visible contrasting characters forming laws of inheritance. He selected and crossed homozygous tall pea plant with genotype 'TT' and a homozygous dwarf pea plant with the genotype 'tt'. F_1 generation consists only of tall plants having genotype Tt. The character 'T' for tallness is dominant over character 't' for dwarfness. Thus, Mendel's experiment showed that traits may be dominant or recessive. **(2½ Marks)**

(b) In Mendel's experiment, different traits were—tall and dwarf plant, round and wrinkled seeds. In F_2 generation, some plants were tall with round seeds and other were dwarf with wrinkled seeds. Other combination was dwarf plants having round seed, that were independently inherited. **(2½ Marks)**

22. The power of a lens is defined as the reciprocal of its focal length. It is represented by the letter 'P'. The power 'P' of a lens of a focal length 'f' is given by

P = — (where f is in meter)

The S.I. unit of power of a lens is 'Diopter'. It is denoted by the letter 'D'. **(1 Mark)**

Lens A of focal length +10 cm is a convex lens.

$$f = +10 \text{ cm}$$

or $$f = +\frac{10}{100}\text{ m}$$

Now, $$P = \frac{1}{f} = \frac{1}{+\frac{10}{100}} = +\frac{100}{10} = +10\text{D}$$ **(1 Mark)**

Lens B of focal length –10 cm is a concave lens

$$f = -10 \text{ cm}$$

or $$f = \frac{-10}{100} m$$

Now, $$P = \frac{1}{f} = \frac{1}{-\frac{10}{100}} = -\frac{100}{10} = -10\text{D}$$ **(1 Mark)**

Lens A, convex lens, will form virtual and magnified image of an object placed 8 cm from the lens. **(1 Mark)**

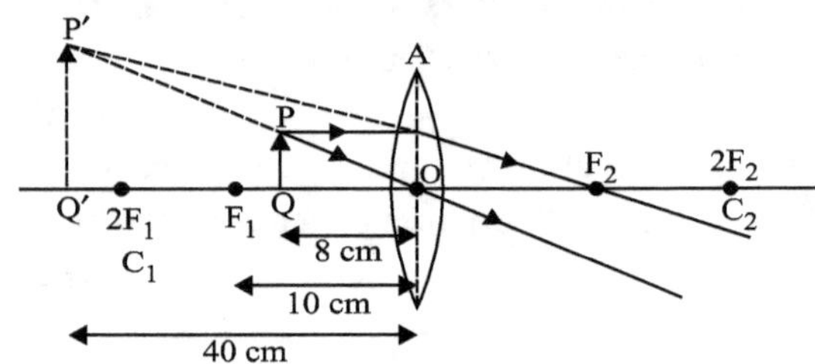

(1 Mark)

The focal length of convex lens is positive.

The focal length of concave lens is negative.

As power $= \dfrac{1}{\text{Focal length (in m)}}$

So, power of the convex lens is positive. Power of the concave lens is negative.

23. Yes, even if the one half of the convex lens is covered with black paper it can still produce complete image of the object. Because rays coming from the object can be refracted by other half lens and form a complete image.

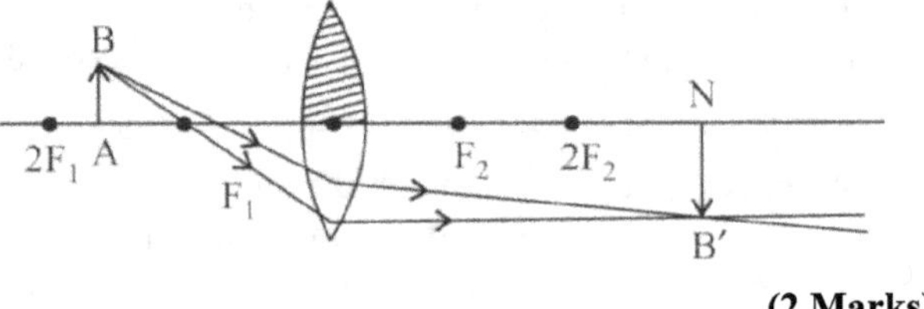

(2 Marks)

Given focal length (f) = +20 cm, $h_0 = 4$ cm, $u = -15$ cm

Lens formula : $\dfrac{1}{v} - \dfrac{1}{u} = \dfrac{1}{f}$

$$\therefore \quad \frac{1}{v} - \frac{1}{-15} = \frac{1}{+20}$$

$$\Rightarrow \quad \frac{1}{v} = \frac{1}{20} - \frac{1}{15}$$

$$\Rightarrow \quad \frac{1}{v} = \frac{3-4}{60} = -\frac{1}{60}$$

$\Rightarrow \quad v = -60$ cm **(1 Mark)**

Also, $m = \frac{h_i}{h_0} = 4$

$\Rightarrow \quad h_i = 4 \times h_0 = 4 \times 4 \text{ cm} = 16 \text{ cm}$ **(1 Mark)**

The image formed is erect, magnified and virtual.

(1 Mark)

Note

(a) When a symmetric lens is cut along the optical axis in two equal parts. Intensity of image formed by each part will be same as that of complete lens. Focal length is double the original for each part.

(b) When a symmetric lens is cut along principle axis in two equal parts. Intensity of image formed by each part will be less compared to that of complete lens. Focal length remains same for each part.

24. Ciliary muscles helps in the adjusting the focal length of the eye lens by changing the curvature of the eye lens.

(1 Mark)

Due to the gradual weakening of the ciliary muscles with ageing, the near point gradually recedes away. This condition is called 'presbyopia'. Person suffering presbyopia should use convex lenses. **(1 Mark)**

(a) Akshay is suffering from myopia or near sightedness. Concave lens is used for myopia. **(1 Mark)**

(b) Values displayed by teacher are scientific temperament, proactiveness, attentiveness. Values displayed by Salman are kindness, caring nature, helpful and value of friendship. **(1 Mark)**

(c) Akshay can express his gratitude by thanking them, helping them and studying well. **(1 Mark)**

25. (a) Red litmus remains red and blue litmus turn red.

(1 Mark)

26. (d) Common salt is added to favour precipitation of soap.

(1 Mark)

Note

The soap formed remains in suspension form. It is precipitated as a solid deom the suspension by adding common salt.

27. (a) P and Q **(1 Mark)**

28. (c) **(1 Mark)**

29. (b) **(1 Mark)**

30. (b) Focal length of the mirror can be find by measuring MS. **(1 Mark)**

31. (d) In case of convex lens, when an object is placed at infinity, then image is formed at the focus of the lens. Thus, device X is a convex lens of focal length 8 cm. **(1 Mark)**

32. (d) When a ray of light enters a glass slab, it bends towards the normal. Thus, angle of refraction is less than the angle of incidence. Also, the angle of emergence is equal is equal to the angle of incidence.

(1 Mark)

33. (b) The emergent ray bends at an angle to the direction of incident ray. **(1 Mark)**

34. When $NaHCO_3$ is added to acetic acid, CO_2 gas is evolved. **(1 Mark)**

$$CH_3COOH + NaHCO_3 \rightarrow CH_3COONa + H_2O + CO_2\uparrow$$

CO_2 gas evolved can be tested by passing it through lime water. It turns lime water milky. **(1 Mark)**

$$\underset{\text{Lime water}}{Ca(OH)_2} + CO_2 \longrightarrow \underset{\text{white}}{CaCO_3}\downarrow + H_2O$$

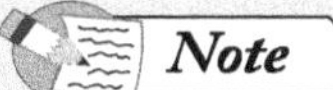

Note

Lime water turns milky on passing CO_2 gas due to the formation of calcium carbonate. However on excess of CO_2, solution again becomes clear due to the formation of calcium bicarbonate.

$$CaCO_3 + CO_2 + H_2O \longrightarrow \underset{\text{(water soluble)}}{Ca(HCO_3)\ (aq)}$$

35. (a) Fine screw should be moved to focus the slide.

(b) Budding in yeast

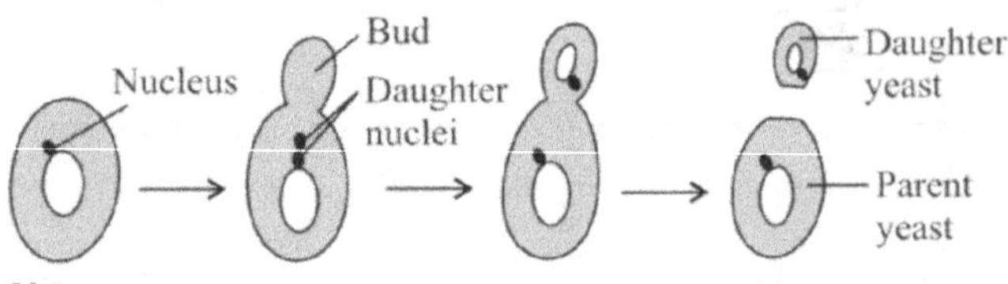

(2 Marks)

Note

Budding is a type of aexual reproduction in which a bud is develops as an outgrowth due to repeated cell division at one specific site. The bud develops into tiny individuals and when fully mature detach from the parent body and becomes new independent individuals.

36. Lens formula : $\frac{1}{v}-\frac{1}{u}=\frac{1}{f}$

$$\frac{1}{24}-\frac{1}{-12}=\frac{1}{f}$$

$\Rightarrow$ $f = 8$ cm

When object is between F and 2F, image is formed beyond 2F. So, if the object is moved away from the lens, image will move towards the lens. So, screen should also be shifted towards lens. **(1 Mark)**

The magnification is given by

$$m=\frac{v}{u}$$

When object is moved away from the lens, the object distance (u) increases and the image distance (v) decreases. Thus, the magnification will decrease on moving the object away from lens. **(1 Mark)**

2014-2015

Solved Paper Term-I

Time Allowed : 3 Hours ***Maximum Marks : 90***

General Instructions:

I. The questions paper comprises of two Sections, A and B. You are to attempt both the sections.

II. All questions are compulsory.

III. All questions of section A and all questions of Section B are to be attempted separately.

IV. Question numbers 1 to 3 in Section A are one mark questions. These are to be answered in one word or in one sentence.

V. Question numbers 4 to 6 in Sections A are two marks questions. These are to be answered in about 30 words each.

VI. Question numbers 7 to 18 iin Section A are three marks questions. These are to be answered in about 50 words each.

VII. Question numbers 19 to 24 in Section A are five marks questions. These are to be answered in about 70 words each.

VIII. Question numbers 25 to 33 in Section B are multiple choice questions based on practial skills. Each questions is a one mark question. You are to select one most appropriate response out of the four provided to you.

IX. Question numbers 34 to 36 in Section B are questions based on practical skills. Each question is a two marks question.

SECTION - A

1. Nickel(II) nitrate is prepared by heating nickel metal with liquid dinitrogen tetraoxide. In addition to the nitrate, gaseous nitrogen monoxide is formed. Write the balanced equation.

2. State and define the unit of resistance.

3. What are endocrine glands?

4. A student constructed a box type solar cooker. He found that it did not work efficiently. What could this be due to? Give any four possible mistakes in the construction and operation of the cooker.

5. How was petroleum formed?

6. What are the limitations of the energy that can be obtained from the oceans?

7. One method of joining railway lines is the 'thermite' reaction. Iron (III) oxide and powered aluminium are mixed together, and heated until the reaction starts. After the reaction has started it becomes red hot. The melted iron runs into the gap between the railway lines.

(a) From this reaction what can you conclude about the reactivity of aluminium compared to iron ?

(b) Is the reaction exothermic or endothermic ? Give a reason for your answer.

8. What would happen if all the hydrogen present in the sun is converted into helium?

9. State the principle of the electric motor and give its diagram.

10. Balance the following chemical equations :

(a) $HNO_3 + Ca(OH)_2 \rightarrow Ca(NO_3)_2 + H_2O$

(b) $NaOH + H_2SO_4 \rightarrow Na_2SO_4 + H_2O$

(c) $BaCl_2 + H_2SO_4 \rightarrow BaSO_4 + HCl$

11. A particle having a charge of 1.6×10^{-19} coulomb is moving with a speed of 3.5×10^7 m/s in a magnetic field of 4T. Calculate the force experienced by this moving charged particle?

12. Which animal or plant hormone is associated with the following?

(i) Increased sugar level in blood

(ii) Changes at puberty in boys

(iii) Inhibits growth of plants

(iv) Rapid development of fruits

(v) Dwarfism

(vi) Goitre

13. (a) Identify the substances that are oxidised and the substances that are reduced in the following reactions.

(i) $ZnO(s) + C(s) \longrightarrow Zn(s) + CO(g)$

(ii) $CuO(s) + H_2(g) \longrightarrow Cu(s) + H_2O(l)$

(b) Name the oxidising and reducing agent in the following reaction:

$$2H_2S + SO_2 \longrightarrow 2H_2O + 3S\downarrow$$

14. Iqbal treated a lustrous, divalent element M with sodium hydroxide. He observed the formation of bubbles in reaction mixture. He made the same observations when this element was treated with hydrochloric acid. Suggest how can he identify the produced gas. Write chemical equations for both the reaction.

15. Three resistors are connected as shown in the following figure. Through the resistor 5 ohm, a current of 1 A is flowing.

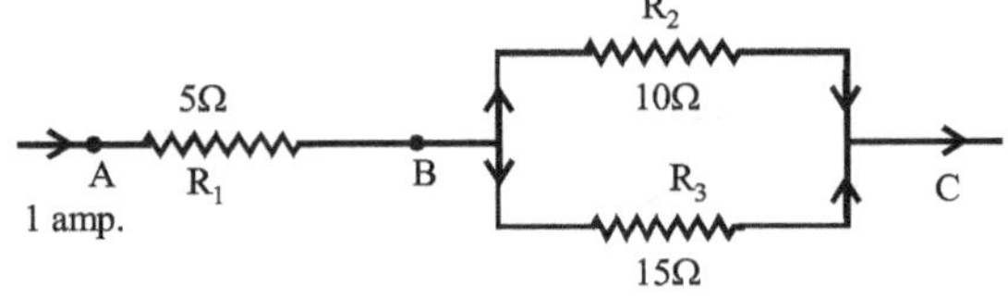

(a) What is the total resistance?
(b) What is the potential difference across AB and AC?
(c) What is the current through other two resistors?

16. State Ohm's law. What is the nature of graph between current and potential difference? What does it indicate?

17. Discuss the functions of Cytokinins.

18. What are the differences between the transport of materials in Xylem and Phloem?

19. Mayank's father never bothered to check the brand/ contents of the salt he had purchased form the market. Mayank noticed that her sister had developed swollen neck. The doctor advised her to eat iodised salt.

Answer the following questions based on above passage.

(i) Name the disease from which Mayank's sister suffered.
(ii) Why has the doctor advised her to eat iodised salt?
(iii) How will this incidence influence Mayank's attitude towards health?

20. Explain Joule's law of heating. What does it imply? A potential difference of 250 volt is applied across a resistance of 500 ohm in an electric iron. Calculate (a) the current (b) heat energy produced in joule in 10 sec ?

21. Describe the activity that shows that a current-carrying conductor experiences a force perpendicular to its length and the external magnetic field. How does Fleming's left-hand rule help us to find the direction of the force acting on the current carrying conductor?

22. (a) A compound *X* of sodium forms a white powder. It is a constituent of baking powder and is used in some antacid prescriptions. When heated, *X* gives out a gas and steam. The gas forms a white precipitate with limewater. Write the chemical formula and name of *X* and the chemical equation for its decomposition on heating. What is its role in baking powder and in antacids?

(b) Name the constituents of baking powder. What is the function of each constituent of baking powder in the manufacture of cake.

23. Name the following:

(a) A metal that catches fire in open air and gives off white fumes
(b) A metal that forms two types of oxides and rusts in moisture; write their formulae also
(c) A metal used in stainless steel.
(d) A metal used in long distance cables wires
(e) A metal added to gold to harden it

24. How do the guard cells regulate opening and closing of stomatal pores ?

SECTION - B

25. In an attempt to demonstrate electrical conductivity through an electrolyte, the following apparatus (Figure) was set up.

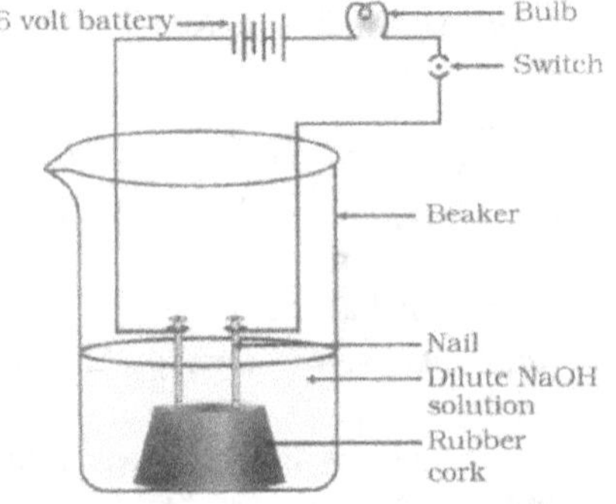

Which among the following statements(s) is (are) correct?
(i) Bulb will not glow because electrolyte is not acidic
(ii) Bulb will glow because NaOH is a strong base and furnishes ions for conduction.

(iii) Bulb will not glow because circuit is incomplete
(iv) Bulb will not glow because it depends upon the type of electrolytic solution.
(a) (i) and (iii) (b) (ii) and (iv)
(c) (ii) only (d) (iv) only

26. During the preparation of hydrogen chloride gas on a humid day, the gas is usually passed through the guard tube containing calcium chloride. The role of calcium chloride taken in the guard tube is to
(a) absorb the evolved gas
(b) moisten the gas
(c) absorb moisture from the gas
(d) absorb Cl^- ions from the evolved gas

27. Observe the experiment set-up carefully:

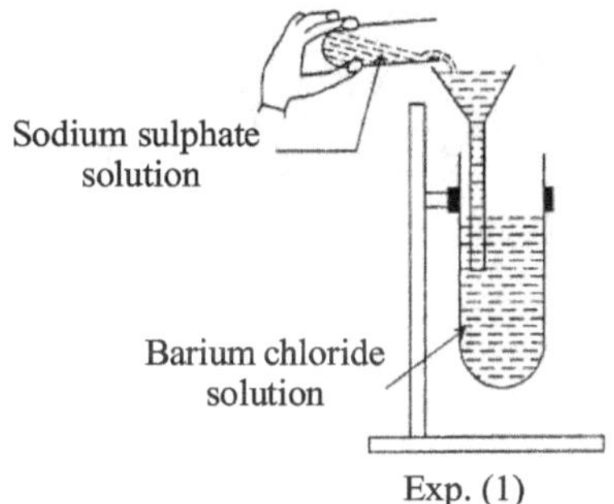

Exp. (1)

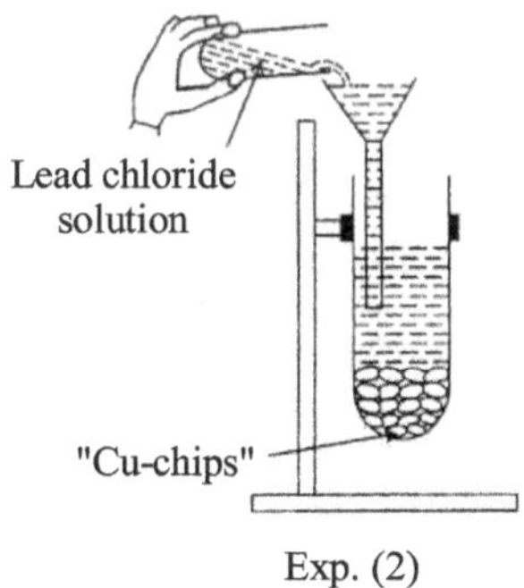

Exp. (2)

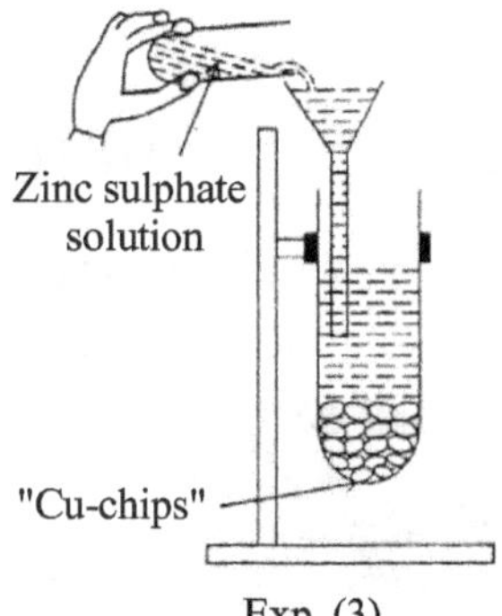

Exp. (3)

In which experiment an insoluble precipitate is formed and of which substance ?
(a) Exp 1, Na_2SO_4
(b) Exp 2, $CuCl_2$
(c) Exp 3, $CuSO_4$
(d) Exp 1, $BaSO_4$

28. If a few drops of a concentrated acid accidentally spills over the hand of a student, what should be done?
(a) Wash the hand with saline solution
(b) Wash the hand immediately with plenty of water and apply a paste of sodium hydrogen carbonate
(c) After washing with plenty of water apply solution of sodium hydroxide on the hand
(d) Neutralise the acid with a strong alkali

29. A student collected the samples of acids such as : hydrochloric acid, acetic acid and bases such as sodium hydroxide and magnesium hydroxide from the science laboratory. He put 10 drops of each of the above sample solution on a watch glass and tested with a 1–2 drops of the following indicators as given below; and recorded his observations :

Sample solution	**Red litmus solution**	**Blue litmus solution**	**Phenolphthalein solution**	**Methyl orange solution**
A. HCl solution	No colour change	Changes to red	Colourless	Changes to red
B. CH_3COOH solution	No colour change	Changes to red	Changes to red	Colourless
C. NaOH solution	Changes to blue	No colour change	Changes to light pink	remains as it is
D. Mg $(OH)_2$ solution	No colour change	Changes to red	Changes to light pink	Colourless

The correct observation is made by a student :

(a) A and B (b) A and C

(c) B and C (d) B and D

30. Observe the experimental set up carefully.

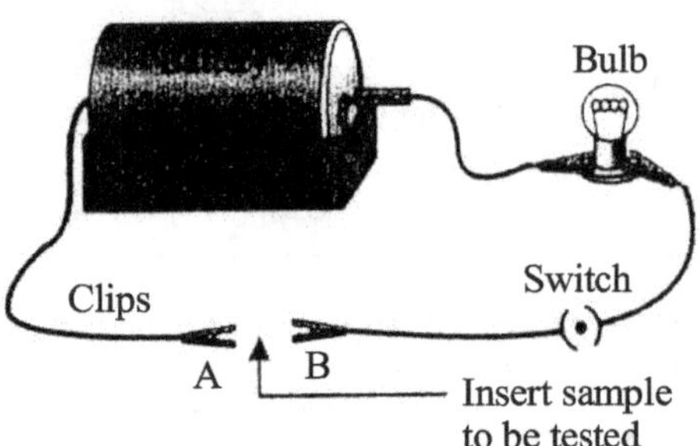

You are provided with four types of metallic wires i.e. silver wire, copper wire, lead wire and iron wire. Which type of metallic wire would you like to put in the circuit between gap of two terminals A and B, so that circuit show maximum conductivity.

(a) Lead

(b) Iron

(c) Silver

(d) Copper

31. In which of the circuits below does a current exist to light the bulb?

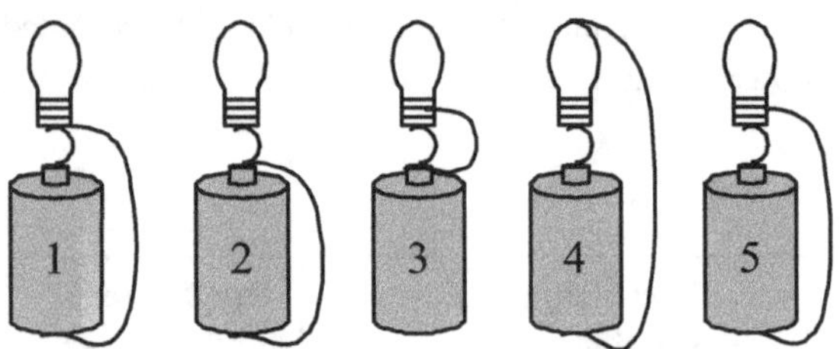

(a) 1 & 5 (b) 4 & 5

(c) 5 (d) 3

32.

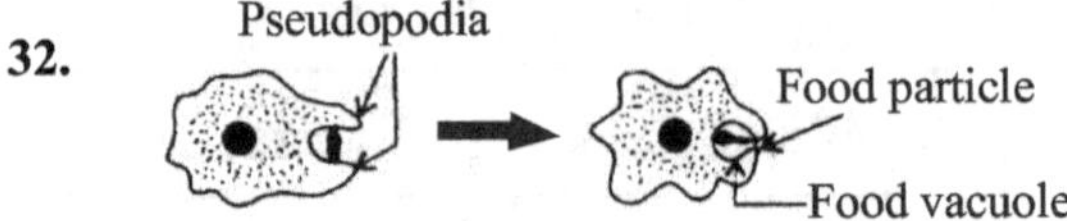

Which activity is illustrated in the diagram of an *Amoeba* shown above?

(a) Ingestion (b) Digestion

(c) Egestion (d) Assimilation

33. From the given picture of the digestive system, identify the part labelled as gastric gland.

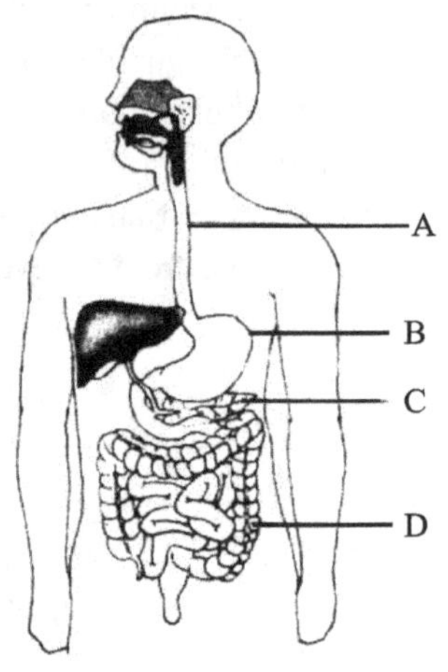

(a) A (b) B

(c) C (d) D

34. The given diagram represents human respiratory system.

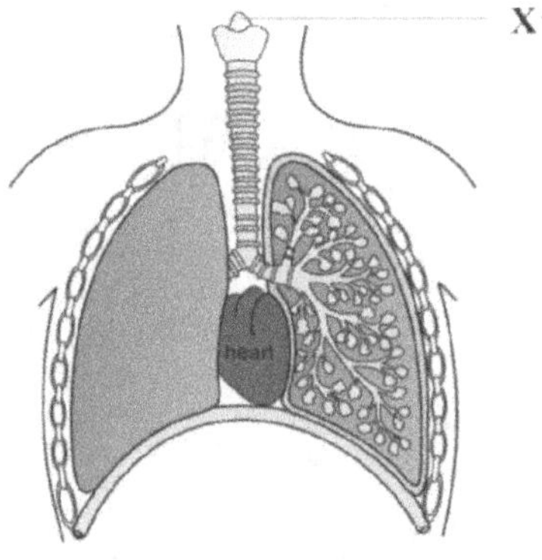

What is X, also write one function of it.

35. Fig. below shows an electric kettle connected to the 240 V mains supply by a flexible cable. The kettle has a power rating of 2500 W.

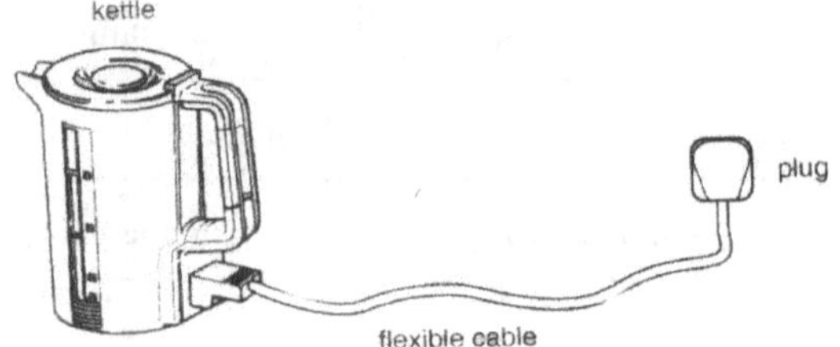

wire diameter / mm	maximum current / A
0.50	3
0.75	6
1.00	10
1.25	13
1.50	15

From the table, select the smallest diameter of wire that can safely be used for this kettle.

(a) 1.00 mm

(b) 1.50 mm

(c) 1.25 mm

(d) 0.75 mm

36. A student took four test tubes I, II, III and IV containing aluminium sulphate, copper sulphate, ferrous sulphate and zinc sulphate solution, respectively. He placed an iron strip in each of them. He found a brown deposit formed in which test tube? Write the chemical equation.

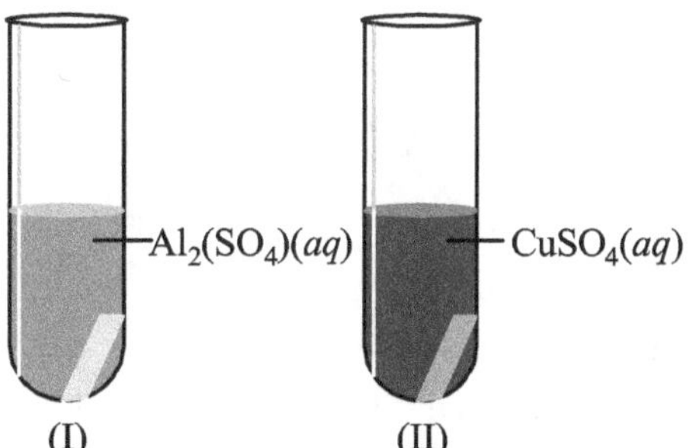

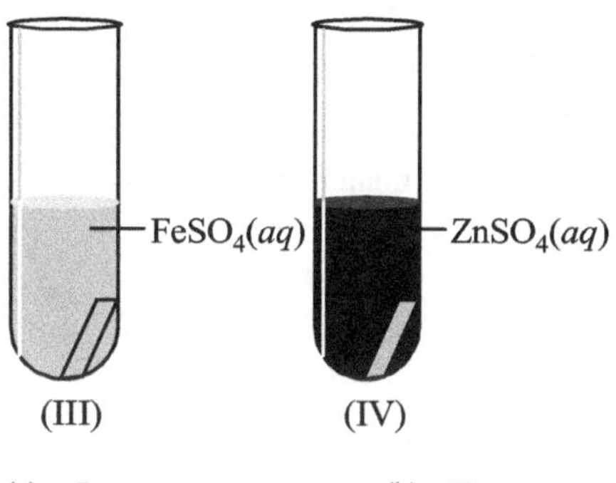

(a) I (b) II
(c) III (d) IV

Solutions

SECTION - A

1. $Ni(s) + 2N_2O_4(l) \longrightarrow Ni(NO_3)_2(s) + 2NO(g)$ **(1 mark)**

2. Ohm is the unit of resistance.
Ohm : If the potential difference across two ends of a conductor is 1V and the current through it is 1A then the resistance R, of the conductor is 1Ω. That is

$$1 \text{ ohm} = \frac{1 \text{ volt}}{1 \text{ ampere}}$$ **(½ + ½ =1 mark)**

3. Ductless glands which manufacture hormones and secrete them directly into the blood stream. **(1 mark)**

Hormones are chemical messengers that are secreted directly into the bloodstream and are transported to different organs and tissues to perform specific function.

4. (i) Instead of a transparent glass he must have used plastic sheet.
(ii) The inside of the box would have not been painted black.
(iii) The reflector must not have been adjusted properly.
(iv) Instead of plane mirror he should use concave mirror for better concentration of rays of reflection.
(2 marks)

5. Petroleum was formed by slow decomposition of sea plants and animals. These plants and animals were buried under the earth's crust millions of years ago. They got covered by layers of sedimentary rocks which cut off the supply of air. In the absence of air these fossils under went a slow chemical change due to high temp and pressure and then turned into new form called as petroleum. It is also known as **Crude Oil.** **(2 marks)**

6. The energy from the ocean can be obtained mainly in three forms- (i) tidal energy (ii) wave energy and ocean thermal energy. But these energy can't be a potential source of energy in future because of the following reasons –
(i) there are very few places around the world which are suitable for building tidal dams.
(ii) the rise and fall of sea-water during high and low tides is not enough to generate electricity on a large scale. **(2 marks)**

7. (a) The reactivity of aluminium is more than that of iron. **(1 mark)**
(b) The reaction is exothermic.
Reason: The reaction evolves heat and due to this it becomes red hot. Since heat is evolved so the reaction is exothermic. **(2 mark)**

The 'Thermite' reaction is

$2Al + Fe_2O_3 \longrightarrow Al_2O_3 + 2Fe + Heat$

since Al displaces Fe from its compound so Al is more reactive than Fe]

8. In case all the hydrogen present in the sun is converted into helium, the temperature and pressure inside the sun will decrease. As a result of this, the sun will collapse due to its own gravity. When the size of sun decreases, its interior temperature will again rise and hydrogen nuclei will get liberated from the helium nuclei. **(3 mark)**

9. Electric motor is a device which is used to convert electrical energy into mechanical energy. **(1 mark)**
Principle : It is based on the fact that when a conductor carrying current is placed in a magnetic field, a force is exerted on it.
So, when a rectangular coil is placed in a magnetic field and current flows through it, then torque is produced and acts on the coil and it rotates. The diagram of an electric motor is as follows.

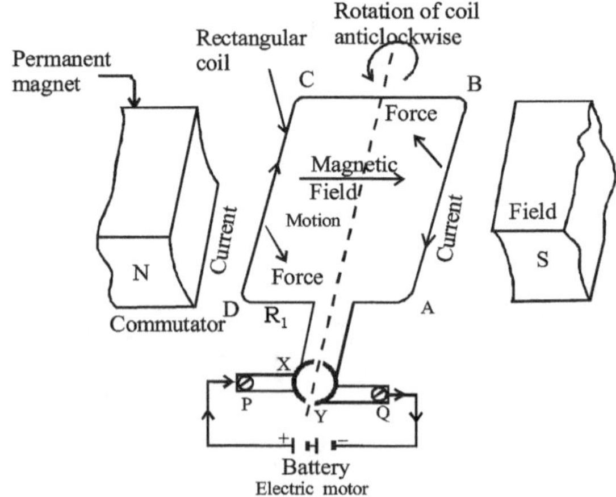

Electric motor

(2 marks)

Direction of force across various arms of the rectangular coil can be find using fleming's left hand rule.

10. (a) $2HNO_3 + Ca(OH)_2 \rightarrow Ca(NO_3)_2 + 2H_2O$ **(1 mark)**

(b) $2NaOH + H_2SO_4 \rightarrow Na_2SO_4 + 2H_2O$ **(1 mark)**

(c) $BaCl_2 + H_2SO_4 \rightarrow BaSO_4 + 2HCl$ **(1 mark)**

11. $B = 4T,\ Q = 1.6 \times 10^{-19} C,\ V = 3.5 \times 10^7$ m/s

$F = B \times Q \times V = 4 \times 1.6 \times 10^{-19} \times 3.5 \times 10^7$

$= 2.24 \times 10^{-11} N$ **(3 marks)**

12. (i) Insulin
(ii) Testosterone
(iii) Abscisic acid
(iv) Auxin
(v) Growth hormone
(vi) Thyroxine **(3 marks)**

13. **(a)**

Reduction (removal of oxygen)

(i) $ZnO + C \longrightarrow Zn + CO$

Oxidation (addition of oxygen)

Therefore the substance

Oxidised = C, Reduced = ZnO **(1 mark)**

Reduction (removal of oxygen)

(ii) $CuO + H_2 \longrightarrow Cu + H_2O$

Oxidation (addition of oxygen)

Therefore the substance:

Oxidised = H_2, Reduced = CuO **(1 mark)**

(b) H_2S is the reducing agent while SO_2 is the oxidising agent. **(1 mark)**

Oxidising agents are the compounds that oxidises the other substance and itself get reduced.

Reducing agent are the compounds that reduces other substance and itself get oxidised.

14. The produced gas can be identified by bringing a burning match stick near the reaction vessel, a pop sound is produced **(1 mark)**

$M + 2NaOH \rightarrow Na_2MO_2 + H_2$ **(1 mark)**

$M + 2HCl \rightarrow MCl_2 + H_2$ **(1 mark)**

The element is a metal

15. $R_1 = 5\ \Omega,\ R_2 = 10\ \Omega,\ R_3 = 15\ \Omega, I = 1\ A$

(a) $\dfrac{1}{R'} = \dfrac{1}{R_2} + \dfrac{1}{R_3}$

$= \dfrac{1}{10} + \dfrac{1}{15} = \dfrac{3+2}{30} = \dfrac{5}{30}$

$R' = \dfrac{30}{5} = 6\ \Omega$

$R = R_1 + R' = 5 + 6 = 11\Omega$

Now, $V = IR = 1 \times 11 = 11V$ **(1 mark)**

(b) $V_1 = IR_1 = 1 \times 5 = 5V$.

Therefore, $V_2 = V - V_1 = 11 - 5 = 6V$ **(1 mark)**

(c) $V_2 = I_1 R_2 \Rightarrow I_1 = \dfrac{V_2}{R_2} = \dfrac{6}{10} = 0.6\ A;$

$I_2 = \dfrac{V_2}{R_3} = \dfrac{6}{15} = 0.4\ A$ **(1 mark)**

16. According to Ohm's law, "At a constant temperature the current flowing through a conductor is directly proportional to potential difference across its ends".

i.e., $V \propto I$

$V = RI$

'R' is a constant called resistance. **(1 mark)**

The graph between current and potential difference is a straight line. It indicates that current is directly proportional to the potential difference and ratio $\dfrac{V}{I}$ is constant.

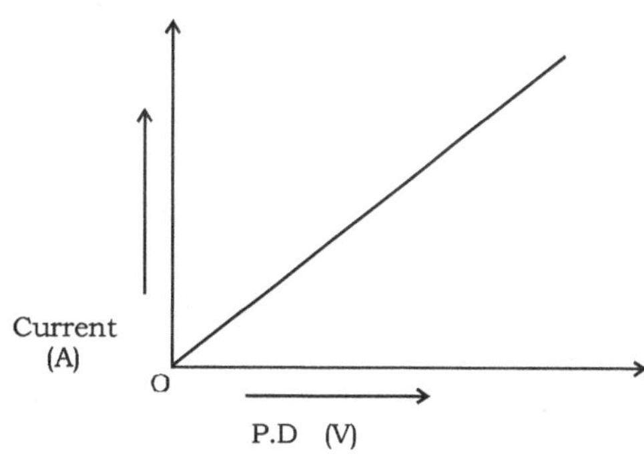

(2 marks)

17. Cytokinins promote cell division, and it is natural then that they are present in greater concentration in areas of rapid cell division, such as in fruits and seeds. These are examples of plant hormones that help in promoting growth. But plants also need signals to stop growing. **(3 marks)**

Phytohormones are also called plant hormones. They are chemical messenger that plays an important role in regulation of cellular activities in plants.

18.

	Transport in Xylem	Transport in Phloem
1	*Components :* It transport water and minerals in plants.	It food transports in plants.
2	*Direction :* The movement is generally unidirectional.	The movement is bidirectional.
3	Physical focus such as transpiration pull are required for transport in the xylem.	The transport of food through the phloem requires ATP (Adenosine triphosphate energy).

(1 × 3 = 3 marks)

19. (i) Goitre/Thyroid related disease. **(1 mark)**

(ii) Iodine present in iodised salt is needed to produce thyroxin hormone. **(2 mark)**

(iii) Mayank would become more careful regarding health, will be conscious of his diet and of people around him. **(2 mark)**

Thyroid stimulation hormone is a pituitary hormone which stimulates the thyroid gland to secrete thyroxine hormone that is responsible for the regulation of carbohydrates, proteins and fat metabolism.

20. Consider a current I flowing through a resistor of resistance *R*. Let the potential difference across it beV (Fig.). Let *t* be the time during which a charge Q flows across. The work done in moving the charge Q through a potential difference V is VQ. Therefore, the source must supply energy equal to VQ in time t. Hence the power input to the circuit by the source is

$$P = V\frac{Q}{t} = VI$$

Or the energy supplied to the circuit by the source in time t is P× t, that is,VIt. This energy gets dissipated in the resistor as heat. Thus for a steady current I, the amount of heat H produced in time t is

H = VIt.

Applying Ohm's law we get

$H = I^2Rt$

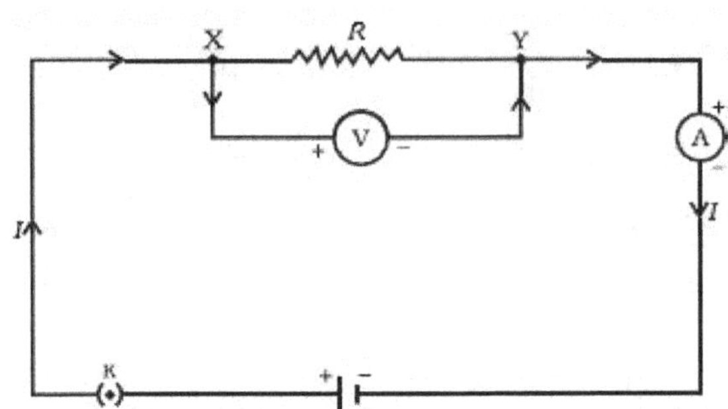

Fig. : A steady current in a purely resistive electric circuit.

This is known as Joule's law of heating. The law implies that heat produced in a resistor is (i) directly proportional to the square of current for a given resistance, (ii) directly proportional to resistance for a given current, and (iii) directly proportional to the time for which the current flows through the resistor. **(1½ +1½ marks)**

V = 250 V, t = 10 sec, R = 500 Ω, H = ?, I = ?, V = IR

$$I = \frac{V}{R} = \frac{250}{500} = 0.5\text{ A}$$

$H = I^2 Rt = 0.5 \times 0.5 \times 500 \times 10 = 1250$ J. **(2 marks)**

Formula $H = I^2RT$ is used if current I, resistance R and time t are known. In some cases, they give us the power P and time t only. In that case heat energy $E = P \times t$.

21.
- Take a small aluminium rod AB (of about 5 cm.) Using two connecting wires suspend it horizontally from a stand, as shown in figure.
- Place a strong horse-shoe magnet in such a way that the rod lies between the two poles with the magnetic field directed upwards. For this put the north pole of

the magnet vertically below and south pole vertically above the aluminium rod.

- Connect the aluminium rod in series with a battery, a key and a rheostat.
- Now pass a current through the aluminium rod from end B to end A.
- What do you observe ? It is observed that the rod is displaced towards the left. You will notice that the rod gets displaced.
- Reverse the direction of current flowing through the rod and observe the direction of its displacement. It is now towards the right.

According to Fleming's left hand rule, stretch the thumb, forefinger and central finger of your left hand such that they are mutually perpendicular. If the fore finger points in the direction of magnetic field and the central in the direction of current, then the thumb will point in the direction of motion or force acting on the conductor.

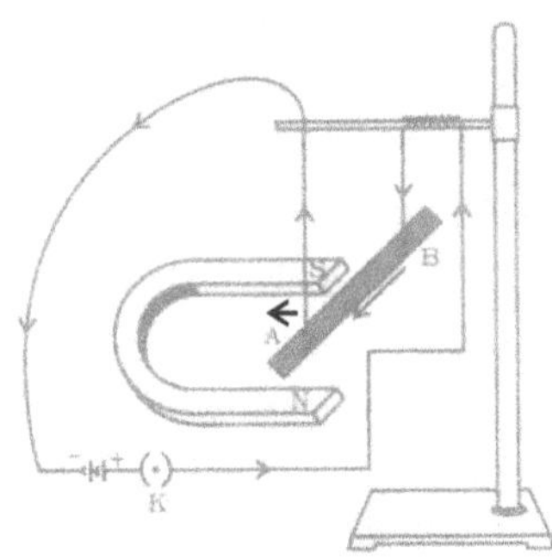

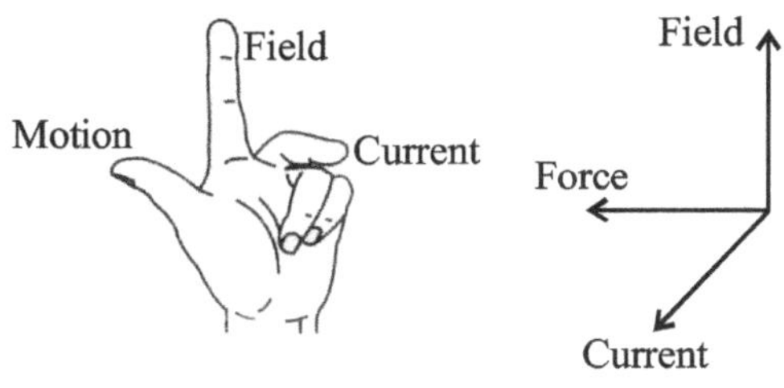

(3 + 2 marks)

Fleming's left hand rule is used to find the direction of force acting on a current carrying wire placed in a magnetic field. Fleming's right hand rule is used to get the direction of induced current produced in a conductor in a magnetic field.

22. (a) 'X' is sodium bicarbonate ($NaHCO_3$). It is a constituent of baking powder and is used as antacid. **(½+½=1 mark)**

When 'X' is heated, it gives out CO_2 and steam.

$$2NaHCO_3(s) \xrightarrow{\text{heat}} Na_2CO_3(s) + CO_2(g)\uparrow + H_2O(g)$$

(1 mark)

When $CO_2(g)$ is passed through lime water, it turns milky due to formation of calcium carbonate.

$$\underset{\text{Lime water}}{Ca(OH)_2} + \underset{\text{Carbon dioxide}}{CO_2} \rightarrow \underset{\text{(White ppt.)}}{CaCO_3} + H_2O$$

Sodium bicarbonate in baking powder makes the cake and biscuits fluffy and in antacid it neutralizes hyperacidity in the stomach. **(1 mark)**

(b) Constituent of baking powder are baking soda ($NaHCO_3$) and tartaric acid (a mild edible acid). **(1 mark)**

Baking soda releases CO_2 on heating and causes the cake to rise/make it soft and spongy.

$NaHCO_3$ on heating forms Na_2CO_3 which is bitter in taste and it is neutralized by tartaric acid.

(½ + ½ = 1 mark)

23. (a) The metal that catches fire in open air and gives off white fumes is sodium. **(1 mark)**

(b) The metal that forms two types of oxides and rusts in moisture is iron. The formulas of its oxides are: FeO; Fe_2O_3. **(1 mark)**

(c) The metal used in stainless steel is chromium besides iron and carbon as it increases corrosion resistance character of steel. **(1 mark)**

(d) The metal used in long distance cables wires is aluminium, because it is a light metal and a very good conductor of electricity. **(1 mark)**

(e) The metal added to gold to harden it is copper. **(1 mark)**

24. The opening and closing of stomotal pores is regulated by guard cells by increasing or decreasing the amount of water in them. When water enters the guard cells, they become turgid. This results in opening of (stomatal) pore. When water exits from the gurad cells, they become flacid. This result in closing of stomata.

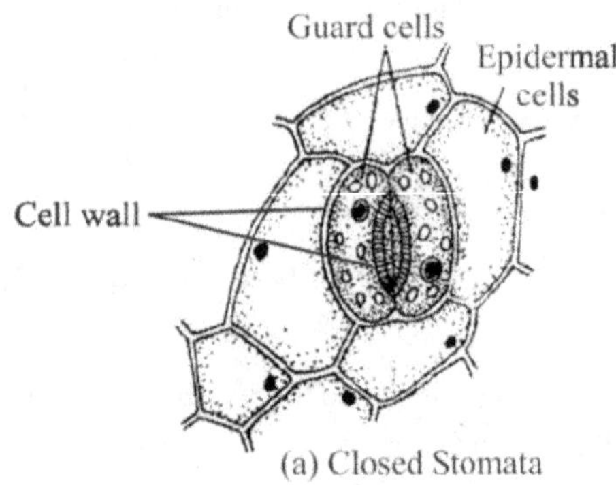

(a) Closed Stomata

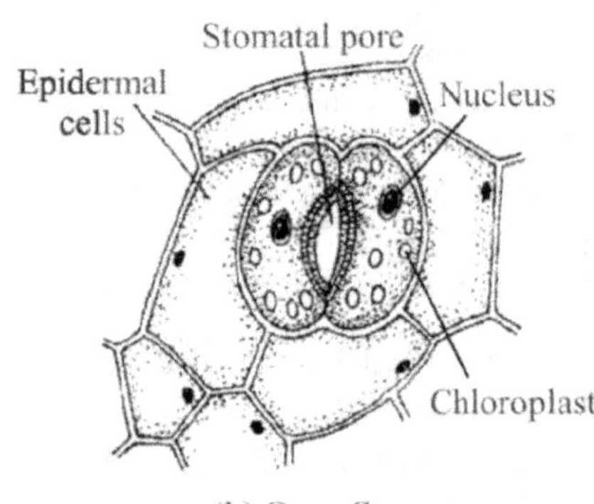

(b) Open Stomata

During closure movement of stomata, guard cells send out K^+ions. Water also passes out. Guard cells become flaccid. Their inner thick walls come to touch each other. The stomatal pore gets closed. **(5 marks)**

Note

Guard cells are specialised plant cells in the epidermis of leaves, stem and other plant organs. It plays on important role in gaseous exchange in plants.

SECTION - B

25. **(c)** Ions are responsible for conducting electricity. **(1 mark)**

26. **(c)** Dry CaCl2 is a moisture absorber. **(1 mark)**

27. **(d)** $Na_2SO_4(aq) + BaCl_2(aq) \longrightarrow BaSO_4(s)\downarrow + 2NaCl(aq)$ **(1 mark)**

28. **(b)** **(1 mark)**

29. **(b)** **(1 mark)**

30. **(c)** Silver is very good conductor of electricity. **(1 mark)**

31. **(c)** In the circuit numbered 5, a current exists to light the bulb because only in this circuit the two terminals of the battery have been joined to two different ends of the filament of the bulb. **(1 marks)**

32. **(a)** Ingestion involves intake of food. **(1 mark)**

33. **(b)** The label structure B represents stomach. Numerous simple or branched glands lie in the mucus membrane of the stomach. The glands are called gastric glands. They secrete gastric juice, HCl acid, protein digesting enzymes, mucus etc. **(1 mark)**

34. **(a)** The label X represents epiglottis. Epiglottis prevents food from entering into trachea. **(2 marks)**

35. **(c)** I = P/V, 2500/240 = 10.4A

The maximum current in the cable is 10.4 A. Therefore, the smallest diameter of wire that can safely be used is 1.25 mm. **(2 marks)**

36. **(b)** $Fe(s) + CuSO_4(aq) \longrightarrow FeSO_4(aq) + Cu(s)$

Activity series of metals:

Al > Zn > Fe > Cu

More active metal displaces less active metal from its compound.

(2 marks)

2013–2014

Solved Paper Term- I

Time Allowed : 3 Hours | ***Maximum Marks : 90***

General Instructions:

(i) Question paper comprises of two sections, A and B. You are to attempt both the sections.

(ii) All questions are compulsory.

(iii) All questions of section A and all questions of section B are to be attempted separately.

(iv) Question numbers 1 to 3 in section A are one mark each, to be answered in one word or one sentence.

(v) Question numbers 4 to 7 are two marks each, to be answered in about 30 words.

(vi) Question numbers 8 to 19 are three marks each, to be answered in about 50 words.

(vii) Question numbers 20 to 24 are five marks each, to be answered in about 70 words.

(viii) Question numbers 25 to 42 in section B are MCQ based on practical skills. Each question is a one mark question.

SECTION - A

1. Give one example of decomposition reaction in which solid and gas are two products obtained.

2. A copper wire of resistivity ρ is stretched to reduce its diameter to half of its previous value. What will be its new resistivity?

3. Which hormone is responsible for the development of moustache and beard in man?

4. Why is fuel oil considered a better fuel than coal in industries? Give any two reasons.

5. Give uses of solar cell.

6. Give reasons for the following :

(a) Metals conduct electricity.

(b) Reaction of nitric acid with metals generally does not evolve hydrogen gas

7. Non-metals do not displace hydrogen gas when reacted with acids/water explain.

8. Heat produced on burning 5.0 g of a fuel raises the temperature of 1.0 kg water from 20°C to 60°C. If the specific heat of water be 4.2 J/g°C, calculate the calorific value of the fuel?

9. List the properties of magnetic lines of force.

10. (a) What is the colour of ferrous sulphate crystals? How does this colour change after heating?

(b) Name the products formed on strongly heating ferrous sulphate crystals. What type of chemical reaction occurs in this change?

11. How does a solenoid behave like a magnet? Can you determine the north and south poles of a current-carrying solenoid with the help of a bar magnet? Explain.

12. (a) How can you obtain pure metal from metals of high reactivity?

(b) Magnesium when reacts with hot water starts floating. Explain.

13. (a) What is rancidity ? What is the general name of chemical which are added to fat and oil containing food so as to prevent the development of rancidity?

(b) Metal X becomes green when left in air, turns black when heated in air. Name the metal and the compounds formed in both the cases?

14. With the help of a chemical equation, explain how a soda-acid fire extinguisher helps in putting out a fire.

15. A poor women live in a village with her 5 years old son. When she switches off one bulb or any other electric appliance in her house all the other appliances get switched off. She did not have any idea as to how to reactify it and could not even spend for an electrician.

Priya doing her electric engineering living nearby decided to do something about this. According to her the series combination for the household connection should be the reason. She called an electrician and had the circuit changed to parallel combination. The problem was solved. She thanked Priya for her help to solve the problem.

(a) What according to you are the values displayed by Priya?

(b) What do you mean by series combination?

(c) Why for household a parallel combination used? Give two advantages.

16. How can three resistors of resistance 2Ω, 3Ω and 6Ω be connected to give a total resistance of (a) 4Ω, (b) 1Ω ?

17. What are hormones? State one function of each of the following hormones:

(i) Thyroxine (ii) Insulin

18. (a) Name the process by which autotrophs prepare their own food.

(b) List three events which occur during this process.

(c) State two sources from which plants obtain nitrogen for synthesis of proteins and other compounds.

19. What is a neurotransmitter? Why the flow of signals in a synape is from axonal end of one neuron to dendrite end of another neuron but not the reverse?

20. Three 250 watt heaters are connected in parallel to a 100 volt supply. Calculate :

(a) the total current taken from the supply.

(b) the resistance of each heater.

(c) the energy supplied in kWh to the three heaters in 5 hours.

21. Define the S.I. unit of magnetic field. "A charge moving at right angles to a uniform magnetic field does not undergo change in kinetic energy." Why?

22. (a) Why is Plaster of Paris written as $CaSO_4 \cdot \frac{1}{2} H_2O$?

How is it possible to have half a water molecule attached to $CaSO_4$?

(b) State one difference between strong electrolyte and weak electrolyte giving one example of each.

(c) When electricity is passed through the aqueous solution of sodium chloride, three products are obtained. Why is this process called chlor-alkali?

23. (a) Distinguish between 'roasting' and 'calcination'. Which of these two is used for sulphide ores and why?

(b) Write a chemical equation to illustrate the use of aluminium for joining cracked railway lines.

(c) Name the anode, the cathode and the electrolyte used in the electrolytic refining of impure copper.

24. (a) Where does digestion of fat take place in our body?

(b) How is small intestine designed to absorb digested food?

SECTION - B

25. Three beakers labelled as *A*, *B* and *C* each containing 25 mL of water were taken. *A* small amount of NaOH, anhydrous $CuSO_4$ and NaCl were added to the beakers *A*, *B* and *C* respectively. It was observed that there was an increase in the temperature of the solutions contained in beakers *A* and *B*, whereas in case of beaker *C*, the temperature of the solution falls. Which one of the following statement(s) is (are) correct?

(i) In beakers *A* and *B*, exothermic process has occurred.

(ii) In beakers *A* and *B*, endothermic process has occurred.

(iii) In beaker *C* exothermic process has occurred.

(iv) In beaker *C* endothermic process has occurred.

(a) (i) only

(b) (ii) only

(c) (i) and (iv)

(d) (ii) and (iii)

26. A colourless and odourless gas is liberated when hydrochloric acid is added to a solution of washing soda. The name of the gas is

(a) carbon dioxide

(b) nitrogen dioxide

(c) sulphur dioxide

(d) sulphur trioxide

27. Observe the following experimental set-up '*A*' and '*B*' carefully and answer in which beaker reaction will occur?

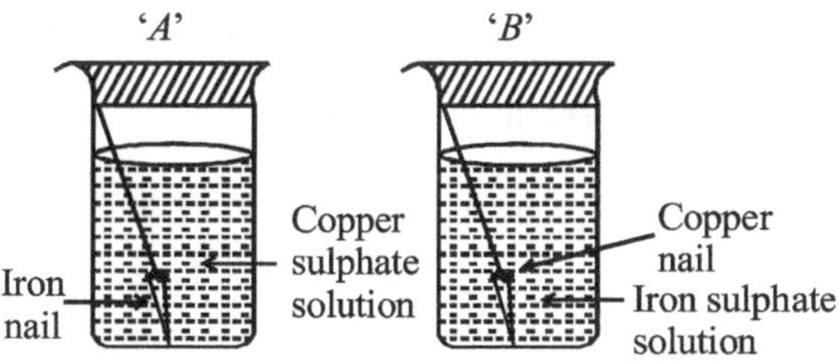

(a) In beaker *A*

(b) In beaker *B*

(c) None of the two beakers

(d) Reaction occur in both beakers

28. While preparing copper sulphate crystals from copper sulphate solution, dilute sulphuric acid is used instead of concentrated sulphuric acid, because

(a) concentrated sulphuric acid is corrosive in nature

(b) dilute sulphuric acid makes large crystals

(c) concentrated acid is ineffective

(d) Both (a) and (b)

29. A fruit juice is tested for its pH value. What could be its possible pH if the colour is changed to red?

(a) Less than 3

(b) More than 8

(c) 7

(d) Between 6.5 and 7.5

30. On adding a few drops of universal indicator to three unknown colourless solutions (*P*), (*Q*) and (*R*) taken separately in three test tubes shown in the following diagrams, a student observed the changes in colour as green in (*P*), red in (*Q*) and violet in (*R*).

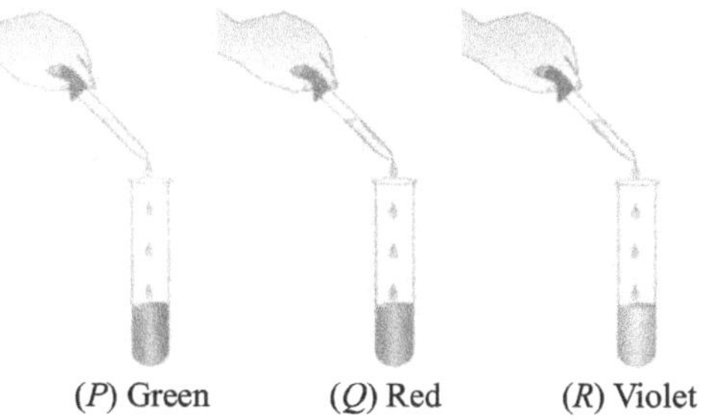

The decreasing order of pH of the solutions taken is :

(a) $P > Q > R$

(b) $R > P > Q$

(c) $Q > P > R$

(d) $R > Q > P$

31. The resistance of an ideal voltmeter is

(a) zero (b) very low

(c) very large (d) Infinite

32. The proper representation of series combination of cells obtaining maximum potential is

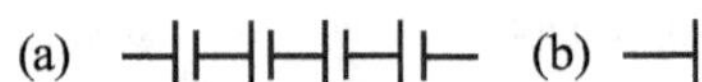

(c) (d)

33. While performing the experiment of Ohm's law, a student has plotted the following graph. The resistance of the conductor will be

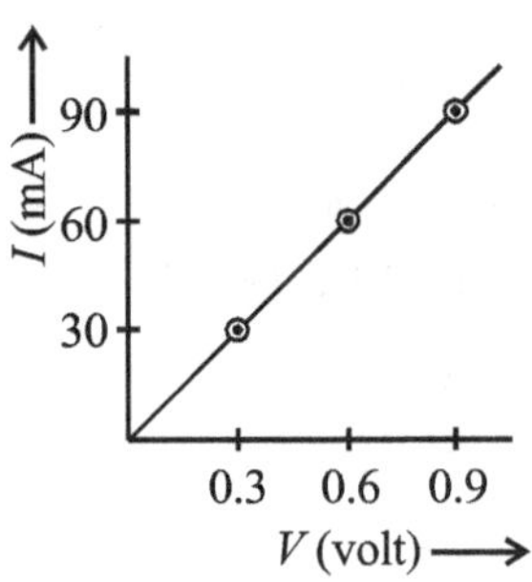

(a) $1000\,\Omega$ (b) $10\,\Omega$

(c) $100\,\Omega$ (d) $1\,\Omega$

34. Four ammeter A_1, A_2, A_3 and A_4 are connected to different resistors in a circuit given here. Maximum current will be recorded by the ammeter:

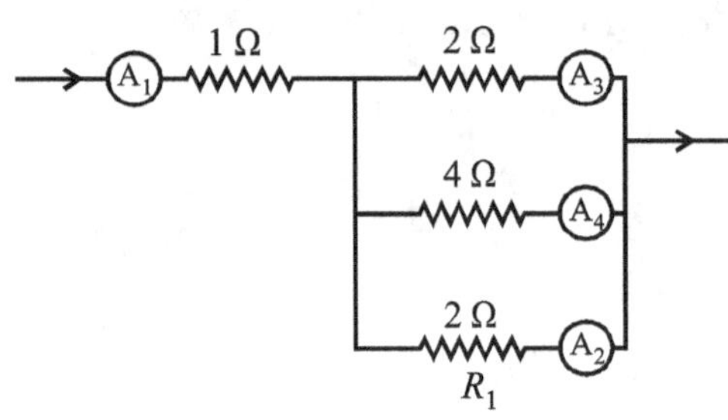

(a) A_1 (b) A_2

(c) A_3 (d) A_4

35. The resistance of a resistor with the following colour code

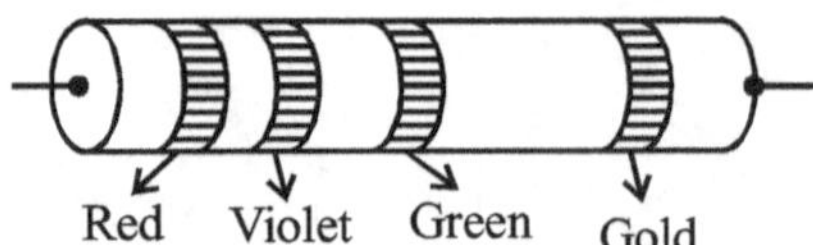

is equal to :

(a) $26 \times 10^4\,\Omega \pm 5\%$

(b) $25 \times 10^4\,\Omega \pm 10\%$

(c) $35 \times 10^5\,\Omega \pm 5\%$

(d) $27 \times 10^5\,\Omega \pm 5\%$

36. Which of the following curve is correct for ohmic circuits ?

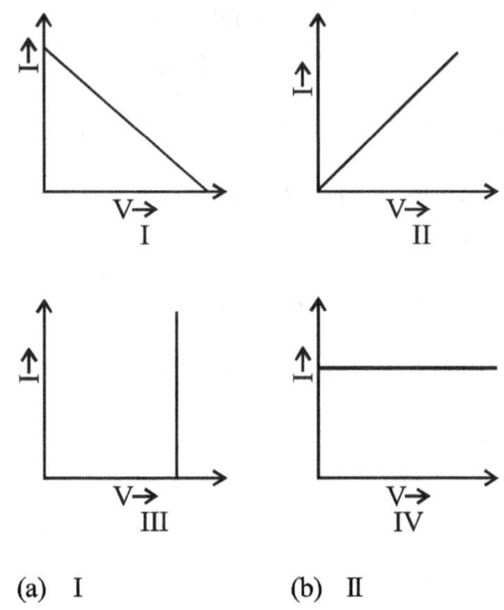

(a) I (b) II

(c) III (d) IV

37. To set up an experiment to show that light is necessary for photosynthesis, leaves should be taken from

(a) Destarched potted plant

(b) Any potted plant

(c) Any plant

(d) Healthy plant

38. For removal of chlorophyll, leaf is boiled in a beaker of alcohol, kept in a water bath. Water bath is essential because

(a) Steam from water bath heats up leaf quickly

(b) Steam from water bath dissolves the chlorophyll

(c) Alcohol is highly flammable

(d) Alcohol is volatile

39. A portion of destarched leaf of a potted plant was covered with a strip of paper. The plant was exposed to sunlight for six hours and then tested for starch. It was observed that

(a) Both covered and uncovered parts turned blue black

(b) Both covered and uncovered parts turned yellowish-brown

(c) Only the uncovered parts turned blue black.

(d) Only the covered parts turned blue black.

40. The given diagram represents the human respiratory system.

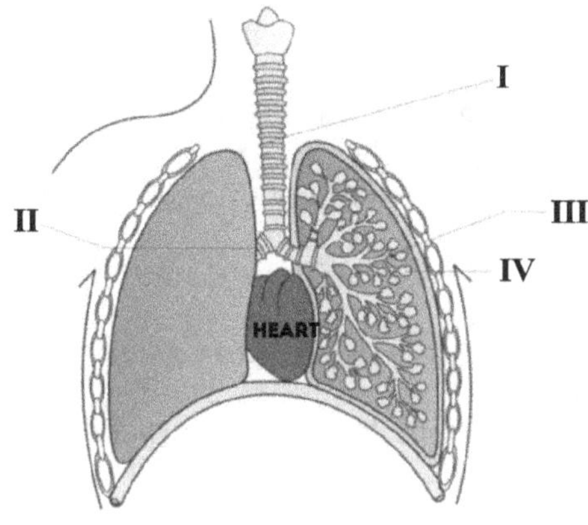

The exchange of gases takes place in which labelled structure?

(a) I (b) II

(c) III (d) IV

41. The function of KOH in the experimental set up to show that CO_2 is released during respiration is to

(a) Enhance respiration

(b) Release oxygen for respiration

(c) Absorb carbon dioxide released by germinating seeds

(d) Remove water vapour from the flask.

42. Connections are made air tight in the experiment to demonstrate release of CO_2 in respiration, otherwise

(a) Partial vacuum would not develop

(b) Oxygen used is immediately replenished

(c) CO_2 evolved will go out in atmosphere

(d) All the above

Solutions

SECTION-A

1. $CaCO_3 \rightarrow CaO + CO_2\downarrow$.

   CaO is solid and carbon dioxide is gas. **(1 mark)**

2. Resistivity will not change as it depends on the material not on the diamater of the wire. **(1 mark)**

3. Testosterone. **(1 mark)**

Hormones are chemical messengers that are secreted directly into the bloodstream and are transported to different organs and tissues to perform specific function.

4. (i) Fuel oil has highest calorific value than coal. **(1+1 marks)**

   (ii) Fuel oil produces less smoke than coal.

5. (i) Used to generate electricity in artificial satellites and space-probes.

   (ii) Used for street-lighting, traffic signals, operation water pumps.

   (iii) Provides electricity to light house near the sea and to off-shore oil drilling platforms.

   (iv) Used for operation electronic watches, calculators, running radio, T.V., etc. **(2 marks)**

6. (a) Metals conduct electricity due to presence of free electrons which can easily move. **(1 mark)**

   (b) It is because nitric acid is good oxidising agent and it oxidises H_2 to H_2O. **(1 mark)**

7. Non-metals do not displace hydrogen gas when reacted with acids/water because they don't have electrons to donate so that hydrogen ion becomes hydrogen gas. Whereas metals have this tendency to loose electrons and displace hydrogen gas from acids or water.

   (2 marks)

8. Here, mass of the fuel burnt, m = 5 g

   Mass of water heated, M = 1.0 kg = 1000 g

   Rise of temperature of water, $\Delta T = (60 - 20) = 40°C$

   Specific heat capacity of water, C = 4.2 J/g °C

   Calorific value of fuel, c = ? (to be calculated)

   From relation of calorimetry, Heat gained by water, Q = Mc ΔT

   Putting values, we get $Q = 1000 \times 4.2 \times 40 = 168000$ J

   From relation, Q = mc;

   We have, $c = \frac{Q}{m}$; Putting values, we get

   $c = \frac{168000}{5} = 33600$ J/g

   Calorific value of fuel, c = 33.6 kJ/g. **(3 marks)**

9. (i) The direction of the magnetic field is indicated by the arrow in the line at any point (Tangent).

   (ii) The field lines come out of the north pole and get into the south pole (closed loops are formed).

   (iii) The strength of magnetic field is indicated by the closeness of the field lines. Closer the lines, more will be the strength and farther the lines, lesser will be the field strength.

   (iv) No two field lines will intersect each other if they intersect there will be two different directions for field at the same point which is not impossible. **(3 marks)**

10. **(a)** The colour of ferrous sulphate crystals is green. On heating, $FeSO_4.7H_2O$ first decomposes to form anhydrous ferrous sulphate ($FeSO_4$) which is white in colour. **(1 ½ marks)**

(b) The products formed on strongly heating ferrous sulphate crystals are ferric oxide, sulphur dioxide and sulphur trioxide.

$$\underset{\text{Greenish-blue}}{2FeSO_4\ (s)} \xrightarrow{\text{Heat}} \underset{\text{Brown}}{Fe_2O_3\ (s)} + SO_2(g) + SO_3(g)$$

(1 mark)

This is a type of decomposition reaction (thermal decomposition) **(½ mark)**

11. A solenoid has a large number of close, insulated circular turns. The magnetic field at the centre of current-carrying circular wire is along the axis; so when current is passed in a solenoid, the magnetic fields due to all circular turns are added and hence the field lines become similar to the field lines for a bar magnet.

(1 mark)

Yes, we can determine the north and south poles of a current-carrying solenoid with the help of a bar magnet. For this, we suspend the bar magnet freely and note its ends pointing along north and south directions and mark on these ends N (north pole) and S (South pole).

Now we bring N-pole near one end of freely suspended current-carrying solenoid; if there is repulsion, then that end of solenoid is N-pole and other S-pole; but if there is attraction, then the end of solenoid is S-pole and the other is N-pole. **(2 marks)**

According to clock face rule, if current around the face of circular wire flows in the clockwise direction, then that face of circular wire will be south pole. If the current around the face of circular wire flows in Anticlock wise direction, then that face will be North pole.

12. **(a)** To obtain pure metal from an ore of high reactivity following steps are involved :

(i) Concentration of ore → removal of impurities

(ii) Electrolysis of molten ore → Metal is obtained at cathode of the electrolytic cell. This metal obtained is pure metal e.g., Na, K, Mg, Ca.

(2 marks)

(b) Magnesium reacts with hot water to form magnesium oxide and hydrogen gas is evolved. It is due to this hydrogen gas it starts floating. Magnesium sticks to the surface of hydrogen bubbles. **(1 mark)**

Metuls which are placed at higher position of the reactivity series are most reactive. Therefore they are not found in free state in nature.

13. **(a)** The oil and fat containing food when left exposed to air reacts with oxygen and gets oxidized forming a toxic chemical called rancid, this process is called rancidity. The general name of the chemicals that are added to prevent this oxidation are called as antioxidants. For example, Nitrogen gas is anti-oxidant. **(2 marks)**

(b) X is copper.

Green compound is due to formation of copper carbonate and black colour compound is due to the formation of copper oxide. **(1 mark)**

Copper articles when left in open green coating of copper carbonate deposited on the surface: when silver a articles are kept in open they acquire black coating of Ag_2S.

14. Soda acid type fire extinguisher contains sodium bicarbonate and sulphuric acid, which are in separate containers in them. When knob of the fire extinguisher is pressed, then sulphuric acid mixes with sodium bicarbonate solution and produces a lot of CO_2 gas, which forms a blanket over the fire and cuts it off from the supply of the air to the burning substance and the fire stops.

$$\underset{\text{Sodium hydrogen carbonate}}{2NaHCO_3} + \underset{\text{Sulphuric acid}}{H_2SO_4} \longrightarrow \underset{\text{Sodium sulphate}}{Na_2SO_4} + \underset{\text{Water}}{2H_2O} + \underset{\text{Carbon dioxide}}{2CO_2}$$

(3 marks)

15. **(a)** Helpful, empathy, problem solving **(1 mark)**

(b) In series combination sum of potential difference across individual apliance is equal to the potential difference applied by the source. **(1 mark)**

(c) same voltage for all appliances, even if one appliance is not working the others can work. **(1 mark)**

16. **(a)** As the total resistance (equivalent resistance) is 4Ω, the 6Ω resistor cannot be in series. So, it must be in parallel with some other resistors.

In parallel connection, the equivalent resistance (4Ω) has to be less than all the resistances. So the resistors of 2Ω and 3Ω cannot be in parallel at one time with 6Ω.

So, the resistors have to be in a mixed combination. Let us consider the combination shown in the figure.

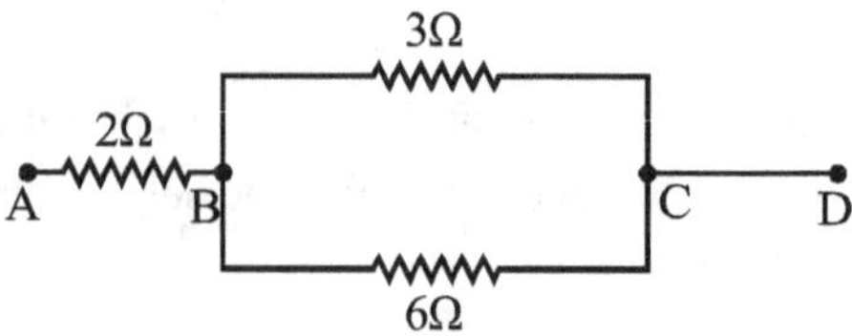

The equivalent resistance between B and C (which are in parallel).

$$= \frac{3\Omega \times 6\Omega}{3\Omega + 6\Omega} = \frac{18\Omega}{9\Omega} = 2\Omega$$

The resistance between

A and D = 2Ω + 2Ω = 4Ω.

So, the combination shown in the figure is true.

(1½ mark)

(b) Here $R_1 = 2\Omega$, $R_2 = 3\Omega$, $R_3 = 6\Omega$, and $R = 1\Omega$

Since the equivalent resistance of the combination is of lesser value than any of the resistors of the combination, it is clear that the resistors should be connected in parallel. It can be further confirmed by using the formula

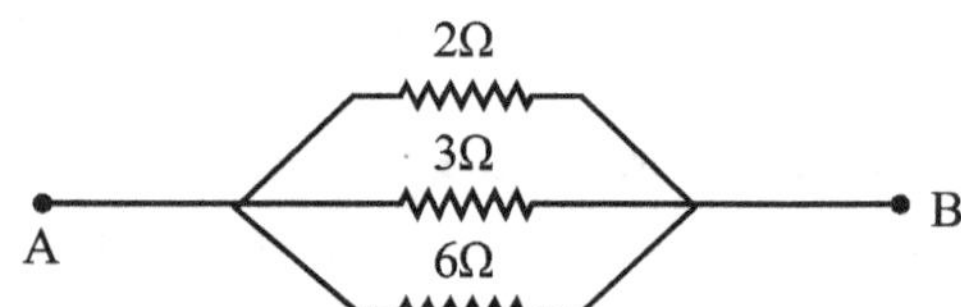

$$\frac{1}{R} = \frac{1}{R_1} + \frac{1}{R_2} + \frac{1}{R_3} = \frac{1}{2} + \frac{1}{3} + \frac{1}{6}$$

$$= \frac{3+2+1}{6} = \frac{6}{6} = 1$$

i.e., $R = 1$ ohm.

Therefore, resistors should be connected in **parallel**.

(1½ marks)

When a number of resistances are connected in series, then their combined resistance is more than the greatest individual resistance. When a number of resistances are connected in parallel then their combined resistance is less than the smallest individual resistance.

17. Hormones are chemical messengers produced by ductless glands which are translocated by circulatory system to other parts for inducing a specific physiological response.

(1 mark)

(i) **Function of Thyroxine:** It controls metabolism of carbohydrates, fats, proteins and provides the best balance for growth. **(1 mark)**

(ii) **Function of Insulin** (secreted by β-cells of islet of Langerhans) : Recognition of glucose by cells for absorption and conversion of glucose into glycogen in liver and muscles. **(1 mark)**

18. **(a)** **Process.** Photosynthesis. **(1 mark)**

(b) **Events.**

(i) Photolysis of water.

(ii) Production of assimilatory power as ATP and $NADPH_2$.

(iii) Reduction of CO_2. **(1 mark)**

(c) **Sources of Nitrogen.**

(i) Nitrate from soil.

(ii) Ammonium ion from soil. **(1 mark)**

Photolysis of water takes place in the presence of sunlight and referred as the breakdown of the water molecule into hydrogen and oxygen.

19. Neurotransmitter is a chemical extruded by an axon terminal for passage of impulse to the next neuron, muscle, gland or organ. **(1 mark)**

As the electrochemical impulse reaches the axon terminal in the region of axon-dendrite synapse, it stimulates the exocytosis of vesicles containing neurotransmitter (*e.g.* acetylcholine). Neurotransmitter attaches to the chemoreceptor sites of the membrane covering the dendrite end of synapse. It creates a new impulse that travels through cell body and axon of the second neuron. At synapse, the axon end does not contain any chemoreceptor sites so that reverse flow of electrochemical impulses is not possible. **(2 marks)**

Synapse also called neuronal junction, the site of transmission of electric nerve impulses between two nerve cells (neurons) or between a neuron and a gland or muscle cell (effector). A synapic connection between a neuron and muscle cell is called neuromuscular junction.

20. Given, power of one heater $(P) = 250$ watt, potential (V) = 100 volt, time $(t) = 5$ hours.

(a) $P = \frac{V^2}{R}$; $R = \frac{V^2}{P} = \frac{100 \times 100}{250} = 40\ \Omega$

The three 250 watt heaters are connected in parallel then total current, $I = I_1 + I_2 + I_3$

$$= \frac{V}{R_1} + \frac{V}{R_2} + \frac{V}{R_3} = \frac{100}{40} + \frac{100}{40} + \frac{100}{40}$$

$= 2.5 + 2.5 + 2.5 = 7.5\,A$ **(2 marks)**

(b) The resistance of each heater is 40 Ω

(1 mark)

(c) The energy supplied to the first heater is

$H = I^2Rt = (2.5)^2 \times 40 \times 5$ Wh, As current flowing each heater is 2.5 A

$\therefore\ H = 6.25 \times 200\ \text{Wh} = 1250\ \text{Wh}$

$= \frac{1250}{1000}\text{kWh} = 1.25\text{kWh}$

Then three heaters in connection = 3×1.25 kWh

= 3.75 kWh energy is used in the circuit. **(2 marks)**

21. S.I. unit of magnetic field is tesla. (T)

The strength of magnetic field at a point is said to be 1T if a charge of 1C while moving at right angles to a magnetic field, with a velocity of 1 m/s experiences a force of 1 N at that point.

The force on a moving charged particle is $F = qBv\sin\theta$

(2 marks)

If $\theta = 90°$, i.e. the particle moves at right angles to the magnetic field, $F = qBv$ which provides the necessary centripetal force for the circular motion of the particle. There is no linear acceleration. So no increase in linear velocity and hence in kinetic energy. **(3 marks)**

22. **(a)** Actually, two formula units of $CaSO_4$ share one molecule of water. So, for the sake of convenience the formula of Plaster of Paris is written as $CaSO_4.\frac{1}{2}H_2O$. It does not mean that half-molecule of water is attached to $CaSO_4$. **(2 marks)**

(b) In aqueous solution, strong electrolyte like H_2SO_4 dissociates completely into its ions; whereas weak electrolyte such as carbonic acid (H_2CO_3) dissociates into its ions only partially. **(2 marks)**

(c) When electricity is passed through aqueous solution of NaCl, the three products formed are : Sodium hydroxide, chlorine and hydrogen.

$$\underset{\text{Sodium chloride}}{2NaCl(aq)} + 2H_2O(l) \xrightarrow{\text{Electricity}} \underset{\text{Sodium hydroxide}}{2NaOH\,(aq)} + \underset{\text{Chlorine}}{Cl_2(g)} + \underset{\text{Hydrogen}}{H_2(g)}$$

In the word chlor-alkali, chlor stands for chlorine and alkali stands for sodium hydroxide. So, the process is called chlor-alkali. **(1 mark)**

23. **(a)** **Roasting :** It is the process in which sulphide ores of the metals are converted into oxides by heating them in the presence of excess air. For example, zinc sulphide is converted into zinc oxide by roasting.

$$2ZnS(s) + 3O_2(g) \xrightarrow[\text{Roasting}]{\text{Heat}} 2ZnO(s) + 2SO_2(g)$$

Calcination : It is the process in which carbonate ores of the metals are decomposed into oxides by heating them in the absence or limited air. For example, zinc carbonate is decomposed into zinc oxide and carbon dioxide by calcination.

$$ZnCO_3(s) \xrightarrow[\text{Calcination}]{\text{Heat}} ZnO(s) + CO_2(g)$$

Out of roasting and calcination, only roasting is used for sulphide ores. This is because it is easier to obtain metal from its oxide as compared to its sulphide.

(2 marks)

(b) $$\underset{\text{Iron(III) oxide}}{Fe_2O_3(s)} + \underset{\text{Aluminium powder}}{2Al(s)} \xrightarrow{\text{Heat}} \underset{\text{Iron metal}}{2Fe(l)} + \underset{\text{Aluminium oxide}}{Al_2O_3(s)} + \text{heat}$$

(2 marks)

(c) Anode – Impure copper

Cathode–Strip of pure copper

Electrolyte–Acidified copper sulphate solution. **(1 mark)**

24. **(a)** Fats are present in the small intestine in the form of large globules which makes it difficult for enzymes to act on them. Bile salts break them down into smaller globules increasing the efficiency of enzyme action. This is similar to the emulsifying action of soaps on dirt. Hence, digestion of fats in the small intestine is facilitated by bile salts.

(2½ marks)

(b) Small intestine is lined by epithelium which is specialised to absorb food. It has mechanisation to increase its absorbing surface area several times. **(i) Villi:** They are transverse folds of intestine wall that not only increase surface area but also reach deep into the lumen of intestine for absorption of digested food. Villi possess blood capillaries and lacetals (lymph vessels) for quick transport of absorbed food.

(2½ marks)

Digestion refers to the biological process that involves the breakdown of large insoluble food molecules into small water-soluble food molecules so that they can be absorbed into the watery blood plasma.

SECTION - B

25. **(c)** **(1 mark)**

26. **(a)** $Na_2CO_3 + 2HCl \rightarrow 2NaCl + CO_2 + H_2O$ **(1 mark)**

27. **(a)** Reaction will occur in beaker *A* only because iron lie above copper in reactivity series thus being more active will displace copper from its salt.

(1 mark)

28. **(a)** Due to the corrosive nature of concentrated acid, dilute acid is used. As the concentrated sulphuric acid can cause severe burns because it can get splashed while boiling. **(1 mark)**

29. **(a)** **(1 mark)**

30. **(b)** **(1 mark)**

31. **(c)** Ideal voltmeter should not draw any current flow source hence its resistance = ∞.

Practically ∞ resistance is not possible, but ideal voltmeter is possible with the help of potentiometer that you will learn in higher classes. **(1 mark)**

32. **(a)** **(1 mark)**

33. **(b)** V=0.3V

$I = 30 \times 10^{-3} A$

$$R = \frac{0.3}{30 \times 10^{-3}} = 10\Omega$$ **(1 mark)**

The slope of I-V graph gives the value of resistance.

34. **(a)** **(1 mark)**

35. **(d)** The value of red, violet and green are : 2, 7 and 10^5. And gold represents a tolerance 5%. Thus $R = 27 \times 10^5 \pm 5\% \Omega$. **(1 mark)**

36. **(b)** For ohmic circuits $V \propto I$ **(1 mark)**

37. **(a)** **(1 mark)**

38. **(c)** A water bath is used for heating alcohol because alcohol is highly inflammable liquid. So, if alcohol is heated directly over a flame, then it will catch fire at once.

(1 mark)

39. **(c)** **(1 mark)**

40. **(d)** In the diagram, label IV represents alveoli. Alveoli are sac like structure present in lungs. They are the site for exchange of gases. The label I represent trachea, label II represents bronchi and label III represents bronchioles. **(1 mark)**

41. **(c)** The KOH has a chemical reaction with CO_2, causing it to become a solid rather than a gas. With KOH, volume would change with respiration because oxygen would be consumed, and CO_2 produced would be turned into a solid, so volume would decrease as oxygen decreases.

(1 mark)

42. **(d)** **(1 mark)**

Delhi 2014

CBSE Board Solved Paper

Time Allowed : 3 Hours ***Maximum Marks : 80***

General Instructions:

(i) The question paper comprises of **two** Sections, **A** and **B**. You are to attempt both the sections.

(ii) All questions are compulsory.

(iii) All questions of Section-A and all questions of Section-B are to be attempted separately.

(iv) Question numbers **1** to **3** in Section-A are **one** mark questions. These are to be answered in **one** word or in **one** sentence.

(v) Question numbers **4** to **7** in Section-A are **two** marks questions. These are to be answered in about **30** words each.

(vi) Question numbers **8** to **19** in Section-A are **three** marks questions. These are to be answered in about **50** words each.

(vii) Question numbers **20** to **24** in Section-A are **five** marks questions. These are to be answered in about **70** words each.

(viii) Question numbers **25** to **42** in Section-B are multiple choice questions based on practical skills. Each question is a **one** mark question. You are to select **one** most appropriate response out of the **four** provided to you.

SECTION A

1. Write the number of vertical columns in the modern periodic table. What are those columns called ?

2. Give the respective scientific terms used for studying :

(i) the mechanism by which variations are created and inherited and

(ii) the development of new type of organisms from the existing ones.

3. Water is a valuable resource List two ways that you would suggest every family member to save this resource.

4. List four advantages of vegetative propagation.

5. Draw a ray diagram to show the path of the reflected ray corresponding to an incident ray which is directed towards the principal focus of a convex mirror. Mark on it the angle of incidence and the angle of reflection.

6. Why is Government of India imposing a ban on the use of polythene bags ? Suggest two alternatives to these bags and explain how this ban is likely to improve the environment.

7. What is meant by biodiversity ? List two advantages of conserving forest and wild life.

8. State the meaning of functional group in a carbon compound. Write the functional group present in

(i) ethanol and

(ii) ethanoic acid and also draw their structures.

9. Write the name and general formula of a chain of hydrocarbons in which an addition reaction with hydrogen can take place. Stating the essential conditions required for an addition reaction to occur write the chemical equation giving the name of the reactant and the product of such a reaction.

10. Based on the group valency of elements state the formula for the following giving justification for each:

(i) Oxides of 1st group elements.

(ii) Halides of the elements of group 13, and

(iii) Compounds formed when an element of group 2 combines with an element of group 16.

11. (a) Define the following terms :

(i) Valency;

(ii) Atomic size

(b) How do the valency and the atomic size of the elements vary while going from left to right along a period in the modern periodic table ?

12. Draw diagrams to explain the regeneration that takes place in each of the body parts of *Planaria* when its body is cut into three pieces. Name any other organism in which a similar process can be observed.

13. List any four methods of contraception used by humans. How does their used have a direct effect on the health and prosperity of a family ?

14. (a) Give the evidence that the birds have envolved from reptiles.

(b) Insects, octopus, planaria and vertebrates posses eyes. Can we group these animals together on the basis of eyes that they possess ? Justify your answer giving reason.

15. A cross was made between pure breeding pea plants, one with round and green seeds and the other with wrinkled and yellow seeds.

(a) Write the phenotype of F_1 progeny. Give reason for your answer.

(b) Write the different types of F_2 progeny obtained along with their ratio when F_1 progeny was selfed.

16. A spherical mirror produces an image of magnification -1 on a screen placed at a distance of 50 cm from the mirror.

(a) Write the type of mirror.

(b) Find the distance of the image from the object.

(c) What is the focal length of the mirror ?

(d) Draw a ray diagram to show the image formation in this case,

17. State the laws of refraction of light. If the speed of light in vacuum is 3×10^8 ms^{-1}, find the speed of light in a medium of absolute refractive index 1.5.

18. Explain giving reason why the sky appears blue to an observer from the surface of the earth? What will the colour of the sky be for an astronaut staying in the international space station orbiting the earth ? Justify your answer giving reason.

19. "Our food grains such as wheat and rice, the vegetables and fruits and even meat are found to contain varying amounts of pesticide residues." State the reason to explain how and why it happens ?

20. State the reason why carbon can neither form C^{4+} cations nor C^{4-} anions, but forms covalent compounds. Also state reasons to explain why covalent compounds:

(i) are bad conductors of electricity ?

(ii) have low melting and boiling points ?

21. (a) Give one example each of a unisexual and a bisexual flower.

(b) Mention the changes a flower undergoes after fertilization.

(c) How does the amount of DNA remain constant though each new generation is a combination of DNA copies of two individuals ?

22. (a) Name the respective part of human female reproductive system :

(i) that produces eggs.

(ii) where fusion of egg and sperm takes place, and

(iii) where zygote gets implanted.

(b) Describe in brief what happens to the zygote after it gets implanted.

23. A student wants to project the image of a candle flame on the walls of school laboratory by using a lens:

(a) Which type of lens should he use and why ?

(b) At what distance in terms of focal length 'f' of the lens should be place the candle flame so as to get

(i) a magnified, and

(ii) a diminished image respectively on the wall ?

(c) Draw ray diagram to show the formation of the image in each case.

24. (a) List three common refractive defects of vision. Suggest the way of correcting these defects.

(b) About 45 lac people in the developing countries are suffering from corneal blindness. About 30 lac children below the age of 12 years suffering from this defect can be cured by replacing the defective cornea with the cornea of a donated eye. How and why can students of your age involve themselves to create awareness about this fact among people.

SECTION - B

25. When you add about 2 mL of acetic acid to a test tube containing an equal amount of distilled water and leave the test tube to settle after shaking its contents, then after about 5 minutes what will you observe in the test tube :

(a) A white precipitate settling at its bottom,

(b) A clear colourless solution.

(c) A layer of water over the layer of acetic acid, or

(d) A layer of acetic acid over the layer of water.

26. A student adds a few drops of ethanoic acid to test tubes X, Y and Z containing aqueous solutions of sodium chloride, sodium hydroxide and sodium carbonate respectively. If he now brings a burning splinter near the mouth of the test tubes immediately after adding the ethanoic acid in each one of them in which of the test tube or test tubes the flame gets extinguished ?

(a) X and Y (b) X and Z
(c) X and Z (d) only Z

27. In order to study saponification reaction we first prepare 20% solution of sodium hydroxide. If we record the temperature of this solution just after adding sodium hydroxide flakes to water and also tests its nature using litmus, it may be concluded that the process of making this solution is :

(a) exothermic and the solution is alkaline.
(b) endothermic and the solution is alkaline.
(c) endothermic and the solution is acidic.
(d) exothermic and the solution is acidic.

28. While studying saponification reaction for the preparation of soap, the teacher suggested to a student to add a small quantity of common salt to the reaction mixture. The function of common salt in this reaction is to :

(a) reduce the alkalinity of the soap,
(b) reduce the acidity of the soap,
(c) enhance the cleansing capacity of soap, or
(d) favour precipitation of soap.

29. A student takes about 6 mL of distilled water in each of the four test tubes P, Q, R and S, then dissolves an equal amount of four different salts namely sodium chloride in 'P', potassium chloride in 'Q', calcium chloride in 'R' and magnesium chloride in 'S'. He then adds 10 drops of soap solution to each test tube and shakes its contents. The test tubes in which scum (insoluble substance) is formed with soap are :

(a) P and Q (b) Q and R
(c) R and S (d) Q and S

30. A student has obtained an image of a distant object with a concave mirror to determine its focal length. If he has selected a well illuminated red building as object, which of the following correctly describes the features of the image formed ?

(a) Virtual, inverted, diminished image in red shade
(b) Real, erect, diminished image in pink shade.
(c) Real, inverted, diminished image in red shade
(d) Virtual, erect, enlarged image in red shade

31. A student has obtained the image of a distant object on a screen to determine the focal length F_1 of the given lens. His teacher after checking the image, gave him another lens of focal length F_2 and asked to focus the same object on the same screen. The student found that to obtain a sharp image he has to move the lens away from the screen. From this finding we may conclude that both the lenses given to the student were :

(a) Concave and $F_1 < F_2$
(b) Convex and $F_1 < F_2$
(c) Convex and $F_1 > F_2$
(d) Concave and $F_1 > F_2$

32. Study the following four experimental set-ups I, II, III and IV for the experiment, "To trace the path of ray of light through a rectangular glass slab."

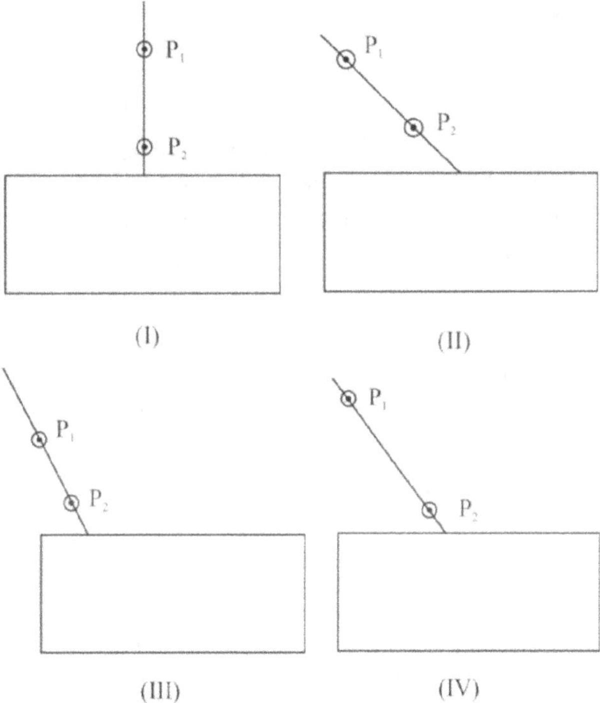

Which of the marked set-ups is likely to give best results (P_1 and P_2 are the positions of pins fixed on the incident ray)?

(a) I (b) II
(c) III (d) IV

33. On the basis of the experiment, "To trace the path of a ray of light through a rectangular glass slab," students of a class arrived at which one of the following conclusions:

(a) Angle of incidence is greater than the angle of emergence.
(b) Angle of emergence is smaller than the angle of refraction.
(c) Emergent ray is parallel to the refracted ray.
(d) Incident ray and emergent ray are parallel to each other.

34. The path of a ray of light passing through a glass prism is shown below :

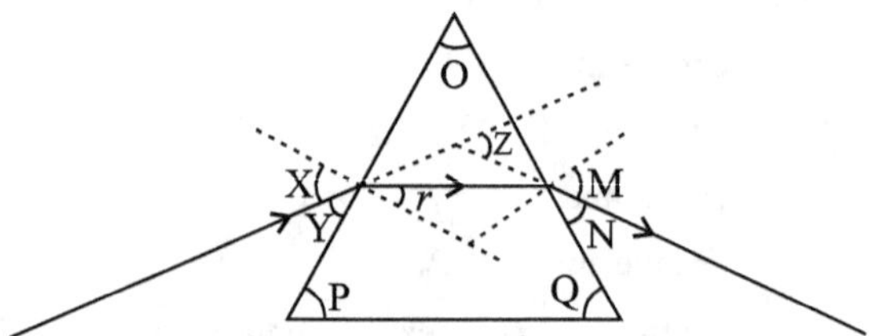

In this diagram the angle of prism, angle of incidence, angle of emergence and angle of deviation respectively have been represented by :

(a) O, Y, Z and N (b) P, Y, M and Z
(c) O, X, M and Z (d) P, X, Z and N

35. A student is observing the diagram showing the path of a ray of light passing through a glass prism. He would find that for all angles of incidence the ray of light bends :

(a) towards the normal while entering into the prism and away from the normal while emerging out of the prism.

(b) away from the normal while entering into the prism and towards the normal while emerging out of the prism.

(c) away from the normal while entering as well as while emerging out of the prism.

(d) towards the normal while entering as well as while emerging out of the prism.

36. A student was asked by his teacher to find the image distance for various object distance in case of a given convex lens. He performed the experiment with all precautions and noted down his observations in the following table :

S.No.	Object distance (cms)	Image distance (cm)
1	60	15
2	48	16
3	36	21
4	24	24
5	18	36
6	16	48

After checking the observation table the teacher pointed out that there is a mistake in recording the image distance in one of the observations. Find the serial number of the observation having faulty image distance.

(a) 2 (b) 3
(c) 5 (d) 6

37. A student has obtained a magnified image of a flame on a screen using a convex lens. To draw the corresponding ray diagram, to show the image formation, which of the following two rays whose paths after refraction are shown he should select ?

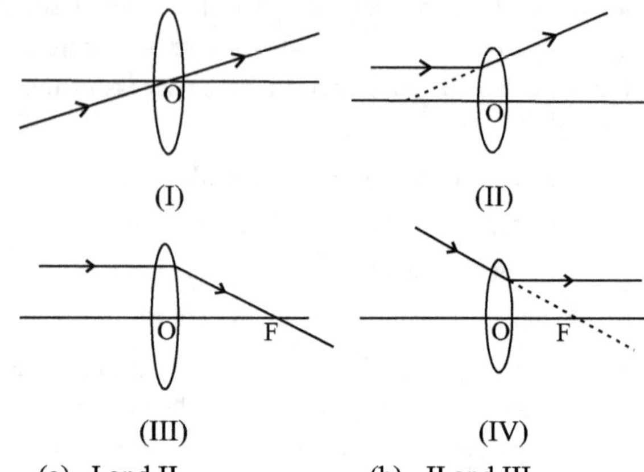

(a) I and II (b) II and III
(c) III and IV (d) I and III

38. Study the following diagrams showing various stages of binary fission in Amoeba :

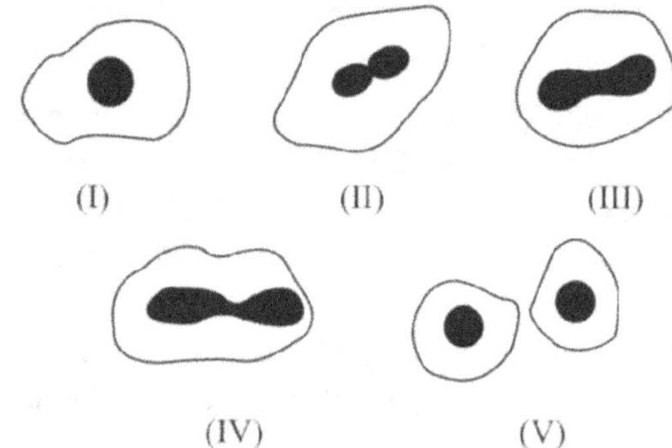

The correct sequence of these diagrams should be :

(a) I, IV, III, II, V
(b) I, III, IV, II, V
(c) I, II, IV, III, V
(d) I, II, III, IV, V

39. Identify the figures showing the process of budding in yeast.

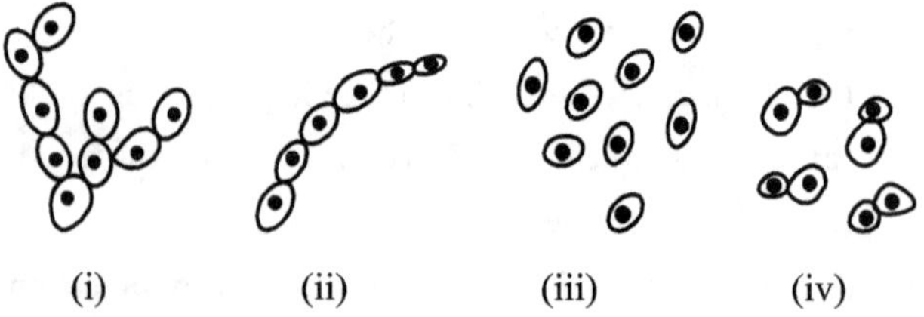

(a) (i), (ii) and (iii)
(b) (ii), (iii) and (iv)
(c) (i), (ii) and (iv)
(d) (iii), (iv) and (i)

40. Which one of the following pairs of vegetables is an example of homologous structures :

(a) Potato and sweet potato

(b) Carrot and radish

(c) Carrot and tomato

(d) Tomato and radish

41. Four students P, Q, R and S differently reported the following set of organs to be analogous :

P. Forelimb of a frog and forelimb of a lizard

Q. Forelimb of a bird and forelimb of a human

R. Wings of a parrot and wings of a butterfly

S. Wings of a bird and wings of a bat

The two students who have reported correctly are :

(a) P and Q (b) Q and R

(c) R and S (d) P and S

42. You are asked by your teacher to study the different parts of an embryo of a gram seed. Given below are the steps to be followed for the experiment :

I. Soak the gram seeds in plain water and keep them overnight.

II. Cut open the soaked seed and observe its different parts.

III. Take some dry gram seeds in a petri dish.

IV. Drain the excess water.

V. Cover the soaked seeds with a wet cotton cloth and leave them for a day.

The correct sequence of these steps is :

(a) III, I, V, IV, II (b) III, I, II, IV, V

(c) III, IV, V, I, II (d) III, I, IV, V, II

Solutions

SECTION - A

1. There are 18 vertical columns in the modern periodic table and these are called groups. **(1 Mark)**

2. (i) The mechanism by which variations are created and inherited is known as heredity.

   (ii) Evolution is defined as the process of development of new type of organisms from the existing one.

   (1 Mark)

Note

Evolution is the gradual process of formation of new individuals which takes millions of years and gives rise to biodiversity.

3. The two ways by which we can save water resource are as follows:

   (i) Turn off the tap while brushing teeth.

   (ii) Repair dripping faucets by replacing their washers.

   (1 Mark)

4. The four advantages of vegetative reproduction are as follows:

   (i) Vegetative propagation provides many benefits as the developed offsprings are genetically identical to their parents.

   (ii) This property of vegetative propagation is used in methods such as layering or grafting to grow many plants like sugarcane, roses, or grapes for agricultural purposes.

   (iii) Plants raised by vegetative propagation can bear flowers and fruits earlier than those produced from seeds.

   (iv) Such methods also make possible the propagation of plants such as banana, orange, rose and jasmine that have lost the capacity to produce seeds. **(2 Marks)**

Note

Vegetative propagation is an asexual method of plant reproduction that occurs in its leaves, roots and stem. This can occur through fragmentation and regeneration of specific vegetative parts of plants.

5.

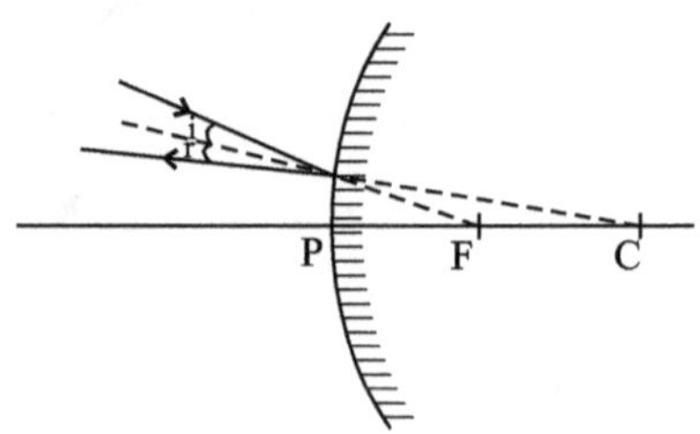

Here i = angle of incidence

r = angle of reflection **(2 Marks)**

Note

If light ray incidents normally on a surface, after reflection it retraces the path.

6. Polythene bags are most commonly dispersed in the environment and have a very slow rate of decomposition. They are very dangerous to sea life. Apart from polythene bags, jute bags and paper bags can be used as they are biodegradable and do not cause pollution. This will also help jute and paper industry to flourish and provide employment to lots of people. **(2 Marks)**

7. Biodiversity is defined as the variety of living organisms that are present in the given ecosystem. It involves all the marine and terrestrial organisms. The biodiversity of an area is measured by counting the number of species that are found in a specific area.

   The advantages of conservation of forest system are as follows:

   (i) It prevents soil erosion and floods.

   (ii) It produces huge amounts of raw materials for the industries.

   The advantages of conservation of wildlife:

   (i) It preserves different kinds of species and thus, maintains the species diversity.

   (ii) It helps in maintaining the ecological balance that is required for supporting life. **(2 Marks)**

8. Group of atoms of different element which impart characteristic properties to the carbon compound are known as functional groups. **(1 Mark)**

   (i) **Ethanol :** Functional group – OH, **(½ Mark)**

   Structure:
```
    H   H
    |   |
H – C – C – OH
    |   |
    H   H
```
   (½ Mark)

   (ii) **Ethanoic acid :** Functional group – COOH, **(½ Mark)**

   Structure:
```
    H
    |
H – C – C – O – H
    |   ||
    H   O
```
   (½ Mark)

Some compounds have same molecular formula but different functional groups therefore they show different physical and chemical properties. For example CH_3OCH_3 and CH_3CH_2OH. Both compounds have different functional groups ether and alcohols respectively but they have same molecular formula i.e. C_2H_6O. This phenomenon is known as isomerism.

9. Alkenes show addition reactions with hydrogen. **(½ Mark)**

General Formula: C_nH_{2n}, where $n = 2, 3, 4, 5, 6.......$ **(½ Mark)**

Essential condition for addition reaction is the presence of double or triple bonds. **(1 Mark)**

Chemical equation:

$$\underset{\text{Ethene}}{CH_2 = CH_2} + H_2 \longrightarrow \underset{\text{Ethane}}{CH_3 - CH_3}$$

(½ + ½ = 1 Mark)

10. (i) **Oxides of Ist group elements:** Group valency of 1st group elements is 1 and valency of oxygen is 2 therefore

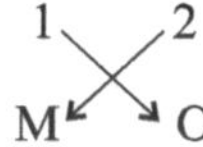

Formula: M_2O **(1 Mark)**

(ii) **Halides of group 13 elements :** Group valency of group 13 is 3 and halogens have valency 1 therefore

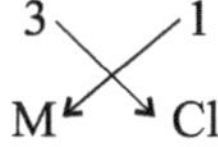

Formula: MCl_3 **(1 Mark)**

(iii) **Group 2 elements combine with group 16 elements:** Group 2 elements have group valency +2 and group 16 elements have group valency –2 therefore

2 ╲╱ 2
M ↙ ↘ A

Formula : M_2A_2 or MA **(1 Mark)**

11. (a) (i) **Valency:** Valency of an element can be defined as the number of electrons that are lost or gained to complete the octet of outermost shell. **(1 Mark)**

(ii) **Atomic size:** Atomic size can be defined as the distance between the nucleus and the outer most shell of an atom. **(1 Mark)**

(b) **Variation in valency across a period:** Valency shown by the elements increases across the period as we move from left to right in the periodic table.

Variation in atomic size across a period: **(½ Mark)**

Atomic size decreases across the period as we move from left to right in the periodic table. **(½ Mark)**

Valency is the combining capacity of an element. For example $_{16}O$, electronic configuration is (2, 8, 6) and it requires two more electrons to complete its octet. Hence it will show valency of –2.

12. Many fully differentiated organisms have the ability to give rise to new individual organisms from their body parts. If the individual is cut or broken up into many pieces, many of these pieces grown into separate individuals. For example: Simple animals such as *Hydra* and *Planaria* can be cut into any number of pieces and each piece grows into a complete organism. This is known as regeneration.

Regeneration is carried out by specialised cells and such cells proliferate and make large number of cells. From these mass of cells, different cells undergo changes to become various cell types and tissues. These changes take place in an organised sequence referred to as development.

Diagrammatic representation of the process of regeneration in Plannaria:

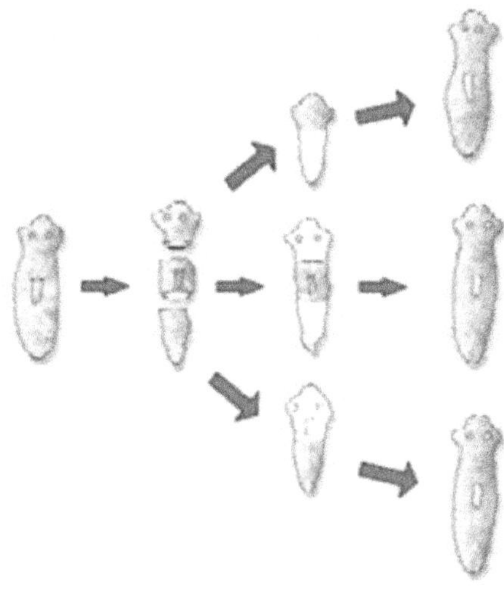

(3 Marks)

Regeneration is not the same as reproduction, as most organisms would not normally depend on being cut up to be able to reproduce.

13. The four contraceptive methods to control the size of human population are as follows:

Oral pills: Oral pills change the hormonal balance so that eggs are not released and fertilisation cannot occur.

Barrier method: In this method, the fertilisation is prevented by using barriers such as condom.

Surgical method: This method involves the surgical removal of vas deferens in males and fallopian tubes in females to block the entry of sperms into the female reproductive system.

The removal of vas deferens is called vasectomy in males and in female's removal of fallopian tube called tubectomy.

Natural methods are also used as contraceptive methods which work on the principle of avoiding the chances of ovum and sperms meeting.

Contraception helps in family planning for a couple. It also helps to maintain space in their children according to their will so that family resources are utilized properly. Contraception helps in taking care of mother and child health as well as parents give more attention to their children. **(3 Marks)**

Contraception aims for prevention of pregnancy as it prevents the meeting of egg and sperm and stops formation of egg.

14. (a) In birds, feathers, for example, can start out as providing insulation in cold weather. But later, they might become useful for flight. In fact, some dinosaurs had feathers, although they could not fly using the feathers. Birds seem to have later adapted the feathers to flight. This, of course, means that birds are very closely related to reptiles, since dinosaurs were reptiles. **(1½ Marks)**

(b) Even an intermediate stage, such as a rudimentary eye, can be useful to some extent. This might be engouh to give a fitness advantage. In fact, the eye-like the wing-seems to be a very popular adaptation. Insects have them, so does an octopus, and so do vertebrates. And the structure of the eye in each of these organisms is different-enough for them to have separate evolutionary origins. **(1½ Marks)**

Fossils are dead remains of plants and animals that are buried under rocks and soil for about several years ago.

15. (i) In F1 progeny, round and yellow seeds are obtained. This cross represents law of dominance.

Law of dominance states that one pair of inherited trait will be dominant over the other pair of inherited trait and independently expressed themselves in a hybrid.

(ii) When F1 progeny are selfed the different types of F2 progeny obtained are:

The phenotypic ratio obtained is as follows:

9: 3: 3: 1

9 round and yellow

3 wrinkled and yellow

3 round and green

1 wrinkled and green

Parents	RRyy	X	rrYY
Gametes	Ry		rY
F1		RrYy (All Round yellow) ↓ Selfing	
	RrYy		RrYy
Gametes	RY, rY, Ry, ry		RY, rY, Ry, ry

F_2 generation	RY	rY	Ry	ry
RY	RRYY Round yellow	RrYY Round yellow	RRYy Round yellow	RrYy Round yellow
rY	RrYY Round yellow	rrYY Wrinkled yellow	RrYy Round yellow	rrYy Wrinkled yellow
Ry	RRYy Round yellow	RrYy Round yellow	RRyy Round green	Rryy Round green
ry	RrYy Round yellow	rrYy Wrinkled yellow	Rryy Round green	rryy Wrinkled green

(3 Marks)

16. (i) As magnification is negative, the image formed by mirror is real. Hence, it is a concave mirror. **(½ Mark)**

(ii) Magnification $m = -v/u = -1$

$\therefore \quad u = v = -50$ cm

Distance of the image from the object

$v - u = -50 - (-50) = 0$ cm **(1 Mark)**

(iii) By using mirror formula:

$1/f = 1/v + 1/u = 1/(-50) + 1/(-50) = -1/25$

$\therefore \quad f = -25$ cm **(½ Mark)**

(iv)

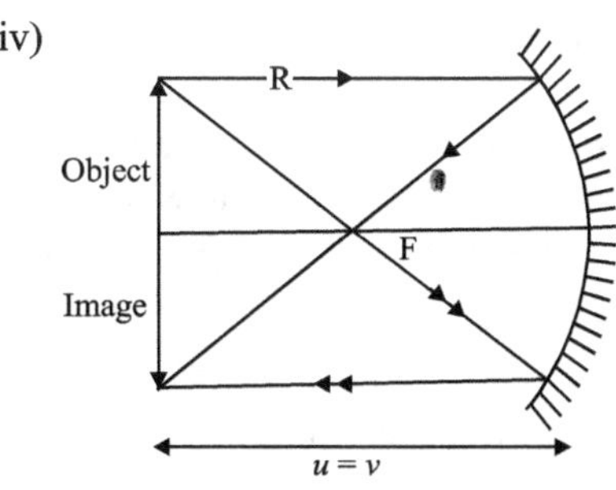

(1 Mark)

Note

If a spherical mirror produces an image m times the size of the object (m = magnification) then u, v and f are given by the following

$$u = \left(\frac{m-1}{m}\right)f,\ v = -(m-1)f$$

and
$$f = \left(\frac{m}{m-1}\right)u$$

17. (i) There are two laws of refraction:

(a) The ratio of the sin of the angle of incidence to the sin of the angle of refraction is constant. This is known as Snell's law. Mathematically, it can be expressed as:

$\sin i / \sin r = n_{12}$

Here, n_{12} is the relative refractive index of medium 1 with respect to medium 2.

(b) The incident ray, the refracted ray and the normal to the interface of two media at the point of incidence lie on the same plane. **(2 × 1 = 2 Marks)**

(ii) Given, $c = 3 \times 10^8$ m/s,

Refractive index, $u = 1.5$

Absolute refractive index

$$= \frac{\text{Speed of light in vacuum}}{\text{Speed of light in medium}}$$

Speed of light in medium

$$= \frac{\text{Speed of light in vacuum}}{\text{Refractive index}}$$

$$= \frac{3\times10^8}{1.5} = 2 \times 10^8 \text{ ms}^{-1}$$ **(1 Mark)**

18. The clear sky appears blue because the molecules in the air scatter blue light (smaller wavelength) from the sun more than they scatter other colour (larger wavelength). **(1½ Mark)**

For an astronaut staying in the international space station orbiting the Earth, the colour of the sky will be black because the light reaching it does not scatter. **(1½ Mark)**

19. A large number of pesticides and chemicals are used to protect our crops from pests and diseases. Some of these chemicals are washed down into the soil, while some enter in the water bodies. From the soil, they are absorbed by plants along with water and minerals; and from water bodies, they are taken up by aquatic plants and animals. This is how these chemicals enter the food chain. because these chemicals cannot decompose, they accumulate progressively at each trophic level and their concentration increases. This increase in the concentration of harmful chemicals with each step of the food chain is called biomagnification. That is why food grains, such as wheat and rice, vegetables, fruits and even meat are found to contain pesticide residue. **(3 Marks)**

20. Electronic configuration of carbon is (2, 4). Therefore it requires four electrons to complete the octet. It cannot form C^{4+} because removal of four valence electrons requires a large amount of energy. The cation formed will have six protons and two electrons which make atom highly unstable. It is also unable to form C^{4-} anion as its nucleus has six protons which is unable to hold ten electrons. Therefore carbon will only able to form covalent compounds in which it attain noble gas configuration by sharing of electrons. **(3 Marks)**

(i) Covalent compounds are bad conductor of electricity due to the absence of free electrons. **(1 Mark)**

(ii) Covalent compounds have covalent bonds which are weak bonds. Therefore lesser energy is required to break the bond. Hence covalent compounds have low melting and boiling points. **(1 Mark)**

Note

Ionic compounds are found in crystal form. They have crystalline packed structure in which atoms are held by ionic forces. Electrostatic or ionic forces are much stronger than van der waal forces or forces that are present in covalent bond. Consequently ionic compounds have comparitively higher and sharp melting and boiling points than covalent compounds.

21. (a) Unisexual flowers are those which contain either stamen (male reproductive part) or pistil (female reproductive part). For example: Cucumber, pumkin, watermelon, papaya. Bisexual flowers are those flowers which have both stamen and pistil in the same flower. For example-Hibiscus, rose, lily, etc. **(1½ Mark)**

(b) A flower undergoes certain changes after fertilization. The zygote divides several times to form an embryo within the ovule. The ovule develops a tough coat and is gradually converted into a seed. The ovary grows rapidly and ripens to form a fruit. The petals, sepals, stamens, style and stigma may fall off. **(1½ Mark)**

Reproduction is defined as a biological process in which an organism gives rise to young ones (offspring) similar to itself. The offspring grow, mature and in turn produce new offspring.

(c) During sexual reproduction, the reproducing cells or germ cells have half the number (amount) of chromosomes and DNA as compared to somatic or body cells or non-reproducing cells. As the offspring receives one DNA copy from each parent, this complex mechanism helps to maintain the amount of DNA constant in an individual. **(2 Mark)**

22. (a) (i) Ovary produces egg in females.

(ii) Fusion of eggs and sperm takes place in the fallopian tube.

(iii) Zygote gets implanted in the uterus of the female reproductive system.

The diagram below shows Female reproductive system.

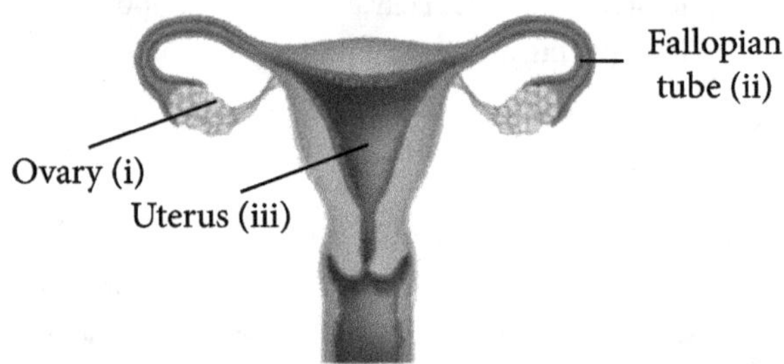

(3 Marks)

(b) The zygote formed after fertilisation in the follopian tube is implanted in the uterus. It divides repeatedly to form a mass of cells known as embryo. This embryo gets attached to the inner layer of the uterine cavity, i.e., endometrium. It becomes thick every month and is supplied with blood to nourish the embryo. Soon it gets covered by rapidly dividing uterine cells. This leads to pregnancy. Within a span of some months, the embryo starts developing limbs and begins to resemble a miniature being. When all parts of the embryo can be recognized, it becomes a foetus. The mother gives birth to the baby when the foetus fully develops. **(2 Marks)**

23. (a) He should use a convex lens as it forms real images. **(1 Mark)**

(b) He should place the candle flame between F and 2F (the focus and center of curvature of lens) to get the magnified image on the wall while the diminished image is obtained when the object is located at a distance greater than 2F. **(2 Marks)**

(c) The ray diagram for the formation of the magnified image is shown below:

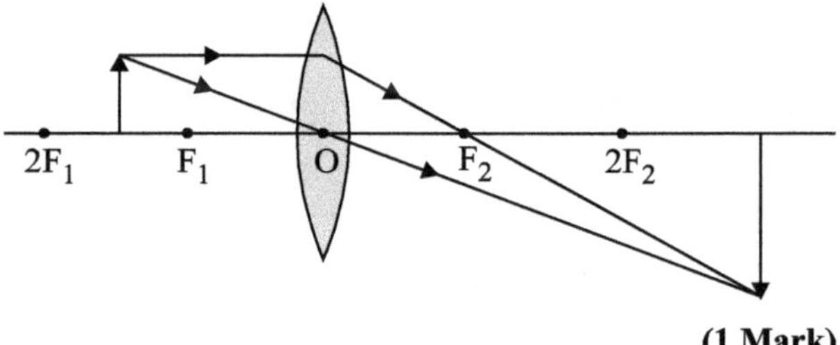

(1 Mark)

The ray diagram for the formation of the diminished image is shown below:

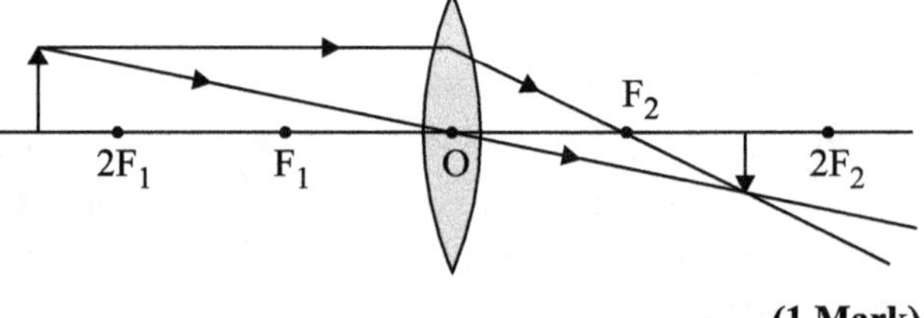

(1 Mark)

Image formed by concave mirror may be real or virtual, may be inverted or erect, may be smaller, larger or equal in size of the object. Image formed by convex mirror is always virtual, erect and smaller in size.

24. (i) The three common refractive defects of vision are as follows:

Myopia (short-sightedness): A person with myopic eye can see nearby objects clearly but cannot see far off objects distinctly. It is corrected by using spectacles having concave lenses of appropriate power. **(1 Mark)**

Hypermetropia (far-sightedness): A person with hypermetro pic eye can see far off objects clearly but cannot see near by objects clearly. It is corrected by using spectacles having convex lenses of appropriate power. **(1 Mark)**

Presbyopia: This is due to a lessening of flexibility of crystalline lens as well as weakening of cilliary muscles. This defect is corrected using bifocal lenses of appropriate power in which the upper part consists of a concave lens (to correct myopia) and the lower part consists of a convex lens (to correct hypermetropia). **(1 Mark)**

(ii) Eyes of a dead person can be donated to the person having corneal blindness. It will help him/her see the world. We can also register ourselves to eye donation camps who can preserve our eyes after our death and donate them to the needy. **(2 Marks)**

An another defect of the eye which usually comes in old age is the cataract. The medical condition in which the lens of the eye of a person becomes cloudy resulting in blurred vision. It decreases the vision of the eye and can lead to total loss in vision.

SECTION - B

25. (b) A clear colourless solution is obtained when acetic acid is mixed with distill water and allow to settle for sometime. **(1 Mark)**

26. (d) Only Z **(1 Mark)**

$CH_3COOH + Na_2CO_3 \longrightarrow CH_3COONa + CO_2\uparrow + H_2O$

Carbondioxide evolve will extinguish the flame.

$CH_3\ COOH + NaOH \longrightarrow CH_3COONa + H_2O$

$CH_3COOH + NaCl \longrightarrow CH_3COONa + HCl$

No evolution of CO_2 in the other two cases.

27. (a) The solution is exothermic as large amount of heat is evolved when NaOH pellets are dissolve in water. The resulting solution is alkaline. **(1 Mark)**

28. (d) The function of common salt in the saponification reaction is to favour the precipitation of soap. **(1 Mark)**

29. (c) R and S **(1 Mark)**

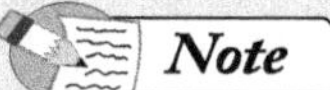

P	Q	R	S
NaCl	KCl	$CaCl_2$	$MgCl_2$

On adding soap solution to these test tubes scum formation results in test tube R and S as these test tube contain calcium and magnesium salt which causes hardness of water.

30. (c) To obtain the focal length of the mirror, the object should be taken at infinity. Therefore the image formed by concave mirror would be real, inverted and diminished in size. **(1 Mark)**

31. (c) As the image formed is real, so the lens is convex. As image distane (v) is increasing hence object distance (u) should be decreasing. Using lens formula.

$$\frac{1}{v} - \frac{1}{u} = \frac{1}{f}$$

Focal length in second case should be less than the focal length in first case. **(1 Mark)**

32. (b) To trace the path of ray of light through a rectangular glass slab, the angle of incidence of ray of light should be between 30° to 60°. **(1 Mark)**

33. (d) The incident and emergent ray are always parallel to each other. **(1 Mark)**

34. (c) Angle of incidence is the angle made by the incident ray with the normal to the surface of the prism. Hence, X represents the angle of incidence.

Angle of deviation is the angle made by the emergent ray with the incident ray. Here, Z represents the angle of deviation. **(1 Mark)**

35. (a) When a ray of light enters a glass prism, it travels from a rarer medium to a denser medium, So, the ray of light bends towards the normal. When the ray of light emerges from the glass prism, it travels from a denser medium to a rarer medium. So, the ray of light bends away from the normal. **(1 Mark)**

36. (b) Observation number 3 is incorrect because the focal length of the lens in all other observations is 12 cm. In observation number 3, the focal length comes out to be 13.26 cm. **(1 Mark)**

37. (d) A convex lens converges the refracting ray. Therefore, rays I and III represent the path of the refracting ray from a convex lens. (converging lens). II and IV show the refracting ray being diverged, the ray diagrams are incorrect. **(1 Mark)**

38. Option (c) is correct. **(1 Mark)**

Binary fission is a type of asexual reproduction in which a single organism (parent cell) divides into two daughter cells that are identical to their parent.

39. Option (d) is correct **(1 Mark)**

During budding in a yeast, a single cell develops a protrusion wherein the nucleus divides to give rise to two daughter nuclei. One of the daughter nuclei migrates to the protrusion to form a bud. This bud then grows in size and may undergo budding while attached to the parent cell. Thus, budding results in a chain of cells.

40. Option (b) is correct. Carrot and radish both are underground roots. **(1 Mark)**

Homologous organs are those organs which have similar structures but different functions.

41. Option (c) is correct. **(1 Mark)**

Analogous organs are not anatomically similar organs but they perform similar functions. It is result of convergent evolution.

42. Option (d) is correct. **(1 Mark)**

Delhi 2013

CBSE Board Solved Paper

Time Allowed : 3 Hours ***Maximum Marks : 80***

General Instructions:

(i) The question paper comprises of **two** Sections, **A** and **B**. You are to attempt both the sections.
(ii) All questions are compulsory.
(iii) All questions of Section-A and all questions of Section-B are to be attempted separately.
(iv) Question numbers **1** to **3** in Section-A are **one** mark questions. These are to be answered in **one** word or in **one** sentence.
(v) Question numbers **4** to **7** in Section-A are **two** marks questions. These are to be answered in about **30** words each.
(vi) Question numbers **8** to **19** in Section-A are **three** marks questions. These are to be answered in about **50** words each.
(vii) Question numbers **20** to **24** in Section-A are **five** marks questions. These are to be answered in about **70** words each.
(viii) Question numbers **25** to **42** in Section-B are multiple choice questions based on practical skills. Each question is a **one** mark question. You are to select **one** most appropriate response out of the **four** provided to you..

SECTION - A

1. How many vertical columns are there in the modern periodic table and what are they called ?

2. What is speciation?

3. Why should biodegradable and non-biodegradable wastes be discarded in two separate dust bins ?

4. "The chromosomes number of the sexually reproducing parents and their offspring is the same." Justify this statement.

5. "A ray of light incident on a rectangular glass slab immersed in any medium emerges parallel to itself." Draw labelled ray diagram to justify the statement.

6. We often observe domestic waste decomposing in the bylanes of residential colonies. Suggest ways to make people realise that the improper disposal of waste is harmful to the environment.

7. List and explain any two advantages associated with water harvesting at community level.

8. Write the name and the structural formula of the compound formed when ethanol is heated at 443 K with excess of conc. H_2SO_4 State the role of conc. H_2SO_4 in this reaction. Write chemical equation for the reaction.

9. Why homologous series of carbon compounds are so called? Write chemical formula of two consecutive members of a homologous series and state the part of these compounds that determines their (i) physical properties, and (ii) chemical properties.

10. Given below are some elements of the modern periodic table:

$_4Be$, $_9F$, $_{14}Si$, $_{19}K$, $_{20}Ca$

(i) Select the element that has one electron in the outermost shell and write its electronic configuration
(ii) Select two elements that belong to the same group. Give reason for your answer.
(iii) Select two elements that belong to the same period. Which one of the two has bigger atomic size?

11. Write the number of periods the modern periodic table has. How do the valency and metallic character of elements vary on moving from left to right in a period? How do the valency and atomic size of elements vary down a group?

12. (a) Explain the process of regeneration in *Planaria*.
(b) How is regeneration different from reproduction ?

13. Write two examples each of sexually transmitted diseases caused by (i) virus, (ii) bacteria. Explain how the transmission of such diseases be prevented ?

14. Tabulate two distinguishing features between acquired traits and inherited traits with one example of each.

15. "The sex of a newborn child is a matter of chance and none of the parents may be considered responsible for it." Justify this statement with the help of flow chart showing determination of sex of a newborn

16. Mention the types of mirrors used as (i) rear view mirrors, (ii) shaving mirrors. List two reasons to justify your answers in each case.

17. An object of height 6 cm is placed perpendicular to the principal axis of a concave lens of focal length 5 cm. Use lens formula to determine the position, size and nature of the image if the distance of the object from the lens is 10 cm.

18. State the difference in colours of the sun observed during sunrise/sunset and noon. Give explanation for each.

19. (a) What is an ecosystem? List its two main components.

(b) We do not clean ponds or lakes, but an aquarium needs to be cleaned regularly. Explain.

20. (a) Define the term isomers'.

(b) Draw two possible isomers of the compound with molecular formula C_2H_6O and write their names.

(c) Give the electron dot structures of the above two compounds.

21. (a) List three distinguishing features between sexual and asexual types of reproduction.

(b) Explain why variations are observed in the offsprings of sexually reproducing organisms?

22. (a) Identify A, B and C in the given diagram and write their functions.

(b) Mention the role of gamete and zygote in sexually reproducing organisms.

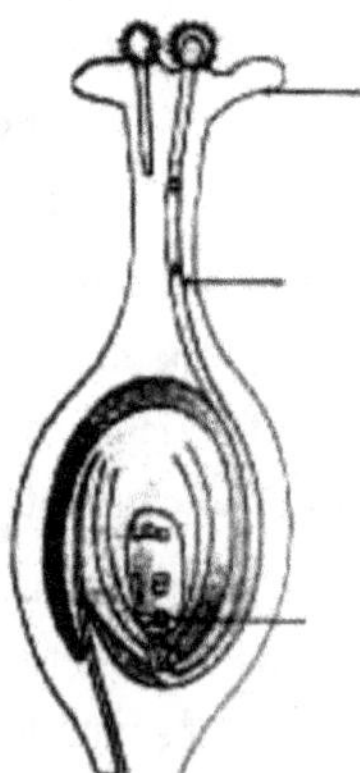

23. (a) State the laws of refraction of light. Give an expression to relate the absolute refractive index of a medium with speed of light in vacuum.

(b) The refractive indices of water and glass with respect to air are 4/3 and 3/2 respectively. If the speed of light in glass is 2×10^8 ms^{-1}, find the speed of light in (i) air, (ii) water.

24. (a) A person cannot read newspaper placed nearer than 50 cm from his eyes. Name the defect of vision he is suffering from. Draw a ray diagram to illustrate this defect. List its two possible causes. Draw a ray diagram to show how this defect may be corrected using a lens of appropriate focal length.

(b) We see advertisements for eye donation on television or in newspapers. Write the importance of such advertisements.

SECTION - B

25. A student takes 2 mL acetic acid in a dry test tube and adds a pinch of sodium hydrogen carbonate to it. He makes the following observations:

I. A colourless and odourless gas evolves with a brisk effervescence.

II. The gas turns lime water milky when passed through it.

III. The gas burns with an explosion when a burning splinter is brought near it.

IV. The gas extinguishes the burning splinter that is brought near it.

The correct observations are :

(a) I, II, and III (b) I, III and IV

(c) III, IV and I (d) IV, I and II

26. In an experiment to study the properties of acetic acid a student takes about 2 mL of acetic acid in a dry test tube. He adds about 2 mL of water to it and shakes the test tube well. He is likely to observe that:

(a) the acetic acid dissolves readily in water

(b) the solution becomes light orange

(c) water floats over the surface of acetic acid

(d) acetic acid floats over the surface of water

27. A student prepared 20% sodium hydroxide solution in a beaker containing water. The observations noted by him are given below.

I. Sodium hydroxide is in the form of pellets.

II. It dissolves in water readily.

III. The beaker appears cold when touched from outside

IV. The red litmus paper turns blue when dipped into the solution

The correct observation are:

(a) I, II and III (b) II, III and IV

(c) III, IV and I (d) I, II, and IV

28. Read the following statements :

I. When a red litmus paper is dipped into reaction mixture of a saponification reaction, it turns blue and the reaction is exothermic.

II. When a blue litmus paper is dipped into reaction mixture of a saponification reaction, its colour does not change and the reaction is exothermic.

III. When a red litmus paper is dipped into reaction mixture of a saponification reaction, its colour does not change and the reaction is endothermic.

IV. When a blue litmus paper is dipped into reaction mixture of a saponification reaction, its colour does not change and the reaction is endothermic.

Which of the above statements are correct:

(a) I and II (b) II and III

(c) III and IV (d) I and IV

29. Hard water required for an experiment is not available in a school laboratory. However, following salts are available in the laboratory, Select the salts which may be dissolved in water to make it hard for the experiment

(1) Calcium Sulphate (2) Sodium Sulphate

(3) Calcium Chloride (4) Potassium Sulphate

(5) Sodium Hydrogen Carbonate

(6) Magnesium Chloride

(a) 1, 2 and 4 (b) 1,3 and 6

(c) 3,5 and 6 (d) 2, 4 and 5

30. A student focussed the image of a distant object using a device 'X' on a white screen 'S' as shown in the figure. If the distance of the screen from the device is 40 cm, select the correct statement about the device.

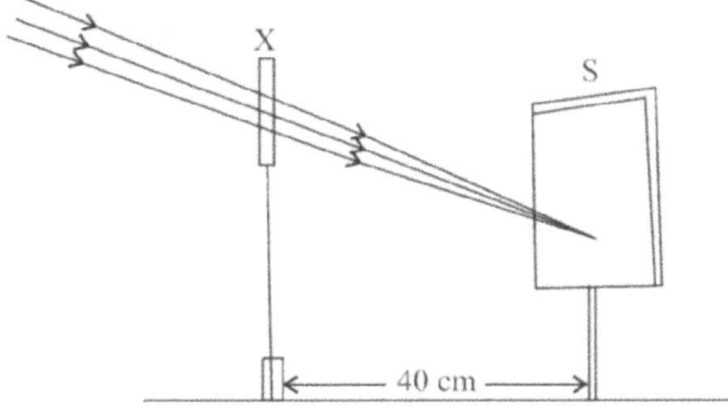

(a) The device X is a convex lens of focal length 20 cm.

(b) The device X is a concave mirror of focal length 40 cm.

(c) The device X is a concave mirror of radius of curvature 40 cm.

(d) The device X is a convex lens of focal length 40 cm.

31. A student obtained a sharp image of a burning candle, placed at the farther end of a laboratory table, on a screen using a concave mirror. For getting better value of focal length of the mirror, the subject teacher suggested him for focussing a well illuminated distant object. What should the student do?

(a) He should move the mirror away from the screen.

(b) He should move the mirror slightly towards the screen.

(c) He should move the mirror as well as the screen towards the newly selected object.

(d) He should move only the screen towards the newly selected object.

32. After tracing the path of rays of light through a glass slab for three different angles of incidence, a student measured the corresponding values angle of refraction r and angle of emergence e and recorded them in the table given below:

S.No.	$\angle i$	$\angle r$	$\angle e$
I	30°	20°	31°
II	40°	25°	40°
III	50°	31°	49°

The correct observations are:

(a) I and II (b) II and III

(c) I and III (d) I, II and III

33. Select from the following the best set-up for tracing the path of a ray of light through a rectangular glass slab:

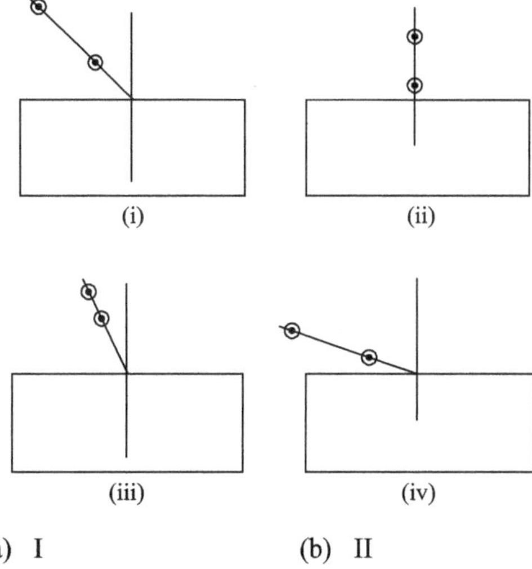

(a) I (b) II

(c) III (d) IV

34. While performing the experiment to trace the path of a ray of light passing through a glass prism, four students marked the incident ray and the emergent ray in their diagrams in the manner shown below.

The correct path of the rays has been shown by:

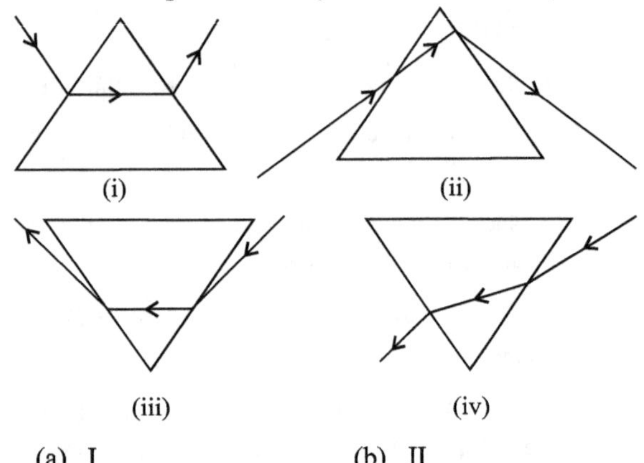

(a) I
(b) II
(c) III
(d) IV

35. In an experiment to trace the path of a ray of light through a glass prism for different values of angle of incidence a student would find that the emergent ray:

(a) is parallel to the incident nay
(b) perpendicular to the incident ray
(c) is parallel to the refracted ray
(d) bends at an angle to the direction of incident ray

36. Study the following ray diagrams:

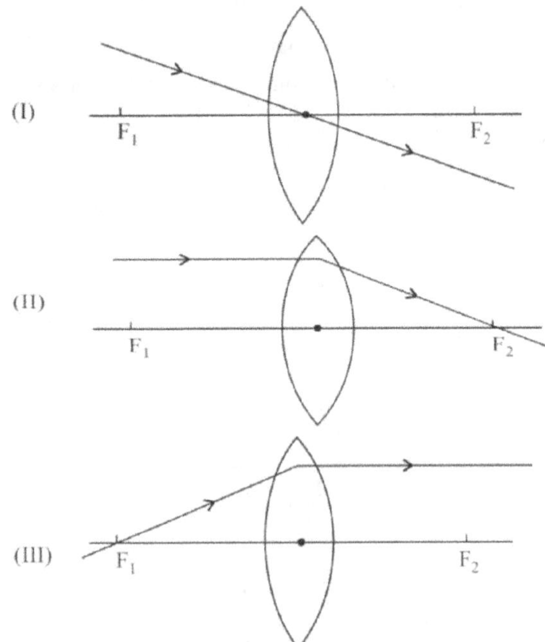

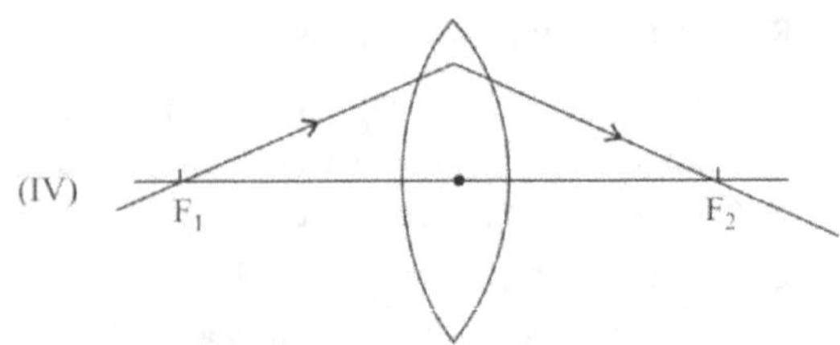

The diagrams showing the correct path of the ray after passing through the lens are:

(a) II and III only
(b) I and II only
(c) I, II and III
(d) I, II and IV

37. Out of the five incident rays shown in the figure find the three rays that are obeying the laws of refraction and may be used for locating the position of image formed by a convex lens:

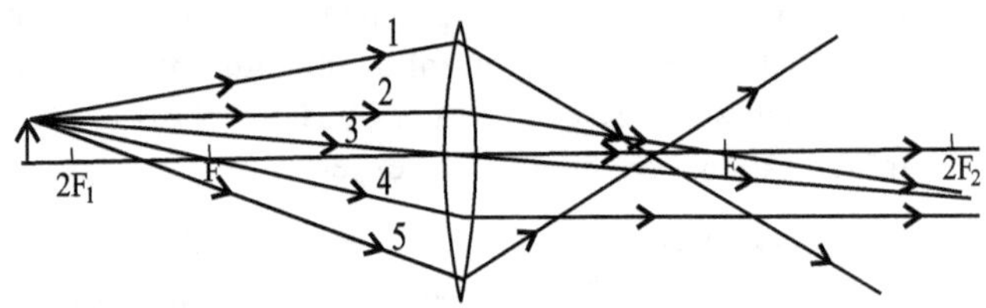

(a) 1, 2 and 3
(b) 2, 3 and 4
(c) 3, 4 and 5
(d) 1, 2 and 4

38. A student after observing a slide showing different stages of binary fission in *Amoeba* draws the following diagrams. However these diagrams are not in proper sequence :

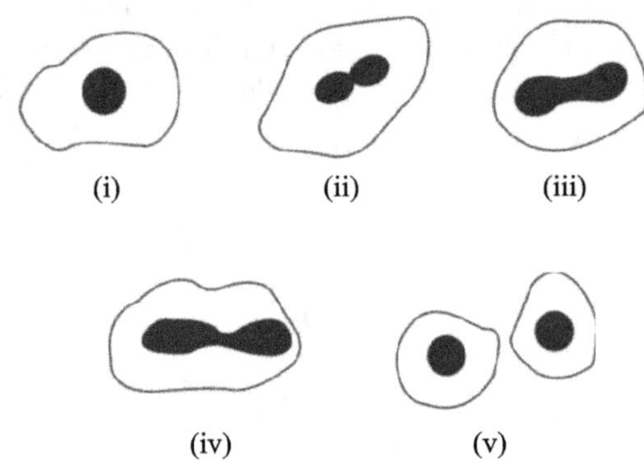

The correct sequence is :

(a) (i), (v), (iv), (iii), (ii)
(b) (i), (iii), (iv), (v), (ii)
(c) (i), (v), (iii), (iv), (ii)
(d) (i), (iv), (v), (iii), (ii)

39. Select the correct statements for the process of budding in yeast :

I. A bud arises from a particular region on a parent body.

II. A parent cell divides into two daughter cells, here the parental identity is lost.

III. Before detaching from the parent body a bud may form another bud.

IV. A bud when detaches from the parent body grows into a new individual

(a) I, II and III (b) II, III and IV

(c) III, IV and I (d) IV, I and II

40. Study the different conclusions drawn by students of a class on the basis of observations of preserved / available specimens of plants and animals.

I. Potato and sweet potato are analogous organs in plants.

II. Wings of insects and wings of birds are homologous organs in animals.

III. Wings of insects and wings of bats are analogous organs in animals.

IV. Thorns of citrus and tendrils of cucurbita are analogous organs in plants.

The correct conclusions are:

(a) I and II (b) II and IV

(c) I and III (d) III and IV

41. You have potato, carrot, radish, sweet potato, tomato and ginger bought from the market in your jute bag. Identify two vegetables to represent the correct homologous structures.

(a) Potato and tomato

(b) Carrot and tomato

(c) Potato and sweet potato

(d) Carrot and radish

42. In the figure, the parts marked A, B and Care sequentially:

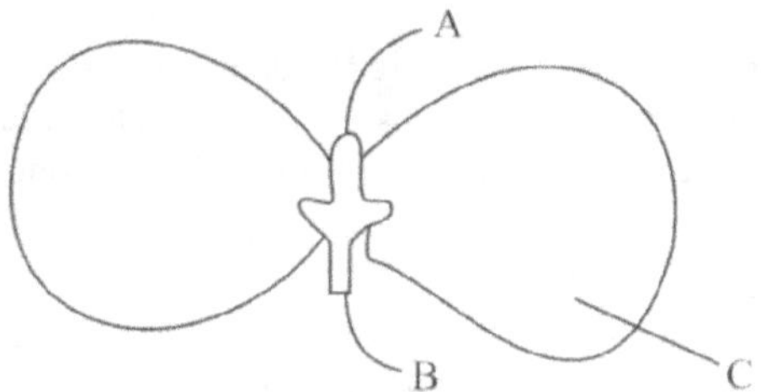

(a) Plumule, Radicle and Cotyledon

(b) Radicle, Plumule and Cotyledon

(c) Plumule, Cotyledon and Radicle

(d) Radicle, Cotyledon and Plumule

Solutions

SECTION - A

1. There are 18 vertical columns in the modern periodic table. Vertical columns are known as groups. **(1 Mark)**

2. Speciation refers to the process of formation of new species from existing species/parent species. **(1 Mark)**

A species is a group of organisms with similar characteristics and can interbreed to give fertile offspring.

3. Biodegradable and non-biodegradable wastes should be discarded in two separated bins as this helps in effective treatment and disposal of these wastes. Biodegradable wastes can be easily disposed by natural way of composting while non-biodegrable wastes can be sent for safe disposal or recycling. This helps in protecting the environment from pollution. **(1 Mark)**

4. Number of chromosomes is halved during gamete formation by the process of meiosis. So, the number of sex chromosomes is half the number of chromosomes in somatic cells during gamete formation.

   During fertilisation, haploid male and female gametes are fused to form diploid zygote. **(2 Marks)**

Meiosis is also called reduction division. It is a type of cell division that reduces the number of chromosomes in the parent cell by half and produces four gamete cells.

5. The emergent ray CD is parallel to the incident ray AB, but it has been laterally displaced by a perpendicular distance CN with respect to the incident ray.

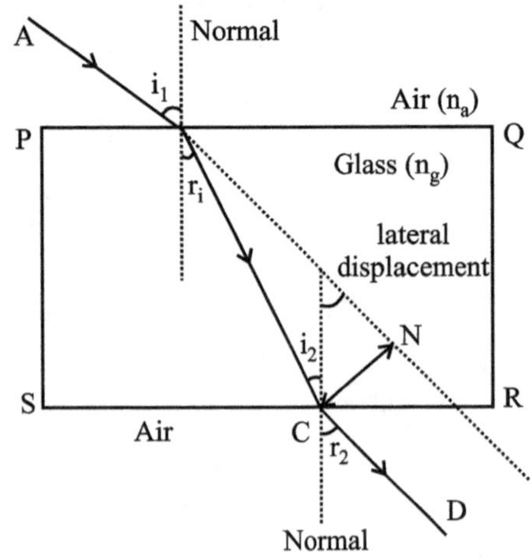

(2 Marks)

6. Following ways are suggested to people realize that the improper disposal of waste is harmful to the environment are as follows :

   (i) Improper disposal of waste will serve as a breeding ground for mosquitoes and will create favorable conditions for the spread of various diseases.

   (ii) Improper disposal of waste will release harmful gases in the environment. It will make the environment unclean and unhygienic for normal living of the organisms.

   (iii) The waste will flow to water bodies along with the rain water and becomes threat to aquatic organisms.

   (2 Marks)

7. Two advantages associated with water harvesting at community level are:

   (a) Over exploitation of water resources will be reduced.

   (b) Helps to recharge the natural wells and provides moisture for vegetation over a wide area. **(2 Marks)**

8. $\underset{\text{Ethanol}}{CH_3CH_2OH} + \text{Conc. } H_2SO_4 \xrightarrow{443\,K} \underset{\text{ethene}}{CH_2 = CH_2} + H_2O$ **(1 Mark)**

   Structural formula of Ethene : $H - \overset{\overset{H}{|}}{C} = \overset{\overset{H}{|}}{C} - H$ **(1 Mark)**

   Concentrated H_2SO_4 acts as a dehydrating agent in the reaction. **(1 Mark)**

9. Members of the homologous series have the same general formula and functional group therefore they are said to belong to the same homologous series.

   CH_3OH and CH_3CH_2OH are the two consecutive members of alcohol homologous series. **(1 Mark)**

   (i) Physical properties are determined by nature of alkyl group and length of the carbon chain. **(1 Mark)**

   (ii) Chemical properties are determined by the nature of the functional group. **(1 Mark)**

10. (i) Potassium (K) has one electron in the outermost shell.

    $_{19}K \Rightarrow (2, 8, 8, 1)$ **(1 Mark)**

(ii) Be and Ca belongs to the same group (group 2) of the periodic table.

$_4Be \Rightarrow (2, 2)$

$_{20}Ca \Rightarrow (2, 8, 8, 2)$

Both Be and Ca have two electrons in the outermost shell therefore they must be belong to group 2 of the periodic table. **(1 Mark)**

(iii) $_9F$ and $_4Be$ belongs to 2nd period of the periodic table.

$_9F \Rightarrow (2, 7)$

$_4Be \Rightarrow (2, 2)$

Be has larger size than fluorine. **(1 Mark)**

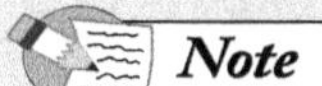

Numbers of electrons present in the outer most shell of an atom determine the group to which that element belongs. Number of shells in an atom determine the period to which that element belongs.

11. Modern periodic table has seven periods.

Valency across the period : Valency increases and then decreases along the period.

Metallic character across the period : Metallic character decreases across the period on moving left to right in the periodic table.

Valency in a group : Valency in a group remain same for all the elements.

Atomic size in a group : Atomic size increases on moving top to bottom in a group. **(3 Marks)**

Valency remain same in the group. For example group 2 elements shows common valency +2. However elements of some groups can show other valency along with group valency. For example phosphorus, an element of group 15 can show +3 and +5 valency and tin, an element of group 14 can show +2 and +4 valency.

12. (a) Simple animal such as *Planaria* can be cut into any number of pieces and each piece grows into a complete organism and this process is termed as regeneration. This process is carried out by specilised cells as these cells proliferate and make large number of cells. From this mass of cells, different cells undergo changes to become various cell types and tissues. Such changes takes place in an organised sequence referred to as development.

(b) Regeneration is not the same as reproduction, since most organisms would not normally depend on being cut up to be able to reproduce. **(½ Marks)**

Diagrammatic Representation of stages of regeneration in *Planaria*:

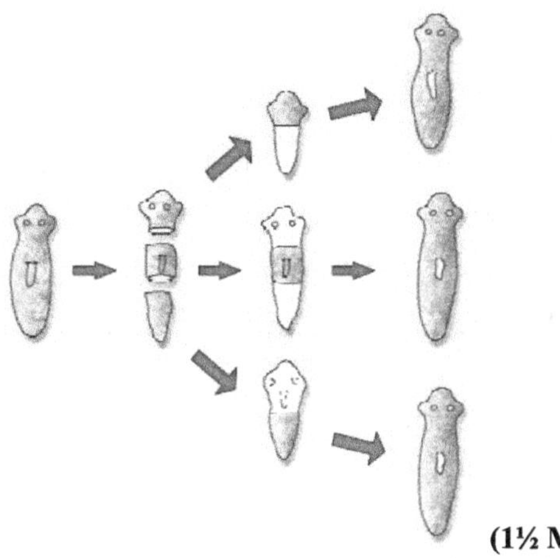

(1½ Marks)

Asexual reproduction involves the production of offspring from a single parent without the involvement of gamete formation.

13. (i) Virus → Viral infections include hearts and HIV-AIDS

(ii) Bacteria → Bacterial infections include gonosrhoea and syphilis. **(1½ Marks)**

Prevention of transmission of STDs:

- Having sex with infected or any unknown person should be avoided.
- Sharing of infected needles, syringes must be avoided.
- Proper sterilization of surgical and dental instruments before use.
- Avoid blood transfusion from infected person as, the blood should be tested before transfusion.
- Proper medical treatment should be provided to the pregnant women to protect the child from infection.

(1½ Marks)

Sexually Transmitted disease (STDs) refer to a condition passed from one infected person to another through sexual contact.

14.

Acquired trait	Inherited trait
(i) Acquired trait cannot be passed from one generation to another generation.	(i) Inherited traits can be passed on from one generation to another generation
(ii) Acquired traits or characteristic are because of the change in somatic cells.	(ii) Inherited traits or characteristics are because of the change in genes.
e.g. Low in weight due to starvation, if a mouse's tail gets cut, the cut tail is an acquired trait.	e.g. Brown eyes and curly hair.

(3 Marks)

15. Human chromosomes have a maternal and a parental copy (sex chromosome) and 22 pairs of autosomes.

Females have a perfect pair of sex chromosomes, both called X. While males have a mismatched pair in which one is a normal-sized X, and one short Y chromosome so, females are XX chromosomes whereas men are XY Half the children will be boys and half will be girls. All children will inherit an X chromosome from their mother regardless of whether they are boys or girls.

Thus, the sex of the children will be determine by what they inherit from their father. A child who inherits an X chromosome from her father will be a girl, and one who inherits a Y chromosome from him will be boy.

Sex determination in human beings :

Gametes:	XX		X	XY
Zygotes:	XX	XY	XX	XY
	↓	↓	↓	↓
Offsprings	Female	Male	Female	Male

From the above genetic cross, the sex of the child is not dependent on both the parents and is a matter of chance.

(3 Marks)

16. (i) A convex mirror forms an erect, virtual and diminished image of an object placed anywhere in front of it. Thus, convex mirrors enable the driver to view much larger traffic behind him that would not be possible by a plane mirror. **(1½ Marks)**

(ii) A concave mirror is used as a shaving or make-up mirror because it forms an erect and enlarged image of the face when it is held closer to the face. **(1½ Marks)**

17. A concave lens always forms a virtual and erect image on the same side of the object.

Image distance, v = ?

Focal length, f = – 5 cm

Object distance u = – 10 cm

Using lens formula

$$\frac{1}{f} = \frac{1}{v} - \frac{1}{u}$$

$$\frac{1}{v} = \frac{1}{f} + \frac{1}{u} = \frac{1}{-5} + \frac{1}{-10}$$ **(1 Mark)**

$$= \frac{-1-2}{10} = \frac{-3}{10}$$

$v = -3.3$ cm **(1 Mark)**

$$\text{Magnification} = \frac{\text{Size of the image}}{\text{Size of the object}} = +\frac{v}{u}$$

$$\Rightarrow \quad \frac{h}{6} = \frac{3.3}{10}$$

$$\Rightarrow \quad h = \frac{6\times3.3}{10} = \frac{19.8}{10} = 1.98 \text{ cm.}$$

Size of the image is 1.98 cm. **(1 Mark)**

The image is virtual or erect and at a distance of 3.3 cm in front of the lens.

18. At sun-rise and sun-set most of the blue light and shorter wavelengths are scattered away by the particles in the atmosphere as the light from the sun near the horizon passes through thick layer of air and larger distance. The light that reaches our eye is of longer wavelength (red colour) giving a reddish appearance. **(2 Marks)**

At noon, sunlight travel a shorter distance and contains all the wavelengths of light which combine to form white colour. **(1 Mark)**

The colour of the scattered light depends on the size of the scattering particles. Very fine particle scatter mainly blue light while particle of larger size scatter light of longer wavelengths. If the size of the scattering particles is large enough, then the scattered light may even appear white.

19. (a) All the interacting organisms in an area together with the non-living constituents of the environment form an **ecosystem.**

An ecosystem consists of biotic components consists of living organisms human, rat, dog, tree etc. and abiotic components consists of temperature, rainfall, wind, soil and minerals. **(1½ Marks)**

(b) A pond or lake is a natural ecosystem. They are self-sustaining and complete, in them, all the organisms of the food chain are available in a pond or lake. If any organism dies, there are decomposers for decomposition of dead remains. On the otherhand, an aquarium is an artificial and incomplete ecosystem. The abiotic components are not supplied naturally to it. It may not have all the biotic components in it. If a fish dies in an aquarium in the absence of decomposer, it will lie there as a decaying body, polluting the water of the aquarium. This is the reason that an aquarium below needs to be cleaned regularly. **(1½ Marks)**

20. (a) Isomers are the compounds that have same molecular formula but different structural formula. **(1 Mark)**

(b) **Molecular Formula :** C_2H_6O

Isomers : CH_3OCH_3 and CH_3CH_2OH

$$\begin{array}{c} H \quad\;\; H \\ | \qquad\; | \\ H-C-O-C-H \\ | \qquad\; | \\ H \quad\;\; H \end{array} \quad \text{and} \quad \begin{array}{c} H \;\; H \\ | \quad\, | \\ H-C-C-OH \\ | \quad\, | \\ H \;\; H \end{array}$$

Dimethylether ethylalcohol

(2 Marks)

(c) **Electron dot Structures :**

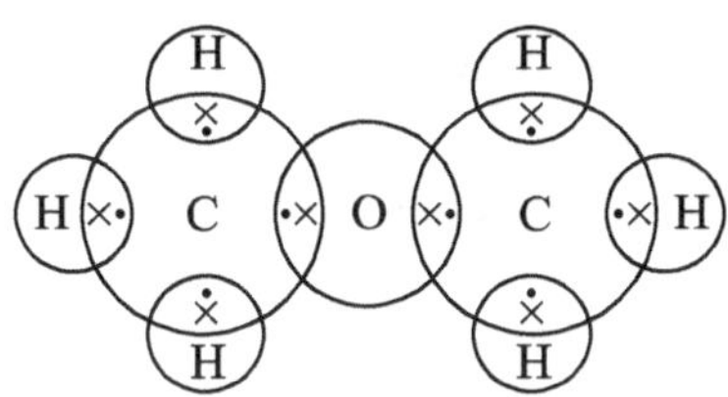

Dimethylether

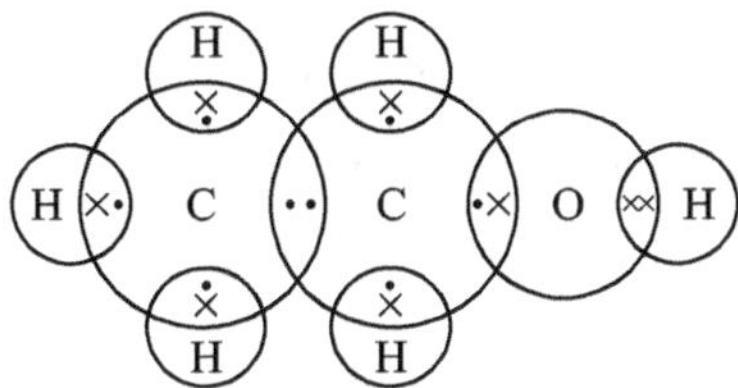

Ethyl alcohol

(2 Marks)

21. (a)

Sexual reproduction	Asexual reproduction
1. It involves a two parents.	1. It involves only a single parent.
2. Gametes are formed.	2. Gametes are not formed.
3. Fertilisation takes place.	3. Fertilisation does not occur.

(1½ Marks)

(b) The variations are observed in the offsprings produced by sexual reproduction are because of:

- Two parents are involved, who are different from each other. One set of chromosomes comes from the male gamete and the other comes from the female gamete and the fusion of male and female gametes results in variations among individuals and produces dintinct individuals.
- The male and female gametes are formed by meiotic division that allows crossing over and recombination which further results in variation in the genes of offspring. **(3½ Marks)**

22. (a) In the given figure, A represents stigma, B represents Pollen tube, C represents female-germ cell.

- Stigma is sticky surface where the pollen lands and later germinates.
- Pollen tube carries the pollen from stigma to the egg cell in the ovary for fertilisation. **(2 Marks)**

(b) The gametes play an important role in sexually reproducing organisms as they carry a genetic instructions that is a haploid set of chromosomes that the new organism needs to grow, develop and complete its life cycle. These gametes upon fusion result in the formation of zygote, which develops into a new individual.

Zygote is the diploid cell formed by the fusion of male and female gametes during fertilisation in sexual reproduction.

Zygote is the first stage in the development process of an organism and contains the complete sets of genetic information of both the parents, essential for the growth of the new organisms. **(3 Marks)**

23. (a) Laws of refraction of light:

(i) The incident ray, the refracted ray at the point of incidence and the normal all lies in the same plane for the two given medium.

(ii) The ratio of sine of angle of incidence (i.e., sin i) to the sine of angle of refraction (i.e., sin r) is always constant for the light of given colour and for the given pair of media.

Mathematically, $\frac{\sin i}{\sin r}$ = constant = n_2

(2 × 1 = 2 Marks)

The constant 'n' is called refractive index of the second medium with respect to the first medium.

Absolute refractive index of the medium is given by

$$n = \frac{\text{Speed of light in vacuum (c)}}{\text{Speed of light in media } (v)}$$ **(1 Mark)**

(b) Given refractive index of water $n_A = 4/3$ and refractive index of glass, $n_B = 1.5$

Speed of light in glass = 2×10^8 m/s

$$n_B = \frac{\text{Speed of light in air}}{\text{Speed of light in glass}}$$

$$\Rightarrow 1.5 = \frac{c}{2\times10^8}$$

$\Rightarrow$ Speed of light in air c = $2 \times 10^8 \times 1.5$

= 3.0×10^8 m/s **(1 Mark)**

Speed of light in water

$$n_A = \frac{\text{Speed of light in air}}{\text{Speed of light in water}}$$

$$\Rightarrow \frac{4}{3} = \frac{3\times10^8}{\text{Speed of light in water}}$$

$\Rightarrow$ Speed of light in water = $3\times10^8 \times \frac{3}{4}$

= 2.25×10^8 m/s **(1 Mark)**

Note

When light travels from medium (1) to medium (2) then refractive index of medium (2) w.r.t. medium (1) is called its relative refractive index.

$${}_1\mu_2 = \frac{\mu_2}{\mu_1} = \frac{v_1}{v_2}$$

where, v_1 and v_2 are the speed of light in medium 1 and 2 respectively.

24. (a) The person is suffering from hypermetropia. **(1 Mark)**

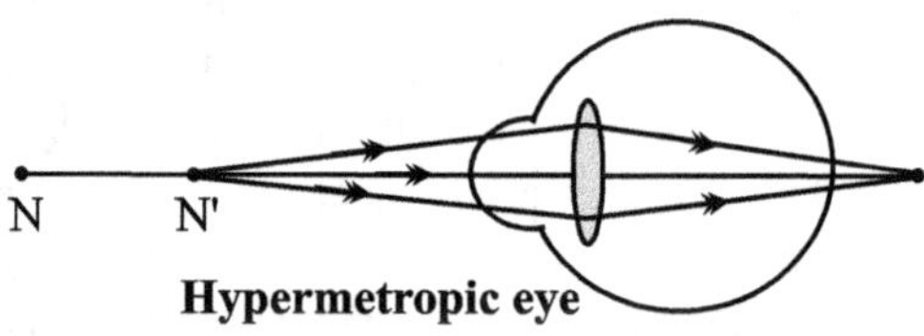

Hypermetropic eye

This defect can be corrected by using convex lens of appropriate focal length

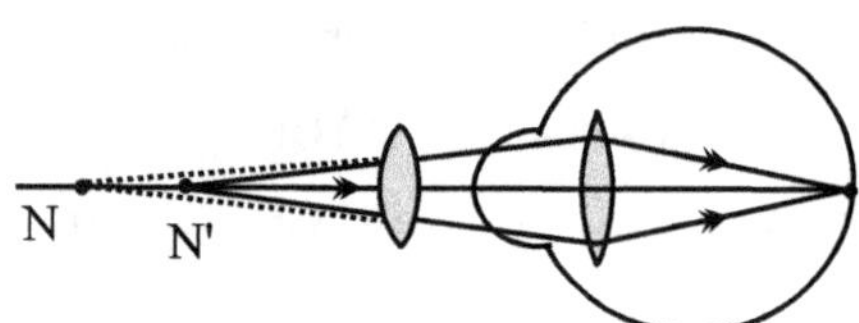

Correction for Hypermetropic eye **(1 Mark)**

Two possible causes:

(i) Greater focal length of the lens.

(ii) Eye ball becoming smaller. **(½×2=1 Mark)**

Calculation of Power of the lens

$$\frac{1}{f} = \frac{1}{v} - \frac{1}{u} = \frac{1}{-50} - \frac{1}{-25}$$

$$= \frac{-1+2}{50} = \frac{1}{-50} \text{ cm}$$

$\Rightarrow f = 50$ cm

$P = \frac{100}{50} = 2$ D power of lens. **(1 Mark)**

(b) Eye donation advertisements are important as:

(i) They make the people aware about donation of organs after their death.

(ii) Sympathetic nature towards others.

(½×2=1 Mark)

A normal eye can see the objects clearly, if they are at a distance greater than 25 cm. This distance is called least distance of distinct vision and is represented by D.

SECTION - B

25. (d) I, II and IV are correct observations. **(1 Mark)**

$CH_3COOH + NaHCO_3 \longrightarrow CH_3COONa + CO_2 + H_2O$

CO_2 gas is released during the reaction with brisk effervescence. CO_2 gas also turn lime water milky due to the formation of calcium carbonate.

$$\underset{\text{Calcium hydroxide or lime water}}{Ca(OH)_2} + CO_2 \longrightarrow \underset{\text{Calcium carbonate (milky appearance)}}{CaCO_3} + H_2O$$

CO_2 gas also has extinguisher property.

26. (a) Acetic acid readily dissolves in water. **(1 Mark)**

27. (d) Correct observations are I, II and IV. Dissolution of sodium hydroxide in water is an exothermic process. Therefore beaker should be hot instead of cold. **(1 Mark)**

28. (a) I and II observations are correct observations. **(1 Mark)**

Due to presence of base in the saponification reaction red litmus paper turns blue. When sodium hydroxide is used, a hard soap is produced while potassium hydroxide results in a soft soap.

29. (b) Calcium and magnesium salts causes hardness of water. **(1 Mark)**

30. (d) As the image is focused on the screen placed behind the device X, Thus, device X is a lens, but cannot be a mirror. As convex lens forms the image of the distant object at its focus. So, device X must be a convex lens of focal length 40 cm. **(1 Mark)**

31. (b) As the image distance is increased, the object distance would decrease and thus the mirror-screen distance should be decreased. Therefore, the mirror should be moved towards the screen. **(1 Mark)**

32. (d) Angle of emergence should be nearly equal to angle of incidence. Also, angle of refraction should be less than angle of incidence. Hence, all three observations are correct. **(1 Mark)**

33. (a) For tracing the path of a ray of light through rectangular glass slab, angle of incidence should be between 30° and 60°. **(1 Mark)**

While tracing the path of ray of light through a glass slab, the angle of incidence is generally taken between 30° and 60°. If the angle of incidence is less than 30°, bending of light at glass-air interface will be less. If angle of incidence is greater than. 60°, the emergent ray may emerge from the side surface.

34. (c) When light goes from rarer to denser medium, it bends towards the normal. When light goes from denser to rarer medium it bends away from the normal. Hence, correct figure is (III). **(1 Mark)**

35. (d) As the light get refracted two times at different angles, the emergent ray bends at an angle to the direction of incident ray. **(1 Mark)**

36. (c) The light rays passing through the optical centre of lens remain undeflected.

The light rays parallel to principal axis passes through the second focus of the lens.

The light rays passing through the first focus become parallel to the principal axis after passing through the lens. **(1 Mark)**

37. (b) Ray parallel to principal axis passes through the second focus of the lens.

Ray passing through the optical centre goes undeflected.

Ray passing through the first focus of the lens goes parallel to principal axis. **(1 Mark)**

38. The none of the sequence mentioned in the above options are correct. Binary fission is a type of asexual reproduction in which an organism divides into, each carrying one copy of genetic material.

Diagrammatic Representation of stages of binary fission in *Amoeba* :

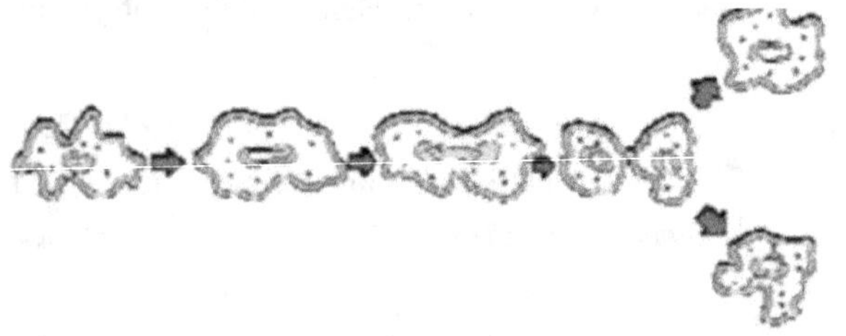

(1 Mark)

The correct sequence of binary fission in Amoeba is: I, III, II, IV and V.

39. (c)

40. (c) I and III

Analogous organs are those which do not share a common ancestor but perform common functions. Wings of insect and bats both perform the same function of flight but are not common in origin. Hence, wings of insects and wings of bats are analoogus organs in animals. **(1 Mark)**

41. (d) **(1 Mark)**

Homologus structures perform different functions but have same origin.

42. (a) In the given figure, the parts marked A, B and C are Plumule, Radicle and Cotyledon. **(1 Mark)**

www.ingramcontent.com/pod-product-compliance
Lightning Source LLC
LaVergne TN
LVHW080209180826
845678LV00023BA/1985

9788119181131